BIBB
COUNTY
ALABAMA

BIBB COUNTY ALABAMA

THE FIRST HUNDRED YEARS, 1818–1918

by

Rhoda Coleman Ellison

THE UNIVERSITY OF ALABAMA PRESS

Tuscaloosa

Manufactured in the United States of America

First Paperback Printing 1999

1 2 3 4 5 6 7 8 9 / 07 06 05 04 03 02 01 00 99

∞

The paper on which this book is printed meets the minimum requirements of American National Standard for Information Science–Permanence of Paper for Printed Library Materials, ANSI Z39.48-1984.

Cover design by Gary Gore

Library of Congress Cataloging-in-Publication Data

Ellison, Rhoda Coleman, 1904–
Bibb County, Alabama.
Bibliography: p.
Includes index.
1. Bibb County (Ala.)—History. I. Title.
F332.B5E44 1984 976.1'82 83-5875
ISBN 0-8173-0987-X

To My Sister
Connie

CONTENTS

ILLUSTRATIONS

Photographs

Maps

PREFACE

The history of Bibb County during its first hundred years is in many ways representative of the experience of central Alabama during that period. Set close to the middle of the state, the county shares the physical characteristics of the adjoining areas both on the north and south. It possesses in its northern section a mineral district and in its southern valleys fertile farming country. As a result of this dichotomy, its citizens have sometimes voted with the hill counties and sometimes with their Black Belt neighbors. Each of the two sections has grown in step with the surrounding counties. Bibb's foundries were established in the same years and by the same ironmasters as Shelby's and its coal mines in the same decade as Jefferson's. Its farmers planted the same crops and faced the same problems as those in Perry, Autauga, and Tuscaloosa. Like Tuscaloosa, though less successfully, it endeavored to stimulate river transportation for both its industrial and its agricultural products.

Created in 1818, while Alabama was yet a territory, Bibb has a history as old as any of its neighbors. The legislature formed it in the same year as Shelby, Autauga, and Tuscaloosa counties and one year before Jefferson and Perry. (Hale was constituted in 1867 and Chilton in 1868.) All this area was invaded by the same rush of settlers from the Atlantic seaboard into the former Creek Indian lands. Life in central Alabama counties through the nineteenth century had many parallels; often only the names of the families were different. Today Bibb, still heavily forested, may be closer to its heritage than some of its more urbanized neighbors. In any case, its story during the first century after settlement by the white man seems significant for all this section of the state.

I came to the writing of this history quite naturally. As a descendant of pioneer Bibb families, I was brought up on tales of the settlers: who entered which land from the government and who built which houses. Especially I was regaled with traditions of the second generation—its soldiers, outlaws, and politicians. For a number of years now I have enjoyed the adventure of searching the records, which in some cases correct oral history as well as add richly to it. I have discovered a variety of sources, including county, state, and federal documents and record books; county newspapers; church minutes; individuals' account books; letters; diaries;

family collections of notes and memorabilia; and the published works of Alabama scholars in certain fields.

I am indebted to the holders of the records for graciously making them available to me, especially the staffs of the Alabama State Department of Archives and History; the University of Alabama Library Special Collections; the Birmingham Public Library Rucker Agee Map Collection; the Bibb County Probate and Circuit Clerk's offices; and the *Centreville Press*; as well as numerous friends, most of whose contributions I have been able to acknowledge in my notes. I am especially grateful to Bibb Countians who have lent me valued old pictures and maps for use as illustrations.

It would be impossible to name all those who have encouraged this undertaking or assisted me in various important ways. Although it has been a happy experience, I could never have carried it on to completion without their concern and help. I have been dependent most of all on the support of my sister, Connie Tullis Ellison, who has been the moving force back of this book from beginning to end.

Rhoda Coleman Ellison
Centreville, Alabama

BIBB
COUNTY
ALABAMA

1

THE LAND AND ITS INDIANS

BIBB IS ONE OF the oldest counties in Alabama, older even than the state. Along with its twin, Shelby County, it was created from Montgomery County on February 7, 1818, by an act of the Alabama territorial legislature, assembled at Huntsville.[1] Thus it was one of the first thirteen counties to be added to the seven already constituted when Alabama was still a part of the Mississippi Territory. It was originally named Cahaba (for many years spelled Cahawba) for the river that flows throughout its entire length. This name was changed to Bibb by the state legislature on December 4, 1820, following the sudden death of Alabama's first governor, William Wyatt Bibb, a native of Georgia who had earlier represented that state in the United States Senate. He had served less than seven months when he died on July 10, 1820, from injuries received in a fall from his horse.

During the period after the American Revolution, the area that was to become Bibb County had been part of three different territories in succession. First it was claimed by Georgia. When Georgia ceded to the newly established United States government all lands west of the Chattahoochee, east of the Mississippi, south of Tennessee, and north of the Spanish possessions, Congress organized it on April 7, 1798, as the Mississippi Territory. After May 12, 1812, when an act of Congress annexed all the region lying east of the Pearl River and south of the thirty-first degree of latitude, the Mississippi Territory included all lands of the present states of Alabama and Mississippi. Following the admission of Mississippi as a state, Congress on March 21, 1817, established a separate government for the eastern section of the former Mississippi Territory and named it Alabama Territory.

Montgomery County, from which Cahaba (Bibb) was created by the Alabama territorial legislature, was one of six counties carved in 1816 out of the extensive county of Monroe. This large area, approximately three-fourths of the state, had been opened for white settlers by two Indian treaties. In the Treaty of Fort Jackson, August 7, 1814, at the end of the Creek War, the Creeks surrendered all their claims west of the Coosa River, and the whole of their cession was incorporated as Monroe County by Governor David Holmes of Mississippi on June 29, 1815. The remaining Choctaw lands east of the Tombigbee were added to this region after they were ceded to the United States in the Treaty of the Trading House, October 21, 1816.[2] Thus, Monroe stretched like a huge irregular triangle between the remaining Indian lands, marked off from them by the Tombigbee and Coosa rivers. It extended from a point just below the Tennessee River to the Florida line; the Cahaba River flowed southwest and south near its center to join the Alabama. Cahaba was the central county in this triangle, located approximately halfway between the two large river systems in the foothill region between the Appalachian Mountains and the Black Belt, often called the Shortleaf Pine Belt.

When the county was formed, it was much more extensive than it is today, stretching as far east as the Coosa River. The legislative act that established it defined it as bounded "on the north by Shelby County, on the west by Tuscaloosa County, on the south by a line to be drawn from the headwaters of Five Mile Creek to the upper end of the ridge dividing the waters of the Cahawba from those of Mulberry Creek and thence by a direct line to the Coosa River, opposite the mouth of Hatchet Creek; and on the east by the Coosa River."[3] During the first half-century after its creation, it shrank considerably, as did the other early counties, in the process of the establishment of other county units. The twenty-two counties of 1819, the year of statehood, were eventually increased by partition and addition to sixty-seven. Cahaba retained the territory extending to the Coosa for less than a year. When St. Clair was created in November 1818, Cahaba lost this eastern area to Shelby, to compensate to some extent for the northern section Shelby had given to the new county.[4]

Perry took the next large bite when it was formed between Dallas and Cahaba on December 13, 1819. The presence of more settlers made it possible by this time to define the boundary in terms of early homesteads. It was described as running from "the source of the main stream of Mulberry Creek, and from thence down said creek to the ford, on the wagon road leading from Hazlett's to the pleasant valley; thence a direct course to where the road leading from Thomas Lindsey's to William Lovelace's crosses the Cahawba valley road; thence along said road to Major John Mahom's, and leaving him in the county of Cahawba, thence a direct course to where the boundary line of the county of Tuskaloosa crosses Roup's valley creek."[5]

Through the years, the exact position of the line between this county and Tuscaloosa has often been debated. An act approved by the state legislature on January 15, 1828, ordered the boundary to be established so as to leave Captain James Hill in Tuscaloosa County, but three years later a new law reversed this decision: "Edward Calvert, Grief Ragsdale, Benjamin Hubbert, John A. Bagby, Robert Hill, Hamilton Kile, and James Hill, at their present residences, or as many of them as can be so included, without taking any others, shall, by this act, be taken from the county of Tuscaloosa and be added to the county of Bibb."[6]

Although further adjustments were made, Bibb's borders remained fairly stable afterward until Reconstruction days, when in the 1867–68 session the legislature appropriated the southeastern segment next to Autauga to help form Baker, now Chilton County. As a result of all these changes, Bibb's shape became that of a pyramid squared off at several places. Its position on the state map was shifted slightly west of center and its area reduced to the present 635 square miles.

The chief natural feature is the scenic Cahaba River. More than a century ago, it was described in the following manner by a U.S. government engineer:

> The Cahaba River is formed at the northern boundary of Shelby County, by the East and West Cahaba, which take their rise in the southwestern part of St. Clair County, and flows in a southwesterly direction to Centreville. . . . From Centreville its direction is a little west of south for a distance, when it takes a southerly course to the Alabama. Above Centreville the river is a series of ponds and falls, the first fall occurring 400 feet above the ferry at Centreville, and amounting to 2.6 feet. Below that place it consists of pools and rapids, the fall in any one of the ponds not exceeding four inches.
>
> For about six miles above Centreville, according to Professor Tuomey's Survey of Alabama, the bed of the river is Silurian rock, and in this formation occur the principal iron-ore deposits, marble and hydraulic limestone. Above this is a narrow strip of sandstone; when this is passed the coalfields are reached and extend to the source of the river.
>
> Below Centreville the bed of the stream for about 45 miles is principally gravel and sand.[7]

The Cahaba has long been considered a fisherman's paradise. A hundred years ago, before the practice became illegal, it was not uncommon for residents to catch numerous sturgeons in fish traps. The river and its edge are also the home of some unusual plants and wildflowers. One of these is the Alabama croton, one of the rarest shrubs in the United States.[8] Except for a single location in southern Tennessee,[9] it grows only along the banks of the Cahaba in Bibb County, where it seems especially adapted to

Cahaba lilies, blooming in May north of the first falls of the Cahaba River. This wildflower grows in Alabama only in the Cahaba and in Hatchet Creek, Clay County. (Courtesy of Mrs. Loyd Owens)

the harsh environment of shale and limestone bluffs. Its buds open in late February or early March near the River Bend bridge.[10] Before the damming of the Black Warrior raised the waters of that river near Tuscaloosa, the plant could be found there also, in rock formations quite similar to those on the Cahaba; the two rivers are thought to have once been one river system. Another rare specimen is a spider lily, *Hymenocallis coronaria,* locally called Cahaba lily, which grows from the bulbs lodged between the rocks in the shallow water and blooms in the month of May. This wildflower, now listed as an endangered species, is found infrequently from Florida to North Carolina, but chiefly in Alabama in the Cahaba and Little Cahaba Rivers.[11] Its Cahaba habitat extends for several miles above the bridge at Centreville, a point from which the southernmost vestiges of Appalachian rock gradually recede underground. In late May or early June, the blossoms stand tall above the water in a spectacular display of gleaming white. In some years, a few miles below the Piper bridge, where the Cahaba is comparatively wide, they cover almost the entire breadth of the river.

Numerous small streams help to drain the county, flowing directly or indirectly into the Cahaba. Among the creeks are Schultz, Haysop, Hill's, Cane, Six Mile, Blue Guttee (or Blue Girth), Affonee, Beaver Dam, Shades

("Shades of Death" on old maps), Sandy, Gully, Caffee, Big Ugly, Little Ugly, Mud, Mulberry, Copperas, Oakmulgee, Millpond, Four Mile, Haggard, Alligator, Hurricane, Johnson, and Elam. The General Highway Map of Bibb County (1976) also shows such "branches" as Bear, Clear, Miller, Furnace, and two Licklogs, one flowing into Haysop and the other into Affonee. One of the most interesting streams is Six Mile Creek, whose main current suddenly drops underground for a short space at a large hole, known as "the sinks." Another tributary of the Cahaba is the Little Cahaba River, formed by the confluence of Mahan and Shoal creeks. Its upper run, above Bulldog Bend, includes an exciting challenge for canoeists, an abrupt four-foot fall.

Some of these streams, cutting deep into the earth, have left the general surface rugged, especially in the northern part of the county. That section possesses large coalfields, besides deposits of iron ore, dolomite, limestone, barites, and other minerals, and several areas of Bibb are currently being explored for oil. About three and a half miles northeast of Centreville, to the east of Alabama 25, is a distinctive natural feature, the mineral springs known as Gary (formerly Brown) Springs, whose water is valued for its medicinal properties. They are said to have been discovered in 1844 by William Jones on land then owned by settler Jesse Brown and were later developed by a Selma physician, Dr. Thomas P. Gary. Near Six Mile are some caves from which saltpeter was once extracted. Almost a century ago, the following division of the county's lands was reported: "It has been estimated that the hilly pine lands total 325 square miles; the Cahaba coalfield, 125 square miles; Roup's valley, 100 square miles; woodland, all."[12] Eighty-five percent of the county is still heavily forested with pine, especially loblolly, and several species of oak as well as hickory, walnut, mulberry hackberry, tulip poplar, gum, cedar, and dogwood. As a result, lumbering is the largest industry.

When the first white settlers made their way into the region more than a century and a half ago, attracted by the unusual water resources and the pleasant valleys of the Cahaba, they found a virgin forest far more magnificent than the present woodlands. Even at the beginning of the twentieth century, virgin pine still stood near Blocton that measured ninety-nine inches in circumference. Government agents who made the first survey noted enthusiastically in 1820 both the luxuriance of the trees and the beauty of the Cahaba. One surveyor reported in his field notes at a point on the river opposite the present Gary Springs road intersection with Alabama 25: "River here looks beautiful, is about 10 chains (660 feet) directly across the stream, is about 7 or 8 feet deep and has a beautiful bottom of solid rock and on the north side a considerable bluff of rock. Neither side of the river is ever inundated. Growth is most luxuriant, is interspersed with a rocky surface, growth mulberry, sugar tree, maple, white and red oak, post oak, ———Ash, lind, and maiden [hair fern?]."[13]

The early settlers were indebted for the conservation of these seemingly boundless natural resources to their Indian predecessors, the Creeks, so called for the many waterways on which they lived. The Indian tribe or confederacy of kindred tribes, of which the Muskogees, or Creeks, were perhaps the most numerous, is thought by some scholars to have migrated to Alabama from the north and west not long before the Spaniards came in the early sixteenth century.[14] Although the Indians settled principally on the Coosa and Tallapoosa rivers, they fanned out also to the west along the Cahaba. Here, remote from the center of Creek culture, the Upper Creeks established a few villages on the eastern banks of the Cahaba or nearby at the forks of its eastern tributaries. Although they probably hunted west of the river, they did not build there because of the proximity to the Choctaw lands. In the Treaty of Mount Dexter, concluded on November 16, 1805, the boundary between Creek and Choctaw ground was described as the watershed between the Tombigbee River and the Coosa and Alabama rivers.[15] This ridge has been identified as one running north and south almost parallel to the Black Warrior and Tombigbee rivers and standing about a mile and a half from the Tuscaloosa County line. Mulberry Baptist Church, located in Beat 3 about sixteen miles southwest of Centreville on Alabama 25, is said to be "situated immediately on the dividing ridge between the waters of the Cahaba and Warrior Rivers.... The waters from the east side of the original building flowed into the Blue Girth and thence into the Cahaba, while the west side flowed into Five Mile Creek and into the Warrior."[16] The Creeks apparently obtained permission for one exception to the restrictions of this treaty. They set up a trading post near the present town of Tuscaloosa, called Black Warrior Town, later burned by General John Coffee during the Creek War.[17]

These Creeks who made the banks of the Cahaba and its tributaries their home for around three centuries before the white settlers intruded on them were instinctive conservationists. They made judicious cuttings of some trees while retaining those on the banks of streams to prevent erosion. A study of artifacts has revealed that each wood had its special use.[18] When it was available, cypress was the favorite material for canoes, but larger craft were hewed from poplar. The Creeks constructed their bows and their house frames of cedar, once abundant in this section. They found gum useful for making drums; dogberry and hackberry for baskets; elm, sycamore, and tulip poplar for spoons; but oak chiefly for firewood. Besides felling certain trees in carefully chosen locations for these purposes, the Creeks in the Cahaba valley, as elsewhere, necessarily cleared patches of woodland near their villages for the cultivation of crops. The first settlers found such clearings and planted their own crops in them. Yet to those land-hungry immigrants the forest seemed to have been barely touched by the red men.

The Indians also kept a balance in wildlife by hunting only for what they needed, never merely for sport. The Creeks considered the deer and bear most important for clothing, but valued the bear also especially for its fat.[19] In addition, they ate raccoons, squirrels, rabbits, and wildcats and sewed skins together for clothing; raccoons were also used to make pouches. Their favorite food was the wild turkey, and one Creek village traditionally located in the county indicated the popularity of this fowl by taking the name "Pinhoti" (also spelled "Penootaw" and "Pensatau"), meaning "turkey home."[20] All these animals as well as panthers and wolves were still to be found in northern Bibb in 1871, when the Blocton area was settled.[21]

The Creek Indians lived by both hunting and farming, but when white settlers encroached on their traditional hunting grounds, they turned more and more to farming. Although they owned their individual houses, the land always belonged to the tribe. The community planted and harvested together, each family raising enough for its own members and storing the excess in common storehouses. David Crockett, who assisted General John Coffee in burning Black Warrior Town, recorded that "there was a large field of corn standing out and a pretty good supply in some cribs. There was also a quantity of dried beans which were very acceptable to us."[22] Corn was the Creeks' principal crop, though they also raised kidney beans, squash, pumpkin, melons, and cane. Besides using corn for food, they beat it to a pulp and substituted it for deer brains when dressing skins.[23] They taught the white men their method of pounding corn into meal. In 1977 a Bibb collector of Indian artifacts uncovered on a hill between Haysop and Affonee creeks a hollowed-out heart pine log apparently used to contain the corn, and nearby he located the tools that must have been used.[24]

Today, around a century and a half after the Indians' retreat westward, no remains of their villages can be discovered in Bibb County. Now those locations must be sought chiefly on early maps, which, however, do not always agree. Various state maps represent the Upper Creek towns in this area as Penootaw, or Pensatau, and Ischooka; and oral tradition adds Osoonee. John Melish in sketchy maps published in 1818 and 1819, showing Andrew Jackson's targets in the Creek War of 1813–14, placed Penootaw on the east bank of the Cahaba River near what was in 1818 actually the lower boundary of Cahaba County, next to Dallas.[25] By 1820 he had revised his spelling, listing "Upper Pensotau, 13 houses, Lower Pensotau,

28 houses." Lucas's 1822 map of Alabama assigns Penootaw Town to the same location, which by that year was in newly created Perry County. Yet both R. S. Tanner's 1822 map of Alabama and Draton's 1827 "Statistical and Historical Map of Alabama" place these Indian ruins a few miles north of present Centreville on the thirty-third degree of latitude. Although none of these early cartographers show Schultz Creek, the general position of the burned village as indicated by both Tanner and Draton indicates a location opposite its confluence with the Cahaba River. This position would bear out the local tradition as recalled by older citizens and reported to Owen.[26] A much later map, however, Cowperthwaite's 1850 "Stage and Steamboat Route Map," places "Pensotau" at the fork of Six Mile Creek and the Little Cahaba.

Both Ischooka (Oschooka) and Osoonee belong to local tradition, though variously located. Ischooka also appears on Melish's map of 1820 at the fork of the Cahaba with an eastern tributary just below Freeman's Survey Line, which crosses the Cahaba River today about two miles east of West Blocton. On Melish's 1818–19 map, where it is spelled Osehcoco, this village is represented as a small one by the drawing of three tepees. Osoonee, or Old Osonee Town, is also claimed by Bibb oral tradition but fails to appear on maps of the state. According to Owen, who tapped the memory of old citizens early in this century, it stood on the east bank of the Cahaba about one and a half miles above the influx of Shades Creek, a location that would be close to the Shelby line in the northeastern corner of Bibb. Royce, however, in the 1920 *Handbook* of the Alabama Anthropological Society, reported it as probably in Shelby; it is possible it spread across the line into both counties.

After the War of 1812 began, the pressure on the Creeks in Alabama from advancing white settlers increased, and so did the hostility between red and white men because many of the Creeks were allied with the British. Clashes resulted on July 27, 1813, in the Battle of Burnt Corn in Conecuh County and reached a climax on August 30, 1813, in the massacre at Fort Mims in newly formed Clarke County. Although the upper Cahaba villages were remote from these scenes of bloodshed and probably dispatched no warriors to the Red Sticks, the Creek war party, they were doomed after the cry for help went out to the neighboring states. That cry was answered by four armies of volunteers, chief of which was that of middle and west Tennessee, led by Andrew Jackson, at that time major general of the Tennessee Militia. Jackson marched through Huntsville, crossed the Tennessee River, and cut a road through the wilderness to the Creek country. After a series of lesser engagements, he defeated the Red Sticks decisively, assisted by General John Coffee, at the battle of Horseshoe Bend on the Tallapoosa, March 27, 1814.[27]

Then, determined to complete his conquest, Jackson wrote on April 23 from Fort Williams: "Tomorrow I detail 600 men under the command of Brigadier General Johnston to scour the Cahauba with instruction after dispersing any bodies of the enemy that still manifest symptoms of hostility, to unite with me at Fort Deposit."[28] General Johnston, traveling up the river, burned Penootaw on April 29 and Tullavahajaj, or Mudtown, on May 1, according to Melish's map of 1818–19. Meanwhile, Captain Gordon had destroyed Osecoco. The Indians along the Cahaba River in this area probably responded like those at Mudtown and Black Warrior Town the preceding October and had already fled when the soldiers appeared. General Coffee wrote to his wife on October 24, 1813, that he had burned three Indian towns and never seen a native.[29] The Creeks, peering through the dense forest, possibly saw the canoes that the white men sent back down the Cahaba, laden with their booty of stored corn and Indian wares confiscated from the trading village of Mudtown.

After their homes were destroyed and their food stores stolen, the Creeks apparently did not linger long in the Cahaba valley. No legends about early settlers' problems with them have survived in Bibb or adjoining Shelby. The Treaty of Fort Jackson on August 9, 1814, which forced the Creek cession of all claims west of the Coosa, noted the destitution of the entire Creek nation and promised "to furnish gratuitously the necessaries of life, until the crops of corn can be considered competent to yield the nation a supply."[30] The treaty also required all Creeks west of the Coosa River to move to the east side, thus clearing the area for white settlers. Some of them found wild horses and cattle, apparently left behind by the Indians in their hurried exodus.[31]

Those few Indians who were discovered living in the Bibb area are thought to have been friendly Choctaws who had moved from their nearby territory on the west. According to tradition, they established a camp called Chitopeni on the Little Cahaba at the confluence of Shoals and Mahan creeks.[32] Evidence of Indians in the neighborhood in the early 1820s appears in the minutes of Enon Baptist Church and in the traditions of Sandy Methodist Chapel, organized before 1825. According to a story handed down by early settlers, some Indians lingered in a camp near a spring on the present Charles England farm, just below Centreville, until they were finally pushed out by the whites in the early 1840s.

Although no remains are extant of Indian villages in the county today, collectors of artifacts continue to find evidence of temporary camps, especially on the Cahaba River and at the forks of its tributaries. Because the riverbed in southern Bibb, where the rock formations end, has shifted during a century and a half, camp relics have been uncovered at some distance from the present river course. These include Indian bowls, pottery shards, game stones for contests like pitching horseshoes, and other stones for making scores; fireplaces and graves have also been discovered. Several Indian skeletons have been dug up from time to time near the river. In the excavations incidental to the erection of the bridge at Abercrombie in 1911, a number of bodies were unearthed, all apparently buried in sitting positions and their bones well preserved.[33] Two years later, field-workers on the Goodson farm below Brent found a large earthen jar that contained skeletons of a man and a child, also thought to be Indians.[34]

Besides these relics, a few other reminders of the Indian past remain in Bibb County. One is the former ball field, traditionally said to have been used by the Creeks, located on the east side of the Cahaba just below Centreville, where a racecourse was laid out during Reconstruction days.

But the most enduring legacy of the red men in Bibb is the names they gave a few of its streams. Most of these names are today considered more likely to be Choctaw than Creek. An early state archivist ventured the opinion that the euphonious word *Cahaba* was a corruption of the Choctaw *Oka Aba*, meaning "the river above," and may have been assigned to this river by some Choctaws living down on the lower course of the Alabama.[35] Two of the three creeks whose Indian names survive flow through that part of the county west of the Cahaba, either in or near Choctaw territory, and are thought to be Choctaw in origin. They are Affonee and Haysop. An Indian etymologist has concluded that Affonee may be derived from Choctaw *afana*, meaning "staked," or even more likely from Choctaw *nafoni*, "bones."[36] Haysop, spelled Haysoppy on La Tourette's Map of Alabama, 1844, may be a corruption of Choctaw *hush apa*, meaning "black gum tree," though other possible derivations include Choctaw *ahe*, "potatoes," plus *sipi*, "old," and also Choctaw *ahe*, "potato," plus *osapa*, "field." Concerning the first suggested source of the name, the black gum tree may have been called *hush apa* by the Indians because birds *(hushi)* liked to eat its berries *(apa)*.[37]

East of the Cahaba, in the larger area settled by the Creeks, one stream has a name that can be identified as Hitchiti, a dialect of the Creek confederacy. This stream, flowing through the southeastern corner of Bibb, is Oakmulgee, meaning bubbling water, from *oki*, "water" and *mulgi*, "boiling."[38] Today the word is perpetuated in the designation of the Oakmulgee Division of the Talladega National Forest in this region of the county.

By the time the first settlers reached the well-forested and well-watered area that was destined to become Bibb County, few red men were left except for the occasional bands of Choctaws. After October 1816, when the Treaty of the Trading House required the peaceful Choctaws to sell their remaining claims east of the Tombigbee, including the strip west of the Cahaba, all the land that was to be incorporated in 1818 as Cahaba County was open to white immigrants.

2

ARRIVAL OF THE SQUATTERS

AROUND 1815 OR 1816 white settlers began making their way into present Bibb as well as other Alabama lands opened by the expulsion of the Indians. For several years, the tide of immigration rose, in spite of the impossibility at first of buying land. The land had to be surveyed before it could be sold, but the immigrants were impatient. They rushed in during this period of "Alabama fever," laid claim to tracts, and became squatters. U.S. census figures show that in 1816 Monroe County, that huge central triangle which composed the entire Creek cession, already had 3,593 unauthorized inhabitants. In 1818 newly created Cahaba County alone had 1,280 residents, and in 1820 it had almost tripled that number to 3,676, as many as all of Monroe had possessed four years earlier.

In an attempt to stop this illegal appropriation of public lands, President James Monroe in December 1815 had ordered the removal of the squatters, even sending in soldiers to burn their cabins. But Congress responded to the resulting protests, and by an act of April 16, 1816, permitted those who had immigrated into the Creek cession before February of that year to remain until the land on which they had settled was offered for sale. Later arrivals, however, were allowed to stay on the same terms. A surveyor for the U.S. government, in approving this clemency, said in 1817: "Many of these unhappy people have expended almost the whole of their little all in reaching the forbidden land; and are utterly incapable of returning, if they wished to do so."[1] The result of this generous policy was that many of the early settlers remained squatters for years.

John Coffee, surveyor-general for the northern half of the Alabama Territory, appointed Benjamin and Hardy Clements to lay the section lines in the western Alabama region that included Cahaba and Tuscaloosa counties. They are said to have arrived from South Carolina with only their horses, saddles, surveying instruments, and the clothes on their backs.

Their work in Tuscaloosa County was interrupted by an Indian attack, but their survey of Cahaba County was apparently without incident, though their field notes of December 1818, made three miles above the present Sandy community near Centreville, record that a recent hurricane had torn down trees for a distance of half a mile.[2] The original section line they surveyed through Centreville passes along what is now the eastern boundary of the Norman Meigs and Hal Cottingham home lots in the residential area created in the 1880s as Aldine.

While the Clements brothers were determining this section line in 1820, a land office was opened in nearby Tuscaloosa. In the same year, Congress passed an act calculated to expedite land sales. It provided that not merely whole or quarter sections be offered but also half-quarter sections, priced at a minimum of $1.25 per acre in cash, a far more reasonable rate than speculators had been demanding. But only gradually did county settlers respond to this encouragement. In a period of commercial instability, many were glad to postpone the day of purchase as long as possible. Moreover, most of them must have lacked the necessary means. Because they had financed their journey by spending much of the cash realized on the sale of their old homes, they often arrived almost if not entirely without funds. Charles C. H. Collier told of reaching the Falls of Cahaba with only twenty-five cents in his pocket.[3]

The valley of the Cahaba must have looked very desirable to those financially depleted, land-hungry immigrants. A more disinterested eye than theirs, that of a U.S. government surveyor, saw it early in 1817, and from his description his supervisor wrote this report to the acting secretary of war on March 12, 1817: "The Cahaba is said to be navigable for Boats to its Falls, distant from Ditto's Landing, just below Chickasaw Island, on the Tennessee, almost 120 miles; and in the neighborhood of the Falls, both above and below, there is said to be a valley of very inviting land, with the finest Springs, & the fairest prospect of health."[4] The cotton land in Virginia and the Carolina Piedmont, from which most of these immigrants originally came,[5] had lost much of its fertility and also lacked the number of streams found in central Alabama. It appeared to the small farmers there that they could improve their economic status by pushing on to this new, cheap land.

Some of the settlers of what was to be Cahaba, later Bibb, County were first attracted to this "valley of very inviting land" when they were fighting the Indians with Andrew Jackson in 1814. They made mental note of rich lands along the Cahaba River or on certain of its creeks and planned to return with their families. Long ago, Kevin Cunningham Mahan related the tradition of how the Mahan brothers and their soldier-companions, including Lindzeys, Fanchers, Massingales, Ragans, and Smiths, made their

An original settler, Obadiah Langston, a native of Kentucky (1799–1888). (Courtesy of Harold K. Cottingham)

way through this area toward the Cumberland valley in Tennessee. He said:

> Rather than tackle the job of running boats on the Mississippi up stream, they decided to follow the not any too safe Indian trails, or just strike out right up through the woods of Mississippi Territory in the direction the wild geese flew in the spring.... They made a compromise of trails and directions, and, after following what was known as the Tuskaloosa trail, took to the woods. When they reached the confluence of three creeks, known today as Mahan, Shoal, and Mayberry creeks, which together make the Little Cahaba River, they found an Indian camp well stocked with swine, horses, cows, and corn; also, says rumor, there were here a goodly number of comely Indian maidens, and not too great a number of bucks with highly developed fighting proclivities.[6]

Twelve of the eighteen soldiers in this traveling band chose to remain with the Indians but had disappeared by the time the others eventually returned with their families. The descendants of many of these as well as other veterans of the War of 1812 and the Indian wars were later able to claim bounty lands for their military services.[7]

The usual pattern of migration seems to have been for one or more members of a family to precede the others by a year or more. Among many families of which this was said to be true were the Averys, Clarks, Clements, Mahans, Mayberrys, Pratts, and Wards. According to tradition in the Ward clan, David Ward had selected land on Six Mile Creek before his father and older brothers followed him from South Carolina, and only after a house was near completion did sixteen-year-old Daniel return in August 1819 in an ox-wagon to transport the mother and younger children with their possessions, only to find that his mother had died a few days earlier.[8] Sometimes four brothers pioneered together, as did Elisha, Charles, John, and William Cottingham with their father, Elisha, North Carolinians who had resided briefly in Tennessee. South Carolinians Joab and John Pratt were followed shortly by two other brothers, Hopkins and Absalom.

It is interesting to speculate upon which roads these first settlers traveled into the new country along the Cahaba.[9] John Melish's Map of the United States, 1818, indicates two likely routes. One of these, called the Federal Road, connected Richmond with New Orleans, passing through Raleigh, Columbia, Athens, and Milledgeville, and entering Alabama around present-day Phenix City. Because it traversed the Creek Nation in eastern Alabama, it was considered dangerous, but many newcomers, like the Ezekiel Smith family from Georgia and the Steeles from South Carolina, are said to have traveled it, the Steeles camping at Montgomery before turning northwest to Bibb. It was probably along this rough way that Ezekiel, Theophilus, and Joshua Miller brought their household goods on ox-drawn slides from Georgia around 1820.[10]

The other route, usually followed by Tennesseeans and those who "touched Tennessee," as the pioneers referred to an interval of residence there en route, was a spur of the Kentucky Trace that ran south to Huntsville. From Huntsville an old Indian trail led past Ditto's Landing on the Tennessee River through Elyton (now Birmingham) to Mudtown, the Indian village site on the Cahaba just north of present-day Bibb. This road would have been familiar to Jackson's veterans and must have been used by many pioneers traveling to the valleys of the Cahaba and the Black Warrior. For some time, this old Huntsville Road was only a horse path. Many settlers, like Joseph Ray of neighboring Shelby County, a Tennesseean who had served under Jackson during the Creek War, brought their families on horseback and their goods on packhorses down this trail.[11] After the immigrants had gradually cleared the trees on their march, the way for a while became a stump road, sometimes called a barrel road because travelers, like the Miller brothers on the Federal Road, could pull their possessions along it in barrels by means of horses or oxen. After these roads would permit four-wheeled vehicles, most pioneers traveled in wagons, often wagon trains, driving their stock ahead of them with the help of slaves, if they owned any. Once they left the beaten way, they were forced to depend on Indian trails or paths of their own blazing.

Travelers responded to the journey differently, according to their luck or disposition. In 1818 a pioneer gave an enthusiastic account of his venture through the wilderness from the nearby log-cabin village of Tuscaloosa. He wrote: "The autumnal leaves and nuts were clattering down everywhere. Shellbarks, hickory nuts, and chestnuts strewed the ground, and grapes, muscadines, persimmons and various kinds of wild autumnal fruits were plentiful. . . . We killed plenty of deer, turkey, ducks, wild pigeons, and had the music of great gangs of wolves around our camp every night. The entire trip was delightful beyond description."[12] Some of the adventurous immigrants to Cahaba County must have found a similar enjoyment in this wild new country, especially after the anxiety of the journey was over. Yet most of them probably suffered difficulties on the way like those Sara Jane Lide Fountain encountered when she migrated with her family from South Carolina to Dallas County in 1835. The roads were rough and muddy, her oxen gave out, and her little wagon broke down.[13] The caravan in which she traveled covered from ten to eighteen miles a day. Like her, Cahaba immigrants were probably fearful of the Indians at the trading posts in the Creek Nation but, also like her, probably found them to be either friendly or harmlessly drunk.[14]

When Cahaba County settlers finally reached their destination, they must have followed the pioneer practice of choosing a tract of land and indicating their claim to it by girdling a few trees and perhaps laying the first four logs of a house, preferably near a spring. Until they had time to build a house, they slept in the same tent that they had camped in along the way. It was the custom to drive four corner posts into the ground and several small saplings between them, then pound the enclosed ground until it was hard enough to serve as a floor, afterward covering the space with the tent.[15] The urgent business was not building a house but raising the first corn crop in fields gradually extended by girdling more trees. This common method of clearing a "new ground" produced a ghost-like appearance from the rows of skeleton trees but saved the settlers a great deal of labor because in a few years the timber fell without the use of an ax.[16] Neighbors then assisted in the arduous work of removing the fallen trees at a "log-rolling," more appropriately called a "log-toting," after which they burned them.

Sometimes it was difficult to survive until the first crop was made because many of the squatters found themselves stripped of resources at the end of the journey. Robert Sterrett was one who apparently never recovered financially or perhaps physically. After arriving in future Cahaba County in 1816, he died in March of the following year leaving an insolvent estate. His tombstone records these dates and the fact that he was "about 31 years old." The Cahaba County orphans' court in February 1819 appointed Gabriel Benson, Charles Coleman, and Ezra Tate as commissioners to adjust the claims of his creditors.[17]

When the settler eventually found freedom to build, he constructed his house of peeled logs, roofing it with slabs made from split timber and flooring it with logs split into two pieces, turning the flat side upward. The first structures in Cahaba County must not have been very different from those described by William Ely in nearby Tuscaloosa on June 2, 1821. In a letter to his wife, he complained that the houses were "without a single Pane of Glass, with scarcely a saw'd board or Plank, Nail, or any other iron about them, all with wooden Chimneys and fire Places.... Some... are raised from the ground high enough for Hogs, Cats & fowls to go under. ... I have sometimes been very much annoy'd by the growling, squeaking, barking, squalling, and cackling of those animals under the floor where I slept."[18]

Ely, a businessman and philanthropist accustomed to the amenities of Hartford, Connecticut, would have made a poor pioneer. Even the first governor of Alabama lived in a two-room log house built with an open hall, or "dog-trot." Examples of one-unit log cabins built in this county may be seen today in the Stewart cabin, which was moved to Tannehill

State Park; and in the Merchant stagecoach inn from Randolph, now removed to Brierfield State Park as a tourist attraction. A double cabin built in 1846 by John H. Ward near the old Post Road in Bibb County was torn down and reassembled in Tuscaloosa in 1946 by Dr. Byron Arnold, who later presented it to the YMCA.

The construction of such pioneer homes was not uncommon in Bibb throughout the nineteenth century. In writing of the house his father hewed out of the wilderness five miles northeast of Centreville around 1880, Charles Collier Dailey described the type that many settlers built: "The first unit of the old home was one large room, about 18 x 20 feet, with a shed type of porch on the front. There was a huge rock chimney and fireplace in one end and a door on the opposite side. . . . For ventilation, aside from the doors, there was a high window with shutters on each side of the fireplace. There were no glass windows. . . . [A later addition] was a large log room, built just far enough away to leave a 10-foot open hallway, commonly called 'The Dog Trot.' My older brother and my father cut the logs and hewed them smooth on two sides and hauled them out of the woods. They also split the pine boards to roof it."[19] Neighbors were invited to the traditional house-raising because enough men were needed to lift and notch the logs. Later, after the logs had "seasoned and settled," the owner chinked the cracks with mud. To accommodate further increases in his family, he eventually enclosed both the front and the back shed porches as bedrooms. The Dailey home, like that of many an early settler, was eventually covered by heart pine boards. This house today faces Alabama 25 on the northeastern edge of Centreville's present town limits and is known as the Bradley house.

According to the accounts of administrators of estates, these early homes in Bibb boasted little furniture except a few beds and "cheers." Each bed was provided with a mattress constructed of broom sage, crabgrass, or corn shucks.[29] In a county home as late as the 1880s, a large shuck mattress was still placed on the bed cords, topped by a tremendous "feather bed" made from the feathers of geese, which were plucked twice each summer for this purpose.[21] Members of the older generation can still recall a mournful folk song:

> Go tell Aunt Rachel, go tell Aunt Rachel,
> Go tell Aunt Rachel the old gray goose is dead,
> The one that she's been saving, the one that she's been saving,
> The one that she's been saving to make her feather bed.

Many of the hardy first-comers erected their log homes in isolated situations, often with the hope of claiming as much land as possible. Yet,

Rock and mud chimney of the century-old Creel house, owned and occupied now by W. A. and Etta Creel Posey, and located off Bear Creek Road about two miles from the Tuscaloosa County line near Pearson. (Courtesy of Mrs. Josiah Kennedy)

without close neighbors, they were vulnerable to frontier crime and to Indian attacks. On December 22, 1818, U.S. Army veteran John Neel reported to the secretary of war from the Falls of Black Warrior that "a remenant of Hostile Creeks" had passed through this general area on their journey to find land on which to settle beyond the Mississippi. "They crossed the rivers Allabama & Cahabia," Neel wrote.[22] After alleged but unspecified "outrages on our Citizons" about forty "interpriseing men" followed them across the Warrior eight miles above the Falls, discovered them "incamped in a beaver ruen well fortyfyed by Nature," and, in a series of skirmishes in which they were aided by a detachment of the U.S. Army, killed a number of the displaced natives and dispersed the others. The *St. Stephens Halcyon* of September 26, being informed that these Indians were Seminoles who had been pushed out of Florida, alerted its readers concerning their presence on the Black Warrior and the Cahaba. It reported, "The inhabitants are in great consternation, leaving their farms and collecting into bodies, in order to defend themselves."[23]

The need for security as well as for neighborliness in a strange country undoubtedly encouraged a number of loose settlements, not villages but areas where farm clearings were within a mile or two of each other, a mile often being considered necessary "elbow room." The first settlements in the county were probably almost simultaneous with the great rush of pioneers who were hoping to claim cheap, fertile land. Today, those first locations that can be identified with any degree of certainty are those that left family graveyards or a history of churches or that appear in official county records. In the orders for road building in the first county court minutes, May 1818, most of the references are to rivers, creeks, landings, for example, George Mayberry's landing, John Canterbury's landing; and to individual residences or business places such as William Deason's (east of the river), King and Smith's store on Hazlett's Creek (now in Shelby County), Taber's Mill (on Schultz Creek just west of later Scottsville), and Maple's Store, near present Maplesville.

Allusions are made, however, to two settlements: the Mulberry Settlement on Mulberry Creek, now in Chilton County; and Hill's Settlement, which grew up at the headwaters of Hill's and Schultz creeks near the Tuscaloosa line, not far from Johntown today. In 1825 James (Jake) Hill received a patent to an entire section (around 640 acres). Farmlands of this large settlement were cleared not only by the Hill family but also by others, including John Goodson, William Calvert, Jackson Caffee, Robert Woods, and Thomas and Milton Kessee.[24] In the Hill-Oldham Cemetery, the oldest marked grave is that of William Green Hill, the two-year-old son of James and Jane Calvert Hill, who died in 1823. The early importance of Hill's Settlement is documented by the establishment of the Mars post office in 1823; James Hill was the first postmaster.

Other loose collections of farm clearings were established within a few years. Taber's Mill, referred to in the May 1818 county court minutes, was the beginning of Taber's Settlement, headed by Revolutionary veteran William Taber and his son, Nathan. By February 1830 the area along Sandy Creek east of Centreville was called Suttleville in these minutes because the clan of John Suttle occupied so much of it. The oldest marked grave and the oldest church are both in the section of eastern Bibb near Brierfield that was later to be known by the name of Carlton Hill. Thomas Carlton is mentioned in the county court minutes of February 1818, and Isaac Carlton deeded the church its lot in 1829.[25] Both the grave, that of Robert Sterrett, today enclosed by a fence in the middle of a hundred-acre soybean field, and the picturesque Cahaba Valley Baptist Church, a few miles distant on the Little Cahaba River, bear the date 1817. Also such early graves as that of John Mahan (1820) on Mahan Creek, Lucinda Green (1821) near Woodstock, and Martha and Wiley Coleman (1822) in the Centreville Memorial Cemetery west of the Cahaba must be indicators of pioneer homesteads.

Among many groups of farm clearings throughout the woods, only one early village existed. It sprang up shortly after the territorial legislature on February 7, 1818, chose the Falls of Cahaba as the temporary site of the county seat, and by May 1818 it was referred to in the orphans' court minutes as Centerville,[26] for which a later variant spelling was Centreville. Like Tuscaloosa at the Falls of Black Warrior, it was often designated by its location instead of by its name. Before the area was honored by the legislature, it had attracted settlers because it was believed to be at the head of navigation of the Cahaba. An old resident defined the situation of the town in this way: "It is located on the Cahaba River, near the upper end of the fertile farming lands known as the Cahaba valley, and the lowest point at which the shelving rock cross the river, and for miles above is known as the river falls. The original location of the town was on the first bluff of the river, with the major part of the buildings on the west side of the river."[27]

The name Centreville, though explained in several ways, was probably derived from its position in a land survey. A resident of nearly a century ago tersely noted that the town was "a village between two points, thus the center previously settled and later agreed on for the county seat."[28] The statement of the first county sheriff, Andrew Henshaw, seems to bear out this explanation. In his report to the governor on June 2, 1818, concerning his division of the county into three militia districts, he indicated that he could not consider the Falls of Cahaba as the center, though it had been designated so, but instead he "considered the local situation of the county. . . . I think it proper to state, that the present boundaries of the County is ill adapted to the location of the Country having the 1st falls of the Cahawba the Centre."[29] Yet, even if no such designation had been made, the residents at the Falls possibly would have preferred the name of Centreville as a matter of policy. The legislative act which made it the temporary seat of justice required that the citizens later elect commissioners to choose a permanent site in or near the center of the county. Any place that aspired to that honor would surely wish to identify with the center, even though to do so would be, as Sheriff Henshaw complained, an inconsistency. Citizens of other counties have tried the same name magic. When Marion County was selecting a new county seat in 1880, advocates of a certain location in unsettled woods tried to attract support by naming it Center.[30]

This frontier village of Centreville was the seat of government during the first few years of the county's existence, initially as Cahaba County and not quite three years later as Bibb. The task of bringing order and a degree of civilization into the numerous widely scattered settlements was not an easy one, but the squatters went to work to organize their county administration. Meanwhile, their choice of a permanent seat of justice through commissioners elected at the polls had to wait for a decade.

3

EARLY COUNTY GOVERNMENT

THE FIRST STEPS toward organizing the government of Cahaba County were taken within three weeks after the territorial legislature's act of February 7, 1818, that created this administrative unit and located its temporary seat of justice at the Falls of Cahaba. In the next half-dozen years, its citizens began shaping a county out of the wilderness.

To expedite the process, Governor William Wyatt Bibb appointed the first officers on February 28, 1818. In these and later appointments, he was apparently approving recommendations sent or brought to him at St. Stephens, the territorial capital, by residents of the county. Sheriff Andrew Henshaw on June 2, 1818, sent him a list of proposals, some of which the governor acted upon.[1] The settlers first named to office included John Canterbury, chief justice; John Cates and James Smith, justices quorum; Andrew Henshaw, sheriff; Ezra Tate, clerk of the superior and county courts, later in the year assessor. In other 1818 appointments, William Ratcliff became treasurer but resigned shortly to follow Tate as clerk; Oliver C. Cleveland became coroner and George Mayberry ranger. In the fall of that year, two other justices, Henry W. Stevens and Littlepage Sims, were added.

By the end of 1819, Gabriel Benson had succeeded Canterbury as "first judge," to be followed in 1820 by Andrew Lusk. Meanwhile, Charles A. Dennis and Agrippa Atkinson had taken Stevens's and Sims's seats on the county court. Three years later, the legislature voted to change the unwieldy judicial system by replacing the five justices with one judge. Judge Lusk was succeeded on January 1, 1824, by Thomas Crawford, who kept his seat until the summer of 1836. Sheriffs of the 1820s were John Henry, Hugh Henry, William E. Lawler, and James W. Davis, the last of whom later served many years in the legislature from Bibb. These were the chief county officers during the period of initial settlement.[2]

In May 1818, when the court held its first session, a courthouse had already been provided on the west side of the river to accommodate its members. According to the minutes, the first meeting was "held at the Court House of Cahaba County, Alabama Territory." No description of this first county building has survived, but it was probably similar to the original courthouse of Shelby, the neighboring county that had been established on the same day as Cahaba. At its first seat of justice, Shelbyville, near present-day Pelham, the citizens built a courthouse twenty-four by twenty feet and eight feet high, at a cost of $53.[3] The government of Conecuh County, also formed in 1818, began life in a one-room building constructed of rude chestnut logs; the judge sat behind a table, which rested on a dirt floor. Its second courthouse, built in 1820, was made of pine logs, had increased in size to twenty by thirty feet, and boasted two doors. The jurors reportedly had to repair to the woods for privacy while reaching their verdicts.[4] These structures suggest the likely pattern of the first courthouse in Cahaba County.

The first jail is not difficult to visualize because specifications appear in the county court minutes of August 1818. It was ordered that "there be built at or near the Falls of Cahaba a jail sixteen feet square of Timbers ten inches square, foundation of like Timbers and floored above of like Timbers one story and a half high roof of plank nailes one."[5] Two Revolutionary War veterans, Charles Coleman and John Wallace, were appointed by the court to receive subscriptions and take proposals for its construction. It must have been completed before the end of the year, for in February 1819 the county court minutes record an application to the territorial treasury for $24.40, the cost of provisions for certain slaves confined in the county jail for the past sixty-one days on a charge of murder. Officials were reimbursed for taking care of prisoners; for example, James Mahan, constable, for guarding and returning to prison five slaves and Stephen Potts for "victualizing" prisoners and guards.[6]

It is not known how effective incarceration in this first jail was. According to Alabama humorist Joseph G. Baldwin, who practiced law in Sumter County in pioneer days, the log jails "held no one but Indians, who had no friend outside who could help them, and no skill inside to prize out."[7] Perhaps the log building on the west bank of the Cahaba could not hold its prisoners, for in less than three years the county was accepting new sheriff John Henry's offer of a building valued at $185 to be used as a jail. At the same time, the sheriff was ordered to "lay off jail liberties so as to embrace as nearly as possible the houses on both sides of the Cahaba River at the Falls."[8]

Even earlier, the sheriff had laid out the precincts of the county. In a period when all male citizens, with a few exceptions like judges and ministers of the gospel, were required to serve in the militia, these precincts were the equivalent of military beats, and until 1824 were called "captains' companies." Sheriff Henshaw laid out three military beats, which he described to Governor Bibb on June 2, 1818:

> Sir: Agreeable to my instructions, I have divided the County of Cohawba into three Captains Companies, & designated their respective beats and boundaries as follows: (viz) all that part of the County laying east of Cohawba river, & southerly of Six Mile Creek, to constitute one Company containing sixty-five effective men, to renderveaux at Mr. George Maburys. All that part of the County situated Northerly of Six Mile Creek & northeasterly of a line drawn northwest from its *confluence* with Little Cohawba to the County line, to constitute one Company, to renderveaux at John Mahans, Containing sixty effective men. All that part of the County situated west of Cohawba river and southerly of the above line, runing from the mouth of Six Mile Creek, to constitute one company containing fifty-two men to renderveaux at the Court House or Mr. John Canterburys.[9]

The captains of the first two companies, chosen by "voluntary elections," were reported as William Lewis and John Lovelady, respectively. Henshaw, who was apparently offended that he was not consulted about those offices, recommended Leven Watkins to command the company at the courthouse. These appointments were approved by August 1818, when William Watkins was substituted for Leven Watkins.[10] Oliver C. Cleveland, a veteran of the War of 1812, was named major of the county regiment.

A number of officers were apportioned to each militia beat in addition to the commanders. These included at least two justices of the peace and one constable. The need for law enforcement officers in these new settlements was underlined in a letter to Governor Bibb from Henry W. Stevens, headed Cahaba valley and dated October 27, 1818, protesting: "William W. Capshaw is not yet recommissioned as Justice of Peace, in Cahawba County, which leaves our part of the country in the same situation as when I last saw you, one Justice only and him a sot of a Dutchman, altho' we have half the population of the County."[11]

The justices that convened in the log courthouse had jurisdiction over several courts. Sometimes they sat as the superior court, sometimes as the orphans' court, but most of their business was transacted in the court of revenue and roads. In its early days, the court disposed of revenue in short order, simply agreeing to levy a county tax equal to one-third of the territorial tax in effect, and calling for occupational licenses when they were due. Roads, however, were a regular topic on the agenda. The first ones cleared through Cahaba County, whether by family efforts or county labor, must have been little more than the stump roads the pioneers had hacked out following Indian trails, but they did permit communication of some sort, both among the scattered farms and between the neighboring county seats.

The early minutes of the county court are full of petitions for such roads, most of them leading out from the courthouse on the west side of the Cahaba toward various points on the county boundaries. Many of these routes were traveled throughout the nineteenth century, and some are still used today. In May 1818 the court granted, among others, these requests: "the petition of Andrew Henshaw et al. for a road leading from the Court House of Cahawba County down the west side of the Cahawba River to the Dallas County line so as to intersect the road leading to the Dallas Court House.... the petition of Benjamin Stewart and others for a road leading from the Court House of Cahawba County by Taber's Mill and Hill's Settlement to the line between the Counties of Tuskaloosa and Cahawba so as to intersect a road leading thence to the Falls of Black Warrior." The first of these routes joined the road that led through Selma to the town of Cahawba, the state capital from 1820 until 1825, and the second passed toward Tuscaloosa, the capital from 1826 until 1847. U.S. surveyors determining the section line in 1820 commented in their field notes on the well-beaten way running west of Centreville. County Road 9 by Scottsville and Johntown approximates this old roadway today.

On the east side of the river, one of the first orders of the court was to grant "the petition of John Mahan and others for a road from the Court House of Cahawba the nearest and best way by Smith's Mill, Captain G. Johnson's on Six Mile Creek, King and Smith's Store on Hazlett's Creek and so on to the line of Shelby to intersect a line leading from thence to the court house of Shelby."[12] In February 1819 another road, the one that led toward "the seat of Justice of Montgomery County," was ordered to be extended. The removal of the county seat for a brief period in the mid-1820s to a new location nine miles east of Centreville occasioned an additional rash of orders for passageways through the woods to and from that place, for example in February 1824 "the road leading from Bibb County Court House to the line of Tuskaloosa County near James Hill's first Precinct." This move also necessitated new river crossings, as revealed by the application of Hopkins Pratt to establish a public ferry near River Bend, "on the road leading from Bibb County Court House to Hills Settlement at the place known as Hargiss Ford," a petition that was granted upon his giving bond and security.[13]

To carry out the public roads program necessary in a frontier state, Alabama law required male citizens eighteen through forty-five years old to donate their services for as many as ten days a year or to furnish mules, or in lieu of either service or mules, to pay ten dollars to the county. When a road was to be opened, the men who resided in that area were ordered to begin work on it as soon as the jury appointed to view the layout and mark the road made its report. An overseer, also of that section, was named by the county court to supervise the labor of clearing the way and later of attempting to keep it in passable condition. As late as the 1850s, Bibb boys might greet the first call to road service as passage rites to manhood.[14]

The fords of rivers and creeks fell under the care of the road force, too. The limits of responsibility were often defined as the middle of a stream, as, for example, in May 1824 road repair in the third precinct "extending from the middle of Cahawba River to the middle of Hurricane, Hopkins Pratt, overseer." The river was not spanned by a bridge until 1846, when one was built at Centreville, and so traffic usually had to cross through the water. Although toll ferries existed, the ford was essential. Some hint of what was involved in the upkeep of a ford appears in the county court minutes of February 1819, which record this order: "that the overseers of the road on both sides of the Cahawba River be notified forthwith to contract their hands at the present used ford on said river at Centreville and open out the same as also to prepare the banks for the passage of wagons, working either way from the center of said River."

Among the numerous duties of the county court was the issuing of permits for ferries and determining proper fees to be charged the passengers. The first ferries ordered by the court were operated at the river landings of planters George Mayberry and John Canterbury.[15] A ferry at the Falls was evidently transporting settlers earlier because from the time of the first session the court regularly received petitions to manage it. Ferry rates were listed in the minutes of February 1819: "Drivers $1.00; man and horse 12½¢; led or drove horse 6¼¢; footman 6¼¢; cattle 6¼¢; sheep, swine or goats 3⅛¢; 2-wheeled carriage or cart 50¢."

Another perennial responsibility of the pioneer government was that of issuing licenses for numerous vocations and in some cases setting prices. The frontier occupations requiring county permits extended from ministers and attorneys-at-law to hawkers or peddlers and tavern-keepers. The term "tavern" had a wide range of meanings, all the way from hotel to mere grog shop. By the time of the court session of July 28, 1820, fourteen tavern licenses and one hawker's license had been issued. The February 1819 minutes identify the tavern-keepers as Jonathan Mulkey, Asher F. Stone, Stephen Potts, Pleasant Henderson, Noah B. Coker, Holly W. Middleton, Thomas Carlton, Richard Chandler, James Root, Greenberry Grisham, Alexander Spear, John C. Anderson, Henry W. Stevens, and Eaton Walker. The hawker was Coleman Allen, a "moonlighting" schoolteacher.

Taverns in the broadest sense of the term were probably few in the new settlements; as elsewhere in pioneer days, farmers who lived near the road would take in strangers and give them what was sometimes called "dry entertainment," board and lodging without alcoholic beverages.[16] The county approved certain tavern charges for food and drink supplied to man and beast but not for lodging. In May 1818 the rate for dinner was thirty-five cents, for supper and breakfast each twenty-five cents, and for horse feed per day fifty cents. Inflation was at work on the frontier, however. By 1819 horse feed had risen to a dollar and by 1822 to $1.12 ½. Also by 1822 the tavern-keeper was allowed to charge thirty-seven cents for each dish at a meal. The price of domestic spirits remained steady at twelve and a half cents per half pint, but that of foreign liquor dropped from thirty-seven and a half to twenty-five cents.

Of course, the officers who met in the log courthouse also bore responsibilities for the political and social welfare of the county. They were authorized to call county elections and to preside over them. They called the first such election in July 1818 for the purpose of naming a representative to the Alabama territorial legislature in St. Stephens, a position won by Littlepage Sims. This election, Sheriff Andrew Henshaw certified, was "begun and holden at the Court House in Centerville."[17] Sims was approved also to represent Cahaba County at the first state constitutional convention in Huntsville, and, according to family tradition, was joined at his home for the horseback journey to northern Alabama by the delegate from Dallas, William Rufus King, future U.S. senator and vice-president.[18] In subsequent balloting in 1819, Sims was elected to represent his county as state senator at the new capital, Cahaba, where he was accompanied by Jonathan Jones, elected representative in the lower house.

Littlepage Sims, who thus emerged as the first political leader in the county, was a native of Virginia who had fought at King's Mountain. He held several offices on the Tennessee frontier before pioneering to Alabama. In Tennessee he had assisted in organizing Blount County and obtained from the governor the coveted appointments of both sheriff and tax collector. He filled a vacancy in the state senate for the second session, June 29, 1795, to March 27, 1796. In 1812 he moved on to Indian land near Ditto's Landing in Madison County, then still in Mississippi Territory. But, when Bibb was created as Cahaba County in 1818, he was on hand by November to become a justice quorum, the next year following this beginning with more important offices. He married as his second wife a widow, Mrs. Mary Sherrill Taylor, sister-in-law of Governor John Sevier of Tennessee. Sometime after the expiration of his term in the state senate in 1821, Sims restlessly moved on to Shelby County, where he died in 1830, leaving a wife, eight children, and six

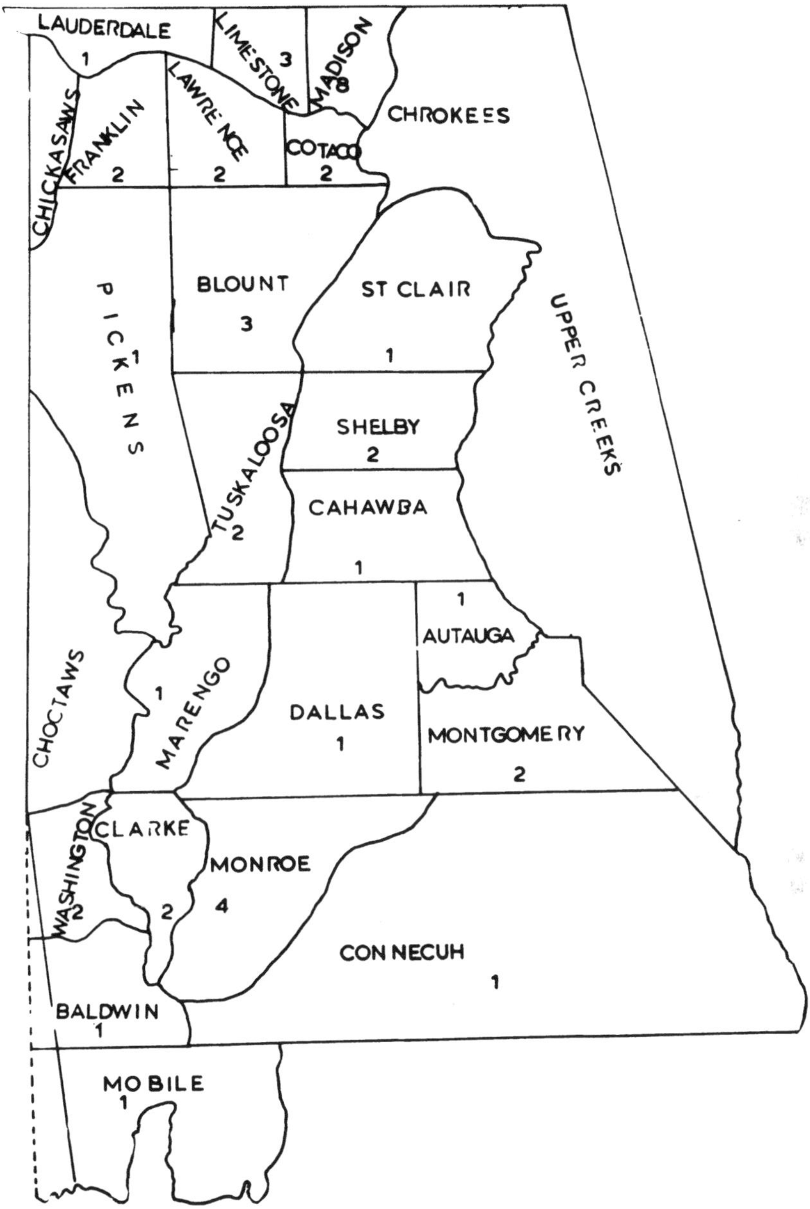

Map of Alabama, 1818, showing the number of county delegates elected to the state constitutional convention of 1819. William Letford, comp., *Alabama Congressional and Legislative Representation, 1819 to 1960* (Montgomery, n.d. [c. 1960]), p. 2. (Courtesy of Alabama Department of Archives and History)

slaves.[19] Evidently he was a pioneer to the end, for family tradition relates that he died on a surveying party in the area of Old Elyton. Unlike Sims, Jonathan Jones served as Bibb's representative for many terms.

When Sims and Jones won in the election held at the courthouse, no other ballot box existed in the county. To encourage countywide participation, the state legislature gradually added other polling places. In December 1819 it named Noah B. Coker's house in the present Antioch community; in December 1820 the home of Henry Stevens, who wrote from "Cahaba Valley," and of John Allen, in the southern section near the Perry County line; in December 1822 Daniel Williams's house on Mulberry Creek (now in Chilton County); in December 1823 Matthew Cox's home in eastern Bibb instead of Noah Coker's, and added Ezekiel Miller's residence near Schultz Creek; and in December 1824, as an eighth polling place, the house of Colonel James Moore in the Brierfield area. In such informal settings, the white male citizens gathered at regular intervals to cast their votes for elective offices, often making a difficult journey on horseback through woods and streams.

The county court from the beginning had jurisdiction over orphans and the poor, as well as over those less personal matters of roads and fords, ferry and tavern rates, and ballot boxes. The uncertainty of life on the frontier, where violence, accidents, and malaria abounded, must have produced many orphans. When the officers assembled under the name of the orphans' court, they dealt with the problem of survival for those who lacked any other recourse. At the original session in May 1818, one of the first items of business was the naming of Charles Coleman, John Mahan, Sr., and John Wallace as "overseers of the poor in their respective Captains' Companies in which they now reside." Each of these former Revolutionary soldiers was expected for a period of twelve months to report cases of need in his own precinct. In situations where no other disposition could be made, the county later, and well into the twentieth century, used a county poorhouse, but in the early years, before one was established, the overseer of the poor was paid by the county for providing this service.

For indigent orphans, the court usually preferred the time-honored indenture system, which was probably sometimes little better than slavery, even though it may have been the kindest solution possible on the frontier. Not only orphan boys were indentured but little girls also. In 1819 Polly, Lucretia, and Priscilla Childers, whose father had died and whose mother was unable to care for them, were "apprenticed by indenture until the age of sixteen years," Lucretia to John Stegner and Polly and Priscilla to Willis Smith.[20] Sometimes the court resorted to this system for those who were not actual orphans. In March 1822 William Elgin was reported as "not by his parents likely to be brought up in Honest ways," and it became the responsibility of the overseer of the poor in his district to find someone as a "suitable master" whom the judge could approve.[21] Until the overseer could do so, he kept such waifs in his home and the county paid him for "victualizing poor orphans."

In those days, more than a century before the modern federal welfare and social security programs, the county was responsible for the care of its neglected poor. When appealed to, it intervened in family situations of various sorts. A good example is the case of Mary Giles, who was referred to the court by the overseer of the poor for her precinct early in 1822. He reported that she was "poor and by reason of age and bodily infirmity so impotent as not to be able to support herself." Her son and sons-in-law, who were said to be capable of maintaining her, had failed to do so for the past month. The court fined them eight dollars and court costs, warning them that any failure to provide for her in the future would result in further fines.[22] The officials also sought to right the wrongs inflicted on other deserted women, as is evident in bastardy cases.

The county tax, even when supplemented by state appropriations and the labor required of its citizens, was a paltry sum with which to accomplish all that was needed in the interest of order, justice, and humanity in the newly settled country. Cahaba County could only begin and Bibb County not quite three years later continue, as best it could, the business of opening roads, issuing licenses and permits, presiding over polling places, and finding means of support for orphans and the poor. As long as so many restless squatters continued to move on westward, citizenship remained unstable. Operation of any effective programs was difficult before land ownership became common.

4

MRS. CHOTARD'S RIVER TOWN

BECAUSE MANY SETTLERS delayed recording their deeds in the U.S. Land Office in Washington or in some cases never did so at all, it is difficult to determine their actual dates. Yet apparently the history of private landownership in Bibb County began between 1821 and 1823. During those years, a few erstwhile squatters entered tracts from the government in the northern section of the county, and other citizens invested in an ambitious real estate project in the southern area.

The earliest certificate from the regional land office at Tuscaloosa that has been located is an entry of eighty acres by Joselin Green on September 26, 1821.[1] Either at the same time or within the next year and a half, Benjamin S. Green, John Green, and William Caffee also entered eighty acres each, their subsequent patents appearing under the date of June 2, 1823.[2] At this time, before the final definition of county boundaries, the Greens were considered to be residents of Tuscaloosa County. All these purchases were widely separated tracts along Caffee Creek in the area now south and west of Woodstock. By 1826 the entry of lands in the eastern section of the county along the Little Cahaba River and Mahan Creek had been recorded by Edward Mahan, by James Fancher for the firm of Fancher and Mardis, and by men named Garner and Mardis. Of these, Mahan and Fancher were considered residents of Shelby County in the mid-1820s before the Shelby-Bibb line was adjusted.

Meanwhile, Centreville, in the southern part of the county, would probably have remained a squatters' village for some time had it not been for the intervention of a remarkable woman, Mrs. Sarah F. Chotard. By 1822 she had won possession of a land grant, the quarter section on which the village of Centreville was growing up. She hoped to make a fortune by having the site surveyed and developing it into a major commercial river town. This sort of enterprise was not unusual in the early days of settlement. In the Tennessee valley, for instance, large stock companies had likely town sites surveyed, hoping to provide the location for the great commercial city of northern Alabama.[3] And, over in Tuscaloosa, William Ely, of Hartford, Connecticut, had just sold the first town lots to the squatters there, after Congress donated that land to provide support for a charitable institution in Connecticut.

Mrs. Chotard, however, did not enjoy the advantage of representing a stock company or a charitable institution. The true story of who she was and how she obtained possession of the quarter section of land varies considerably from the romantic legend long circulated in the county. According to this legend, she was a glamorous Frenchwoman who met and charmed her future husband at a ball in New Orleans celebrating General Andrew Jackson's triumph over the British in January 1814. In one version, her husband was an officer in Jackson's army and in another a fictitious son Henry was, and General Jackson gave her this land in appreciation of the military services of her husband or her son, as the case might be. According to another story attempting to explain the alleged gift, she was Jackson's French interpreter during his military tour in New Orleans. Yet none of these often contradictory traditions is verified by the official records.

Mrs. Chotard was born Sarah F. Williams in the colony of Virginia, according to a tradition that has not been controverted.[4] By 1793 she had married Henry Willis, a Revolutionary veteran, and it was through him that by a lengthy chain of events as his widow she was later able to claim the land grant in Bibb. Willis was apparently a South Carolina resident whose pioneering spirit had already taken him to Georgia and from there to the future state of Mississippi, then a part of the Louisiana Territory, still owned by Spain.[5] Like many of his countrymen of that period, he sought to acquire free or cheap public lands. Because the Spanish government was making a generous offer to any settler who would reside on and cultivate a tract in the Louisiana Territory, Willis had traveled to the Natchez District in the spring of 1791 to try his fortune. He was granted a warrant of survey, signed by the Spanish governor, for 800 arpents (672 acres) of land on Bayou Sara. In addition, he purchased from another settler an adjoining tract of 500 arpents (432 acres), making a total of more than 1,100 acres. At the end of the year, he journeyed home, reportedly intending to return shortly. What delayed his return is not known, but late in 1794, three years later, he died in Charleston, South Carolina. His will, dated September 24, 1794, made his young widow and his infant son, Lewis, heirs to his property, all of which the widow inherited after the son's early death.

Sometime afterward, the widow, Mrs. Sarah F. Willis married her second husband, John Chotard LaPlace, a member of a French family that had come as refugees to New Orleans from San Domingo during the insurrectionary period there (1791–1804).[6] After the United States government purchased the Louisiana Territory from France in 1803, Mrs. Chotard and her husband attempted to sell the land in the Natchez District, but the land office did not honor their claim to it because Willis had not fulfilled the conditions of residing on it and cultivating it. Fifteen years later, apparently after Chotard's death, Mrs. Chotard and a daughter of Willis by a previous marriage, Mrs. Josiah McComas, began petitioning Congress to satisfy the claim. They were refused at first, but, by dint of continuing appeals, they finally won. The land they claimed in Mississippi had long since been sold by the U.S. government, but, in lieu of it, an act of Congress on May 4, 1820, authorized them to enter without payment around 1,150 acres (a little less than two sections) in any land office in Mississippi or Alabama.[7]

Mrs. Chotard then began a search for attractive lands available for town sites. Her first objective seems to have been a tract in Monroe County, where lots had already been laid out on the banks of the Alabama River for the town of Claiborne. When the land officer refused that location to her, she carried her petition to Congress and her lawsuit to the courts, but this time she lost. In *Chotard* v. *Pope*, Judge William Wirt ruled that the government had intended her grant to be vacant rural lands rather than town lots already surveyed.[8]

By 1822, a year before this unfavorable verdict, Mrs. Chotard had located as another part of her grant the quarter section in Bibb County already cleared and occupied by the straggling little village of Centreville.[9] She must have seen several advantages in this location. According to tradition, she expected that its position near the center of the state might recommend it as the future site of the capital. In the previous year, when the usual flooding of the town of Cahaba by the Alabama River was more serious than in the past, speculation had begun that the capital would need to be relocated.

Yet an even more significant reason for Mrs. Chotard's choice of the location at the Falls of Cahaba must have been that it was at the head of navigation on the Cahaba River. From the moment that the first U.S. government surveyor saw this site in the spring of 1817, he expected that here, as also at the Falls of Black Warrior, an important commercial town "would spring up at no distant day."[10] Mrs. Chotard, residing with her daughter in the booming little river town of Tuscaloosa, saw the prediction beginning to be fulfilled there. She must also have heard of the budding traffic in flatboats during certain seasons between Centreville and Mobile. These conveyances, typically forty feet long and twelve feet wide, built with a covered section in which the oarsmen (more accurately called polemen) slept and cooked, could carry from fifty to a hundred bales of cotton to market.[11]

By the end of the decade, Bibb farmers were depending on a fleet of these heavy barges. John Logan, a colorful character who had migrated from North Carolina by way of Tennessee to Centreville by 1828,[12] came to be called "captain" of the flatboats. Besides these vessels, it was hoped that steamboats from Mobile would soon travel up to Centreville, especially after the first one reached Montgomery in 1821. Snags and sandbars in the Cahaba, however, were especially hazardous when the river was low. For that reason, plans to improve the channel must have been under discussion in the early 1820s, though the act to incorporate the Cahaba Navigation Company was not approved by the state legislature until January 10, 1827.[13]

One further attraction in this location may have been its recent acquisition of mail service, a further promise of communication for the prospective commercial city. The first post office in the county was established at Centreville in 1821, the first local postmark bearing the date of February 1, 1821. Only half a year earlier, in the summer of 1820, William Ely had complained to his wife in Hartford, Connecticut: "I wrote you a few lines from the Falls of the Cahawba River about 10 days ago, and sent it 40 miles to a Post Office, by a private Conveyance, to be forwarded thence by Mail, but whether it will ever reach you or not is quite uncertain."[14] A map of postal routes in Alabama in the early 1820s shows the Falls of Cahaba in a strategic position at the crossroads of the two chief lines: the east-west road from Augusta, Georgia, to Tuscaloosa, and thence by a spur to Columbus, Mississippi; and the north-south road from Washington, Tennessee, to Cahaba and St. Stephens.[15] Bibb's mail service, only by horseback before the first stagecoaches in 1830, was irregular and painfully slow, but Centreville's location on the route was advantageous.

Because of government red tape or her dilatoriness, Mrs. Chotard's patent to this land was not issued until October 10, 1823, but by the fall of 1822 the intrepid widow had apparently come to Centreville and employed Thomas Crawford as her surveyor. The squatters had probably built their shops on the riverbanks where they could be accessible to the flatboat traffic, sometimes using them also as residences, and erecting public buildings and other residences to the rear on the west side of the river. It is impossible to locate the sites of either shops or residences before Mrs. Chotard introduced lot ownership. Only on rare occasions is a privately owned house mentioned in the records, as when the county court minutes of April 1820 note a temporary move of the sessions to "the east bank of Cahawba River at the House lately occupied by Henry Moody," and those

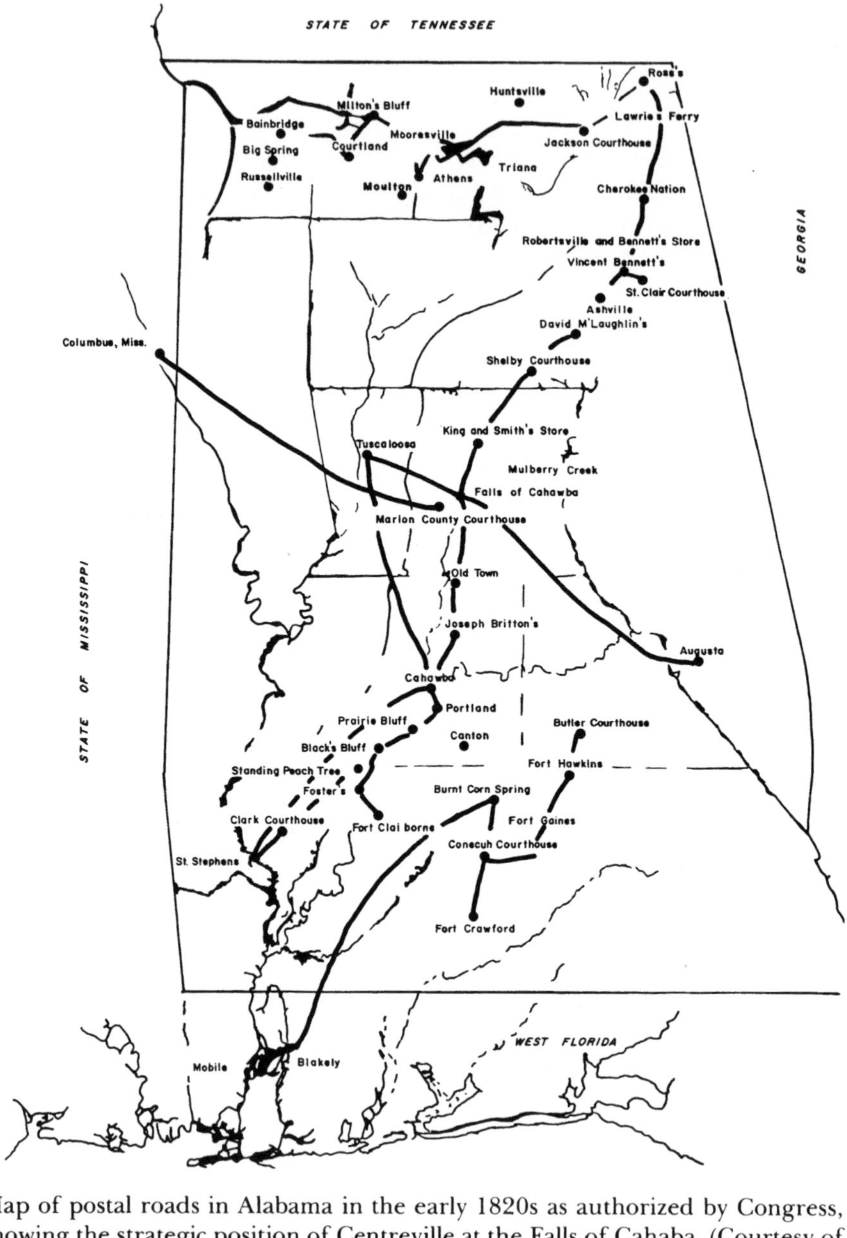

Map of postal roads in Alabama in the early 1820s as authorized by Congress, showing the strategic position of Centreville at the Falls of Cahaba. (Courtesy of Alabama Department of Archives and History)

of July 1820 record the payment of house rent to Stephen Potts for a similar use. The original village had undoubtedly grown up in its first few years without any preconceived plan, but now Mrs. Chotard, through the labors of Crawford, set about putting it in order, apparently without regard to any of the log cabin claims already staked out. He signed the plot of her town on Christmas Day 1822.[16] In one margin he wrote two names, "Centerville" and "Williamsburg," as if she might be planning to choose between them.

Evidently some problems had arisen in completing the survey, however, for only a week later, on New Year's Day 1823, Mrs. Chotard was appealing for assistance to none other than the popular hero, General Andrew Jackson, at his home in Tennessee. It is not known how she had become acquainted with him, but he was obviously on friendly terms with both her and her daughter, Eliza Chotard McGee, with whom she was then living in Tuscaloosa. Mrs. Chotard must have been around fifty years old at this time, and her request of the general in her New Year's Day letter reveals that she was still exercising the aggressiveness and tenacity that had kept her land claim alive for three decades.

According to Jackson's reply of March 3, she had urged him to instruct General John Coffee, director of the U.S. Public Land Surveys in northern Alabama, to run a line midway across her quarter section. Jackson stoutly refused to do this, assuring her that Coffee lacked authority for such a line from Congress or from the commissioners of the land office at Washington. He continued in a softer tone: "I have just received from General Coffee the Plott of the Town of Centreville, with your polite and generous offer for me to choose a Block of lots in said Town. I thank you, my dear Madam, for this evidence of your generosity and friendship, but I cannot accept this liberal offer from you, permit me to suggest to you to present them to your daughter, Eliza. It will afford me more pleasure for her to possess them than to possess them myself." At the beginning of this year in which he was about to emerge as the popular presidential candidate of the new Democratic party, the canny master of the Hermitage added: "My wants are but few, time is rolling on, and my locks having grown gray with age, toil, and ill health, gives me notice that these few wants will be of short duration." He concluded with wishes for her success in her lawsuit (apparently the one concerning the Claiborne tract), and he gave the town of Centreville his blessing in these words: "I hope your Town will grow and prosper like the rose."[17]

Unlike the original village that straggled along the riverbanks and dotted the space to the west, the map of this new town that was expected to "grow and prosper like the rose" compactly covered the full area of Mrs. Chotard's quarter section, 105 acres of which were described as west of the Cahaba River and 55 east of it. Today, that part west of the river extends north to the Lovelady and Olon Belcher residences on Birmingham Road, and east of the river to the northern boundary of the George Howard Young home lot on Montevallo Road. Its southern boundary is Walnut Street, or Alabama 82. It extends west to include most of the Olon Heights Shopping Center and east roughly to Montevallo Road (Alabama 25). In that space of 160 acres, Crawford created 265 lots in six short east-west blocks and five longer north-south blocks.

The streets bore names of military heroes, chiefly those of the recent War of 1812, as do the older streets in the city of Montgomery, chartered four years earlier. Those running north and south were named Washington, Jackson, Coffee, Carroll, and Hynes, and the short east-west streets were labeled Decatur, Lawrence, Perry, Hull, and Bainbridge. The streets were certified to be 100 feet wide and the alleys 12 feet wide. The Cahaba River ran diagonally in a southeasterly direction across Carroll and Coffee streets. The most unusual feature of this town plot today is that, except in one block, it ignored the river, whole lots being laid out in the water as well as on the land.

The first entries in Bibb County Deed Book A record the sale of lots beginning in late November 1823 in this recently surveyed town of "Centerville." The usual size of a lot was half an acre and the usual price was $100, but corner ones were valued at a higher rate and so were the much larger lots on the two most western streets, Washington and Jackson, perhaps expected to be the sites of public buildings. In the first sales, dated November 29 and 30, 1823, John Hunt and N. J. and J. C. Canterbury bought two of these larger lots, numbered 33 and 11 respectively. Jonathan Potts, who bought two spacious ones on the west, numbers 5 and 26, was charged a total of $1,823. Sheriff John Henry acquired a quarter-acre lot on the east side of the river for $100 but had to pay $2,000 for the adjoining one on the corner of Hynes and Perry. Among others, Dr. David R. Boyd and S. W. Davidson purchased lots on the east bank and Charles Cottingham one on the west side.

Of the twenty-one lots sold during the first year, thirteen were located west of the Cahaba and eight east. It would be interesting to know how many investors in this real estate were purchasing the sites on which they had already established their businesses or homes and how many were speculating on future sales. A number of the lots were sold and resold quickly, and others continued to be disposed of only gradually. Of the 265 laid out so hopefully, only 23 were sold in Mrs. Chotard's name. Her ambitious project must have been a disappointment to her, for, in general, outside capital did not rush in to invest in Centreville. Among the few exceptions were the commissioners of Tuscaloosa, who bought two lots later. But, at the time of her death in the capital city of Cahaba on June 11, 1824, only six months after the sale opened, she may not have realized the extent of the failure of her river town project.

Although Mrs. Chotard's enterprise was not the financial success she had hoped for, it may have given stability to the community during the mid-1820s when the county seat was moved for a few years to another location. One evidence of its spirit then was its offer to provide the site of the new state capital, just as Mrs. Chotard had hoped it would, after the flood of 1825 temporarily devastated the town of Cahaba. But the only vote Centreville received for this honor in the legislature was cast by Bibb's representative. Tuscaloosa overwhelmed all the other candidates, including Montgomery, Selma, Greensboro, Autaugaville, and Wilson's Hill (Montevallo).[18]

When Centreville failed to win the state capital in 1826, it had already lost the county seat, at least for a short period. The 1820s were the decade in which Bibb's seat of government was on the move, and its comings and goings may reveal the first power struggle in the county.

5

SEARCH FOR A PERMANENT COUNTY SEAT

THE SELECTION OF a permanent seat of government was one of the chief concerns of the 1820s, a problem for both the legislature and the county settlers. When the territorial legislature created the early county units, it designated the site of a seat of justice for immediate use but called on the residents to make their own choice through elected commissioners as soon as feasible. For a full decade after Cahaba County was formed on February 7, 1818, its citizens failed to select a permanent county seat, and for several years they continued to take their legal problems to the log courthouse on the west bank of the river without confirming either this or any other site as even a temporary seat of justice.

Such delay was apparently not unusual in pioneer counties; other examples are Shelby and Pike.[1] Year after year, the legislature prodded and the citizens failed to follow its instructions. Evidently in many cases the commissioners could not agree, finding themselves caught in a tug-of-war among the sections of their county. Such a hassle occurred in neighboring Perry County, where in 1819 the five original commissioners nominated four different locations, each holding out for his choice throughout a long day until sundown. Only then did they agree on Muckles Ridge, soon to be renamed for the famous Revolutionary general of South Carolina, Francis Marion. By May 22, 1822, town lots in Marion were being sold at public auction.[2]

The process in this county lasted much longer. Nearly two years after its formation, the territorial legislature, meeting in Huntsville, took the initiative into its own hands. By an act of December 17, 1819, it provided for an election of five commissioners on the first Monday of March 1820.[3] These five men, each to be paid three dollars a day for his services by the county treasurer, were authorized to select a suitable site for the seat of justice as near the center of the county as possible, at least within four miles of it. If they could not agree on a permanent location, they were instructed to name a temporary one. The courts were to continue their sessions at the Falls of Cahaba until such a selection could be made. When no action was taken during the following year, the lawmakers by act of December 20, 1820, ordered the sheriff to hold an election for new commissioners if those elected had not chosen a site by Christmas Day of 1821. The county court minutes of July 1821 state that the commissioners made their report but, oddly enough, do not reveal what it contained, though possibly they reached an impasse.

Finally, on November 27, 1821, despairing of obtaining results by their more democratic method, the legislators appointed three commissioners to fix a temporary seat of justice at the center of the county or at the nearest eligible place within four miles of the center by April 1, 1822. Each was to receive ten dollars compensation from the county treasury.[4] These three men went to work and completed the assignment by the deadline. They were Henry W. Stevens, Agrippa Anderson, and Ansel Sawyer, each probably representing one of the militia precincts of the county. All were prominent in local affairs. In December 1820 Stevens's house had been named one of the county polling places. Earlier in the same year, Atkinson and Sawyer had both become county officers, the former a justice in the court and the latter the county surveyor.

The place they selected, probably under pressure from residents of eastern Bibb, was at the intersection of the Elyton-Selma and Tuscaloosa-Montgomery roads, nine miles east of Centreville and approximately halfway between Centreville and present-day Randolph. The area was then chiefly woods. The Antioch Baptist Church, which now for many years has given its name to this community, was not established until 1833.[5] Probably the only house there at the time of the selection was that of Noah B. Coker, who later owned the land. The fact that his residence was one of the first polling places in Bibb, along with the courthouse in Centreville, suggests that the location was convenient to a sufficient number of settlers in the eastern part of the county. The western section had temporarily lost in the political tug-of-war.

Just when most of the court functions were removed from Centreville to the new location, which took the name of Bibb Court House, is not known. The first record of an official session at the "Temporary Seat of Justice," as it was always called in the county court minutes, is that of the circuit court in September 1822. Probably Coker provided temporary quarters in his tavern residence at the crossroads to accommodate the justices and those citizens who found it necessary to travel the raw new roads to meet with them. County court minutes of the mid-1820s are full of petitions for roads to Bibb Court House, and by 1825 a horseback postman was traveling them to bring mail for Judge Andrew Lusk to dispense, probably from the courthouse. Judge Lusk, Centreville's first postmaster, had been authorized to assume the same position in the new county seat.

Coker, who had been licensed as a tavern-keeper in May 1819, may have erected the building later known as the courthouse before or during the years when the courts met there, or he may have added to its original structure later because it continued to house overnight travelers between eastern Bibb and Centreville. Either originally or eventually, it had two stories; nine or more rooms, measuring about sixteen feet square; and a wide hall, probably a "dog trot" but later enclosed. Those who were present when this ancient structure was torn down a few years ago to provide material for pioneer houses at Tannehill State Park report that it was constructed of heart lumber planed by hand and fitted tongue-in-groove. One room bore above its door the sign "Travellers' Room," and many were numbered with red paint. Today the spot where the building stood at the then important crossroads is empty of any reminders of its former significance; even the chimneys of handmade bricks have been moved.

It was December 30, 1823, before an attempt was made to provide the county with any funds to construct a public building. On that day, the U.S. Congress passed the motion of Senator William Rufus King of Alabama: "that the Commissioner on Public Roads be instructed to inquire into the expediency of granting a pre-emption to one quarter section of land to each of the counties of Bibb, Conecuh, Henry, Pike and Covington, in the State of Alabama, for the location of their respective seats of justice."[6] Thus encouraged, the state legislature a year later, by act of December 15, 1824, appointed John Hunt, James Moore, and William White as agents to select a quarter section of land to be sold with the object of applying the funds to the erection of public buildings.[7]

The new commissioners chose for this government entry a quarter section where their predecessors had agreed to locate the temporary county seat.[8] They laid out lots but failed to sell any of them, perhaps because they had neglected to carry out the formality of entering the land and receiving legal title to it. Probably also the general lack of enthusiasm resulted from the discovery of a serious handicap in the new location: water was scarce. Today, evidence of futile efforts to find an adequate supply appears in the number of wells attempted in the neighborhood, two of them close to the courthouse site.

For this reason and others, such as the economic loss the community of Centreville had suffered, discontent with the "Temporary Seat of Justice" increased until the legislature was petitioned to allow a change. To remain impartial in the matter, the lawmakers at the session of 1827–28 passed an act authorizing an election on the first Monday in February in which the citizens were to choose a permanent seat of justice by voting for either Bibb Court House or a site east of the river at the Falls of Cahaba. In the event that the latter location received the larger number of votes, Commissioners James Moore and William White were ordered to withdraw their application for the quarter section they had never entered so that one might be selected in its stead at the Falls.[9]

The result of this election was the return of the seat of justice to Centreville, not to the old site but to a new one on the eastern hilltop above the mosquito-infested riverbanks. The return was not immediate, for the legislative act that authorized the election also ordered "that the present place of holding courts in said county shall continue to be the place of holding courts therein, until the commissioners report . . . that there are sufficient buildings and accommodations at the site selected." According to the county court minutes, the sessions continued to be held at Bibb Court House (soon to become Bibb Old Court House on the maps) until May 1829. At that date, no public buildings had yet been completed in the new Centreville, but the polling place for the first county precinct had been renamed "the courthouse near the falls of Cahawba." Among other polling locations listed were Old Court House, Hill's precinct, the Big Spring, Coxes, and Pope's, three others being illegible.

Meanwhile, in 1828 a commission composed of Samuel W. Davidson, David L. Lipscomb, and William H. Wilson had been appointed to establish this new permanent seat of justice. They conducted the operation in an eminently businesslike manner, as Chairman Davidson's journal reveals.[10] They applied for and duly entered the quarter section on which most of the chosen site lay.[11] After making a Tuscaloosa bank loan of $200, subsequently covered by another loan from a Mobile bank, they paid the government $181.25, the price of the thirty-six and a quarter acres at $1.25 an acre. They also bought from James B. Clark for $15.57 approximately twelve and a half acres on the south side necessary to complete the entire site. Clark had entered this adjoining quarter section by patent of August 13, 1830. According to tradition, this entire hilltop had been cleared and for some years cultivated by squatter Abisha Camp.[12]

The January 21, 1832, act of incorporation defined the town limits in the following manner: "Beginning at the junction of the first branch, above John Henry's dwelling house, with the river Cahawba, thence up said branch to the boundary line of the tract of land on which the seat of justice is located, thence with the boundary line of said tract . . . running north and continuing round said tract of land to the place where the road leading from the county ferry on Cahawba river to the Court House intersects the boundary line, thence with said road to river Cahawba, thence up said river to the beginning."[13] In terms of present ownership, the tract of land on which the new town was built extends through the Kennedy and Moore property on the south, up the hill on the east to Martin Williams's home lot, to Mrs. Fred McGee's residence on Valley Street on the north, and to the western boundary of Brady Belcher's lot on the side of the hill above the river (the eastern limits of the old town). The act of incorporation added the east bank of the river.

This relatively modest area was surveyed with the assistance of a slave furnished by Revolutionary veteran George Mayberry for no cost except $5.75 board. Mayberry also received a fee of $4 for "work on streets" and George W. Howard $1.75 for carrying the surveyor's chain, according to entries in Davidson's journal of 1830. The town was laid off in seventy-eight lots around a spacious courthouse square, surrounding which the city fathers a few years later planted chinaberry trees, popular at that time for their shade. In 1831 the principal streets of Montgomery were shaded by "pride of china trees."[14] Most of Centreville's streets, like those in the city of Cahaba, were named for other trees—Walnut, Chestnut, Pine, Cedar, Locust—and the two running north and south from the square were called Valley and Market.

The chinaberry trees endured for the rest of the century—until the hard freeze of 1899, after which the editor of the local newspaper published this obituary:

> The Big Freeze of last Winter was too much for the dear old hollow, gnarled and knotted China Trees of Centreville. They had ceased to put forth leaves or blooms, Most of them are sixty years of age and the sap no longer flows in their veins, and their branches are withered. They have, for lo, these many years, furnished shade for village loungers; berries for the small boy's pop-gun, and served as hitching posts for the horses of country visitors; no protection was thrown round them. It is a wonder that they have lasted so long.
>
> But the day of their usefulness is over. ... Farewell, old trees! How emblematic of human life. We are all growing old! The places that know us, will soon know us no more.[15]

Meanwhile, as soon as the survey had been completed in 1829, one lot was set aside for the county jail and another for an academy. On May 15 the commissioners placed the following advertisement in the newly founded Tuscaloosa *Alabama Intelligencer*:

> VALUABLE LOTS
>
> On Monday, the first day of June next, the Lots in the part of Centreville, contiguous to the site selected for the public buildings of the county of Bibb will be sold on the premises to the highest bidder.

> Centreville having now become the permanent seat of Justice for the County of Bibb, and situated at the highest point of navigation of the Cahawba River, in the centre of a fertile, populous and healthy country, this property offers greater inducements than any of the kind now offering for sale, in the middle region of the state. A liberal credit will be given; and terms made known on the day of Sale.

Unfortunately this advertisement, for which the commissioners paid $2.50, failed to attract any bidders. The first sales were made on September 5, 1829, and were listed in "The Final Report of the Commissioners of the Permanent Seat of Justice" as follows:

> Number 3 (the present Davidson-Leeper home lot) to Jonathan Potts, $54.
>
> Number 5 (corner lot occupied now by part of old bank building) to Thomas Crawford, $90.
>
> Number 6 (north section of former bank building lot) to S. W. Davidson, $49.
>
> Number 9 (location of present jail and courthouse annexes) to Jacob Dominick, price unlisted.
>
> Number 19 (J. T. Fuller home lot) to Enoch Carson, $36.
>
> Number 23 (eastern section of Rock Building lot) to George W. Howard, $35.
>
> Number 33 (Southland Furniture Company lot) to J. W. Clark, $49.
>
> Number 34 (Scarborough Service Station lot) to L. Lowe, $62.[16]

The sale continued through 1834, eventually bringing in $2010.67½, according to the meticulous account in Davidson's journal. The prices ranged from $104 for Lot 10, the southern half of the People's Bank lot today, eventually sold to Jacob Dominick, to $3.50 for Lot 40, an unidentified location east of the hilltop business section, bought by Alexander Hill. The only space allotted to a church was one third of Lot 76 on Cedar Street, today next to Kate Dailey's shop, which was sold to the Methodist Church for $5.

The expenses incurred by the commissioners for land and buildings totaled $2785.22 and thus exceeded the returns on the sale of lots by $767.34½, an amount that was paid from county taxes. The highest cost was for labor on the two-story frame courthouse, $475 earned by Enoch Carson and Daniel Sneed; $168 was also due George W. Howard, either on the same project or on the academy. The next most expensive item was lumber, $414.29½, billed by William Summers and William E. Sawyer. Although most of the material, such as shingles, hinges, and even lumber, was bought locally, an order of nails was transported from Mobile by river freight, costing $1.50 to the town of Cahaba and the same amount from there to Centreville. Chairman Davidson followed the history of some of those nails further by noting that Thomas Glass was paid $3.00 for "nailing the court house floor." The log jail was built on the lot back of the present People's Bank by Absalom Pratt, who earned $180 for his labor and his logs. Edward Kennedy recalled playing in its ruins when he was a child, after it had been replaced by a rock jail.

The courthouse was apparently not completed before 1832, the year in which the town was incorporated. Funds came in slowly from the real estate sales, and much time was required to procure the building materials. They often had to be ferried across the river or, perhaps more often, brought up the stream to the Falls of Cahaba. The commissioners purchased one flatboat from Absalom Pratt for $45 and later apparently another from Henry Youngblood for $40. County funds were requisitioned to replace one of these boats, which must have been worn out by the time the courthouse was completed, for, according to Davidson's entry, "Old ferry flat sold, $15." No picture of this third courthouse survives, but its timbers endured in a new location for many years after the structure was replaced in 1859 by a brick building. The 1832 courthouse was sold that year and rebuilt on what is now Magnolia Circle, just off Montevallo Road, where it burned in 1930, around a century after it first appeared on the brand-new courthouse square.

Shops and residences gradually rose around that new square. Businesses migrated there from Old Centreville, which kept its identity for a time as West Centreville. Anthony Stoutenborough erected one of the first stores. This enterprising German emigrant had settled in the village on the west bank of the river by 1826, when his name appears as an official of the projected Cahaba Navigation Company in its act of incorporation.[17] Although he reportedly came to Bibb without any means, by 1834 he was able to invest in several lots in the new county seat east of the river. Some of these he resold, but on Lot 70 (now the location of Maddox Florist Shop, 456 Walnut Street), which he bought from the original purchaser, Jacob Newell Mayberry, he erected a two-story frame building that had a large basement. There he opened a grocery-saloon and the first hotel in the new hill town. This building, which later housed the general mercantile business of J. S. and Edward Kennedy, was consumed in the town fire of 1903 and rebuilt of brick and stone.[18]

The 1830s became an era of building. As officials moved into the new courthouse, citizens began erecting the antebellum homes that still ornament Centreville. By 1834 George W. Howard was constructing for Dr. David R. Boyd and his wife, Theresa Coleman Boyd, the two-story plantation residence on the west side of the river, now 228 Walnut Street. Four years after Boyd's death in 1835, his widow married Howard, and the home has been owned ever since by their descendants, today by a great-granddaughter, Emily Cooper Cleveland, and her husband, Howard Cleveland, Jr., who remodeled it.

The partnership of Carson and Howard built two residences on the east side of the Cahaba, one for John Henry and the other for S. W. Davidson. The two-and-a-half-story house, including a half-basement, at 476 Walnut Street just east of the town square was erected in 1837 for Henry's use as a stagecoach inn and residence. In 1853 Josiah S. Kennedy, after renting it for a few years from the Masonic Lodge, which had acquired it after Henry's death in 1843, purchased it for the same use. The Kennedy family continued to operate it as a hotel until 1900, and it remains in the family today as the residence of Mrs. Josiah M. Kennedy. The Davidson-Smitherman house, now the home of Gladys Pittman Leggett and her husband, Reuben Leggett, stands high on the hill southeast of the town square at 167 Third Street. It contains not only two and a half stories but a large brick basement that house servants occupied during slavery days. This house and a hundred surrounding acres were sold to Bettie Howard Smitherman, wife of Thomas J. Smitherman, in 1869, after which their family occupied it for three quarters of a century.[19]

Another plantation residence was built by George W. Howard for Jacob Newell Mayberry at an undetermined later date, possibly after the death of Howard's partner, Enoch Carson, in 1846, because tradition connects only Howard's name with its erection. A specialist who examined it reported: "Details in the house indicate that it was built later than the Kennedy house and the Davidson-Smitherman house."[20] This two-story frame residence, now the home of the Charles England family, was known for nearly a century as the Moren house, after Dr. E. H. Moren bought it in 1867. A storm in 1946 destroyed its quaint observatory and belltower, from which a rope was suspended to the first floor, a survival from the days when field hands were summoned by this bell at noon. This house stands at the end of a long driveway just off Alabama 219, south of the juncture of that road with Highway 82 at the foot of Market Street.

Although these four antebellum homes have survived (along with the much later Davidson-Leeper residence, erected in 1880), one building that was called the showplace of Centreville has not. Anthony Stoutenborough, who was evidently successful with "Tonteen," erected what was then considered a lavish residence at the corner of Walnut and Cedar streets, the present location of the Dalton Murphys' home. It was said to possess solid mahogany stairs, mirrored walls, and marble mantels, and to be lighted by chandeliers. According to the recollection of an old-timer in 1900, the original cost of the building was $10,000, but the builder is not recorded.[21] Probably Stoutenborough transferred his hotel quarters

Mayberry-Moren-England house, Centreville, built in the 1840s by George W. Howard for Jacob Newell Mayberry and occupied for over half a century by the Moren family. Photographed in 1929 before a storm destroyed its observatory and bell tower. (Reproduced by photographer Andrew Russell from an old newspaper print)

from the second story of "Tonteen" to this house, for, after he sold it in June 1849 to Jacob Newell Mayberry and his wife, Mary Coleman Mayberry, they operated it as a hotel. After Mayberry's death in December 1851, this hotel was bought by Dr. James W. Crawford, and at some date before the Civil War it was unfortunately destroyed by fire, said to have resulted from the carelessness of servants. Its dinner bell was afterward given to the Kennedy House on the square, where its sound continued to be familiar until the end of the century. Stoutenborough apparently left the county about the time of his sale to the Mayberrys, for his name does not appear in the 1850 U.S. census.

During the same decade when the first substantial buildings, both public and private, were rising around the new county seat, some residents of northern Bibb were constructing commodious homes. One of these, that of the Green family, still stands on a country road near Woodstock, not far from Alabama 5. It looks down impressively from a slight eminence above the quiet lane, framed by ancient oak trees and surrounded by green pastures. John Green and his son John E. Green began building the house in the spring of 1830 and completed it four years later, according to family tradition.[22] They moved into it in the spring of 1834,

Green plantation house near Woodstock, built in 1830–34 by John Green and his son, John E. Green. (Courtesy of Mrs. Josiah Kennedy)

immediately after which the son returned to South Carolina to marry Sarah Echols James and bring her to join the family in the big house. All the building material was either hand-sawed or hewed out with a broadax, and the broad heart pine boards of random widths in the walls and floors of the spacious rooms were fitted tongue-in-groove, as was common at that time. Like all of Bibb's large antebellum homes, it originally had a separate kitchen house. Because of a tradition that travelers on the Elyton-Selma road changed their horses there, some older citizens still refer to the Green home as Halfway House. Several generations of the Green family lived in this country home until 1939, the last descendant to do so being Mary Green Caffee.

Another ancient house in northern Bibb was the Brick House, as it was called. During the first half of the twentieth century, it was still standing near Johntown. The date of construction of this brick residence, probably the first in the county, is unknown. It is said to have been originally the home of James Hill, possibly the early settler, the first of that name, who was a political power in his region of the county. He died in 1842, reportedly murdered by a neighboring landowner in a dispute over property ownership. Although no full description of the house is now available, several Bibb Countians remember it when Dan Belcher owned it, first as an impressively large two-story residence and later as a great shell before it was torn down.

The construction of these and other new buildings, mostly "plank houses," was evidence of the gradually increasing prosperity in the county and especially in the "Permanent Seat of Justice" that had been created after a decade of indecision. During most of the rest of the century, this village remained the population center. Country people converged on it every Saturday by horseback or wagon to hitch their horses to the chinaberry trees on the courthouse square and afterward to "trade" and listen to the news as well as witness any fight that might occur. Sometimes these combats were undertaken in the impersonal spirit of prizefights, though encouraged by frequent recourse to the bottle.

One such fight survived in oral tradition into the twentieth century. According to the story, a pugnacious and well-liquored countryman called Sweet William stepped out in front of the expectant crowd on the courthouse square and announced, "I can whip any man that lives in Centreville." When his boast was met with silence, he continued in a louder voice, "I can whip any man that lives east of the Cahaba River." Still he got no takers. Finally he called out, "I can whip any man that lives west of the river." After that challenge another sturdy countryman, known as Uncle Jimmy Steele, stepped forward, declaring, "*I* live on the west side of the river!" Thereupon the two combatants took themselves off down the hill, perhaps to avoid interference from "the law," as the sheriff is still frequently called. After a while, Uncle Jimmy returned in quiet satisfaction, alone.[23]

The pioneer tradition of the Saturday fight, so vividly described by A. B. Longstreet in *Georgia Scenes* in 1835, continued to be observed in Centreville for many decades. The Six Mile *Bibb Blade* of May 27, 1880, commented casually: "About a half dozen fights took place at Centreville and adjoining neighborhoods last Saturday. No serious damage done except to Sam Howard, colored, who was cut very severely with a knife."

After the conclusion in 1828 to return the county seat to Centreville, it remained there. Only once was any attempt made to move it again, and that occurred thirty years later, when a new courthouse was being planned. By this year of 1858, the population of Randolph had increased greatly because of the coming of the first railroad, and the village enjoyed new commercial importance. Inspired by this development, partisans of eastern Bibb again called for a countywide referendum on the relocation of the county seat. On May 3, 1858, voters went to the polls to choose between Centreville and Randolph; the result was recorded in a contemporary diary: "Centreville triumphant!"[24]

6

PIONEER LIFE AND OCCUPATIONS

THROUGH MOST OF THE antebellum years, Bibb remained frontier country and its inhabitants lived like pioneers, not much less so in the county seat than in the scattered clearings. Change came slowly to this area during the nineteenth century, and some aspects of pioneer life linger in the memory of older citizens today. These features were especially marked during the first two decades of settlement.

A large proportion of the inhabitants lived on small, isolated farms, raising their own foodstuff, making the material for their clothing, and seldom traveling outside the confines of the county. Their simple fare is suggested by the survival among the older generation today of certain linguistic connotations: milk, meaning buttermilk; bread, cornbread; peas, the black-eyed variety; potatoes, yams; greens, turnip greens or collards. Bacon (pork) and greens was a favorite Alabama dish, often comprising the whole meal.[1] Homemade molasses was the usual sweetener, rather than commercial sugar. Even at the end of the century, a country hostess might inquire, on serving coffee, if the guest preferred "long or short sweetening." A physician who began practice in Bibb County in the early 1930s testifies that the chief diet in the rural areas at that time was still "sow belly, sorghum syrup, cornbread, and turnip greens," to which he attributed the normal blood pressure he found common then.[2]

Material wealth during the early decades consisted chiefly of those things necessary for family sustenance, for cash was short. Even in neighboring Perry County, which had the advantage of extending into the fertile Black Belt, most of the settlers were originally "poor as a church mouse," according to a Marion citizen writing in 1844. Of planters who by that time had become large landowners, he named one who once "kept a small country tavern on the roadside and was in the humblest circumstances. He still occupies his former location, but his first residence has become a negro cabin, his next his kitchen, and his present residence would do honor to a nabob."[3] Bibb, because of its relatively small valleys and largely hilly terrain, could not produce planters by such spectacular self-promotion. The climb was slower and more limited, and a degree of pioneer equality continued to be maintained among the white settlers.

From the first days of settlement, certain differences were apparent in economic status but few in life-style. One measure of the original standing of a settler appears in the appraisal of estates. To settle the estate of a deceased person, the administrator was required to obtain an impartial evaluation of his or her possessions and file it with the court. Among the first few administrators' records, the total value assigned individual estates varies from $1771.16½ (William Latham, October 24, 1821) to $18,083.18½ (Wiley Coleman, February 14, 1823).[4] The chief difference in the possessions of these two men lay in their holdings in slaves (Latham had none, Coleman thirty-seven valued at $6,000) and in notes indicating loans to fellow citizens (Latham $390, Coleman $4,500). Neither owned land in Bibb at a time when almost all settlers were still squatters.

The possessions of these and other immigrants in the early 1820s differed more in quantity than in type. They consisted mostly of livestock and primitive farm implements, plus some simple furniture and farm products. These items drawn from the inventory of William Latham's estate are characteristic of both possessions and appraisal values:

Twenty head of shoats	$10.00	One bed, furniture and bedtick	25.00
Forty head of hogs	95.00	Four dittoes	each 20.00 to 30.00
One cow and bull yearling	18.00	Three cheers	1.00
Two heifers	24.00	One lot of bells	4.00
One large bay horse	60.00	One lot of puter	13.00
One small black mare	60.00	One lot of earthing ware	1.37½
One sorrel mare	50.00	Delph ware	1.62½
One wagon, gears, bridles, etc.	85.00	Tin ware	9.00
Four ploughs, two cleavers	2.50	Three bottles, jug, pepper mill	1.00
Six hoes, two mattocks and frow	4.00	One coffee mill	2.00
Four axes, two wedges, piece of iron	9.25	Two wheels, one clock reel	6.00
One sithin cradle	3.00	Two hills potatoes	17.50
One man's saddle and bridle	8.00	One lot of fodder	25.00
One woman's saddle	15.00	Cotton crop	200.00
One rifle and shotbag	15.00	Two cribs of corn	280.00

Latham's cash on hand consisted of $51.81½ "in spicer" and $10 in bank notes.

The will of Zephaniah Clements, whose estate was appraised on March 9, 1822, at $7,087.50, reveals the pioneer estimate of the essentials for two life situations.[5] Clements, who had already made a settlement on his oldest son, bequeathed to each of his other nine children typically "one Negro Girl named———, one Horse, one Cow and Calf worth ten dollars, and one bed and furniture worth fifty dollars," occasionally substituting a sow and pigs for the cattle and in one case a mule for the horse. These were the necessities for starting life in one's own home. For the use and support of one family of servants designated to cultivate his plantation until his debts should be paid and the estate settled, these items were purchased from that estate: two oxen (worth $60), a handsaw and "sundries," one smoothing iron, a box of tools, jugs, two barrows, ten shoats, one sidesaddle, a loom, 200 bushels of corn and also "150 buckets of corn."

Among all these utilitarian holdings in the early 1820s were few books and fewer frivolous objects. Usually a man's library was valued at a dollar and probably included little more than the family Bible. Zephaniah Clements owned books valued at $4, one of which was *Sheridan's Dictionary*. Besides books worth $1.50, William Smitherman's administrator listed one vanity item, a "looking glass." The settlers had little time for anything but work during those rugged early years. Even those who owned slaves must have labored beside them in the fields, following a practice common throughout the Deep South in pioneer days. Many lacked schooling as well as leisure for reading.

These hard-working farmers did not usually provide their heirs with a last will and testament; in this respect, Zephaniah Clements was an exception. But they found other uses for the lawyers who moved into the county with them, as well as for the physicians and those settlers of other practical occupations. According to Joseph G. Baldwin, a fledgling attorney who migrated from Virginia to Sumter County around 1830, this newly opened area of central Alabama promised to be "a legal Utopia, peopled by a race of eager litigants," who offered "exhilarating prospects of fussing, quarreling, murdering, violation of contracts."[6] The first two lawyers licensed to represent the "eager litigants" were Horatio G. Perry and William G. Gill. Both appeared at the August 1818 session of the intermediate court, presided over by Justice John Canterbury, to take the oath, Gill producing a previous license. Among others who joined them at the bar within the next decade were Lewis Cammack, Lewis Kennedy, and James B. Clark, the only one who remained permanently to practice in Bibb County.

Like Baldwin, these young men, who traveled on horseback through the woods to confer with their clients and to represent them at Bibb's shifting county seat, must have found pioneer legal practice an adventure, sometimes a comic one, even if not as remunerative as expected. The circuit court records of the 1820s provide an introduction to their clients and incidentally afford a lively index to the life of the times. The commonest charges brought before the court were those of trespass and theft, often judged unjustified. When James Henry accused Charles Reach of refusing to return a valuable "cow beast commonly called a steer," valued at $150, the court assessed the plaintiff $11 and court costs."[7]

Like other frontier counties, Bibb had its share of fights. Sometimes the combatants used the savage bowie knife, nicknamed the "Arkansas toothpick," whose use the state legislature tried to suppress by enacting a law on June 30, 1837, to tax the sale of each at $100. But frequently, when tempers flared, sticks were the readiest weapon. Many of these fights found their way into court, and in at least one case actually began there. Jonathan Potts sued John Risinger for $500 for "violently and with a stick attacking him a severe blow on the back of the neck," apparently in the same court fray for which Potts was later admonished by his brother elders of the Centreville Presbyterian congregation.[8] The case was tried by Judge Reuben Saffold of Montgomery, and the judgment rendered at the April term, 1830, was a fine of sixty-four cents and court costs, a total of $13.37½, hardly the vindication of his reputation that the elder must have hoped for.

Pioneer women went to court, too, and in some cases they also were concerned with clearing reputations. Annie Johnson, said to be under twenty-one years of age, sued Nancy Fancher and her husband, Richard, charging Mrs. Fancher with "uttering and publishing these false scandalous defamatory English words," that is, accusing Annie of stealing a quarter from Nancy's reticule (a small woven handbag). Annie won a judgment of $50. In addition, the defendant was made responsible for court costs of $44.77, of which $16.40 was required for the expenses of witnesses, for example Nancy Carleton for "two days and twenty-six miles," $3.04. Because of interest and other fees, the cost of charging Annie with filching twenty-five cents amounted to $101.74, a judgment that was satisfied on October 13, 1830.[9]

In an age of arduous labor necessary to clear the wilderness and cultivate "new ground," settlers naturally looked for a few diversions, some of which were illegal. Retailing strong drink in certain quantities and operating gambling devices in public places were subject to penalties by circuit court. In *The State* v. *Charles Franklin*, tried in circuit court in the fall term of 1828, the defendant was charged with both "retailing spiritous liquor" and playing "a game of cards to the evil example of all others in like case offending . . . at a store house." The case was dropped because Franklin, like many other defendants, could not be found in the county. Noah Coker, not a fly-by-night but a prominent citizen whose house was one of the first two designated polling places, was fined a dollar in the spring term of 1830 for selling rum, brandy, whiskey, and gin in smaller quantities than a quart. Gambling devices were popular and varied. Young John Logan was convicted of "exhibiting a gaming table called Chuckaluck—at other times a gaming table called and known by the name of Equality." Like Franklin, he vanished temporarily before the judgment of twenty dollars could be collected and probably before his lawyer could pocket his fee.[10]

Pioneer physicians must have spent even more time on horseback than did the lawyers. In a day before roads and bridges were adequate, the family doctor depended on his faithful saddle horse to carry him to cabins in farm clearings many miles distant. There he not only prescribed treatment but also dispensed his old-fashioned remedies from his satchel, a traveling drugstore of the kind used throughout the nineteenth century. Judged by modern standards, he was severely limited in his recognition of the ailments he faced and in his methods of treatment. It is instructive to read the reported causes of death in Bibb as late as 1850: dysentery, fever, dropsy, consumption, bleeding, croup, jaundice, heaves, cancer, whooping cough, scrofula, sore head, worms, quinsy, lockjaw, accidents of drowning and burning, and, occasionally, old age.[11] The list says much about both frontier conditions and the problems of the attending physician.

Like the early nineteenth-century lawyer, the doctor usually learned his skills by apprenticeship with an older practitioner, afterward being subjected to a state medical examination. Sometimes he found a way around this requirement. An act "for the relief of William Dunlap," approved by the legislature on January 7, 1835, made it "lawful for William Dunlap to enroll his name as practising physician without undergoing an examination before the medical board.... Provided that the provisions of this act shall not be construed as to extend out of the limits of Bibb County."[12]

The first two physicians known to have practiced in Bibb are Drs. Joshua West and David R. Boyd. West enjoyed the additional distinction of being an ordained Methodist preacher who gave his services to the local churches of Bibb and Shelby. He was a Virginian, born in Rockingham County in 1771. Licensed to practice medicine in 1812, he emigrated six years later to Cahaba County, where he first settled near Centreville, later moving to Montevallo. He is said to have rendered service to hundreds of families in Bibb and Shelby counties until his death at the age of ninety-one years.[13] Boyd was fated to have a much briefer career. A native of Surrey County, North Carolina, he practiced his profession in and around Centreville from the early 1820s until his untimely death in 1835 at the age of thirty-three. He served as Bibb's representative in the lower legislative house in 1831–32 and was state senator at the time of his death.[14]

The account book in which Dr. Boyd and his unnamed successor made note of their patients' bills, writing in the graceful shaded penmanship of the period, reveals a great deal about pioneer medical practice in Bibb and life in the decade between the mid-twenties and mid-thirties.[15] A present-day pharmacist, on examining the many types of medication prescribed, is impressed by the large number that treat stomach disorders. Bates Antibilious Pills probably leads the list, followed closely by those distasteful century-long favorites calomel, castor oil, and Epsom salts. To prevent infection from the common cold, the pioneer doctor ordered "gum foetid," the evil-smelling asafetida, which was customarily worn in a small sack around the neck. Those patients already stricken were issued a blister plaster.

For malaria, so prevalent every summer and fall, Dr. Boyd prescribed sulfate quinine or Peru bark, a cheap substitute. Unfortunately, according to Dr. J. Marion Sims, who set up practice in Montgomery County in 1835, physicians were not yet aware of the need to prescribe quinine in the beginning of the disease, but instead weakened the patient, often disastrously, by attempting first to reduce the fever by bleeding and purgatives.[16] When Boyd took Hiram Elam into his home for two days' treatment, he administered an emetic followed by both Peru bark and sulfate quinine.[17] Physicians understood even less how to cope with typhoid fever and with epidemics of the dreaded yellow fever, which decimated families. Although Bibb churches, like the Schultz Creek Baptist congregation in 1841, observed proclamations of the governor for fasting and prayer for the removal of the pestilence from their midst,[18] Bibb doctors continued to perform venesections (bloodletting) on those who were stricken. Dr. Boyd did so regularly for a variety of ailments, though his successor was more inclined to use dry cupping, which required the pressure of a highly heated cup against the skin rather than an incision, as in wet cupping.

The exigencies of frontier life made other demands on the physician and his medicine satchel. Seneca snakeroot was required for snakebites and also possibly for what was judged to be high blood pressure in a period without instruments for checking pressure. This medication was usually accompanied by a cathartic or paregoric or the popular Bateman's Drops. Wormseed oil, followed by a cathartic or an emetic, was evidently considered necessary in cases of intestinal worms, which struck the planter's wife as well as his slaves. Dr. Boyd "cleansed teethe" and frequently extracted them. On other occasions, he was a surgeon, setting broken bones and amputating mutilated fingers, afterward dressing them for many weeks. The violence of the period is reflected in the number of times he was summoned to sew up and dress wounds, suffered usually by the settler himself, though sometimes by his son or his slaves.

The charges for these medications and services were predictably modest, varying from twelve and a half cents for "gum foetid" to eight dollars for certain "accouchements." A "nocta visit" was fifty cents more expensive than a day call, which was usually listed at one dollar if without prescription. Even a "visit and attention for 8 hours" cost Ebenezer Leeth only six dollars. When the doctor was summoned to ride his horse some distance out in the country, fording creeks and possibly also either fording the river or crossing it at his own expense by ferry, if one was available, he expected a proportionately higher fee. Yet a round trip of sixteen miles below Centreville at night to the home of Bird Griffin, for whom he sewed up and dressed a wound and dispensed tincture of myrrh, Epsom salts with tincture opium, and a box of Lee's Antibilious Pills, cost his patient only twelve dollars. In 1836 Vardy Johnson's account included the simple entry "To ride 12 miles, $3.00."

In spite of the modesty of the charges, bills were frequently not paid for months or years, if at all. Times were hard and money scarce in the 1820s and early 1830s. Cotton receipts were accepted in lieu of cash; at two cents a pound, James Lewis on January 22, 1830, had to produce a receipt for 820 pounds. Barter was common. John Tucker, who had incurred a bill of sixty-one and a half cents on December 29, 1830, began to meet the obligation on May 21, 1832. "by 1 venison Ham in part, 50¢." Barney Kornegay, whose charges for 1829 and 1830 amounted to $3.50, came to Dr. Boyd in 1832 with sixty-two and a half pounds of beef valued at three cents a pound and produced the balance of his debt in cash. Pioneer women made payments in kind, too, sometimes by their own handwork and sometimes by possessions that should have been necessities to them. Mrs. Berry, whose "fractured radius" Dr. Boyd had set, made a partial payment "by 2 pare of socks, $2.00," but never submitted a further remittance. On the other hand, Mrs. Prudence Starling met her obligation of $18.50 in full "by one work oxen," a transaction that should have involved a real deprivation for a frontier widow. All these early settlers, physician and patients alike, were struggling to survive and prosper in the difficult conditions of the central Alabama frontier.

The merchants, who plied their trade from the earliest days of settlement, were involved in the same struggle. Some of these ambitious immigrants reached the rural areas throughout the nineteenth century by peddling their wares on foot or in wagons. In the 1820s and 1830s, the peddler was often the only merchant that housewives in the farm clearings ever saw. The county tax for the privilege of "hawking and peddling" for a year was ten dollars when Coleman Allen, a settler from Tennessee, paid the fee in March 1819, according to the county court minutes of that date. This peddler's business evidently was not successful because five years later, in October 1824, he listed himself in a bill of divorce as currently a schoolteacher who was "defraying many of his old debts which unfortunately he had contracted trading in merchandise."[19] In 1831 another peddler's failure to pay the state tax resulted in a suit for $2,000 by Anderson C. Whatley, apparently an irate rival. According to the plaintiff's statement, the defendant "on May 31, 1830, used a certain waggon commonly called a Pedlars waggon for pedling [*sic*] from house to house and did sell goods and merchandise as a pedlar at the house of David B. Currie."[20]

These early local peddlers were later joined by picturesque foreign immigrants, five of whom, all having German names, were registered at Centreville hotels on one day in 1850.[21] A Bibb Countian has described the type who periodically visited his father's house a few miles north of Centreville later in the century.

> They were either Austrian or German Jews who came to this country and started their new life peddling dry goods and other light weight merchandise to the farmer population. They would leave their family in Europe until they could make enough money to bring them to America. . . . They worked until they could get enough money to buy a horse and small wagon to travel in. Then they could carry a much bigger pack. They were stocky and well-muscled fellows as a rule, and it was amazing the load they could carry on their backs in those canvased covered packs.
>
> One would frequently spend the night at our house and pay his night's lodging ($1.00) in goods. My mother would thus get a new linen table cloth, yard goods, thread, etc.[22]

During the first decade of settlement, small stores sprang up at various crossroads and in the village of Centreville, often in residences. Some of these, popularly known as "doggeries," specialized in whiskey and a few staple groceries, and others also offered a limited supply of general merchandise. Often these roadside doggeries became centers for meeting and lounging, and, according to an antebellum jury report in the then adjoining county of Autauga, they were "a fruitful source of evil, a terror to the community where they were located, and calculated to demoralize the young men and youth of our country."[23] A deacon in the Antioch Baptist Church who wished to express the ultimate in contempt made a comparison to a doggery.[24] Yet the settlers had to depend on these shops or the peddlers for the few necessities that they were unable to raise on their farms or create with their own hands. Items of a more elegant nature had to be imported by boat from Mobile. Two old bills charged to Josiah S. Kennedy in the spring of 1835 reflect dress materials that could be purchased in this age of homespun and their prices:

8 yds gingham 4.00	8 do gingham 2.50
1½ do do [ditto] .47	1 bunch Braid .13
2 hanks silk .25	11½ yds callico 11.38
3 yds Brochileu 4.50	1 dress stock 1.50

The second bill carries an additional charge for a copy of Josephus,[25] followed by a statement that the whole was "settled by Jonathan Moody's note."

In addition to farmers, lawyers, physicians, and tradesmen, the county possessed many kinds of artisans and workmen. It had architect-contractors like Enoch Carson and George W. Howard from North Carolina, blacksmiths and wagon-makers like the Mahans from Tennessee, millers like the brothers Ezekiel and Theophilus Miller from Georgia, flatboat captains like John Logan from North Carolina, and many others. Thomas Crawford provides an example of the pioneer ability to function effectively in several vocations and civic offices. Although he had been a linen weaver before migrating from North Carolina after service in Andrew Jackson's army,[26] he became the surveyor of Mrs. Chotard's river town in 1822. In 1824, the year after the state legislature introduced the new system of single county judges, he was the first citizen to be elected to that office in Bibb and filled it afterward for fourteen years. While still serving in this capacity, he was chosen to represent the county in the state senate also. In a letter to his wife, Mary Davidson Crawford, written in the senate chamber on January 12, 1830, he indicated how active he was in that body: "My favorite bill to destroy land speculation will be taken up by the Senate today. I expect to have to make a hard argument in favour of it. I think it will pass. A bill which I introduced to restrain tippling, however, passed the Senate yesterday."[27]

At home, Judge Crawford was one of the officials of the proposed Cahaba Navigation Company in 1826–27 and a moving spirit in planning the academy building in 1833–34, serving as treasurer of that project. He was also a devout elder in the Centreville Presbyterian Church and clerk of its session from its establishment in 1824 until the year before his death in 1844. Like most other settlers of every occupation, he was first of all a farmer and landowner. In many ways, he is a distinguished representative of the county's pioneers.

7

EARLY CHURCHES

AMONG THE INSTITUTIONS that took root on the Bibb frontier, one of the earliest and most influential was the Christian church. It seems to have been planted and nurtured originally in the rural areas of Alabama rather than in the larger towns, where community life did not depend so much upon it. A missionary who visited the state in 1828 described Montgomery as a town of "about twelve hundred inhabitants, of which only four or five are professors of religion. They have a meeting house which is not yet finished though commenced several years ago. They have no regular preaching, sometimes none at all for five or six weeks together." The nineteenth-century church historian who quoted this report commented: "In truth, for two decades and a half the place was openly and shamelessly immoral."[1] He gave no better account of the town of Cahaba, former state capital, where he said no denomination was strong enough to build a house of worship until after 1848, when one was erected for Baptists, Methodists, and Presbyterians to use by turn.

It was different in the backwoods. Many of the settlers brought with them a bias in favor of one denomination or another, and, after they had erected their own log homes, they often began planning a church building. These sanctuaries were rude, simple structures that had dirt floors and stick-and-mud chimneys to accommodate open fireplaces. To escape the discomfort of the split-log benches, the congregation gathered outdoors when weather permitted at a "stand," which might be either a brush arbor or simply the shade of large trees. Records of all denominations in the pioneer days show a preference for these outdoor settings in summer.

Some early congregations were able to schedule worship services only when a missionary passed through the area, and throughout the century most of them settled for a sermon only once a month. The scarcity of resident ministers in the 1820s may be reflected in the number of marriages performed ("rights of matrymony cellebrated" or "sollomnised") by justices of the peace. The first two ministers of the gospel licensed by the county court were Joshua West, Methodist, in August 1818 and William Hanod, Baptist, in November 1818. By the mid-1820s Isaac Suttle and Moses Crowson were signing many marriage certificates. A large number of these weddings required the consent of the bride's parents because she was under legal age. Both boys and girls often married in their teens; an example is future Probate Judge Jackson Gardner at nineteen and Margaret Bolling at fifteen, who were later the parents of ten children.

Strong rivalry existed among the denominations. The race during the nineteenth century in Bibb, as in the state as a whole, was chiefly between Baptists and Methodists, though the former sprinted ahead in the number of sanctuaries and communicants. The Presbyterians were represented by the U.S.A. church (later U.S.) in Centreville and by the Cumberland branch in the rural sections. These Protestant groups were the most numerous also in the state during antebellum days, the Baptists possessing 805 congregations in 1860, the Methodists 777, and the Presbyterians 135.[2] All denominations accepted slaves as members.

The Baptists established the earliest churches in the county. The first on record are Cahaba Valley (1817), Bethel (1818), and Enon (Rocky) and Rehobeth (both 1819)—all constituted before the name of the county was changed to Bibb.[3] The first pastor of Cahaba Valley was Moses Crowson; of Bethel, William Callaway; of Enon and Rehobeth, Isaac Suttle. All were local residents. Cahaba Valley created Enon as an "arm" by releasing a group of its own communicants to become charter members of the new congregation. In response to the same practical system, numerous other Baptist churches sprang up over the countryside, creating a web of arms. Mount Moriah came into existence in 1827 in the Hill Settlement, sponsored by Sardis Church across the Tuscaloosa line. According to its minutes of July 1824, the Sardis Church "agreed to arm of church at Bro. Calfee which shall have the liberty of holding communion when necessary."[4] From its organization in March 1827, this congregation, led by Reverend Joab Pratt, met in the home of John Goodson until the completion of a house of worship on Goodson's land in June of that year.

Pratt, a vigorous horseback evangelist, was also in charge of the Sardis Church, from which he extended an arm to create at least five other churches during the next five years. In Bibb these included in 1830 both Haysop, which he initially led, and Schultz Creek, whose first pastor was Reverend John E. Summers, probate judge in the 1840s.[5] Mount Gilead, headed first by John Dennis, dates from 1832. Both Antioch and Mount Zion were constituted in 1833, Antioch under the leadership of Enoch Hayes, and Mount Zion, an arm of Enon, presided over by George Everett. By the time the county was fifteen years old, it possessed these nine Baptist churches within its present boundaries.

Cahaba Valley Baptist Church, located in the Carlton Hill area near Brierfield. Organized in 1817, it was the earliest in the county. (Courtesy of Mrs. Josiah Kennedy)

The history of Enon is probably representative. Its conference minutes, which are available in full from its origin in 1819, when Alabama was still a territory, reflect the life of both the church and the rural society of the pioneer period. The usual business at these monthly congregational meetings, besides the appointment of messengers to the district or association meetings, was to accept new members and give letters of dismission to old ones. The latter practice was so common that it reflected the instability of the pioneer settlements, from which many newcomers soon moved on westward. In antebellum years, nothing is recorded about financial commitments to the once-a-month preacher or to other causes, such as missions, though one member left the church "on account of Bro. Dennis being favorable to the missionary."[6]

Legends abound concerning the poor pay for ministers of all denominations, the most apocryphal surely being Frank Gist's story of "the good Baptist brother, whose name I have forgotten, who served Rocky Mount for five years with only a mess of turnip greens for his pay."[7] Undoubtedly cash was scarce in rural areas. For 1874, the year after a financial panic, sixteen members promised (and most of them paid) to their pastor, J. M. Langston, amounts varying from fifty cents to two dollars, except for one five-dollar donation. The fifty-cent pledges of two enterprising women, Martha Johnson and Fannie Arnold, were "paid in cloth," probably homespun.

Not business matters but disciplinary problems occupied most of the attention at these monthly meetings. The churches of all denominations maintained rigid standards of conduct and attempted to enforce them on the members by threatening "unfellowship," or expulsion, apparently a dreaded penalty. In the early years at Enon, individuals frequently brought charges against fellow members, and the church conference attempted to judge the case and when possible to effect reconciliation, both assisted by a committee. If their own committee failed, they requested the "helps" of representatives from sister churches. Some of the charges were difficult to adjudicate. In September 1821 a member brought an accusation against another to the effect that his wife had borne an Indian child and moreover had given it medicine to destroy it. A committee composed of Charles Coleman, Isaac Suttle, Thaddeus Perkins, John Armstrong, and Hardy Thompson cleared the brother of wrongdoing after hearing testimony on both sides, but the accuser persisted until he drove the couple temporarily out of the church.

On other occasions, it was charged that a brother "got drunk and presented a pistol," but in one such case he was duly forgiven some months later after "presenting himself for taking off his coat to fight."[8] Confessions were encouraged. "Brother David Terry became his own accuser for having been Intoxicated the Church agreed to bare with him."[9] Drunkenness and fighting were the commonest charges, but in the 1840s several members came under criticism, and one unrepentant sinner was expelled, for "playing in those plays common amongst young people," plays that "we consider not becoming professors of religion."[10] The church also did not hesitate to intervene in an attempt to bring reconciliation within a family, as when a married couple was charged with "living separately" and a father and son were allowed "5 (five) days to settle a land difficulty between them."[11] In these ways, the church upheld its position as arbiter of morals and manners in the community. Whether it was a Baptist, Methodist, or Presbyterian congregation, it kept close watch on the life-style of its members.

Like the Baptists, who gradually covered the county by extending arms to form other churches, the Methodists also maintained a system peculiarly suited to the conquest of the frontier: the circuit and its tireless circuit rider. Lorenzo Dow was apparently the earliest Methodist and, in fact, the earliest Protestant minister to make his way through central Alabama. He is said to have crossed it around ten times between 1803 and 1812 on his journeys to the already settled Tombigbee country farther south. Although Bibb was only Indian territory at that time, he seems to have left an impression on later settlers, for his name appears on several gravestones in the county: Lorenzo Dow Stewart in Mount Carmel Cemetery; Lorenzo D. Canterberry, Kinard Cemetery; and possibly Lorenzo R. McCary (born 1808), Centreville Memorial Cemetery.[12] But, although Dow was a dedicated traveling preacher, he was not a circuit rider. He chafed at the ties of the Methodist connection and withdrew from the New York Conference to follow his own mystic, eccentric calls to missionary labors, whether in Ireland or the "Tombeckbee."

The first regularly appointed circuit rider to penetrate the wilderness of new Cahaba County was Ebenezer Hearn in April 1818. Young Hearn was commissioned by the Tennessee Conference, which included Madison County, to make preaching appointments throughout this section south of Huntsville and to organize Methodist congregations, then called societies. After meeting the Methodists who had moved into Jones Valley, near the site of future Birmingham, Hearn turned his horse's head in a southwesterly direction and made his next stop at Hill's Settlement, in Cahaba County. He then traveled about twenty miles to the Falls of Cahaba, where the village of Centreville was being built on the riverbanks as the first county seat. Here he probably preached and at least left an appointment to be filled on his second round a month later, before moving on to Wilson's Hill (Montevallo), where he organized his first society.[13] Later in the year, he returned to Centreville on three other rounds, preaching on each occasion. In 1819 Centreville became a preaching station in the new Cahaba Circuit, of which he was appointed as pastor for that year.

Just where the circuit rider preached in Centreville is not recorded. In 1818, when Hearn on leaving Centreville paid his first visit to Tuscaloosa, which he described as a town of board shanties and two log cabins, he was permitted to preach in one of the log cabins, a tavern.[14] During the warm months, the Methodists near the Falls of Cahaba probably gathered in a brush arbor, as did the local Presbyterians. When the new town of Centreville was surveyed on the hill east of the river, the Methodists bought a small lot on the corner of Cedar Street and what is now First Street, South, on which to build a house of worship.

Beginning with Thomas Stringfield in 1819, a number of circuit riders followed Hearn on the Cahaba Circuit, usually in twos, a senior and a junior partner. As was the Methodist custom then, they were appointed by the regional church conference for a term of only a year of full-time labor on each circuit. They sometimes served as many as fifteen or twenty preaching appointments. In their strenuous schedules, they were supported by local preachers like Joshua West, who has been noted as one of Bibb's earliest physicians, and B. L. Defreeze. These circuit riders, like their Baptist counterparts, were hardy pioneers of strong and sometimes eccentric character. One who left his impression on the county was Walter McDaniel, admitted to the Alabama Conference in 1834 and appointed to serve slave missions for a period in the 1840s. He was later remembered in Bibb as "a pioneer of Methodism, a Greek scholar, a devout man, who would just as soon beat religion into the sinner as preach it into him."[15] The United Methodist Church at Brent is named for the son of this "skillful controversionalist," as the historian of Alabama Methodism has called him.[16] Among other pioneer circuit riders later remembered in Bibb are John Starr, John Faust, Charles McLeod, and John Meggs.

In 1832, when the Cahaba Circuit was organized, it contained eight Methodist churches besides the one in Centreville, but by 1835 churches were numerous enough in Bibb to form the Centreville Circuit, though the Montevallo church was retained for a time. By 1840 Methodist "societies" had sprung up over most of the county. The minutes of the second quarterly conference of the circuit for that year give an incomplete list when they name the sixteen member churches that had sent representatives: Cottingham's (Wesley Chapel), Mahan's, Reed Springs, Salem, Ashley's, Mount Zion, Ebenezer, Camp Branch, Crowson's Chapel, Dunlap's, Yellow Leaf, Riggins', Cox's, Six Mile, Sandy, and Centreville. In 1860, when the Centreville congregation was disbanded for a period, the circuit was renamed for the Randolph church.[17]

Sandy Creek settlers built one of the earliest Methodist churches, allegedly while Indians still lived in the neighborhood. According to tradition, they assembled in a brush arbor on McSpadden Campground (near Gary Springs) for some years before erecting this log sanctuary. Its date is not known, but in the summer of 1825 it was recorded that the congregation of Enon Baptist Church, still without a building of its own, held two sessions in Sandy Creek Meeting House.[18] In 1840 it was agreed that the Centreville Circuit should sell McSpadden Campground and that James W. Bishop should receive from Joseph Hinds the funds arising from this sale and should "apply one-third of the money aforesaid to reparing the church at Centreville, the other remaining two-thirds to building a church at Sandy Meeting House."[19] The project at Sandy evidently went slowly. Two and a half years later, a committee was nominated "for the church to be built on Sandy": Jefferson Dominic, Martin Dominic, David Kersh, James Bishop, Nelson Kersh, Presley Rottenberry, and B. L. Defreeze.[20] On July 26, 1843, these trustees bought the church lot of 1.13 acres from James and Sarah Bishop for $16.37½.[21] A structure of a later date, 1880, was dismantled in 1910 for the erection of the present picturesque house of worship, the fourth on this site.[22]

Like their Baptist and Presbyterian brothers, the Methodist preachers,

Randolph United Methodist Church (now a community center), built probably before 1860, the year in which Randolph became head of the Methodist circuit in the county. The second story was added later for the use of the local chapter of the Masonic lodge. (Courtesy of Mrs. Josiah Kennedy)

exhorters, and class leaders attempted to enforce strict social as well as moral standards, but their list of social taboos may have been the longest. As early as 1837, they were trying to influence their members through the introduction of the Sunday school. "There is one Sabbath School in this circuit at Davis, though not very prosperous," it was recorded in 1837, but by 1844 six such schools existed; Number 1 (Sandy) reported two superintendents, seven teachers, one librarian, twenty-eight pupils, and 150 volumes.[23] In 1837 it was also noted that, though forty-one church members had been received on the circuit, fourteen had been expelled. Some of the reasons for those expulsions may appear in the resolution of March 4 of the same year: "Resolved: That the following practices be particularly attended to... practices of dram drinking, attending the race ground, going to dancing parties, or suffering our children to do so, attending circuses, theatres,... breaking the Sabbath, the neglect of class meeting, and the indulgence of superfluous ornaments." A complaint against D. H. Norwood for "retailing spirits" was dismissed "after hearing Brother Norwood's acknowledgement and his promise not to retail spirits any longer than to get shut of his present stock of liquor now on hand."[24]

While the Baptist and Methodist preachers were carrying their faith chiefly to the rural communities, a group of Presbyterian emigrants from Tennessee and the Carolinas gathered quietly in Centreville and established the first church of their denomination in Bibb County. The date was February 7, 1824, and the place was "the new house of Robert Fleming," which, according to tradition, was located on the western edge of the village.[25] The families from which the thirty-two charter members came bore the names of Potts, Davidson, Crawford, Henry, Peters, Wallace, Majure, Wilson, Moore, Fleming, Clark, and Woodruff. Jonathan Potts, Thomas Crawford, and Alex Clark were chosen to be the first elders. Reverend Henry White, a Presbyterian missionary, drew up the bond of union.

For the next several years, this devoted group continued as a congregation without either a church building or a regular pastor. Its members met for "divine service," always including an "action sermon" followed by the sacrament of communion, whenever a missionary preacher was available, regardless of the day of the week, for which he was paid an honorarium of five dollars. But a missionary sent out by the Associated Reformed Presbytery of South Carolina, who called himself a "cecessionist," passed Centreville by in February 1827 and chose to preach in the plantation home of one of its members. Reverend Henry Bryson recorded in his journal: "20 Tu. This day I turned into the Cahaba river and went into the falls of it at a little town called Centreville and went on 5 miles below this on the river and stayed at cousin Johnathan Potts. 21 W. This day I rested and preached here at night."[26]

The organization that furnished the Centreville congregation with its traveling preachers was the Missionary Society of the Alabama Presbytery, an auxiliary of the American Home Missionary Society. In 1829 it began doing so on a regular basis. Missionary Thomas Davis was engaged "to labour for the ensuing four months in the counties of Bibb and Shelby," and to preach once each month in Centreville. Three years later, on March 8, 1832, when the Presbytery met in Centreville, the congregation called its first pastor, James N. Carothers. Carothers was received in May as minister in charge of the churches of Centreville and Elbethel. After a vacancy from 1833 to 1836, the pulpit was filled by Reverend Robert Caldwell of Tennessee on a half-time basis for a year and a half. The membership continued to grow, as newcomers were added such as the Neeleys, Mrs. Mary Howard, Thomas Glass, and James T. Simpson, all from South Carolina.

Meanwhile, the congregation had erected a church before it could obtain its first pastor. Until they were able to build, its members met in a variety of settings, beginning with private homes, in one of which they heard a sermon on March 14, 1824, on the appropriate text "Fear not, little flock." In the summer months of 1826 and 1827, they preferred to gather "at a stand prepared for the purpose," described on August 11, 1827, as "a stand in a grove on the west end of town." But, on the first Sunday in October 1829, Thomas Crawford, clerk of the session, recorded triumphantly: "Assembled for the first time in the new Presbyterian Church erected by the congregation of Centreville."

According to tradition, this sanctuary was constructed on land owned by Mrs. Nancy Hunt, possibly the site now of the Bibb County High School's Ninth Grade Building. At a time when the new county seat was being planned on the hill east of the river, the Presbyterians conservatively chose to build west of the river in the original community. They continued to use this building at least until March 26, 1854, when the session was recorded as meeting in it. A citizen writing at the turn of the century recalled that this wooden structure remained after all the others around it had fallen into decay.[27] In 1859, at a cost of $4,000, the Presbyterians built their present brick church on the courthouse square. Robert Fleming, a charter member, and Dr. J. W. Crawford, son of another original member, were the trustees in charge of it construction.

Like other denominational groups, the Centreville Presbyterians kept a careful record of infractions by members and the action taken by elders in each case. The two commonest charges were drunkenness and profanity, sometimes accompanied by "boisterous behavior on the streets of Centreville." During the Reconstruction period, B. F. Glass failed to follow the usual pattern of appearing before the session to express his penitence and so was summarily excommunicated. The charges against him were listed as these: "1. constant neglect of church attendance. 2. retailing intoxicating drinks to the great scandal of the church. 3. preparing a bowling alley to aid in demoralizing the community."[28]

The Cumberland was the most numerous branch of Presbyterians in the county, four out of the five Presbyterian congregations reported in 1850 being of that persuasion.[29] The Cumberlands, unlike their mother church (U.S.A.), preached universal atonement, a doctrine that was popular on the democratic frontier. All of Bibb's churches of this faith were members of the Elyton Presbytery. The one at Green Pond has had the longest but the most checkered history. Green Pond is located in the northern corner of the county, an area whose prosperity early gained it the name of Kingdom Beat. The community took its name from a pond, now long since drained, that was said to have been covered by perpetual green moss.[30] According to tradition, the church was established there in 1827, inspired by a camp meeting held the preceding fall by two preachers, J. L. Guthrie and John Williams, in a barn belonging to Solin Green, about three miles from the present community.[31]

The church was named Bethany, and for a short time Guthrie was its

Green Pond Presbyterian Church, organized in 1832 as a Cumberland church. The pulpit and pews in the present sanctuary were built by the family of the Reverend S. G. Oglesby, pastor in the 1870s. (Courtesy of Mrs. Josiah Kennedy)

pastor. After a period of eclipse by a short-lived Presbyterian Church U.S.A., Bethany was reorganized in 1832 with forty-eight members. After another period of inactivity, it was revived by Robert Oldham, who became its pastor on the day of reorganization, September 16, 1846. He was followed ten years later by H. W. Jones and then a year subsequently by W. W. Moore, who remained with the church until 1871 except for the last year of the Civil War, when he served as a chaplain in the Confederate Army. Over a hundred years later, the small but loyal congregation (now Presbyterian U.S.A.) still meets in its quaint sanctuary just off the main thoroughfare in Green Pond.

Other Cumberland Presbyterian churches established in the county were Smyrna at Mars, 1833; Bethel at Six Mile, 1834; Pleasant Hill, northwest of Centreville, 1841; Scottsville, 1846; and many years later, in 1879, Friendship at River Bend.[32] These churches endured many vicissitudes. At Mars, in Hill's Settlement, Smyrna was reactivated in 1846 as Spring Hill, followed by Mount Moriah in 1853. The Scottsville congregation disbanded by the fall of 1850, after which one of its elders was given the same position in the Pleasant Hill Church. The Six Mile congregation, which originally worshipped in a log building near the creek bank and later in a frame structure just below the present site of the local Baptist Church, remained active until the early twentieth century. The Six Mile and Pleasant Hill congregations cooperated in planning joint events, including "protracted meetings" that sometimes lasted nine days.[33] Reverend Robert Oldham, son-in-law of James Hill, was instrumental in organizing all these churches except Bethany, founded by Eli Berger, and Friendship, established by S. S. Oglesby.[34]

Pleasant Hill is the only Bibb church that survived in this original fold. When the county's Cumberland shepherd, Robert Oldham, organized it in 1841, he undertook to serve as the first pastor and continued in that post for ten years. The original thirty-three members represented these families: Pearson, Steele, Shropshire, Lightsey, Nichols, Woodward, Green, James, Stringfellow, and Woodruff. The first elders were Samuel Pearson, William Nichols, David Lightsey, and J. S. Green. John Steele, who had earlier served Cumberland congregations at Bethel, Lebanon, Jericho, and Six Mile, donated the church lot, on which trustees Martin P. Steele, Felix Shropshire, and William Green planned the first sanctuary, a log house. Besides the original brush arbor, three buildings have stood on the same grounds, where monthly services are still conducted today.

In its early years, Pleasant Hill had to cope with many of the problems of other county churches. It often felt called upon to chastise its members for their misconduct. When "Brother John Lewis was reported to have been intoxicated and also had been betting on horse racing," the session, after a month of forbearance, voted to suspend him.[35] Three women who confessed that they had participated in a dance were placed on probation. The most certain candidate for instant dismissal was any woman who allegedly had "been delivered of an illegitimate issue." A very different problem that faced the session was that of paying the preacher, especially during the critical years of the Civil War and Reconstruction. In October 1867 W. W. Moore received in lieu of his salary these donations: "Corn—25 bundles; fodder—400 bundles; cotton—950 pounds."

Until the Centreville Presbyterians built their brick sanctuary in 1859, none of Bibb's church structures was impressive. The U.S. census reporter for 1850, Robert McIlvain, a Bibb lawyer, valued the property of the five Presbyterian, ten Methodist, and eighteen Baptist churches at $250 each. The congregations had increased in membership but done little to improve their physical facilities since the days of settlement. Even in the first two decades after the Civil War, the buildings were described as open, sometimes, at both ends, and therefore hot in summer and cold in winter. Like that other early institution, the school, the Bibb church was not concerned with physical comfort. Nevertheless, it kept its hold on the people, and to the end of the century it was the dominant influence on community life.

8

ANTEBELLUM SCHOOLS

THAT OTHER CIVILIZING institution of pioneer days, the school, left fewer records in Bibb than did the church. It was sometimes presided over by the same authority who occupied the pulpit on Sundays, but it generated less enthusiasm in a fairly bookless society. In fact, it made only slow progress in the county throughout the nineteenth century.

One detriment to interest in education was the lack of an organized public school system in Alabama until 1854 and the failure of any program for funding it adequately before the next century, in spite of early attempts by the legislature. In 1819 the first state constitution allocated the sixteenth section in each township for the use of the schools and authorized the election of local commissioners to survey and lease the land and apply the proceeds to education.[1] The first record of the appointment of such commissioners in Bibb appears in the county court minutes of February 1831, but no subsequent mention is made of their activities. In some cases, the sixteenth section was poor and of little value for lease. In other cases, where the lands were leased for ninety-nine years or sold outright, with the object of supporting the schools on the interest of the funds invested, the financial panic of 1837 wiped out that investment.

Following the legislative act of March 6, 1848, the schools had to depend on county tax money, apportioned to them according to their enrollment. For example, in 1850 Bibb reported 400 pupils and its schools received only $816 in public funds.[2] These funds were designated to cover the tuition of the poorer pupils, as a result of which the common schools came to be called "pauper schools." No public money was provided for building costs or the salaries of teachers. They supported themselves on tuition fees collected from patrons, who paid only for the days their offspring actually attended classes. One illiterate but enterprising farmer as late as 1890 kept a stick on which he notched those days, and, when the head of the Centreville school, Jesse Dean Cooper, came to collect, he brought out the stick and paid accordingly.[3]

Another discouragement to the development of adequate schools was the irregularity of pupil attendance. For boys and girls who could handle a hoe little time was available throughout farming season to indulge in book-learning. The custom of dropping out of school each year at planting time in the spring and again at corn-gathering and cotton-picking season in the fall was not uncommon even in the early twentieth century. Only after the row crops were "laid by" in early July, and again after cotton picking was finished, often not until January, were there brief intervals for schooling.

An ambitious pupil, Jasper James, who lived in the area called Affonee in southern Bibb, left a record of typical interruptions in his dairy. On October 11, 1857, he commented ruefully: "I went to school exactly 20 days this year if I dont go more than that I will soon be grown and no Education." By mid-December he had added twelve more days. He kept an account of his attendance in certain other years: 1847, 29 days; 1854, 16 days; 1855, 63 days; 1856, "45 or 50 days." Among Bibb farm boys, Jasper was probably unusual in his determination to continue his education at home. He describes himself, like young Abraham Lincoln, "while the family are all abed . . . sitting around the pine knot fire deeply buried in some Book."[4] When "the book peddler Stephens" passed by, his father, Alexander Hill James, bought the "cabinet Library," a collection of "twenty volumes, neatly bound by the author of Peter Parley's tales cost $8.00 and some cents." In these books and others in his earlier library, which included such diverse titles as *The Adventures of Robinson Crusoe* and *The Young Bride's Book*, he continued the education he had begun in various little schoolhouses in the woods.

Most boys and girls in Bibb attended school in a one-room log house in the woods or an abandoned field, a type called throughout the South the "old field school." Following the Southern custom, a group of neighboring farmers agreed to build and support a school in a spot convenient for all of them. As in the case of pioneer homes, the site they chose was usually near a spring and also, if possible, close to a shady grove for play and a "switch" orchard for discipline. The field school, like the church, was typically a rather primitive building and remained so throughout the nineteenth century.

A Bibb native, writing of the country school he attended near Rocky Branch, several miles north of Centreville, in the last decade of the century, described a one-room structure quite similar to the type in antebellum days. Although many rural schools in the 1880s and 1890s were simple "plank houses," this building was constructed of logs; a big rock chimney was at one end and a door at the other. "For additional ventilation," the erstwhile pupil recalled, "a long window was cut in one side by sawing three logs out. This opening had a shutter made of plank which hinged down inside and afforded a sort of table for pupils to practise writing in their copy books."[5] The feature that he remembered most vividly was the spring that gave its name to the school: "Sycamore Spring had a pine box where the water bubbled out of the ground beside a small bluff. A rustic trough made by splitting a hollow sourwood sapling carried the water about twenty-five feet to a large trough hewed out of a big pine log. There the livestock could get a refreshing drink. The sourwood trough was almost grown over with moss and algae. McDuffey's Fifth Reader gives a picture (an old wood cut) exactly like Sycamore Spring, trough and all."[6]

The first known references to a schoolhouse in Bibb appear in the records of the Centreville Presbyterian Church from 1826 through 1829, during which time it was "the usual place of worship." This building was located in "Old Centreville," west of the Cahaba. A deed by Nathaniel Woodruff to Samuel Woodruff, dated November 7, 1830, describes a certain tract of land in Fraction 6 of Section 23, containing four acres, "beginning on the west margin of Cahawba River at a Spring known as the School House spring."[7] This spot can be identified now as approximately opposite 149 Riverview Road, somewhat more than half a mile above the river bridge. It was blessed with an excellent spring, possibly the old schoolhouse spring, for at least three quarters of a century before the river swallowed it during the disastrous tornado of 1973.

Unfortunately, the school whose pupils drank from the spring did not leave any records that have been discovered, but it was probably presided over by anyone who chose to try to collect tuition fees from the local patrons. Because in many cases little was expected of an instructor besides the ability to read and "cipher," almost anyone may have been acceptable, even Coleman Allen, the peddler, who in his 1824 bill of divorce called himself a schoolteacher.[8]

Many field schools sprang up in Bibb throughout the antebellum years, most of them leaving not even a reference to the schoolhouse spring. Those accessible to the Affonee area in the 1850s, as listed in Jasper James's diary of September 6, 1857, were ruled with one exception by males, in some cases local farmers who tried a stint between their crops. The one exception was the widow of Judge Thomas Crawford. Jasper recorded: "I went to school to Mrs. Crawford 1847, George Creel 1850, H. Wooley 1851, J. W. Moreland 1852, D. W. Yeager 1853, J. Walker 1854, W. J. Rousseau 1855, D. W. James 1856, R. C. Corley 1857."

The location of Jasper's school is not always specified; he described one as "over on the other side of nowhere." But on February 28, 1858, he wrote: "I am going now to a Mr. Corley down hear at the little schoolhouse in the woods not far from the Hurricane branch. This place not famous for good scholars at all." He was head of his class and was therefore allowed to "give out the lesson."The principal subjects were grammar and "Davies arithmetic,"for which he had bought textbooks in Centreville on August 1, 1856. He worked out a number of his problems in his diary by a method he called "operation according to Smiley." Jasper's school apparently did not require public speaking by the pupils, but on May 1, 1858, he attended and heartily approved such a program "at the schoolhouse on the road leading from Centreville to Marion."Field schools were sometimes the scene of community celebrations. On July 3, 1858, at a schoolhouse in the neighborhood of James Mason, Jasper heard Captain T. W. Gantt read the Declaration of Independence and John Pratt give an oration, after which there was "music fiddles banjoes accordeons."

More information is available about the schools that were dignified by the name of academy. Each of these boasted trustees and was incorporated by the state legislature. Four academies were established in Bibb during the antebellum period, at Centreville, Six Mile, Green Pond, and Sandy, respectively.[9] By far the earliest was the Centreville Academy, established after the county seat was moved to the hill east of the river in 1828. The commissioners who created the new town reserved a lot for an academy, Number 37, on Walnut Street, now diagonally opposite the post office. They also appointed a building committee, two of whose members are known to have been County Judge Thomas Crawford and William B. Norris because they signed the detailed specifications drawn up on January 25, 1833.[10]

The first specification reads: "The building shall be forty feet long twenty two feet wide with a wall of twelve feet in height between sleepers and joists."The contract was awarded to the new partnership of Enoch Carson and George W. Howard, who agreed to build the academy as specified and to "furnish the Blocks and dry the plank wood being furnished for the sum of two hundred and fourteen dollars, $^{50}/_{100}$." They also contracted to make for the schoolhouse four benches and two writing desks with drawers. All bills for labor and material were paid during the following year, as agreed upon. Funds for building the academy, like the courthouse and jail, were designated to come from the sale of lots in the new town, but it was later found necessary to complete that amount with a small sum from county taxes. The school was in operation at least by 1837, when the Centreville Presbyterian Church records refer to divine service "at the Academy Building" on July 9.

This two-room frame structure has had better luck than several other

Centreville Academy, constructed in 1834 by Enoch Carson and George W. Howard, is probably the oldest school building in the county. It stands now at the rear of the Mayberry-Moren-England house, where it was moved in 1876 to serve as dining room and kitchen. (Courtesy of Mrs. Josiah Kennedy)

historic school buildings in Bibb, all of which have been destroyed by fire. It has continued to survive, though in a different location and use. After a new schoolhouse was erected in 1852, this building served various purposes, including church gatherings, until Dr. E. H. Moren bought it in 1876 for $150 and moved it back of his home (the present Charles England residence). His family used its two large rooms for many years as dining room and kitchen, an area that was frequently separated from the main residence throughout the nineteenth century because of the danger of fire. In the twentieth century, it provides commodious storerooms for its owners. It is probably the oldest surviving school building in the county.

Centreville was indebted to the local chapter of Freemasons for its new schoolhouse in 1852. After withstanding a certain amount of suspicion and antagonism, typical in the 1830s and 1840s, this fraternal order became an important social and moral influence. Lodges were chartered in Centreville and Green Pond and later in other communities. Friendship Lodge Number 83 was organized at Centreville on July 12, 1847; Lovick P. Ramsey was worshipful master, John W. Hays senior warden, and L. W. Wilson junior warden; the charter was issued on December 4,

1847.[11] One of the first concerns of the Masons in this village, as in other communities in Alabama, was to encourage education by sponsoring an academy bearing its name. On May 3, 1851, the membership elected seven trustees for this purpose: J. W. Cleveland, L. W. Wilson, Felix Shropshire, E. H. Bernhard, A. D. Potts, James W. Crawford, and Josiah S. Kennedy. The original purpose was to construct a building for housing the school and the lodge and also to subsidize the teacher's salary by collecting tuition fees. The building was to be impressive for its day: "The trustees shall select a suitable convenient location for the Institute and contract for the speedy erection of a suitable building of these dimensions to wit, fifty feet long by 40 feet wide, two stories high twenty windows, ten above and ten below, one room below, benches, desks, tables, &C. Three rooms above, one hall forty-five feet long, the other ten feet equally divided, the Hall furnished with stands &C necessary for a Masonic Lodge sealed above & below, painted & neatly furnished in a workmanlike manner, the Cost not to exceed two thousand dollars."[12]

To defray some expense of this ambitious project, the trustees were authorized to sell for $1,400 their current meeting house, later known as the Kennedy hotel, which the lodge had bought in 1847 on the death of its first owner, former sheriff John Henry. The trustees selected a site on the hill above the town, now known as the O. C. Oakley lot, and bought it from S. W. Davidson. On it B. F. Parsons erected the new building in which the academy was to be continued under the name Centreville Masonic Institute. It was ready for occupancy on November 1, 1852. On that day the thirteen pupils in the academy were marched up the hill by their principal, A. C. Collins, who taught the boys, and his daughter Ann, who was in charge of the girls.[13] Bibb County boys and girls were to study in that schoolhouse until 1894, when it burned and Principal Jesse Dean Cooper shortly replaced it with another building that has served as a residence during the present century.

Little is known about the teachers at the original academy before A. C. Collins and his daughter, though the names of Amanda Parker, Lelias Law, Gamble, and Post have survived in tradition. Possibly James Knox was in charge in 1850 because this teacher was boarding at the Mayberry Hotel in Centreville during that year.[14] By the late 1850s, Mrs. S. K. Jennings had come to the Masonic Institute. She and her husband, editor of the *Central Enquirer*, boarded at the Kennedy House. Mrs. Jennings was the former Margaret West of Marion, a graduate of Judson College. A long poem that she had composed, entitled "Music," was read at a community gathering at the courthouse in 1858 and afterward printed in her husband's newspaper. Dr. E. H. Moren, who visited her classes as a member of the school board, reported that she instructed her pupils in French.

When she left around 1860 to teach in Plantersville, the memory of her accomplishments lived on.

Another notable antebellum teacher was DeWitt Logan, but it is not clear whether he followed Mrs. Jennings at the Institute in 1861 or came after the war. In any case, he had earlier gained experience at a number of field schools in Bibb. In 1850 this twenty-two-year-old pedagogue was rooming at the farm house of Mrs. Rachel Moore in the Sandy community, and in 1860 he gave his address as the new railroad town of Randolph.[15] By 1861 he was probably teaching at either Sandy or Centreville because he and his wife, Sarah, daughter of Probate Judge Jackson Gardner, became members of nearby Mount Zion Church in March of that year. Logan's pupils described him with some awe as "that teacher whose height was seven feet six, or six feet seven, in his stocking feet."[16] He was a stern disciplinarian, who had the reputation of whipping his pupils if they had not prepared their lessons. He conducted what was called a "blab school"; that is, his pupils studied aloud, a custom that was continued at the institute until Jesse Dean Cooper, a graduate of Bucknell University, succeeded him in 1869.

One difficulty that the institute must have suffered at the end of the 1850s was the competition of a new school operated by Reverend and Mrs. H. A. Smith, two of those "Yankee schoolteachers" who left a tradition of learning in many parts of the South. A native of New Hampshire, he came to be pastor of the new brick Presbyterian Church, erected in the courthouse square in 1859, but he was also eager to set up a school. He was a graduate of Amherst, and his wife, Hannah Hitchcock Smith, of Vermont, was an alumna of Mount Holyoke.[17] Because the old courthouse was being replaced by a new one, Smith assisted by one of his elders, Dr. J. W. Crawford, bought the old building for a residence and schoolhouse and moved it to the Crawford farm, on a site now facing Magnolia Circle. Smith taught the older boys and Mrs. Smith the girls and little boys.

A pupil of Mrs. Smith many years later left an account of her methods and textbooks: "When teaching the alphabet, she would give the child a newspaper and have him stick a pin in a certain letter. She had a class in mental arithmetic which she conducted like a round table discussion.... We studied McGuffey's readers, a spelling book, Cornell's geography, Davies Written Arithmetic, and wrote in copy books. We used slates and had a little piece of sponge tied by a string to the frame to erase our figures.... We studied a primary U.S. history which Mrs. Smith made very interesting by telling us tales of Revolutionary days. My older sisters studied Smith's Grammar and learned to parse."[18] The Smiths, unlike other academy heads, never conducted public examinations at the end of the school term. Yet, even without these demonstrations, their reputation spread, as did that of their daughters, who taught with them. In spite of their Northern origin, they remained in good standing through the war years. In 1872, when the Masons offered the institute for sale, they bought it and managed it until their departure in 1884, when they were succeeded by their son, H. K. W. Smith, a recent Princeton graduate, who had the institute incorporated under the name Centreville Male and Female College. After Smith's two-year tenure, Jesse Dean Cooper resumed control, by 1897 calling the school Centreville High School. He was assisted by his daughter Bessie in the primary department while he refined a college preparatory program that included Greek and advanced mathematics.

Of the three other academies established in Bibb before the Civil War, the oldest was located in the farming community of Green Pond. This school seems to have been indebted to two benevolent organizations of that day. Tradition credits its founding to the Sons of Temperance, a national group that encouraged education as a means of fighting the evil of strong drink. The date was 1846.[19] Evidently the building was considered inadequate, for the Masons, here as at Centreville, provided a new one. The sponsoring chapter, Cold Water Lodge Number 148, some months before receiving its charter on December 4, 1851, was planning to build a combination schoolhouse and lodge. By May 17, 1851, it was agreed that $250 be appropriated for this cause, and a member, Reverend Robert Oldham, donated a quarter acre of land for the site. Members of the building committee were listed as Oldham, Law, Davis, McMath, and Tatum.[20]

The building must have been completed by March 13, 1852, because in the minutes of that date the committee was instructed to pay M. Oldham for his services as builder. The academy used the first floor, and the lodge held its meetings on the second floor. The principal of the Green Pond Academy, a Mr. Meriwether, transferred his pupils to this new facility, where he was soon succeeded by Lelias L. Law. William Wilson Moore, a local Presbyterian minister, headed the school from 1854 until 1867, except for the year 1864–65, when he served as a Confederate chaplain. After a series of short-lived administrations, Andrew W. Hayes, nephew and former student of Reverend Moore, became principal of the academy in 1876 and, except for a year in which he completed his university study, guided the Green Pond Academy and its successor, the Woodstock Academy, for the rest of the century.

During the same prosperous decade in which the Masons built new facilities at Centreville and Green Pond, residents of Sandy, the farming community three miles east of Centreville, organized their own school without any fraternal backing. On October 18, 1853, a group of citizens "residing on Sandy Creek" who were "desirous of being incorporated for the purpose of education" met and elected trustees for that school, to be called Sandy Creek Academy. These trustees included A. R. P. Conwill, J. S. Cleveland, Carter W. Cleveland, J. W. Suttle, David Kirsh, Jacob Lightsey, and Samuel Frazer.[21] The account book of one of those trustees, John W. Suttle, records a donation of $100 to the academy in the same year of 1853, and presumably the venture was underwritten by other trustees also.[22]

The one-room school building must have been completed by 1855, if not before, because Richard Hopkins Pratt, destined to be one of the county's best-known educators, taught there from 1855 to 1858. He came to Sandy carrying a fresh bachelor of arts degree from the University of Alabama. When he resigned his first teaching post in 1858 to go to Six Mile, he may have been succeeded by a man named Montgomery, who is said to have taught at Sandy sometime before the Civil War. Nothing is known about the school during the war or for several years afterward, until Captain Pratt was again in charge for two or three years before 1872. He was followed by Alice Brown and later by Mrs. Conwill, probably Mrs. M. L. Conwill, who was slated to appear on August 18, 1883, on a County Teachers' Institute program to discuss "What Are the Teacher's Trials?"[23]

Like the Sandy school, the fourth Bibb academy was apparently created in the 1850s, but the exact date of its establishment is unknown. This was the Six Mile Academy, founded in the community that took its name from the creek flowing through it. Six Mile Creek appears in the earliest county records as one of the first streams the white man named. One explanation of its name is that its main bed runs six miles before entering the Cahaba River.[24] Several other traditions exist, however, some of them comic. The community was one of the most thriving settlements in Bibb during the nineteenth century, becoming incorporated in 1860. A citizen of Six Mile wrote this account of its origin: "About the year of 1836, when wolves were not scarce in this country and when the deer and turkey were plentiful, and the appearance of a bear would sometimes strike terror to the people of this section, George Leith settled at the present site of Six Mile. He labored for some time almost alone but finally built a mill which drew custom and caused others to settle around him. Among those early settlers were Thomas Soal, Jerry Hayes, W. P. Thompson, J. N. Smith and others."[25]

Although the actual date of the establishment of the Six Mile Academy is unknown, it was functioning before 1858, when thirty-year-old "Hop" Pratt came from Sandy Academy as coprincipal with William Joseph Peters. The school building, erected on a two-acre lot donated by Robert and Louisa Goode, remained in use until it burned in October 1897. It was a wooden structure measuring sixty feet long and thirty feet wide and

Typical one-room country school: pupils of Woolley School, Antioch community, in the 1880s, pictured with J. C. Hicks, schoolmaster. (Courtesy of Vera Hicks)

providing two spacious rooms on each floor, three for classrooms and one offered to the local Masonic lodge for its sessions. The trustees who had the academy incorporated in 1859 were listed in the charter of "The Six Mile Male and Female Academy of Bibb County" as William T. Thomas, Leroy T. McGuire, Ezekiel G. Smith, Simpson W. Hederick, and Pulaski Wallace.[26]

Only two years after the state granted this charter, Richard Hopkins Pratt, who was destined to be the leading spirit of the academy, marched off to the Civil War, and the ambitious plans made for it had to wait until he returned to Six Mile in 1872. After that time, Captain Pratt gave his dynamic leadership to the school until in 1896 he moved up to the position of county superintendent of education, as DeWitt Logan had done before him and Andrew W. Hayes was to do later. During his tenure at Six Mile, no school in the county gave more concerts, held more festive commencements, or fostered more loyal alumni.

The decade of the 1850s was one of relative promise for Bibb County schools. At its beginning, only twenty teachers presided over twenty common schools, which accommodated a total of 400 white pupils, according to the U.S. census of 1850. At that time, only eight inhabitants called themselves teachers: James Knox (age 32), Calvin McConnell (25), Willis Caddell (19), James M. Wade (22), Levi Boidston (51), William Vance (24), DeWitt Logan (22), and James R. Codwide, a native of India (50). By 1860, however, thirty-one residents claimed teaching as their occupation.[27] Most of these presided over one-room institutions where they attempted to instruct pupils of all ages and different degrees of advancement, but, in spite of the difficulty of the task, they were assisting the second generation to rise above the illiteracy that handicapped so many of the early settlers. Even in 1850, the U.S. census recorded 1,137 adult white illiterates in the county.

The progress of education was suddenly halted at the end of the decade, however, by the outbreak of the Civil War. During that conflict, many of the teachers and older students served in the Confederate Army, and those schools that survived did so by what might be called a "holding operation." Afterward, they were shackled by poverty and low morale. The conditions necessary for further development did not return until many years after that war which resulted eventually in allowing schooling for blacks as well as whites.

9

SLAVERY

ALONGSIDE CHURCH AND SCHOOL, another kind of institution existed in the county from the earliest days of settlement: slavery.[1] Because Southerners realized that it was peculiar to their section, they sometimes referred to it as "our peculiar institution." Dr. Basil Manly, well-known Baptist minister and president of the University of Alabama, speaking at the State Baptist Convention in 1860, called slaves "our peculiar property."[2] Although a few voices in the South questioned the institution as immoral, it is doubtful if such a voice was ever heard among white citizens of Bibb, where as early as 1826 its representative in the state senate opposed a bill to prohibit the importation of slaves into the state.[3] It is true that in 1844, when Methodist churches in the Alabama Conference were determining whether to sever their union with their denomination in the North over the issue of slavery, "decided opposition" to the resolution was recorded in the Centreville circuit, the only one except Eufaula in which any dissension was reported.[4] The opposition, from whatever cause it may have stemmed, was soon overridden. Although the county was predominantly Democratic, it possessed a number of Whigs and, later, Union men but no articulate antislavery citizens.

Bibb was never one of the big slaveholding counties, but the ratio of slaves to white residents increased steadily during the antebellum period. Before 1830, slaves in Alabama were found chiefly in the fertile lands of the Tennessee valley and along the Alabama and lower Tombigbee rivers. In 1818 the Alabama territorial census reported for newly created Cahaba County a total population of 1,280, of which 247 were slaves, approximately 20 percent of the total. By 1840 the proportion had grown to 24 percent, by 1850 to 29 percent, and by 1860, the year before the Civil War, to 32½ percent, according to the U.S. census for those years. Yet the 1860 percentage was well below the state average of almost 50 percent. The constant increase in both county and state was the result of the rising importance of cotton in the Southern economy. It has been said defensively that the only cheap, stable labor then available for raising this crop was that of black slaves.

Bibb farmers who found it necessary to invest in more and more slaves in order to produce this valuable staple had several opportunities for acquiring them. They could travel to the slave markets in such nearby Alabama cities as Montgomery. In 1836 Richard Habersham, a visitor from the older and more settled state of Georgia, gave a vivid description of what a Bibb Countian might have seen on Montgomery's main street. After passing a family of Creek Indians selling articles of their own manufacture, this Georgia lawyer "came suddenly upon ranges of well dressed negro men and women seated upon benches. There may have been 80 or 100 all in different parcels. The women were as well dressed as the negro women in Georgia usually are for church. Each had a new light striped cotton handerchief on her head, tied somewhat in the shape of a sugar loaf. With each group were seated two or three sharp, hard featured white men. This was the slave market and the negroes were dressed out for show. There they sit all day and every day until they are sold, each parcel rising and standing in rank as a purchaser approaches. Although born in a slave country and a slave holder myself and an advocate of slavery, yet this sight was entirely novel and shocked my feelings."[5]

For those who found it inconvenient to travel to the city market, it was possible to buy these valuable properties at home. Speculators plied their trade in the rural counties, though perhaps more in the Black Belt than in the hill counties. One early settler later reported: "I came to Perry County in 1832 with Anderson West, who was specializing in Negroes and brought a drove with him at the time.... Every man we met either wanted to buy a 'nigger' or take a drink."[6] Traveling dealers usually transported the slaves in wagons and pitched their tents in different settlements to exhibit their wares. Many runaways advertised for in the newspapers of the period were the property of speculators. During the 1850s, at least one Bibb Countian seems to have raised slaves for the local market, if the term "not a planter but a Negro raiser" has that implication.[7]

Another more common method of adding to one's labor force was to patronize the local slave auctions that were held from time to time by the sheriff. The usual scene of these events was the courthouse steps, though in 1823, after the county seat had been temporarily moved to the present Antioch area, the sheriff was granted authority to hold such sales in the village of Centreville for the convenience of residents west of the Cahaba River.[8]

These auctions were often occasioned by the court's need for funds to clear a debt owed an administrator's estate or to cover a citizen's court costs in a legal case. A settler's slaves were usually his most available property and sometimes his only assets on which the court could levy. The Bibb County circuit court records abound in cases in which slaves were levied on. As a result of a suit by William Fondren's administrators for the purpose of collecting a debt owed to his estate, Sheriff J. W. Davis reported in the usual form on October 13, 1830, to the court then in session: "Levied 17 June 1830 on the following negroes to wit, Charles, Lucy, and Raiford set for sale on the 1st Monday in July next not sold by Lewis Cammack making oath and giving bond and putting in a claim to try eight of said slaves 5 July 1830 and the said Michael Purtle and Mitchell Watkins has no other goods or chattels lands or tenements in my county that I can make the sum of $273.65 ¾ or any part thereof."[9] Yet a quarter of a century later the legal form had not changed. Attorneys Garrott and McIlvain settled the debt of George A. Oden to T. L. Johnson on February 11, 1856, by the public sale of "Jerry a Boy Phebe a girl Jane a girl and her infant child Ben, Sal a girl and her Two Children, the eldest named Jr. and the other an infant having no name, the property of the defendant."[10]

Farm implements were not infrequently lumped with slaves in order to realize the sum due, which included numerous court costs and sometimes board and clothing for the slaves, in addition to the debt. On November 2, 1857, Sheriff W. A. Schoolar recorded: "The within named girl Indiana was bid off by Felix Shropshur for the sum of Eight hundred and seventeen Dollars it being the highest and best bid offered, the crop cut saw bid off by Adam James for two and 05/100 Dollars it being the highest and best bid offered."[11]

Such sales were considered final. If the highest bidder afterward refused to accept and pay for the slave, he would be liable to a suit by the sheriff "for the use of" the owner, and would probably have a judgment rendered against him, as it was against Henry Adams in the spring term of circuit court in 1842. In this suit, which the sheriff won, he claimed a loss because he was subsequently compelled to sell the slave, a boy called Aaron, for $390 instead of at Adams's auction bid of $600.[12]

The slaves that the planter purchased, probably by one of these methods, then usually became his most valuable property, and he was often referred to in terms of their number, for example a "forty-slave planter." When his assets were listed, as in the administration of his estate, usually slaves were named first, followed immediately by farm animals. In Wiley Coleman's estate appraisement, no break appears between "Boy Jacob 75.00" and "Five Sows and Sixteen Piggs 20.00."[13] Yet, though the slaves were considered property like farm animals, they were not necessarily treated inhumanely. Official records give little evidence of violence between master and slave, though admittedly it may not always have reached the courts. A Bibb slave charged with murdering a white man was not automatically considered guilty, as was shown in *The State* v. *Peter (a Slave)*. Peter, who belonged to the estate of Littleton Riggins, had been indicted for killing Martin Walker, a white man, by shooting him with a rifle, but on October 7, 1846, at the fall term of circuit court he was ordered "detained in custody that another indictment may be preferred against him." At the following spring term, he was declared not guilty and released.[14] Also, for Dave, a slave charged with assaulting Michael White, a white man, with a knife, the solicitor entered a "nol pros."[15]

Sometimes a master was suspected of attempting to protect his man from the court, perhaps in order not to lose his services during a long jail term like the one Peter evidently endured. In *The State* v. *Frank (a Slave) and George (a Slave)*, these two blacks, the property of David S. Lipscomb and S. W. Davidson, respectively, were indicted for "burglariously breaking and entering the residence of John O'Brien," from which they were accused of stealing "one pair of boots, two tin buckets, three jugs of whiskey, one piece of bleached domestic, one piece of material for cotton handkerchief, forty pounds of brown sugar, and one pair of slippers." A year elapsed between the robbery and the indictment, and another year passed before the date set for the trial, October 7, 1847. When Frank did not appear on that day, his master, David Lipscomb, was indicted for "taking his slave away," though he later won dismissal of the charge.[16]

Masters usually housed their slaves in log or plank cabins, built along a lane in an area referred to as "the quarters." In most cases, these cabins were ventilated by the chimney of the large open fireplace, on which the occupants cooked, and by the cracks between the logs or boards, daubed with mud in winter. The arrangement around the home of John E. Green and his son, James Green, on their 3,400-acre plantation near Woodstock was typical. A descendant's account enables the reader to visualize the environment of the servants' living quarters: "The place required numerous slaves and mules to work it. The [twelve] old slave cabins were located about a hundred feet north of the dwelling house, and the white overseer's house was located about one hundred feet north of the present well on the southeast side of the house. Across the present highway was a large mule lot, cotton gin, sorghum mill, and a few other smaller buildings. There were a number of large white oak trees scattered around the house place. . . . There was a large back yard which contained several small outbuildings such as smoke house, chicken house, weavers house, potato storage, etc., also fruit trees—figs, plums, pomegranates, and two large grape arbors."[17]

The owner provided his black people with basic care, including food and clothing. The clothes were made from homespun or from osnaburg, the chief product of the Scottsville cotton mill, often called "slave cloth." Planter George Mayberry bought 116½ yards of osnaburg from the Tuscaloosa Manufacturing Company, owners of the mill, on March 20, 1848, at ten cents a yard.[18] Slaves were issued heavy rawhide shoes that could not be bent by hand, advertised in the newspapers as "negro shoes." They were also furnished with cheap blankets, referred to in James and Latham's store advertisements as "planters' blankets."[19] Thus supplied, and usually provided with their noon meal, field hands were expected to work from daylight until dark, but those who were too old to do so were permitted to continue to live in their cabins and receive the same benefits as during their active years.

Even under the kindliest master, however, there was always the possibility of the separation of the slave family after his death. Most owners desired, for both practical and humane considerations, to bequeath their valuable slaveholdings directly to their children. George Mayberry willed several slaves to each of three heirs, and his executor disposed of them in that manner, evidently not breaking all their family ties:

> To Elizabeth Berry—4 slaves—Harry, Patience, White, and Tishey—$1200.
> To Mary Sullivan—3 slaves (viz) Alley, Mary, and Tom—$1300.
> To James Mayberry—4 slaves (viz) Amy, Eliza, Emily, and Kitt—$2275.[20]

But the will of Ruth Tucker, signed on December 17, 1842, was impossible to administer without such a break, and it was more typical: "I do will and bequeath my negroe woman Aggy and four children Matilda Sim Louisa Andy to be equally divided between my six youngest children." Even though a petition by the heirs to sell the slaves, dated January 13, 1846, named also "an infant about four months old, name unknown," an equal arithmetical division would not have satisfied the requirements of fairness, and so an auction was necessary. Aggy and her child, Alfred, evidently the infant, were "bid off" to William Blocker at $401, Sim to George Tucker at $384, Louisa to Jacob Mayberry at $293, and Andy to George Tucker at $177. This sale resulted in the dissolution of Aggy's family, though two of her sons were left together with one of Mrs. Tucker's sons. At the auction of all possessions not designated in the will, held on February 18, 1846, two other human chattels were disposed of: "man slave Ben" to Thomas L. Rasco for $750 and "1 Do [ditto] Arch" to J. R. Colwell, a son-in-law of Ruth Tucker, for $560.[21] Ruth's husband, John Tucker, who died in 1831, had bequeathed nine other slaves "subject to a division into seven equal shares" among his children.

When the owner did not need the labor of some of his bondmen, it was the custom to hire them out to those farmers who had an inadequate work force. On January 5, 1855, a newspaper in nearby Greene County described the lively competition of "Hiring Day," a regular event of New Year's Day. The editor noted: "Negro men ranged, generally, from $150 to $200, though $175 was about the price paid at public hiring for choice field hands. Women and boys brought generally from $90 to $100."[22] Because Bibb was not a Black Belt county, it could not have produced such big business, but hiring was a common practice, beginning in pioneer days. The Bibb County orphans' court records show that it was a convenient way of employing slaves who were the property of minors. When an owner left no will, the court-appointed administrators of an estate divided the slaves, like the other property, among the heirs, appointing a guardian to "use" (that is, hire out) those who were apportioned to minors until they came of age.

Through the proceedings of the orphans' court, the fortunes of Nathaniel Woodruff's hired slaves may be followed for nearly a decade. Woodruff, who farmed around forty acres of land north and northwest of the present Bibb County High School playgrounds, stated specifically in his will of January 11, 1830: "I do not wish the negroes to be sold but to remain the possession of my children." Of his five slaves, he bequeathed two—a man, July, and a woman, Winny—to his wife for the remainder of her life and the other three to his three children when they came of age. "My will is for Newton to have Ephraim, Henry—Cuff, and Martha Ann—Caroline," he dictated, adding that, if there should be any others, they were to be divided according to law. Meanwhile, he wished them, like the land, to be "used." Through the years from 1835 to 1842, these three were leased to different employers each year, the boys at rates that increased to $167 by January 1837, the year of the financial panic, after which their value dropped sharply to $135 by 1840. During this period, rent for the girl Caroline rose, apparently as she grew up, from $12.50 to a peak of $50, decreasing somewhat during the years of financial depression.

Meanwhile, the family had increased and three little boys gradually entered the administrators' accounts. By 1837 "boy Berry" was hired for $40; by 1838 an amount was deducted from the rents "for maintaining a boy Henry"; by 1839 it was reported: "In addition there are 2 small boys, Charles and Henry, barely worth their support and working for their maintenance," and by the following year simply "Charles and Henry, laboring for their support." Their story in the county records ended abruptly in 1842, when a commission appraised the value of the slaves, and Woodruff's widow, now Mrs. Horace Ware, made an accounting to the orphans' court of moneys received and spent.[23]

Whether he was employed on his owner's or some lessor's property, the life of the slave was governed by numerous legal restrictions. These laws reflect the growing apprehensions of the master and the increasing value of the slave in a cotton economy. The master's apprehensions are understandable in the light of contemporary newspaper warnings, especially those concerning bandits called "Murrelites." "Look out for Murrel men!" the Cahaba *Southern Democrat* was exclaiming as early as February 3, 1838. John Murrell was a notorious outlaw whose gang stole slaves and horses, resold them, and then stole them again, sharing the profits with the slaves in return for their cooperation. After his arrest in Tennessee in 1834, he was the subject of a book entitled *A History of the Detection, Conviction, Life and Designs of John A. Murel, the Great Western Land Pirate, together with His System of Villainy, and Plan for Exciting a Negro Rebellion, . . .*, written by Augustus Q. Walton, Cincinnati, and published by Harper and Brothers, New York, 1836. Because of the activities of Murrel and his gang, his name was given to any group suspected of stealing slaves. The Tuscaloosa *Independent Monitor* in the fall of 1857 frightened Bibb slaveowners with the latest rumor:

> Murrelites In Bibb County—By a private letter received, we learn that a gang of men have been discovered in the eastern part of Bibb and west in Autauga, supposed to be organized upon the Murrel plan, and who have been engaged for the last year in tampering with and running off negroes, stealing horses and committing other depredations.[24]

As a result of the growing concern, state laws aimed at protecting the master from the loss of his property became more stringent through the years until they were summarized in the Alabama Slave Code of 1852.[25] The code enumerates many actions forbidden the slave unless he obtained his master's permission, usually required in writing. For example, he was not permitted to enter into any kind of contract. The courts upheld this law in the case of a slave residing near Maplesville, then in Bibb County. Dick, a shoemaker, the property of John Herrington, had lived as a free man following his master's death in the early 1850s. After two white men borrowed $220 from Dick and gave him a promissory note for the amount, Dick's white "adviser," named Davis (probably David E. Davis, a Maplesville lawyer), lost a suit to compel repayment. The Alabama Supreme Court ruled that Dick had no legal right to enter into such an agreement.[26] Also a slave could not own any property or under any pretense keep a dog, unless in a case of necessity his master paid a five-dollar tax. If he sold liquor, not only he but the white man who bought it from him were liable, as Philip Shuttlesworth learned when the Alabama Supreme Court upheld his conviction in Bibb County circuit court for receiving a quart of whiskey without the slave's master's permission.[27]

Among other laws, a slave was forbidden to go beyond the limits of his master's land without his pass or to furnish one to a fellow bondman. Punishment for the first act was set at not more than twenty stripes at the discretion of the justice or ten lashes on the bare back at the order of the owner or overseer, but for the second act the severest punishment was prescribed: a hundred lashes on the bare back. A slave was not legally allowed to assemble with more than four other males off the plantation unattended by his master, nor speak or preach to a group of slaves without the presence of five slaveholders, a law whose violation "must" be punished with thirty-nine lashes on the first offense and fifty on the second, "inflicted by any officer of a patrol company or by order of the justice of peace." Traditionally, the local patrol company, sometimes referred to by blacks as the "patty role," was the most feared law enforcement agency.

It is impossible to know now how strictly such rules were enforced by slaveholders, but some restrictions were clearly violated or circumvented, such as the law against teaching a slave to read, enacted by the state legislature in 1832. This law forbade attempting to teach any slave or "free person of color" to spell, read, or write "upon penalty of from $250 to $500." House servants were more likely to be indulged in this respect than were the field hands. One such case is that of Araminta Davidson, grandmother of Bibb's black educator Henry Davidson, who was taught to spell and read by one of the daughters of her mistress, Mrs. S. W. Davidson.[28]

Also it is difficult to learn now what the slaves in Bibb thought of their life under these laws and other conditions of their bondage. The oral traditions that have been handed down to their descendants are too far removed from the source to be very illuminating. Yet many are confirmed by earlier records from survivors of the antebellum period elsewhere in the state.[29]

Jack Clark of Brent is the grandson of a slave, Richard Hill, who was raised on a plantation near Harrisburg, probably the Robert Hill place because he took the surname Hill after emancipation. A few years ago, when he permitted some of his family traditions to be recorded, Clark said: "I don't think my grandfather ever married in slavery but he had children. He had my father, who was born in slavery. My grandfather was still under another slave master, and so they sold my father, Charlie Clark, to another slave master."[30] Jack Clark's memories agree with the records of black freedmen that the commonest punishment meted out to a slave was for his failure to "keep up on the row," as in "chopping" cotton. "I have heard the old parents talking," he said, "about how they would whip you if you didn't act right. They were so rought on you until they'd hold you almost up to the bossman, then turn you round half way down the field and you'd go back to the other bossman on the other end." He explained,

"There would be two bossmen, one on one end and one on the other, twisting and dragging you with a rope."[31] According to other sources, the slow workman was chastised with his own hoe handle. Jack Clark's wife, Callie Clark, was told in her childhood of another cause for beating. "An old lady told me about slavery. Her name was Annie Rachel. She told me that they beat her and made her wade out in the water in the ponds to get calves and things together."[32] She also told Callie Clark about the fear of the "patty role."

To balance somewhat these rather grim stories, more pleasant impressions are recorded in a few letters addressed after the war to a Bibb planter by some of his former slaves. Writing to Dr. E. H. Moren of Centreville, these freedmen demonstrate the kindly relationship that had evidently existed between them and their master. John Mickil, who had moved after emancipation to Holly Springs, Mississippi, wrote in this homesick strain: "I never feel like I am at home until I get to your house . . . when I come again I expect to stay as long as I live if agreeable with you. . . . Dr., you know you have always told me to be a good boy, & have cautioned me to keep out of bad company. So I have taken your advice as a very good thing for me & shall always think of it & Never forget you. . . . I am the same Boy that I was when I left you."[33] Another former slave, Joseph Davidson, a preacher, corresponded regularly with Dr. Moren from his new home in Wilcox County until the doctor's death in 1886. On April 10, 1884, Davidson wrote: "I showed your letter to some of my white friends down here & they esteemed it much, & also many of my Colored ones and they give you the Praize as being my former owner. I said thats the way we do Business up home."[34]

The master at his best was concerned for both the physical and spiritual well-being of his black people. On a purely practical level, medical treatment was a good investment. The implication of Dr. David R. Boyd's account book in the pioneer years is that the Centreville physician was often summoned as promptly for the slave as for a member of his master's family.[35] For instance, in January 1829 he was called to pay thirteen visits to the "quarters" of James B. Clark, during which he performed a venesection and dispensed emetics, cathartics, quinine, blister plasters, castor oil, a painkiller, and other medications. During six months in 1836, Anthony Stoutenborough required professional calls from Dr. Boyd's successor for ten of his black people, including "visit negro child through rain." Also in 1836 the doctor made nine visits during eleven days to the slaves of Thomas Crawford. At the request of Thomas Stringfellow, he extracted teeth for three servants, the usual remedy for toothache in those days.

The careful owner, like Crawford or Stoutenborough, would not necessarily trust child delivery to the midwife in the "quarters." For services listed as "To visit negro accouchement," Jacob Dominick paid Dr. Boyd eight dollars, the highest fee charged for similar visits to the planter's wife. Among other slave owners who engaged the services of a physician between 1826 and 1836 were John Tucker, Henry Potts, William Caddell, Beverly Belcher, Oliver Cleveland, Jacob Mayberry, Lunsford Lowe, and Sherrod Saunders. The number of calls increased noticeably during the mid-thirties as the slave population began to rise.

The health of his workers was an economic necessity, but the master's encouragement of church attendance and membership must have been more disinterested. Unlike medical attention, however, this concern to bring black people into the rear pews of the churches was limited to relatively few owners in the first two decades. One of the earliest was baptized at Enon Baptist Church less than three years after it was constituted, according to this record: "Being met together on Saturday before the second lords day in April 1821 . . . Received by experience Grace belonging to Thos. Hargis. William Davis, Clerk."[36] When Hargis and his wife withdrew two years later, he withdrew the name of "his black woman" also. Only four other slave members were listed by this rural church.

The Centreville Presbyterian Church, some of whose members had larger slaveholdings, eventually showed an increase in black communicants somewhat proportionate to those holdings. Only two of these, however, were admitted before 1842: Diamond and Lucy, both the property of Thomas Crawford. In November 1831 Diamond's master recorded as clerk of the session: "Diamond, a slave of Thomas Crawford, came before the session and made application to unite himself with this church, and after being examined respecting his doctrinal views and experiential religion and giving satisfactory evidence to the session is received as a candidate for the initiatory ordinance of Baptism. Ordinance of Baptism was administered to George Green [a white man] and Diamond a slave upon the profession of their faith."[37] Twelve years later, other white members began to bring their slaves into membership, and a total of twenty-eight "colored members," each identified by his master's name, were listed on the back page of the record book, including Joseph and Martha, "late servants of Thomas Crawford," and seven servants of S. W. Davidson.

After the new brick Presbyterian church was built in 1859 on the east side of the river, the black members were seated on the balcony planned especially for them, an architectural feature that endured until the sanctuary was remodeled in the mid-twentieth century. The first wedding ceremony that the pastor performed in this church was that of Ellen, slave of S. W. Davidson, and Wesley, slave of Jacob Dennis Mayberry.[38] The records do not indicate any racial division of communicants until April 17, 1864, when clerk of the session James W. Crawford wrote: "This being one of our regular communion days, after a sermon by Rev. H. A. Smith, the sacrament of the Lord's Supper was administered to a few whites and in the afternoon to a large collection of blacks."

Most county churches welcomed slaves on their rolls. Pleasant Hill Cumberland Presbyterian Church is another whose records list such members. Six appear in the early 1860s, each with the name of his master, for example "Sylvia, a slave, property of H. Calhoun," and "Aggy, a slave, property of Isaac Parker." Some of the slave members were buried in the church cemetery, but the rock markers on their graves have disappeared over the years. Not all those who applied for membership in this or any other congregation were the property of its own communicants, but they were required to obtain the approval of their masters in any case. "Creasy, Mary, Emily, Harriett and Nelly, servants belonging to the estate of S. W. Davidson," a Presbyterian, were granted permission by E. H. Moren, administrator, before being received into the fellowship of Mount Zion Baptist Church.[39]

The local church leaders sat in judgment on the conduct of slaves as well as of their masters, both of whom, in good Baptist terminology, they sometimes "found in disorder." At Mount Zion, the case of a slave named Henry indicated they could handle such matters with admirable tact and trust. When it was stated at the July 1859 church conference that Henry, the property of Elias Bishop (a Methodist), had been in disorder, two white members, Henley G. Snead and David A. Griffin, were commissioned to visit him, with instructions to report at the next monthly meeting. On their subsequent announcement that Henry had denied the report, the conference immediately dismissed the charge.[40] At other times, it could be severe, joining with a master to discipline one of his men or women. For example, "John W. Suttle made it known to the church that a servant named Louisa a member of this church belonging to him had been guilty of fornication and on motion was excluded from the fellowship of the church."[41]

Among all its blacks, Bibb possessed few freedmen during antebellum days. One "freedom paper" appears in county records under the date of September 7, 1849.[42] According to its terms, Ben Skener, a twenty-one-year-old mulatto about six feet tall, "stout-made," and weighing one hundred and seventy-five pounds, was to be freed at the request of Shadrick and Nelson Rice. Nelson's father, Henry Rice, had brought Skener to Bibb County from South Carolina in the winter of 1833, afterward keeping him at his house and hiring him out part of the time. Skener may have left Bibb after his emancipation because he is not listed in the U.S. census for the following year.

Laws setting the conditions for an owner's emancipating his slaves were stringent, and after the adoption of the Alabama Slave Code of 1852 they continued to be tightened until it was almost impossible for black people to be willed their freedom. From 1830 to 1860 no free blacks who were heads of households were recorded in the county, according to the U.S. census of those years. The Huntsville *Southern Advocate*, November 24, 1832, published a listing that showed one free black in Bibb, the smallest number for any Alabama county except Fayette, which had none.

The eleven free blacks who may be counted in the 1850 census for Bibb were all labeled mulattoes and listed under the protection of white households. Five mulatto children, including a thirteen-year-old girl in one home, and two children aged two as well as two others aged one year in another, were all recorded with the white family surnames. The census enumerator listed irregularities in one white household, where he noted that two small mulatto children were illegitimate. Only two of the total eleven free mulattoes were adults, both of them women and under thirty. By the year 1860, the number of "free colored" in Bibb had risen to twenty-five, and these included the first male adult, Bert Roe of Mars, twenty-seven years old, a native of Georgia, whose occupation was not specified. A free mulatto woman, Artemis Wires, and her one-year-old son are listed as an independent household in the neighborhood of Centreville. One white resident of the county had a mulatto wife and five mulatto children; and another kept a one-year-old mulatto child in his home, no other members of his family being named.

Obviously, slavery brought social complications to various parts of this rural county, and in a few cases miscegenation seems to have resulted in the freedom of the mulatto offspring. It is impossible to follow the history of these unfortunates any more than that of their slave brothers and sisters, who are numbers rather than names in the census enumeration. After each decade, they vanish from the records and are replaced by others, who also must later either have left the county or escaped the eye of the census-taker, if indeed they did not become nameless numbers themselves. The lot of the free blacks and mulattoes was traditionally thought to have been unhappier than that of slaves because they were said to be socially excluded from both races. Those who achieved economic independence in adjoining Tuscaloosa County appear to have enjoyed a relatively happy existence,[43] but similar opportunities evidently did not arise for free blacks in Bibb.

By the 1850s the "peculiar institution" and the economy it supported were already doomed. Like most Alabamians, however, Bibb Countians were largely unaware of the imminent storm and the revolutionary changes it would bring. They were more conscious of the economic progress of the last two decades. Population and material prosperity continued to grow until the outbreak of the Civil War.

10

ECONOMIC GROWTH, 1835–1860

IN THE QUARTER-CENTURY before the outbreak of war between the slavery-supported South and the increasingly industrial North, the county developed rather rapidly. It grew from a scattering of pioneer settlements that had recently chosen a permanent county seat to a prosperous farming area that was beginning to experiment with industry.

At the beginning of the period, the impact of outside events held back this progress temporarily. In 1837, when Bibb Countians were reading in the *Selma Press* or the Tuscaloosa *Intelligencer* of the accession of Queen Victoria to the British throne and of the formation of the Whig party for the purpose of opposing the policies of Democrat Andrew Jackson, whom Bibb always supported, they read also, with concern, of the crisis in the affairs of the State Bank. In the preceding year, which marked the height of "flush times" in Alabama, the legislature had issued bonds to increase the branches of this bank in Huntsville, Montgomery, and Mobile. The result was the financial panic of 1837, repeated in 1839, and the persistence of hard times for several years, even after the State Bank was abolished. The Bank of Alabama, the Branch Bank at Mobile, and other banking houses won judgments against numerous Bibb citizens for debts, especially in 1841. These obligations were usually satisfied by the sale of property, but in some cases "No goods, chattels, Lands or Tenements [were] found of the defendant to satisfy any part of this fifa."[1]

A letter written by John E. Green from his home near present-day Woodstock on April 18, 1840, reflects the difficulties of these times. It is headed McMaths, Alabama, a post office of which Elisha McMath was postmaster, and it is addressed to Green's brother Benjamin, who had emigrated temporarily to Benton, Salina County, Arkansas:

> Dr. Brother
> ... I am sorry I cannot write you a more flattering account of your bisness than I can doe at this time I believe Henry Strickland will not be able to pay you anything this Spring he has promised ... but I find his onley chance is to borrow the money and that is a bad won for he is now in the Bank and I know of no one that has got money to lend.
> ... Times is harder here I expect than you have any Idea of. Common property fetches nothing when sold there was 500 acres of Houston's land sold the first Monday in March for $80, and that is about a fare aveage of such property at this time Our cotton netted us 5¾ cents. from 5½ cents is what the people has generally got for cotton and we had to give it almost all for baling and roops. baling was 45 cents and roops 20 and there is so many that is not able to pay off these bank debts that it is almost impossible to make a note that will [not?] be discounted.... the only chance I see is for people to live on their own resources and not make any debt that they can help.[2]

The writer, who reported he had experienced "several set-backs with dropsy," did not live to see more prosperous times, for he died in the spring of 1843.

One result of the economic depression following in the wake of bank trouble, both state and national, was the westward migration of a number of Bibb families. Only one generation after settling in Alabama, many had not yet put down roots that would hold them, especially after they became insolvent, and so they moved west for a fresh start, often leaving their land to be fought over by creditors and tax collectors. Salina County, Arkansas (admitted as a state in 1836), was one of these emigrants' favorite destinations. In the fall of 1841, a wagon train organized by Reverend Joab Pratt from among the financially stricken families in his several Baptist congregations headed in that direction.[3] They made their way to the middle of Louisiana and then pushed north, passing a point in Union Parish just below the Arkansas line still known as Alabama Landing, on their way north to Salina County. Today, markers at the cemetery of the Philadelphia Baptist Church, which they founded when they settled there, are said to bear the Bibb County names of Mayfield, Pumphrey, McDaniel, Pratt and Cobb, and the community nearby is called Prattsville.

Still restless, by 1845 Joab Pratt and a number of his fellow pioneers had moved back to the rich land in Union County. Among many other Bibb Countians who early migrated to that county were Thomas and Jane Green Kessee, Ezekiel and Mary Miller and their children, and, after the Civil War, John C. and Maria Pratt Goodson. Through the years, Arkansas remained a favorite escape from the ills at home. So also did Louisiana, which offered cheap, rich lands. Several members of the Steele family moved by 1849 to Bienville Parish, where Robert Steele bought 157 acres of land on January 24, 1850.[4] Others who accompanied him besides his immediate family were Zachariah and Sarah Steele Canterbury as well as Richard J. and Mary Ann Mitchell Steele.

Not all the adventurous emigrants from Bibb pushed west in wagon trains after the panics of 1837 and 1839. In one case, a settler slipped away from his family in the winter of 1838 in a wagon borrowed from a brother-in-law allegedly for the purpose of "wagoning." He was thought to have made his solitary way as far as the Republic of Texas. According to rumors that reached Bibb, he "passed" there for a preacher, filched a gold watch from a pious widow, and eventually murdered Jacob Blanton, another Bibb County emigrant, afterward breaking out of jail twice and escaping finally to Tennessee or Mississippi. The brother of his deserted wife in Bibb advertised this description of him and offered one thousand acres of land for his apprehension and delivery to any jail in Texas: "He has a good voice and sings well, and when he resided in Bibb he frequently taught singing schools. He was then a member of the Baptist church but never attempted to preach. He is six feet one inch high, has a thin sharp looking nose, and is about 45 years old. One of his big toes has been broken, it turns up so as to be plainly seen with a shoe on.... We ask Editors to pass him around, and if he is in the United States let him be found and returned to Texas."[5] Throughout the century, the road west was the usual route for evading both unfavorable economic conditions and the avenging law. But not until the Reconstruction period did an exodus occur comparable to that in the 1840s.

One of the chief incentives for Bibb Countians to move west came with the annexation of Texas on March 1, 1845, followed shortly by the Mexican War (1846–48). The first effect on the county of this conflict was the enlistment of some of its young citizens. Captain John Gorman Barr, of Tuscaloosa, rode into Bibb and recruited a group of farm boys, as reported by the Tuscaloosa newspaper: "Capt. J. G. Barr marched into this city on Saturday morning last, with about half a company of volunteers for the war, from Bibb County. We understand that Capt. Barr has more than a full company enrolled. He left, yesterday morning, for Shelby to bring in another squad. The Bibb volunteers are a sturdy looking set, and to us seem to exhibit an appearance of more than ordinary intelligence. They look like sensible, as well as, stout men. Capt. Barr is encamped, at present, about two miles from the city. His little camp presents a cheerful appearance."[6]

When the roster of the company was completed, the soldiers elected their own officers, including two who can be identified among those "sensible as well as stout men" from Bibb: First Lieutenant John W. Caddell, age twenty-two, and Third Sergeant William C. Mahan, age seventeen.[7] In Mobile they were mustered into the U.S. Army as Company B (the Warrior Guards), 1st Battalion, Alabama Volunteers; Major John J. Seibels of Montgomery was the commander. Before they embarked for Mexico, Governor Joshua L. Martin gave this first Alabama contingent an enthusiastic send-off at the docks. They arrived in Mexico too late for combat but performed garrison duty in the interior until the end of the war, seven months later.[8] On June 28, 1848, after they returned to Mobile, many in poor health, the battalion was paid off, mustered out, and honored by a barbecue dinner given by the city.[9]

During the 1850s, a number of Bibb families emigrated to the new frontier state of Texas, looking to better their fortunes in the virgin farming country. They wrote letters home, sometimes enthusiastic, sometimes disenchanted, about conditions there. A Bibb County boy, corresponding with a friend who had moved with his family to Melorse, Necogdoches County, asked for "a description of your country" and at the same time recorded his own sentiments in his diary: "The western part of our mighty Republic is viewed as a better country than the more civilized states: that it may be, I think I can never leave the place of my birth, to live and die in the far western barbarous country. All criminals that get away go to the west, there to carry on their murderous practices, I love this part of my birthplace. . . . I love the very name of old Bibb; The burial place of my fathers."[10]

One indication of the vanishing frontier that drove some Bibb settlers farther into the wilderness was the first local experimentation in industry. A year before the panic of 1837, which took its toll of emigrants, a water-powered cotton factory had already been established on Schultz Creek seven miles north of Centreville. There the community of Scottsville soon grew up. The original owners of the mill, chartered in 1834 by the state legislature, were residents of the county seat and were said to have invested heavily in the project. After a group of Tuscaloosa men, including David Scott, purchased stock in the company in 1836, a building was erected. In the following year, the Tuscaloosa Manufacturing Company was incorporated by the state legislature with a capital stock of $36,000 and in May the mill began production.[11] But the panic of 1837 endangered it until Scott became the principal owner and director, moving his family to the vicinity. Scott was a former South Carolinian who had reaped profits as a land speculator, based first at Elyton and later at Tuscaloosa, and more recently as a merchant.

The following year, the editor of the Tuscaloosa *Independent Monitor*, probably invited by Scott, made a tour of the plant and shortly afterward introduced it to the public in the columns of his newspaper, saying that he thought half the residents of Bibb and Tuscaloosa counties were unaware of its existence:

> A cotton factory is now in successful operation in Bibb County of this State . . . built of Brick, three stories high and 90 by 44 feet in extent. . . .
>
> In the second story we found the carding and roping operations going forward; and in the third, a multitude of spindles were employed in the finishing work of making cotton yarn. A few hands, men, women, children, seemed to be employed in rather a quiet way in attending to the machinery. . . . In another department the cotton gin is in operation; so that the factory is prepared to take the cotton, either after it is picked, or in the seed.
>
> In the spinning department, there has been in operation, heretofore 500 spindles . . . very soon will be working between seven and eight hundred. There is water power sufficient, we are assured, to work 10,000. . . . The average production per day with 500 spindles has been 430 dozen [spools of thread].
>
> About 20 hands are employed—all white—some males, some females, some large, some small. They are chiefly people of the neighborhood. . . .
>
> A grist mill and saw mill are connected with the works, which are in active and profitable operation.
>
> The place is called Scottsville, in honor, we suppose, of D. Scott, one of the principal proprietors. . . . Their sales are brisk. They contemplate adding a weaving factory to their other works.[12]

From this modest beginning, the industry continued to expand throughout the quarter-century before the Civil War. From 1841, when the sum of capital stock was paid in, the management invested part of its profits in slaves, initially one black family that cost $2,200 but that by the 1850s had so increased in number and in usefulness to the factory as to be valued at $10,000.[13] Poor whites, about three-fourths of whom were women and children, continued to be employed as operatives. In the 1850s Scott brought Joseph Morris from England to take charge of the machinery. For some reason not now known, this prosperous business was offered for sale in a large advertisement in the Tuscaloosa *Independent Monitor* on October 29, 1857, but it was not sold.

The statement published the following year in *DeBow's Review* was impressive.

> Every year since [1841] a dividend of ten per cent has been declared which has been laid out in buying Negroes, land, &c, adding to the buildings and machinery, until the capital stock has increased to $117,000, of which $25,000 is in Negroes, and about $16,000 in goods in the company's store.
>
> The company owns 3,000 acres of land and all the buildings on the place,

> which consists of the factory, a large hotel, a store, blacksmith, carpenter, wheelwright, and boot and shoe shops, a saw mill, grist mill, large flouring mill, a church, and a large number of cottages. No liquor is permitted in the village, and the company will not sell an inch of land to anyone. Its stock has long been over par, and its dividends this year will be at least twelve per cent.[14]

Several other industries were growing in Bibb, though none so ambitious as the Scottsville cotton mill. A few sawmills had early begun making clumsy inroads into the forests. By 1850 William Oakley owned and operated the plant later called the Ashby Brick Works. Weeks Parker was a carriage maker and James W. Owen and J. T. Yancey each made twenty saddles a year valued at a total of $500.[15] A blacksmith like J. C. Campbell required two assistants and 4,000 pounds of iron to achieve an annual product worth $1,313. The forges and bloomeries that supplied Campbell and other blacksmiths were the most promising of these minor industries, destined in some cases to enjoy a longer life than the cotton mill.

The mid-1830s, which saw the origin of the Scottsville factory, also became the era of forge building. Early settlers had been aware of the brown ore and other metals in the rocks of northern and eastern Bibb and tried to smelt them for their own use by crude processes. Eventually they erected a number of forges that anticipated Birmingham's iron industry by several decades. It is difficult to date their establishment precisely, but a letter from Daniel Hillman of New Jersey, one of the ironmasters who pioneered through the South, proves that ironworks were being introduced on the northern edge of the county by 1830. Hillman wrote to his son on August 21 of that year from a spot he dubbed Valley Forge, Bibb County, Alabama: "Shall start one forge for Col. [Ralph] McGehee in about 4 or 5 weeks, and then a sawmill for myself. I can fell about $2000 worth of plank. I can cut timber on Uncle Sam's land, a practice very generally prevailing in this country.... Believe my prospects for making a handsome property."[16] The forge that Hillman built on the Tuscaloosa line near Woodstock was purchased in 1836 by the planter Nathan Tannehill and became the predecessor of the Tannehill Furnace.[17] Nathan's son Marion is listed as an ironmaster in tbe 1850 U.S. census, but by 1860 Moses Stroup, ironmaster from South Carolina, was in charge, giving Mars, Bibb County, as his address. Among his employees were a machinery molder, Thomas Alexander, and a bookkeeper, his son Alonzo.[18] Through the Civil War years, the plant was referred to as the Stroup Furnace.

Among other ironmasters who early made their way into Bibb were Jonathan Ware, his son Horace, and William P. Browne, all New Englanders. Jonathan Ware built the Mahan Forge for Edward Mahan on

Shoal Creek near present-day Brierfield and also the Camp Forge, as it came to be called later, for himself, both reportedly around 1836. The origin of the Camp Forge was connected romantically with "the year the stars fell on Alabama" by James Camp, an 1819 settler from South Carolina, who saw that meteoric display on the night of November 12–13, 1833, while he and Jonathan Ware were camping near the future forge site. Camp always said that they began collecting materials for the forge that year and completed construction two years later.[19] Jonathan Ware had been induced by Edward Mahan to come to Bibb from Cowpens, South Carolina, where he had just set up a forge. He and his son Horace, who later bought him out, moved about in both Bibb and Shelby, setting up forges to supply the planters with the crude implements they needed. By 1840 the U.S. census listed three bloomeries or forges in the county, employing a total of fifteen men and producing annually forty-five tons of iron. These production figures rose notably during the following two decades, as did also the number of forges, which soon included Little Cahaba Forge, Six Mile Forge, and Adams Dam Forge, all built on land that had been owned by Jonathan Newton Smith.

The operation of these first forges was primitive by modern standards and so were the products. The daughter of James Camp, who managed his own forge on Schultz Creek until his death in 1858, a period of nearly twenty years, has given this description of the process: "The forge was run by water power, and the ore crushed by big wheels. When the ore had melted into a large mass of red hot iron it was placed on the anvil under the great upraised hammer. The hammer man usually had a short bar of iron heated red hot, which he welded into the big burning mass with sledge hammers. Then the big hammer, run by water, pounded the iron into marketable shape. My father got his iron ore near Tannehill 15 miles away at first. But he soon found all he could use right on his own farm. He found a ready market for his bar iron.... Tuscaloosa and Marion were chief markets."[20] The hammer man was, of course, a strong and faithful slave. One such slave was Joe, bought by Jonathan Newton Smith for $3,000 at a sale of the estate of a Georgian named Watson. Joe had become an expert hammer man while apprenticed by his first owner for five years to Jonathan Ware.[21]

Some time passed before the production of hollow ware, as a descendant of Edward Mahan made clear. "The first blooms made in these early forges," she said, "were only chunks of iron which could be sold to blacksmiths and other such tradesmen to be heated and hammered in plow point, pots, pans, etc. There was no manufacturing of finished products at this time in Brierfield."[22] Yet in 1851 Edward Mahan and Jonathan

Ware were able to win a prize by their exhibit of charcoal iron blooms at the international show in Sydenham, England.[23]

Another New Englander who pioneered in central Alabama ironworks was William P. Browne, a versatile lawyer who had come from Vermont with a contract to build canals at Mobile and New Orleans. He bought land from Jonathan Newton Smith on which to build the first blast furnace in Bibb. The site was the precipitously steep bank of the Little Cahaba River near Brierfield, a short distance from the Mahan Forge and three miles from the later community of Piper. The dam that Browne threw up across the Little Cahaba at this point and that afterward bore his name was once called one of the wonders of the county. Before it was destroyed by scavengers, Ethel Armes saw it and described it dramatically: "It was fashioned by several tiers of great, solid hewn pine timbers, fourteen by fourteen, their bases resting against the seats cut out in the rock on each side of the river, and fastened together by huge iron belts. The whole made the figure of a beautiful arch, bowing up stream and meeting midway on a tiney little rock island below the shoals."[24]

About a hundred and fifty yards above Browne's Dam, the ironmaster directed slave labor in the building of the only charcoal furnace that went into blast in the county before the Civil War. Horace Ware had constructed his own small charcoal blast furnace in Shelby County near Columbiana reportedly in 1846, the first in central Alabama. By 1850 the Little Cahaba Furnace had set the record for Bibb under its original operator, J. N. Thompson. In 1851 it was described by *DeBow's Review* in an article apparently written the preceding year: "Of the two high furnaces [in Alabama], one is in Bibb County; it has but recently been erected, so that its operations are, as yet, confined to the manufacture of pig iron and hollow ware; the blast is urged by steam power, and the boiler is heated directly from the trundle head. From the convenience and good quality of the ore, and the abundance of fuel, they can scarcely fail of success, under ordinary management."[25] One of Little Cahaba's two stacks was twenty-three feet high and the other almost nineteen.

Although official records continued to refer to it by its original name, the Little Cahaba Furnace soon came to be called Brighthope, a poetic name Kermit Hunter borrowed for his 1978 romantic outdoor drama about the neighboring Brierfield ironworks. Michael Tuomey, state geologist, may have inspired the name when he said, after a visit to this area, "There is enough ore in sight to run a hundred furnaces a hundred years."[26] Because Bibb was so rich in brown ore, coal beds, fire clay, and timber, it ranked among the three Alabama counties that led in antebellum iron production, the other two being Shelby and Talladega.

Bibb's industrial experiments may have been more newsworthy than its farms in the decades just before the Civil War, but livelihood continued to depend chiefly on agriculture. From a varied crop program that in 1840 included rye, corn, wool, wax, and potatoes, among other products, and 268,408 pounds of cotton, the county by 1860 had moved to a greater concentration on its money crop, reporting 8,303 cotton bales averaging 400 pounds each. Improved farm acreage rose almost 50 percent in the final antebellum decade, from 53,411 to 74,705 acres, while 230,542 still remained unimproved. As the mule became more highly valued for cultivating cotton fields, it superseded the ox, the holdings in those two farm animals being almost reversed, from 625 mules and 994 working oxen in 1850 to 1,092 mules and 585 oxen in 1860. The number of horses, however, remained fairly constant and was double that of oxen in 1850 and of mules in 1860. Bibb was still raising wool, demonstrating little interest yet in dairy farming; the aggregate of sheep in 1860 was more than twice that of cows.

All these statistics from the U.S. census of those years indicate an expanding agricultural economy, in spite of the nation's financial panic of 1857. The principal discouragement continued to be the expensive as well as tedious method by which farmers marketed their cotton in Mobile. For example, a cotton receipt for George Mayberry's 1848 crop from Patrick Irvin and Company to Godwin and Davis shows that charges for freight, drayage, weighing, storage, and other services, including a 2½ percent commission and a final deduction for bagging and rope, left only $518.62 of the $602.25 at which the nineteen bales were valued.[27]

At the outbreak of the Civil War, the county was still composed chiefly of relatively small, fairly self-sufficient farms, nearly three-fourths including less than 100 acres each. The 1860 U.S. census reported:

3– 9 acres	19 farms
10– 19 acres	75 farms
20– 49 acres	276 farms
50– 99 acres	254 farms
100–499 acres	247 farms

Only five plantations boasted from 500 to 999 acres, and only two possessed 1,000 or more.

The holdings in slaves were in keeping with these figures. Although 447 citizens were slaveholders in 1860, half that number owned three or less servants. Only thirteen reported forty or more, and of those thirteen only two possessed between one and two hundred. A farmer's slave property usually outvalued his real estate throughout the period. In 1849 eleven slaves of the George Mayberry estate were appraised at $4,125 and the

912 acres of improved and unimproved land at $2,310. When land was assessed for tax purposes, usually at a third to a half of its actual worth, the difference was even wider. In the year 1860, according to the U.S. census, George W. Howard possessed real estate worth $8,000, personal estate (usually understood to mean chiefly slaves) $60,000; James Hill, real estate $12,000, personal estate $45,000; S. W. Davidson, real estate $4,000, personal estate $150,000. As cotton became more and more important in the economy, the work force that cultivated it increased in value.

Like real estate, these human chattels were taxable. Their poll tax rose by degrees from twenty-five cents on each slave under five years old to $1.10 on each between fifteen and twenty, then decreased gradually to twenty cents per head on those between fifty and sixty years of age. A slight tax for the slave registration fund was added, one cent for each slave under ten and two cents for each between ten and sixty years old.[28] Yet, because only a few citizens had made so large an investment in their work force, the real estate assessment outweighed the aggregate personal estate values in the county; for example, in 1850 it reached a total of $498,889 as opposed to $352,355. On all these assets, residents paid state taxes of $3,724 and county taxes of $1,499, no federal taxes being required as yet.[29]

The general prosperity encouraged a much-needed improvement for those residents at the end of the 1850s: the building of a new courthouse. By 1854 the frame structure that had been erected a quarter of a century earlier to serve a much smaller population was evidently deteriorating. In the fall of that year, the county paid the sheriff twenty dollars for the use of Walker Parker, possibly a prisoner, in repairing the courthouse and the fence around it.[30] Shortly afterward, however, the officials must have determined to replace the old structure with a new and larger brick building. By 1858 plans had been made and by the following year the original timbers had been moved. The new courthouse, erected by contractors C. A. Shelby and Son of Talladega at a cost of $13,000, was an imposing one in its day. It was fronted by a large second-story porch under a gabled roof that was supported by four large columns with capitals. Beneath this porch, a spacious entrance was provided on the ground floor. Four tall chimneys rose from the roof. The courthouse area in the center of the town square continued to be surrounded by a fence, and the original chinaberry trees planted to shade visitors to the first permanent county seat provided a setting for the new building.

In the last decade before the Civil War, Bibb citizens must have felt that the county had made considerable economic progress since the days of settlement. It is true that numerous white laborers who owned no farms did not share noticeably in the profits. The average monthly wage paid a

Fourth courthouse, erected in 1858–59 by C. A. Shelby and Son of Talladega and razed in 1902 for the construction of the present courthouse on the same site. Photographed around 1900. (From family collection of author)

farmhand in 1850 was ten dollars. A day laborer with board received fifty cents, and without board one dollar. A female domestic worker earned two dollars a week if provided her board.[31] Obviously white workers competing with slave labor were afforded little opportunity for advancement. In 1860 some 52 percent of all heads of families still earned an annual income of less than $1,000.[32] Most of the farmers, living on their relatively small acreage, enjoyed a measure of economic independence though they were still struggling to improve their lot in life by increasing that acreage. Prospects must have looked good to them at that time.

11

CULTURE, CHANGING AND UNCHANGED, 1835–1860

CERTAIN CHANGES IN life style naturally followed economic development during the 1835–60 period. In order for farmers to convey their cotton to market and for manufacturers to sell their textiles and iron products, transportation and communication facilities were necessarily improved. Increased communication led to wider interest in public events, especially in politics, and brought Bibb its first local newspapers. In a number of ways, the standard of living gradually rose, though for many people home life continued to be simple and isolated as in settlement days.

The most exhilarating evidence of a break through the frontier isolation in southern Bibb came with the whistle of the first steamboat on the Cahaba. This new invention was to supplement but not supersede the flatboats in carrying products to market, for only five ascended from Mobile to Centreville before the Civil War.[1] The dream persisted through most of the century, however. Each steamboat brought a cargo of general supplies, including the specially needed commodity of salt, and returned with as much as a hundred bales of cotton.

The first to excite residents of Centreville and the river plantations to the south was a side-wheeler, the *Marion*, in 1836, the year the Scottsville cotton mill was built. It was a 109-ton boat, constructed in Pittsburgh.[2] That same year, a visitor to Montgomery saw and heard his first steamboat, and the novel sound he described must have been similar to that which broke the frontier silence around Centreville: "One has just now stopped and is grunting at the wharf. They make a singular sound, resembling heavy breathing of a large elephant but ten times as loud. They are all high pressure."[3] The *Marion* returned to Mobile with a hundred bales of cotton.

The next arrival at Centreville, that of the stern-wheel steamer *Irene*, did not occur until 1844, when the effects of the panics of 1837 and 1839 had begun to subside. It was a smaller boat, of only 76 tons, built in Burlington, Ohio, which sank four years later in Mobile without apparent cause. The side-wheeler *Noxubee*, built in Louisville, Kentucky, whose capacity was 108 tons, followed it to Centreville in 1845. Two more sternwheelers, the *Ark* in 1847 and the *Motive* in 1849, tonnage 96 and 67 respectively, discharged their cargoes at the local dock to make room for cotton bales. The *Motive* was destined to become snagged and sink near Mobile the following year. Shortly afterward, the Cahaba River was spanned about sixty-five miles below Centreville by the Alabama Central Railroad bridge, which was to end river traffic until 1880. During the 1850s, Bibb Countians still imported and exported by steamboat on the Alabama River between Mobile and the town of Cahaba. They made journeys overland to Cahaba or sent and received their materials by flatboat there.

Traffic across the Cahaba River in the county continued to use fords and toll ferries most of the antebellum period except at Centreville. There in 1845 George Howard built a wooden bridge, the first of four that have crossed the river at that point. He constructed this bridge, traditionally said to have been covered with wooden shingles, for planter Jacob Newell Mayberry, who operated it as a toll enterprise in spite of local opposition. Howard and S. W. Davidson came into joint possession of it in 1855, after Mayberry's death. Later Dr. E. H. Moren purchased Davidson's half-interest for $1,305 on September 28, 1863, after Davidson's death.[4] Meanwhile, in 1854 at River Bend, Mary Pratt had won permission from the commissioners' court "to keep public ferry on Cahawba River in Bibb on road leading from Noah B. Coker's by way of Hill's Settlement to Tuscaloosa at place where the old Ferry had been run."[5] The intrepid widow of Absalom Pratt continued to operate this ferry through the war years.

The roads to which these crossings gave access remained in a deplorable condition, especially in wet weather. The attempts of the road commissioners and their drafted crew were unequal to the problems. Yet from the early 1830s the stagecoaches labored over the narrow roads, in and out of mud holes, sometimes being extricated from them by the assistance of the passengers. Two stagecoach lines ran through Bibb, one east and west and the other north and south. The latter, from Elyton to Selma, was abandoned some time after the coming of the railroad to eastern Bibb in 1852. For the former road, both *Mitchell's Geography* in 1834 and Morse and Breese's Map of Alabama in 1842 showed a route of 119 miles through the stations of Tuscaloosa, Mars, Centreville, Coosada (Autauga County), and Montgomery. In 1860 two stage drivers gave Mars as their address.[6] Today, this road from Tuscaloosa to Montgomery would be roughly equivalent to that by way of Vance, Centreville, Maplesville, and Wetumpka.

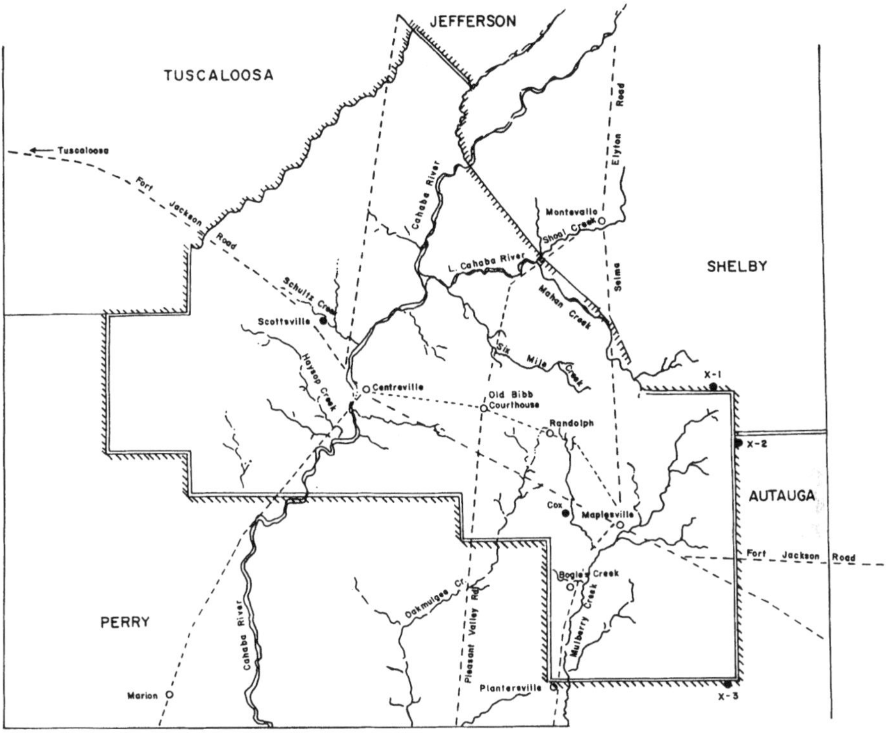

BIBB COUNTY 1849

Map of the county in 1849, showing the principal nineteenth-century roads. (Loaned by Howard F. McCord and reproduced by courtesy of William T. Ogletree)

By the 1850s the coach made regular stops also at Scottsville. According to tradition, when the driver reached the top of a hill a few miles from the village he paused and blew a blast on his horn for each passenger aboard, thus giving the innkeeper notice of the number of guests to prepare for. Place-names in the county still recall the stagecoach days. The horses were possibly changed at Stagestand Hill, near Scottsville. On the Elyton road, the change, usually considered necessary every fifteen miles, is said to have occurred regularly near Woodstock at the old Green house, called Halfway House.

Except for those who journeyed privately by horseback or carriage, the stagecoach was the chief mode of travel during antebellum days. The first ironmasters must have arrived by coach. Bibb's early representatives in the state legislature probably boarded it with their carpetbags en route to Tuscaloosa during the decade before 1845, afterward reversing their direction toward the new capital of Montgomery. The stagecoach resulted in at least one romantic incident at the county seat. One day in the 1850s when the red-wheeled vehicle made its regular stop in Centreville, a young man and a girl stepped off, "manifested a desire to be married," and were immediately accommodated by the necessary official, after which they happily mounted the fold-up steps and continued their journey.[7]

Whether the stagecoach transported ironmasters, politicians, or eloping lovers, it always brought the mail. The group of citizens that thrilled to the driver's bugle watched while he delivered the mailbag to the postmaster and waited while that official handed out letters and newspapers to the appropriate persons or their accommodating neighbors. He carried those items not claimed to his place of business or residence, where he posted a list. After the death of Mars's original postmaster, James Hill, in 1842, the mail was delivered during the remainder of the antebellum period to his son-in-law, Reverend Robert Oldham. Most of the other county postmasters were merchants or clerks. They are listed here following the names of their post offices and the years in which their five-year appointments were made.[8]

> Centreville: 1844–45, Morgan Howard; 1849–50, Morgan Howard (one quarter), Josiah S. Kennedy; 1854–55, Josiah S. Kennedy.
>
> Scottsville: 1844–45, Justin Houghton; 1849–50, David Scott; 1854–55, T. F. Samuel.
>
> Maplesville: 1844–45, Samuel H. Cox; 1849–50, Thomas R. Brown; 1854–55, Wiley Foshee.
>
> Randolph: 1849–50, Jared Cole; 1854–55, John Brown.

By the 1850s all these towns were probably served on a five-day schedule as was Maplesville, whose postmaster, Thomas R. Brown, in a letter to Judge John W. Suttle dated March 8, 1851, objected to his appointment as a road overseer because of his postal duties: "The mail comes hear five days a week."[9] For a few years after 1850, Stephen Caudle was receiving mail at his blacksmith shop for his community near present-day Harmon. By 1859–60 J. Latham had taken charge at Randolph and W. L. Camp at Scottsville, the former a merchant and the latter a clerk, probably in David Scott's commissary. Other post offices, appearing for the first time in the 1860 U.S. census, were Six Mile, Oakleyville near Ashby, Affonee near Harrisburg community, and Benton south of Eoline on the Pondville road. A once-a-week horseback line, called the Blocker route, ran from Centreville to Tuscaloosa along a path similar to that of the railroad in the twentieth century.[10]

By 1855 the Kennedy House in Centreville was able to advertise: "The Tuscaloosa Stages, connecting with the Cars at Randolph, stops at this House." The cars referred to were on the new railroad, the first in the county, completed from Selma as far as the village of Randolph by 1852.[11] It was also one of the first in Alabama, which at the close of the preceding year had possessed only 165 miles of tracks.[12] This new line, which crossed the eastern side of the county from north to south, was part of the system planned to connect the Tennessee valley with Mobile and, significantly for Bibb County, to develop the mineral region. It was originally called the Alabama and Tennessee Rivers Railroad; in Reconstruction days the Selma, Rome and Dalton; and still later the East Tennessee and Virginian, before becoming a part of the Southern Railway System in the twentieth century. It passed by Mahan's Forge, where the community of Brierfield later was established, and near other ironworks, including Brighthope Furnace, giving them all much-needed transportation for their products.

This road was chartered in 1848, but work did not begin on it for several years. Actually it had been projected by A. A. Dexter as the Selma and Tennessee Railroad as early as 1837, when he was writing from "Near Six Mile Creek" to a Selma newspaper on the subject.[13] But it was the day of the steamboat, and railroads did not generate the same amount of enthusiasm. When the tracks were finally laid in the early 1850s, railroad towns were already growing up along the route, chief of which in Bibb was Randolph. Until the Alabama and Chattanooga was built in northern Bibb in October 1868, Randolph drew business from all over the county; and, until the establishment of the Mobile and Ohio through Centreville in 1898, it remained the magnet for the southern half. Cotton and other goods were now carried by wagon on a two-day journey from Centreville to Randolph to be shipped by railroad to Selma, and other goods were received there. Residents of the Bibb county seat made annual or semiannual shopping trips by rail to the Dallas county seat. Most of Bibb was brought securely into Selma's orbit and remained there for the rest of the century.

Along with the improvements in transportation, by steamboat, stagecoach, and railroad, and especially because of the regular mail service by stagecoach, channels of communication were opened to and from the county. One result was the first experiments in newspaper publishing. Like the other weekly sheets of the period, these early papers carried almost no evidence of their locality except legal notices and a few advertisements, and the world news on its pages was quite old. Yet the motive for establishing most Alabama weeklies in the antebellum period was not to carry news so much as to support a political party, often by attacking another one.[14] The journalistic experiment was frequently undertaken during a heated campaign and did not long survive the resolution of the issues being contested.

The *Centreville Advocate*, reported to have been founded in 1843 by James

Mapes, is the first known Bibb newspaper.[15] Unfortunately no copies of it have been located, but Editor Mapes, like most journalists in Alabama during that era, was probably attempting to promote the cause of one of the presidential candidates in the election of the following year. The contest was drawn between perennial Whig candidate Henry Clay and Democrat James K. Polk, who was destined to carry both Bibb and the nation. In 1844, when the annexation of Texas was the chief issue, Alabama's brilliant young orator William Lowndes Yancey toured Bibb as part of his congressional district, campaigning for its seat in that year's special election. He traveled by private conveyance through the entire district, which did not then possess a single mile of railroad. He must have spoken not only in Centreville but also in many other county communities to fulfill his stated plan of making a hundred speeches in the seven constituent counties.[16] His Whig opponent was Daniel E. Watrous of Shelby County, state senator representing Bibb and Shelby, who absented himself from the state during most of the campaign on "imperative business." The Whigs scheduled other speakers to challenge Yancey, men who were fresh in every county. In Bibb a Mr. King stood up to debate him.[17]

No issue of the *Centreville Advocate* has survived to report the encounters, but, according to Yancey's biographer, his "original thought, compact and resistless arguments" and his courage in facing a battery of Whig speakers appealed to the voters.[18] They turned out in unprecedented numbers everywhere to hear the "neatly dressed man, habitually wearing a smile, an admirable relater of anecdotes."[19] who was also capable of vehement invective. As everywhere else in the district, they must have taken him into their homes, refusing any pay for his accommodations. On election day, Bibb contributed to his large majority, though three years later in the presidential race it voted for the Whig ticket.

The second known newspaper was the *Central Enquirer*, reported to have been in existence by 1857 and operated in that year by men named Caddell, Gantt, and Caddell; J. G. Rogers was the publisher.[20] In the preceding year, the gubernatorial contest between the Democrats and the new American party, which had emerged on the demise of the Whig party, had kindled excitement in the county that resulted in a temporary departure from its fairly usual loyalty to the Democratic organization. Bibb became one of twelve counties that gave a majority to the Know-Nothing candidate, Judge George D. Shortridge, in opposition to the victorious contender, Governor John S. Winston.[21] Because the contest was heated in Bibb, it may have given rise to the *Enquirer*; if not, the paper must have been embroiled in the controversy on one side or the other. By 1858 S. K. Jennings was in charge. His political stance is not known, though his literary gifts are on record in his anecdote concerning author John G.

Barr that was reprinted from the *Enquirer* in the October 23, 1858, issue of the New York *Spirit of the Times*. Barr campaigned for the Democratic ticket in Bibb in 1856, and Jennings's admiration for this ardent Democrat is probably significant.[22] In the brief space that an editor of the period sometimes allowed himself for comment, he must have reflected in 1858 some of the political confusion that spilled over even into county elections. A split was growing within the Democratic party between the conservative, or Union, men and the new Southern Rights faction. A Bibb boy took note in his diary: "The August election came off yesterday the 2d inst. I am not able to tell how the election has went. We have no parties now the parties has broke asunder. . . . [Later] The election went as follows: For Sheriff R. N. Oakley for Circuit Clerk J. Shropshur For Tax Assessor J. T. Lawhom."[23]

The split had become wider by May 12, 1860, when the *Central Enquirer* bore on its masthead the stirring slogan "Our Country and Our Country's Honor." Thomas B. Mason, age twenty-three, was then editor, and Willis Caddell, age twenty-eight, was "in charge of collections." This first extant issue of the *Enquirer* carries no editorial comment but probably testifies to the editor's position by quoting "Horse-Shoe Ned," a column from the *Montgomery Mail*, a leading secessionist organ. Allegedly reporting to the *Mail* from the Democratic convention then in session at Charleston, it parodies a Unionist's point of view. Editor Mason evidently copied this ridicule for the enlightenment of the old Whigs of Bibb, most of whom remained opposed to secession until it became a fact; examples are Centreville merchant and postmaster Josiah S. Kennedy and Bibb's perennial representative in the state legislature, James W. Davis, both of whom later lost sons in the Confederate service. The editor's own comments concern agricultural rather than political problems, such as the dry weather and the folly of overplanting cotton. Most of the exchanges he selected deal with such exotic topics as "Wine Growing in Georgia" and "Vegetables on the Moon's Surface," or they are short stories of love or adventure.

Only a few business and professional men advertised in the *Central Enquirer* in 1860, but those merchants who did so listed their wares flamboyantly across its pages. All of them seem to have operated general stores. W. N. Green and Marion Goode of Six Mile offered a variety of dry goods and patent medicines, as did also J. W. Latham of Randolph. In Centreville, Latham and James dealt in everything from flutinas and fifes to double skirts and printed jaconet (a popular cotton textile). Josiah S. Kennedy was the most versatile of the lot; he conducted a variety of enterprises, including a hotel, a blacksmith shop, a gun shop, and a general store. Concerning one type of merchandise that he stocked, this old Whig proclaimed: "The Union Saved by a Late Arrival! J. S. Kennedy has received the following choice brands of fine Liquors." Other merchants at this time were R. D. and William Hicks of Randolph, and Morgan Howard, Jacob Kersh, J. W. Person, Lucius Winship, and Charles Sanford (the last two being natives of Connecticut), who gave their addresses as Centreville in the 1860 census.

The county had increased its roster of professional men by the 1860s, though only one of them advertised in the newspaper. He was Zachary Abney, a young lawyer of Randolph. Other attorneys were Henry Brown, A. S. Hornsby, Robert McIlvain, and Thomas Smitherman, all of Centreville.[24] It would seem that physicians were in greater demand at this time than legal counsel, for, surprising as it may be to people in the late twentieth century, Bibb County possessed twenty-one doctors in 1860, as recorded in the U.S. census of that year. These practitioners, mostly in their twenties and frequently the sons of local farmers, must have pondered this news item in the *Central Enquirer* of May 12, 1860: "Sunflowers bring immunity from malaria, according to Professor Maury of the National Observatory."

Besides an increased number of merchants, lawyers, and especially physicians, the county possessed at the end of the antebellum period representatives of less common vocations and natives of several foreign countries. A confectioner lived in Randolph, and Centreville enjoyed the services of a dancing master and a horse trainer. Natives of six European countries were seeking a better way of life: a ditcher and an overseer from Ireland; a machinist, a brickmason, and a shoemaker from Scotland; a manufacturer from England; a baker and a vineyardist from Germany; and farmers from Austria, Germany, and Italy.[25] All of these added variety, if not a cosmopolitan touch, to the population.

Far from being cosmopolitan, life remained relatively simple and provincial, especially in the rural areas. S. K. Jennings's purportedly true story of a visit by John G. Barr to northern Bibb in 1856, when he was campaigning for the Democratic ticket against the American party slate, begins with a description of the lonely torturous roads and this typical home scene: "The region not being familiar with him, darkness approaching, and the houses being few and far between, he bethought him of seeking a lodging for the night. He reared up his horse in front of a house. There was a calf hitched to the gate, a spinning wheel on the piazza, and an old lady knitting."[26]

In spite of the opportunities afforded by increased facilities for transportation and communication, average citizens did not travel outside the county. They lived out their lives on the farm and made only occasional journeys to the county seat. There they learned somewhat more than in settlement days concerning what wars, military and political, were being waged in the outside world, but at home they continued their simple, self-sufficient life-style. A study of the property listed in the estates of even well-to-do planters reveals much the same type of agricultural and household implements as in earlier days, though often a larger supply of them.

One indicator of the simplicity of antebellum life appears in the tax schedules, such as those in the Bibb County Tax Assessor's Report, 1858. At this time, personal property that was taxable, in addition to slaves and farm animals, included these "luxury items": gold watches, gold safety vest or fob chains, silver watches, clocks, playing cards, jewelry, plate, household furniture, and ornaments over $200 in value, except family portraits; also "vehicles kept for use, not exempt" and bowie knives as well as revolving pistols. One fairly representative planter was taxed for only one of these items, a clock, the most common of these taxable objects. Seventy-one men and women in the county (mostly men) owned gold watches, in nine cases suspended on gold chains. Many more told time by silver watches. One hundred and twenty-six residents were taxed for vehicles not exempt, that is, not used primarily for work. Only four citizens declared they owned jewelry, plate, household furniture, or ornaments valued at more than $200.[27] Incidentally, only three Bibb Countians admitted possessing such weapons as bowie knives and revolving pistols.

Bills and letters surviving from the 1840s and 1850s give glimpses of social customs. Even more than weddings, funerals brought the community together. Home preparation for burial was common throughout the century, before the establishment of the undertaking industry, and it required the services of both family and neighbors. The purchases that James Mayberry made in the week before the imminent death of his ninety-seven-year-old father, the Revolutionary veteran George Mayberry, indicate some aspects of that preparation. On November 4, 1849, the Centreville merchant Charles Sanford billed him for these items:

6 yds. Blea Domestic	1.20
1 yd. Jackonet	.63
1 pr. Stockings 3/6	.44
4 yds Blea Domestic	1.00
5/2 Black Velvet	4.12
2 Paper Tacks	.25
1 C. Brass Do.	.20
1 Doz Screws	.12
1 Bolt Blk Ribbon	.50[28]

Antebellum life had its lighter side in young people's entertainment. A farm boy recorded some of the simple rural pleasures. He attended a barbecue at Six Mile bridge and looked forward to the Fourth of July celebration, including sermon and barbecue at "Old Bethel." On his way home from the cotton patch, he met a friend who was going to "a frolic away over the other side of Haysop" and commented: "Who would believe that fiddling and dancing are becoming fashionable again."[29]

A letter dated June 5, 1860, reflects some of the social interests and customs in the county seat on the eve of the Civil War:

> Dear Sister,
>
> This place is about as dull as it ever gets to be.... We haven't had a picnic, fishing party nor anything else this spring. I generally get a weekly call from Dave B———[Brown], Lucius [Winship], Jack, & sometimes but seldom Tom [Smitherman].... I tell you this is a dry old place. The dancing parties have died out too, but I can't say they died a natural death. They were certainly murdered—the one I mentioned in my last letter was the final one—it ended in a *magnificent female row*. Cousin Prill and Bettie [Howard] had found quite a dislike to Houri[30] the 2nd because she was so unfortunate as to have a sister that married Fred [Mayberry?]. So on the memorable night in question Lucius & Houri fronted Bettie & John G. [Gardner] in the Set—and Bettie when she saw the arrangement flew the track, and so there wasen't other ladies to fill the set. L. & H. had to follow suit.... The Debaters say their next question shall be "Did the Ladies do right in seceding from the party?"
>
> Houri dresses very fine evenings low neck & short sleeves & spreads a large veil over her head & walks the street. All the men are in love with her.... She has joined our bible class sayed a lesson with us Sunday & I must say is not very studious or exceedingly dull—she diden't answer a single question correctly.
>
> ... Everyone is talking of Dave Griffin's luck—drew a lottery prize of 11,500 dollars.... He is now at home, a rich man.
>
> I think you would like Lockett you ought to get acquainted with him he is very gallant—knows just how to please the ladies. Somebody offered me an arm chair in his presence—he jumped around and got me one without arms—said he happened to know Ladies these days diden't like arm chairs. I haven't made me a basque by the pattern you sent me—have not done much sewing lately but think I will like them.[31]

The writer, who demonstrated feminine concern for the little conflicts among her friends and for the new dress styles, glanced light-heartedly at the issue of secession, which had become a real possibility since Alabama had led the bolt of Southern delegates at the Democratic convention in Charleston the preceding month. She could not know that within eight months Alabama would secede from the Union and by the following June all of the beaux who were then calling on her and dancing in the ballroom on the second floor of the Kennedy House, even the lucky lottery winner, would be marching off to war. All would enlist in the first Confederate company from Bibb County, except Lucius J. Lockett, elected captain of the company he himself organized.[32] The lives of all Bibb Countians were destined to undergo sweeping changes during the next four years and afterward the Reconstruction period.

12

IN THE CONFEDERATE ARMY

THE YEAR 1860 ended on a note of excitement in Bibb, though with little foreboding of the reversals of fortune that the new decade was to bring. The presidential election in November had proved the national ascendancy of the new Republican party, which many Southerners expected to work toward outlawing slavery throughout the Union. Alabama's legislature had already voted in February to hold a state convention in the event of a Republican victory, and now in response Governor Andrew B. Moore was calling for such a body to decide the crucial issue of separation from the United States. In the midst of holiday festivities, the adult white males of Bibb, like those throughout Alabama, went to the polls on Christmas Eve to name their delegate.

Although the county possessed Union men, former Whigs in most cases, the majority of its citizens apparently shared the sentiments expressed by Mrs. Martin Kersh, a widow, when she received the news of Abraham Lincoln's election. As her grandson, then eight years old, later recalled, Mrs. Kersh, smoking her pipe by her fireside near Sandy, paused a few moments and then remarked, "Yes, he will try to free our Negroes, but we will give him the fight of his life while he is at it."[1] In this same spirit, the voters chose a delegate who favored immediate secession. He was Dr. James W. Crawford of Centreville, who had represented the county in the state legislature in 1855–56.[2]

Thus, when the fateful vote was taken, 61 to 39, at the state convention on January 11, 1861, Bibb stood with the Black Belt counties rather than with those of northern Alabama and the Wiregrass, where sentiment favored waiting to see if the new president would actually alienate the South.[3] Crawford must have listened impatiently to the "resistance men" and cheered the "fire-eaters," especially the spellbinding orator William Lowndes Yancey, dressed in homespun for the occasion.[4] When the ordinance of secession was passed, followed by the ringing of church bells, the firing of cannon, and the whistling of a steamboat, he must have thrilled, even if uneasily, to the sound of the new name of "Republic of Alabama." Only two months later, Bibb Countians were citizens of a different republic, the Confederate States of America, in which their fortunes were linked with those of other Southern states. While the Provisional Congress was meeting at the temporary Confederate capital, Montgomery, a number of county residents may have traveled there to share in the euphoria of those days.[5]

The enthusiasm spilled over into Bibb and produced its first volunteers for military service shortly after war was declared in April. A company was organized, whose first captain was James L. Davidson. After his resignation a year later, he was succeeded by his first lieutenant, Joseph Caddell, also of the Centreville area, who was followed after his death at Petersburg by the young Randolph lawyer Zachariah Abney. These officers were all in their twenties, like most of the other members of the company. The Bibb Greys, as they were called, procured some tents and camped briefly at Brown Springs, now Gary Springs, where a Captain Pettaway, a cadet from the University of Alabama, came to drill them.[6] It was not a dull time, for the Centreville girls called on them frequently.

The day before the Bibb Greys left for the war zone on June 21, they paraded around the courthouse square to the applause of an ecstatically admiring crowd and then received a silk battle flag ordered by the women of the community from Selma. Bettie Howard, daughter of George W. Howard, had the honor of presenting the banner, standing on the porch of the new Presbyterian Church. Like other young women who were addressing departing Confederate companies in Alabama, she undoubtedly charged the Bibb Greys to do their duty on the battlefield, perhaps in such typical words as these: "We who present the banner expect it to be returned brightened by your chivalry or to become the shroud of the slain."[7] Her fiancé, Private Thomas J. Smitherman, received the flag for the company. That evening, she married him; and the following morning, in the excitement before the departure of most of the company, another romance culminated in the union of Rebecca Carson, daughter of the late Charles Carson, to Private John S. Gardner.

Many citizens accompanied the young volunteers on their triumphant ride to the nearest railroad station, at Randolph. The parting was described two days later by young Josiah McNeil Kennedy, who was chafing because his father had not allowed him to join this company:

> I went to Randolph with the Bibb Greys and witnessed some of the most affecting scenes when they were taking their leave that the State of Bibb ever beheld—women squalling and fainting, old men shaking hands with

> the volunteers and making private and public speeches to them, and shedding crocodile tears. Everyone was crying and carrying on at a dreadful rate save Fate Mayberry, he stood with Jacob leaning on his shoulder and swearing by the powers above he should not part with him as he was his only brother and he would never see him again, more like a statue hewn out of marble than like a living soldier, he seemed deeply affected but never shed a tear while all around them was shedding them by the pint. Fate makes a very fine looking soldier. Jacob had to be held off of the cars while they were starting.[8]

After traveling by rail to Lynchburg, Virginia, the Bibb Greys, as Company F, were enlisted in the 11th Alabama Infantry Regiment and moved to action in the Army of Northern Virginia. Shortly after Christmas, Tom Smitherman was writing from Camp Bull Run, Virginia, that the company, with the rest of their regiment, was stationed about half a mile from the main battlefield, preparing for winter quarters by building log cabins ten by fourteen feet, each to accommodate eight to ten men.[9] The company fought its first major engagement at Seven Pines the following spring. Later, it was also involved at Second Manassas, Gaines Mill, Frazer's Farm, and the Seven Days' Battle around Richmond. When the 11th Alabama surrendered at Appomattox, only 125 of the 1,100 men who joined it during the war were still on its roll. More than 270 fell in battle and about 200 were killed by disease.[10]

During the summer of 1861, five other companies containing large numbers of Bibb men were organized, most of their members volunteering for three years. All five units were mustered into the 20th Alabama Infantry Regiment as Companies B, D, F, G, and H, all of which had already adopted their own special names. Company B, led by a resident of Dallas County, called itself the Phoenix Reds. Company D, an all-Bibb group, enlisted on July 22 at Schultz Creek Baptist Church under Captain Richard Hopkins Pratt of Six Mile, took the name of Bibb Rangers. Company F, composed of Bibb and Perry volunteers, was known as Lockett's Company from the name of its first captain, Lucius J. Lockett of Perry. Company G, led by John W. Davis of Shelby, was called the Cahaba Valley Guards, and Company H, whose later captain was Samuel W. Davidson, Jr., the Perry and Bibb Liners. As part of the 20th Regiment, these companies fought over a large area of the South. They were first stationed in south Alabama near the Gulf, later in Tennessee and Kentucky, and then were sent to Vicksburg, where they were surrendered with the fortress. After parole camp at Demopolis, the regiment suffered severely in the Atlanta campaign and surrendered finally at Salisbury, North Carolina; by that time only 63 of those present had been among the original 1,100 members.[11]

Shortly after these five companies first moved to camp, a Bibb native, then a resident of Mobile, expressed his satisfaction in a letter to a sister in Centreville: "The good old 'state of Bibb' was for a time woefully deficient in her effort to rescue our country from the clutches of Northern Vandals, but from the intensity with which the fires of patriotism are now burning I feel sure that she will make herself both known and felt by our enemies. Her sons were last in the field."[12] The author must have been further gratified during the winter when Bibb volunteers added two other units to the Confederate Army, assigned in February to the 29th Alabama Infantry as Company D and Company H. After two years on duty in Florida and south Alabama, this regiment joined the Army of the Tennessee and during the Atlanta campaign of 1864 lost more than half its members. The survivors fought under General John B. Hood at Franklin and Nashville, and the remnant of about ninety men surrendered in 1865 at Greensboro, North Carolina. Alfred V. Gardner was captain of Company D, called the Bibb Rifles, and, in spite of wounds suffered at Reseca, Georgia, and Franklin, Tennessee, remained in charge throughout the war. Company H was led first by Hugh Latham, probably of the Randolph clan of that name, and later by Berry G. Brown, of Centreville, both of whom lost their lives during the conflict.[13]

The Confederate Congress, in its urgent need to build up an army, passed its first conscription act on April 16, 1862, not quite a year before the United States Congress adopted a similar measure. Shortly after this unpopular bill became law, four new companies, including a large number of Bibb men, joined the Confederate Army. When the 44th Alabama Infantry Regiment was organized in Selma on May 16, 1862, those units were mustered in as Companies B, F, G, and H—not all of which boasted gallant names like those of the preceding year, for war was grimmer business now. The age of some of their officers is noticeably more advanced. Company B, recruited at Scottsville, was led by John A. Jones, a thirty-three-year-old farmer and son-in-law of David Scott, who was eventually promoted to be colonel in command of the regiment. The Scottsville Guards were then led successively by three young men: L. D. Brown, who resigned; Joab Goodson, of Mars, who died near Richmond in January 1865; and James M. Hill, also of Mars. Company F, an all-Bibb unit, was first commanded by Henley G. Snead, listed in the 1860 U.S. census as a forty-six-year-old farmer of the Centreville area. After his resignation and the subsequent wounding and retirement of his successor, William N. Green of Maplesville, young John N. Fondren, another farmer from near Centreville, originally a member of the Bibb Greys, became captain.

Company G, which contained both Bibb and Dallas men, was first led by Thomas C. Daniel, and after his death by Bludford Brown. The captain under whom Company H was organized at Randolph was twenty-nine-year-old Francis Goode, a merchant of Six Mile. The regiment to which these companies were attached suffered severely from disease. It was part of the Army of Northern Virginia, but it was destined to do battle also north of Atlanta and at Chickamauga and Knoxville before surrendering at Appomattox.[14] The military record of John Wesley Lawrence, a young Randolph farmer who was a second lieutenant in Company G, shows twenty-one engagements between Manassas on August 20, 1862, and Darby Town on October 23, 1864, from a number of which he was absent because of illness.[15]

Among the many other companies enlisting Bibb citizens, two were organized in the county during 1864. Company A of the 62nd Alabama Infantry, a regiment composed almost wholly of young men, was commanded by William C. Ward, a schoolteacher from Six Mile, after its original captain, James L. Davidson, became for a time lieutenant colonel of the regiment. These forces saw action only in Alabama. They were twice captured and imprisoned at Ship Island, first after the bombardment of Fort Gaines and later after their exchange and the siege and bombardment of Blakely, being exchanged finally just before the Confederate surrender.[16] Company A of the 9th Alabama Cavalry, the second cavalry regiment assigned that number, was also organized in 1864. It was comprised of Bibb and Autauga men and captained by W. C. C. Cleveland, a thirty-four-year-old farmer from the Randolph area. After fighting around Dalton, Georgia, it served under General Gideon J. Pillow and later with Clanton's Brigade, finally resisting Wilson's Raiders in Alabama and laying down its arms at Gainesville.[17]

The departure of these fourteen companies for camp caused the biggest stir in the county because they took away the largest number of men. Later, Mrs. Eugenia Wallace Logan recalled the excitement and labor of outfitting the Six Mile volunteers in the summer of 1861 to join Company D of the 20th Alabama Infantry:

> The men must furnish their own uniforms so everybody in the whole country around got busy sheering sheep, dyeing and carding the wool, spinning the thread, and weaving the cloth. Ma would be up by daybreak and the whirring of the old spinning wheel would wake me every morning. We had to make their blankets, too. We made six. We had no gray dye for the uniforms so we dyed some wool black and left some white. Then we carded the two colors together to make gray.
>
> After the weaving was finished we met every day at the Six Mile Baptist Church to sew on the uniforms. Every stitch was by hand.
>
> The boys were to leave on Monday morning and on Saturday we could

Two Confederate soldiers, both casualties of the war: Jasper E. James (with dagger) and his younger brother, Monroe James. (Courtesy of Mrs. James M. White)

> not finish our work so we came back on Sunday and worked just as hard as we could until about 12 o'clock and the last piece was finished.
>
> Monday morning every man, woman and child went to Ashby to see the boys off. They left about 8 o'clock.[18]

Military camp outside the county offered less gaiety than the Bibb Greys had enjoyed in the neighborhood of family and friends, but the recruits were relatively carefree even though restless and bored until they were shipped off for active duty. Life in Camp Johnson near Auburn, as described by a member of the Bibb Rangers in the fall of 1861, was probably typical. Jasper James wrote to his father:

> I am happy to state that myself, Monroe, Milton, Pleasant, Arthur and Abe I Avery are well.... Only 54 of the "Rangers" drilled this evening. About 20 was, as usual, left to cook. The remainder are either sick or strolled off to town or somewhere else. The Captain can't do much with the "boys." When they get into service, they will do better or worse.... The water don't agree with many, it being freestone. No other company of our regiment yet arrived. I understand their is 5 companies at Montgomery, but you can hear anything you please. Today you may hear the Confederates have taken Arlington Heights, and the city of Washington is bombarded, and tomorrow you may hear that 6 men of war are in sight of Mobile and that all of the soldiers at this place, and us too, will take the cars for Mobile.... The boys are impatient to leave. They don't care where, so they leave here. We are

> comfortably situated, having built brush harbors [arbors] on both sides of our tents and ditched around them, but I learned that tomorrow we will move three quarters of a mile beyond Auburn.
>
> Major Pettus has been in our camp twice in conference with Capt. Pratt. I think we make rapid progress in tactics. Two young men from other regiments to drill us turn about. We have plenty to eat, sometimes the beef seems to give out about one mess before mealtime again, which is every morning. Sometimes rice . . . such delicacies as beets and cabbage. . . . A parcel of the "Rangers" went today to Auburn, and the "Railroad Hotel," and invited the ladies to favor them with a few tunes on the Piano. They complied, and said they would play for us when we desired. . . . Our Company gets water out of a man's well about 200 yards from our encampment. The dress parade is dismissed and the drums ceased and hundreds of axes may be heard. Our camp is continually infested with cigar and cake sellers, and some of the boys to show their liberality purchase occasionally, but I tell them to save their money for more useful purposes I occasionally give 5 cents to have a shirt washed, for you know I don't understand the business. But I mean to wash some of these days.[19]

Members of the first five Bibb companies spent Christmas away from home in 1861, most of them for the first time in their lives. Their letters gave their families a sometimes poignant glimpse of what that experience was like. Jasper James, who had earlier sent his mother the photograph she requested, "Ambrotype on Glass,"[20] wrote on Christmas Day from Camp Goode near Mobile to his brother Hill:

> In my imagination I see all that is going on at home and how I wish I was there for a season. I fancy Uncle Claiborn is now enjoying his everlasting eggnog which he is a dear lover of. And I can, as it were see you all going thither and thither just where your fancy may lead, while we wretches are confined and no prospect of the least fun. As to the eggnog, we have that. Many are busy beating eggs. As to the whiskey, we have tolerable plenty of that. . . .
>
> There is a great number of the regiment out on the parade ground playing what we call ball pen, and judging from the screaming and squalling they have had their drams. If there is enough sober ones to put the drunk ones in the guard house it will be pretty full by the end of the day.[21]

Those Bibb boys who had been assigned to the 44th Infantry Regiment in Virginia were having a snowball fight shortly after the following Christmas, as Joab Goodson reported enthusiastically: "We ragged rebels had a great sport snowballing. . . . It is a grand sight to see a thousand men with banners (handkerchiefs) flying meet on an open field and with deafening yells engage in a regular snowball battle."[22] Their leaders directed the mock battle from horses.

In the Confederate Army, farm boys from Bibb were learning to perform new chores. They were becoming cooks of sorts, but they missed the accustomed home fare. In northern Virginia, Joab Goodson wrote, "Our regular diet is fresh beef, hard crackers, and cold water," admitting that he longed for sweet potatoes.[23] At bivouac near Knoxville, Jasper James yearned for milk, butter, and honey and from besieged Vicksburg requested his father to send at his next opportunity "a bundle of red pepper, sage and onions."[24]

Necessity taught these boys to wash as well as to cook, for they were early transferred far from hired washerwomen and their homemade clothing was limited. Jasper Fair wrote to his wife from Camp Stonewall: "You ought to see me washing I wash my shirt today. I can wash as well as anybody."[25] In the mountains near Knoxville, where Unionist sympathizers sometimes attacked Confederate soldiers in guerilla fashion, Bibb men had to do their washing at a nearby spring. Lacking a change of clothes, they sometimes needed to perform the chore unclad. Jasper James humorously reported that in this situation he had to flee up the hill from the view of women passing on the path and lie behind a log with his feet badly cut up by the sharp rocks. In the same letter to his parents, he urged, "Send on my breeches. You know the consequences."[26] Only late in 1864, in his last letter home, did he notify his mother not to send any more clothes because the government "furnishes a good many clothes & we draw them, & it seems we will get no commutation for clothes. We can get them as cheap as she can make them."[27]

The soldiers wrote home for many other items. Jasper Fair requested shoes and hand-knitted gloves and also pled for a lock of his young wife's hair, saying, "You can flat it and send it a lettr."[28] Irving Ragland, at his camp in Calhoun County, urged his wife, Nancy, to "send to the hatter shop if you can and Git Me a wool hat for my old one is worn out," explaining that a hat would cost him twenty dollars if bought from the sutler in camp.[29] When Thaddeus Wallace wrote home in 1863 that his old hat was gone, his shoes were worn out, and he was "almost naked for clothes," the hat that his sister packed in his box of provisions was one she had created from an old black broadcloth coat; she decorated the brim and crown with many rows of tiny stitches.[30]

Two of the most urgent needs were for shoes and blankets. Captain Joab Goodson was disturbed on November 30, 1862, by the barefoot condition of many of his men. He tried to console himself by thinking that in the mild fall weather in Virginia "they will fight as well as any," but a month later he recorded that the company had been in combat around Richmond in the snow.[31] The same shortage existed the following August when he returned from sick leave at home. "I was really glad to see the boys. . . . They looked weary and worn, many were barefooted, but still in high spirits and ready for anything."[32]

Blankets were always in short supply. In 1863 the carpets in the state capitol in Montgomery were torn up in an effort to supply Alabama soldiers with adequate covers.[33] Rufus Goodson felt triumphant when, in an encounter with a federal captain at Campbell's Station, Virginia, he "ran him out of his blanket."[34] A soldier's blanket was his chief protection from the elements, even on guard duty, as Jasper James discovered during the campaign near Vicksburg: "When I get hungry I think of all the good things I ever eat in my life, and when I am setting propped up against a tree with my blanket over me thoroughly drenched and dying for sleep, I think of all the dry, warm comfortable houses, shuch pens, fodder houses, gin houses, stable lofts I ever was in in my life."[35] A soldier's blanket might also serve as his shroud, as Jasper's was destined to do after his death in the Battle of Jonesboro on August 31, 1864. The more fortunate Thaddeus Wallace made a coat of his blanket to wear home after his release from prison at Camp Douglas, in Chicago. [36]

Thaddeus Wallace was only one of many Bibb soldiers who suffered imprisonment during the war. Sometimes all the survivors of a regiment were captured and sent to prison, as in the case of those incarcerated at Ship Island after the siege of Spanish Fort and again after the bombardment of Blakely. Of the sixty-eight men in Captain Hop Pratt's company who went into the Battle of Fort Gibson near Vicksburg, only twenty-eight could be counted afterward.[37] Twenty of those missing, including Captain Pratt and young Hill James, had been captured and shipped north to prison at Alton, Illinois. After James was paroled to a camp near Demopolis, he wrote his father of their experience:

> I will begin with the first hour of our imprisonment and give you a brief sketch. We were taken by flank movement of the enemy extended as our forces were falling back. We being some distance in the rear of the retreating column. I will here state that the number captured on that day was about four hundred and fifty.
>
> We were almost perished & entirely worn out when taken. But the enemy regardless of that marched us all night to the river without giving us either rest or "grub." At the river they gave us some rest but nothing to eat save a pease of hard bread to each man at night of the second day. They carried us on an old boat completely riddled by the shots of our batteries to a few miles above Ft. Gibson where we landed & began a march of thirty-five miles across the fertile state of Louisiana to Millikens Bend where we got aboard a large old freight boat on the evening of the sixth of May. . . .
>
> We made a tedious journey on the river to Alton, Ill., where we were confined in the state penitentiary, a dirty filthy hole of about three acres in

> extent & that limited space was about half occupied in old rock building, miserable quarters for convicts. Here our treatment was by no means good. When we went in to the prison we were striped of everything we had save the suit we were then wearing. They even robed us of canteens, pocket knives, pocket books with all the money they contained, in fact everything of value about our persons. The worst is not told. They carried us into this living grave among all sorts of diseases, small pox, erysipalous &c which quickly spread among us, and scarcely one escaped the merciless small-pox & many died from this almost fatal disease.[38]

Captain Pratt was imprisoned again later at Johnson's Island, Ohio, where he occupied himself by carving a complete set of chessmen, which he brought home at the end of the war.

Although disease was especially rampant in the prison, Bibb recruits had become acquainted with it in many forms in camp and soon learned that it was as bad a hazard as enemy fire. William Kennedy lamented in the fall of 1861 concerning the volunteers from Bibb: "How they have suffered. Though yet unknown to the horrors of war, they can show a list of comrades dead, scarcely equaled by that of the most unfortunate company that stood in the deadly breach. Both past and present experience, though, show that country troops lose about three to one from sickness, compared with troops from cities. Out of about 25 Mobile companies now in Virginia, I have not heard of as many as ½ a dozen deaths."[39] Writing to his family on January 10, 1862, Jasper James said: "There is more serious sickness now in the 20th than there ever has been at one time. I suppose some die nearly every day. A man died yesterday about dark of a congested chill, very suddenly, too. He was found dead in his tent. E. D. Perry of our company died the other day. John W. Langston is in a dying state. I heard from him this morning, they say he can't live through the day. Uncle Abe and Aunt Penny are with him at the hospital. . . . There is about thirty of our men at Camp Goode in the hospital."[40] Dysentery and malarial fever were the two most common ailments, and each could be fatal. When the far more deadly smallpox invaded some camps, Alexander Hill James sent his sons a "scab," with which they vaccinated themselves.[41]

By the midpoint of the war, the Confederate Army showed a significant increase in losses other than those from deaths in the camps and on the battlefields. Many of its soldiers were deserting. Persistent illness, small and infrequent pay (typically eleven dollars a month during the last year of the conflict),[42] and most of all the destitution of their families were responsible in most cases.[43] Occasionally other family problems seemed to call a soldier home. The desire to protect his recently orphaned sisters and brothers led Daniel Lightsey of the Bibb Greys, embattled at Richmond, to offer $1,000 to a substitute if one thirty-five years old could be found, but when none was located in Bibb he resigned himself to his situation.[44] Others deserted to protect their families from outlaws in the Bibb hills, frequently thought to be deserters themselves.

Bibb was one of many counties that contributed to the desertions, though by no means as much as did the northern Alabama hill counties, where it was estimated that by the last year of the war 8,000 to 10,000 soldiers were hiding in the woods. Bibb men began deserting as early as 1862,[45] the year of the conscription bill that took heads of households from their farms and businesses and was doubly unpopular because it exempted citizens who were working as many as twenty slaves. In December of that year, Jasper Fair wrote to his wife from camp: "I herds bad news from Bibb yesterday I herds that the conscrip had rebeled and no more would come to Camps there has no conscrips come from bibb since I lift."[46]

Loyal soldiers were troubled by defections from their companies. Perhaps many of them viewed the situation with mixed emotions at first. Writing his parents on January 26, 1863, from bivouac near Vicksburg, Jasper James asked: "Is it expected that men with families will remain in the field and their families probably suffer?... Eight men left us last week. You will see some of them. There is a great deal of discontent now in the army. I fear we will become greatly demoralized." On February 8 he continued in a sterner mood: "You said nothing concerning our absentees who was nearly all our neighbor boys, whom I consider have brought eternal infamy upon themselves and families, and run the risk of losing their lives." By December of that year, the editor of the hometown newspaper was moved to exhort: "Let the women everywhere drive back or frown back the skulkers to their posts in our armies."[47]

On May 15 of the following year, Jasper James described to his parents the traumatic experience of seeing punishment meted out to some absentees from a North Carolina brigade: "I witnessed yesterday the execution of 14 poor fellows who had deserted. It was a solemn scene. They was all tied in a row and fell by the same volley. Think of this, ye mothers & wives when you write letters to your sons and husbands, thus causing them to desert." Something of the emotional climate of the time is indicated in the "gracious revival of religion" that he reported in the same letter as "progressing in the brigade and from all accounts it pervades the entire army."

In another mood, soldiers recorded gallant encounters on the battlefield, as when Edward Kennedy in a bold charge with his company of cavalry fell under his horse but finally freed himself and escaped under enemy fire.[48] They described, not without humor, such front-line adventures as sleeping on the edge of entrenchments filled with water and having to roll over into them "whenever our watch heard a stick break."[49]

They usually reflected courage in line of battle, observing occasionally that only one member of the company "took a slight chill when... the Yankee guns came booming over our heads"[50] or that only two took fright and "skedaddled when we were marching toward the battlefield and the shells were bursting around us."[51] At tragic moments, these boys attempted to comfort homefolks when reporting a brother's death and his hurried interment near the battlefield, his clothes "tolerable clean" and the grave marked by his name carved on a cedar or pine tree at its head.[52]

But the chief burden of the many letters that have survived is the day-to-day camp problems of food, clothing, and sickness. It was these that caused fathers to visit their sons, sometimes to carry provisions and at other times to nurse them in the camp hospital. Through visits and letters, Bibb Countians on the home front shared vicariously in their soldiers' lives during the four years of the war.

13

ON THE CONFEDERATE HOME FRONT

THE WAR YEARS were increasingly difficult for Bibb Countians at home as well as for those at the battle front. Like their soldiers, however, most of them began the period under the Confederate flag enthusiastically, and, in spite of all their hardships and the defection of some citizens, many never gave up hope of victory until the final days.

Enemy forces did not invade the county until the last month of the conflict, but Confederate soldiers were frequent visitors. Among these after the first year were officers who had been dispatched to enforce the much-resented draft law. Protective family members were constantly fearful of them. On July 22, 1862, Jasper James wrote from "bivouac near Knoxville" to his father concerning his young brother: "If the conscript gets after Hill, I want him to come here." In November of that year, after his eighteenth birthday, Hill enlisted in the same company, but whether under pressure is not known. Daniel Lightsey, writing from the Virginia battle zone, expressed anxiety as to which of his neighbors in the Sandy community would be seized next.[1]

Conscript officers were doubly unpopular because they frequently ignored passes of soldiers home on furlough and forced them to return to the army.[2] Archibald Kennedy, son of Josiah S. Kennedy, was wounded in his knee in the first Battle of Manassas and disabled for further military service.[3] On July 5, 1864, his sister wrote to another anxious sister: "No, the conscriting officer did not get Archie," adding with amusement, "He enquired of your whereabouts & said had he only thought of it in time he would have gone to the Judson concert & met you."[4] Many of the soldiers assigned this unpleasant duty were, as is apparent in this case, local boys. One of Bibb's "conscriting officers," Pat Cruise, was so unwelcome after the war that he left home for five years.

Confederate soldiers who were passing through the county on other missions were received far more hospitably. Yet sometimes these men in gray foraged over the countryside much in the manner of men in blue, according to a granddaughter of Elisha Cottingham, whose homestead lay near Pratt's Ferry, on the Cahaba. "Our own soldiers often camped near us and one time took lots of our stuff to live on and exchanged bad horses for good ones," she recalled.[5] Passersby reported seeing Confederate soldiers camping near the Cottingham place in an open field, where they were cooking their supper in groups of five or six around each camp fire.[6]

The presence of soldiers swimming in the Cahaba River en route to their next assignment or visiting in a Bibb County home while recuperating from sickness added much interest, especially for the young women, during the often dull days of the war. Sadness struck, however, when two Confederate soldiers died in Centreville, both on their way home but too ill to complete the journey. One was said to have been a Harrison of Tuscaloosa and the other a Cunningham of Boone County, Mississippi. Both were buried in the Centreville Memorial Cemetery.[7] Another Confederate, an unidentified courier, perished while attempting to swim the Cahaba just below the River Bend bridge, and his funeral was held at the Brick House, built by James Hill.[8]

One Confederate visitor remembered his brief sojourn half a century later. G. W. Dudley of Benton, Missouri, originally a Mississippian, wrote: "In 1864 I camped for a week on the Cahaba River, just outside the limits of Centreville. I was a member of Ferguson's cavalry brigade. . . . On our march to Centreville we passed through a factory town called Scottsville . . . and a large number of young girls lined up by the road and sang 'Dixie' as we passed by. Our camp was near the river east of town. I remember that a peafowl strayed into camp and we cooked it for dinner one day. The meat was very dark but it was not bad eating."[9]

The presence of Confederate troops in the county often stimulated business. S. G. Wilson, owner of a mill on the Montevallo-Centreville road at Six Mile Creek, testified to the active life he and other operators of mills and blacksmith shops led during the war: "Being located on so public a thoroughfare, with the cavalry divisions of Generals Loring, Pillow, Forrest and part of Wheeler's cavalry constantly passing, we were forced to abandon usual work, and shoe horses and feed and house soldiers. We kept the mill running night and day, supplying meal and flour to a large area of the country."[10] Wilson, a native of Memphis who had bought grist and flour mills at Six Mile after giving up the management of the Brierfield Furnace, added small ironworks for converting ore into malleable iron. He used this iron to make horseshoes and also the metal parts of wagons, which he built of native timber, eventually contracting to furnish wagons to the Confederate government.

Numerous other industries sprang up in the county, and those already existing experienced rapid expansion. This industrial boom was the one positive effect of the war on the economy. A saltpeter cave on Six Mile Creek, said to be about twenty-two yards below a natural bridge, was opened for the production of saltpeter for Confederate gunpowder. Bibb's Oliver Frost was one of the managers employed in this enterprise where Confederate authorities reportedly manufactured between five and six thousand pounds of saltpeter during the war.[11] The Scottsville cotton mill, the largest industry in the county at the beginning of the war, was shortly called upon to supply large quantities of material for citizens of Bibb and adjoining counties, who were deprived of Northern-manufactured goods by the federal blockade. The government in Richmond soon pressed it into the Confederate service and turned its looms to weaving textiles for the army.

Ironworks multiplied. They included forges, furnaces, and rolling mills from the Stroup, or Tannehill, ironworks on the Tuscaloosa line above Woodstock to several plants around Brierfield. The Little Cahaba, or Brighthope, Furnace, the only Bibb blast furnace in production at the beginning of the war, had for several years been manufacturing bar iron and turning out hollowware for the farmers of the region. After the blockade, it created the facilities to supply planters with agricultural implements on a large scale. Yet other blast furnaces were needed.

In 1861, while private enterprise was still in control, a resourceful planter from Greensboro, C. C. Huckabee, came to Bibb's mineral district. Assisted by Jonathan Newton Smith, from whom Browne had bought the land on which he built Brighthope, Huckabee seized the opportunity of making a fortune by constructing a blast furnace near the Mahan Forge. He bought a large tract of land from Edward Mahan's son, Jesse, who was spending the war years as an iron inspector and sawmill operator. Huckabee supplied the slave labor and most of the capital and Smith his expertise, gained in watching the building of Brighthope.[12] They bought some of their machinery for the cold blast furnace, later known as Number One, from Montgomery. They also ordered some from Brierfield, Mississippi, the home of Jefferson Davis, a circumstance that has sometimes been credited with inspiring the name eventually given the community, though other conjectures have been made. Whatever its source, the name Brierfield was assigned later by Major W. R. Hunt while he was in charge of the plant, according to General Josiah Gorgas.[13] When it was discovered that wrought iron was more profitable than cast iron, the company constructed a rolling mill near the railroad on Mahan Creek, where it could use the waterpower, and built a tramway from the mill through a brierpatch.[14] The furnace and rolling mill allowed the owners to do a booming business supplying farm implements to hard-pressed Alabama farmers for nearly two years.

Then, as the need for iron to prosecute the war became more acute, all the blast furnaces in the South were placed under contract to supply the Confederate government. George Peacock, in charge of selecting pig iron that could best cast the large guns for the army and navy, reported that Brierfield's sample was the toughest and most suitable. But, because the trade with the planters was more lucrative, Huckabee declined the government's contract and also the alternate offer to lease the plant. As a result, the Confederacy in 1863 purchased the property at a "force sale" for $600,000 in Confederate money and made Major Hunt manager.

The Brierfield ironworks, under the name of Bibb Naval Furnace, greatly increased in productivity during the next two years. The Confederate government immediately poured funds into the plant to improve the facilities and to pay the local white laborers who furnished much of the manpower. It added to the cold blast furnace a large brick stack equipped for hot blast, which it called Number Two, and also constructed a new and more up-to-date rolling mill not far away on Mahan Creek. The entire output was shipped to the Confederate Arsenal at Selma, where much of it was used to build heavy cannon for the navy. Later, General D. M. Maury said concerning his defense of Mobile: "The Brooke guns, of which I had a number, were more formidable and serviceable than any which the Federals used against me. These guns were cast at Selma of iron around Brierfield in north Alabama."[15] This plant was also the most productive in the state, turning out around twenty-five tons of pig iron a day in comparison with twenty-two at Tannehill, fifteen at Shelby Ironworks, and twelve at Brighthope.[16] In addition, its rolling mill, the only one in Bibb County in the Confederate service, reached an estimated daily capacity of ten tons.

Coal mining was another county industry that the war stimulated. The incentive to explore for coal was provided by the state legislature's offer to exempt from the armed services any man who signed a contract to use twenty slaves to dig coal for the Confederate government. Several refugee families from Mississippi and elsewhere mined coal in Bibb. Members of one family that engaged in strip mining with their slaves had fled from Hinds County, Mississippi. After their home and four hundred bales of cotton were burned by federal soldiers, W. H. and Lewis Thompson, two brothers, came into the Cahaba hills, where they were later joined by their father, N. H. Thompson. Lewis Thompson sent his son Julius and his overseer with his ablebodied slaves to mine coal in the Dailey Creek basin for the Confederate government. From the seam that became known by their name, the Thompsons eventually opened three mines, in later years developed as Piper Number 1 and Number 2 and Coleanor. In their primitive operations, they used no explosives but required the slaves to do all the work with pick and bar; mules hauled the cabs to the surface, a method continued in later years. It was a severe life for blacks accustomed to Mississippi cotton fields. Because no pump was available to keep the mines dry, they were forced to carry the water out in buckets and often worked with wet feet. As a result, many became ill and died, as the graveyards around the mines testified.[17]

A few may have escaped, as did some other slaves from their Mississippi refugee owners in Alabama. The Centreville *Central Enquirer* of December 17, 1863, advertised two slaves who were being held in the Bibb County jail. One had apparently languished there for five months, according to this notice:

> Committed to the jail of Bibb County, Alabama, by Robert Keith, a justice of the peace, on the 27th day of July, 1863, a negro man as a runaway slave by the name of Edward. Black color, about 6 feet high, weighs 180 pounds, and says he belongs to Col. Kelley, of Hinds County, Mississippi, and that his master is a refugee, and that he left his master near Jonesboro, Jefferson County, Alabama.
>
> The owner is requested to come forward, pay charges, prove property, and take him away, or he will be dealt with as the law directs.
>
> C. J. Rotenberry, Deputy Sheriff

A resident of northern Bibb during the war later recalled that the slaves whom Mississippi refugees put to work in the nearby Tannehill Furnace often ran away and were caught by bloodhounds kept for the purpose.[18]

The coal obtained by these crude methods was hauled twelve miles to the railroad station at Ashby, a team of four mules with one wagon carrying one ton a day. When the Thompsons returned to their Mississippi plantation after the war, the mines became overgrown with briers until they were rediscovered two decades later. Other refugees who mined this area for the Confederate government were named Brooks and Gaines, Rogers, Carter, and Gholson and Herndon.[19]

A number of Bibb Countians found employment during the war years in industries other than the slave-powered coal mines, but the financial state of the county as a whole declined precipitously. Farming was no longer as successful as it had been in the 1850s. Because most of the ablebodied men were in military service, management was left in the hands of the women and old men. Both taxes and prices rose dramatically. The enactment of the Confederate tax-in-kind in the spring of 1863, amended February 17, 1864, hurt especially the families of small farmers. According to its provisions, a farmer, after reserving out of his crop a certain number of bushels of his products (fifty each of sweet and Irish potatoes, twenty of peas or beans, one hunderd of corn or fifty of wheat), was required to deliver to an appointed depot within eight miles 10 percent of the remainder of his crop of every sort raised during the year and 10 percent of all meat killed.[20]

This 1864 report of Dr. E. H. Moren as administrator of the estate of S. W. Davidson was followed by a statement of receipt at Depot #2, Section 1, 5th Congressional District, State of Alabama, March 10, 1865:

Agricultural Products	Gross Quantity	Quality	Tithe or One-Tenth	Value of Tenth
Corn	2350 Bush.	Fair	235 Bush.	$528.75
Cured Fodder	15000 Lbs.	Fair	1500 Lbs.	33.75
Molasses	300 Gals.	Fair	30 Gals.	150.00[21]

The total tax equaled five or six times the amount required before the war.[22]

Among the depots for receiving the tax-in-kind in Bibb County, one is known to have been a store on the southeastern corner of the square in Centreville and another the Stroup (Tannehill) Furnace near Woodstock. Andrew W. Hayes later recalled going with his older brother to deliver the required supplies to the Stroup Furnace. "We would fill the wagon body full of ear corn," he said, "then put as much fodder on top as we could carry, binding it on with a pole."[23] John M. Green, also of Woodstock, whose family must have carried their product to the same depot, related the family tradition concerning the decline of their fortunes: "Until the year 1860 it was a profitable cotton plantation. When the war commenced they were first required to exchange all gold money, etc., for Confederate paper money, then all taxes kept rising until the war and the grafters got most of it. Back then they had what they called tax in kind, meaning a part of all and everything produced on the farm, and nobody knew where it went or what it was sold for, so at the end of the war the owner had nothing but his cotton and his land, on which he could continue to pay taxes."[24] Although many farmers, like the Greens, were ignorant of the use of the tax-in-kind, it provided for most of the army's food after 1863.[25]

Besides heavy taxation, another burden for some planters was the impressment of some of their slaves into the Confederate Army. In the later months of the war, these laborers were required for such work as digging trenches. J. H. Green received this notice:

Centerville, Bibb Cty, Ala., Nov. 17, 1864.

Mr. J. H. Green

Sir you are hereby notified to furnish one (1) able bodied hand for 12 months, said hand will be hired or impressed at your option by the government "to increase the efficience of the army by the employment of slaves in certain capacities." You will receive $15 per month, rations and clothing furnished by the government or $25 per month rations only furnished by the government. You will deliver me said hand with 4 days rations at Centerville, Bibb Cty—Ala. on the first day of Dec. '64 when you will be [compensated] therefore.

L. E. Starr, Agt Impressment Bibb Cty, Alabama.[26]

Even before taxes had become so exorbitant, prices had risen astronomically and severe shortages of consumer items had occurred. In October 1861, only six months after the beginning of hostilities, Dr. E. H. Moren wrote from Montgomery, where he was representing Bibb in the state senate, that he had just paid $20 for a pair of boots not worth $7. On December 2 of the following year, he reported to his wife that he was sending by W. C. C. Cleveland a few articles she had requested: "1 lb. black tea for which I paid $10.00; two toothbrushes at $2.50 each, six miserable linen Hdks. at $1.25 each, two papers pins at $1.25, 4 papers needles #9 at 28¢, 22 yds. calico at $1.55 yd."[27] After the Confederate dollar, worth 90 cents in U.S. currency in 1861, dropped to 6.3 cents in 1863,[28] inflation pushed prices to even higher levels. In Selma, the favorite shopping city of most Bibb Countians, these prices were advertised in March 1864:

Salt per bushel	$30.00
Calico per yd.	10.00
Women's common shoes per pr.	60.00
Men's rough shoes per pr.	125.00
Cotton card ($1.75 in Connecticut)	85.00[29]

By December 1864 mules, horses, and cattle were costing ten times their price before the war. The cry of "extortion" was raised in Bibb as elsewhere, and is reflected in letters from soldiers at the front: "If reports be true a speculation mania [pervades] the minds of men, who it would never be expected of having turned perfect extortioners. Selling such things as soldiers families are obliged to have at exorbitant prices. Extortion will ruin our country and end the war to our ruin. . . . If we draw money I will send home all I can spare to enable you to buy corn enough."[30] Accounts of the administration of estates show that the value of slaves rose along with other merchantable property, for example those of three leading Bibb planters who died during the conflict: Walter C. Duff, S. W. Davidson, and Robert Hill. On February 26, 1863, Duff's best slaves were appraised at $1,600 each. By the fall of 1864, these official records showed an average value of $2,000, more than double that before the war.

Meanwhile, shortages had become a more critical problem than prices. It made no difference if coffee and sugar cost $20 a pound and flour $300 a barrel if they were not to be found in the stores. The failure of the market to supply some items could be an inconvenience, as was the lack of hats and buggies, according to a good-humored letter of 1864,[31] but some shortages worked such a hardship that they inspired considerable ingenuity in devising substitutes. Andrew W. Hayes recalled:

> Sugar was substituted by honey and molasses; coffee, from rye, barley, okra, and other grains; salt was obtained by bleaching the earth in smoke-houses after the manner of making soap from ashes; soda, from a kind of white ashes secured from the decayed old hollow oak trees; and for matches we had no substitute except the old tinder box, flint and steel. Our main dependence for fire, however, was keeping fire in the open fireplace both winter and summer. I was sometimes sent to our nearest neighbor to "borrow fire." This neighbor lived a mile away, and sometimes the fire would go out just before reaching home. I remember several times when the coal would be nearly gone getting pine straw and kindling a blaze, and so recruiting my coals.[32]

One of the most inconvenient shortages was that of salt. Although most farmers depended on the method of boiling down the brine from soil under smokehouses, some returned to another pioneer practice, that of visiting salt wells for several weeks in the hope of obtaining a year's supply. The chief wells in Alabama were located on the state reservation in Clarke County, near which several privately owned works developed also. Both Alabamians and Mississippians thronged there during the war. The roads were clogged with planters' wagons loaded with containers and provisions, the drivers often accompanied by fifteen or twenty barefoot slaves plodding along on each side.[33] After setting up camp, the planter usually put his slaves to work boring a well. They hauled rock to build a furnace and wood to burn while boiling the brine in a large kettle. The area resounded with the felling of trees for fuel.

A letter to Lucinda Summers James, headed "Clark" County, Alabama, September 21, 1862, describes the frustrations one Bibb farmer encountered there.

> Dear Wife and Children:
>
> This leaves me in the best of health as is all the company. Let M. E. Lette's family know that he is well. We are at Jeffrey's Work, but we are not located

A Bibb County woman whose life almost spanned the county's first century: Lucinda Summers James, 1823–1916; she lost two sons and eight brothers in the Civil War. (Courtesy of Harold K. Cottingham)

yet and I think will have to move. We can get no place here or have not yet. Jackson will be our post office, but for the present write to Gainstown. How glad I would be to see you or to hear from you. We get no news here. . . . Do the best you can. I do not know what to tell you to do. You can tell better than I can, only do the best you can. I write by the fire lite sitting on a log, and it is now beginning to rain. We have no shelter. What we are to do I don't know if it rains. Tell all the children howdy for me & tell them for me, it seems that all the Negroes most of the white ones, has congregated here. You never saw such a stew. Our prospects to make salt is very discouraging. I hope it will soon be better. . . .

Yours affectionately,
A. H. James[34]

The shortage of salt and other necessities was reflected in the *Central Enquirer*. By the end of 1863, area merchants were offering bacon, flour, and other produce for salt, and some who were fortunate enough to possess this scarce staple were trying to barter it for other items. The editor advertised on December 17: "A small quantity of salt for pork, on liberal terms." In the same issue he reflected rather plaintively his want of candles: "WANTED: Beeswax and tallow, for which we will pay the price demanded. Will our friends spare us a little?" It is not known at what point the *Enquirer* ceased publication; in December 1863 it was the only surviving newspaper in Bibb and Shelby counties. The lack of paper and ink drove more than a fourth of Alabama papers out of circulation before the end of the Civil War.

While the formerly well-to-do farmers were struggling to overcome shortages, the poorer families, especially those in which the head of the household was serving in the army, were often facing destitution and even starvation. Their situation deteriorated throughout the war years and early necessitated government relief. In 1862 all county commissioners were authorized to levy for the benefit of the destitute a tax equal to the regular state tax, in addition to which the state appropriated $2 million for the same purpose, to be distributed by the county commissioners in either supplies or money. The state, assisted by the counties, also attempted to furnish meat and salt to the poor through officers during the last three years of the war.[35] The Bibb commissioners on whom these duties fell were L. T. McGuire, R. F. Caffee, J. N. Shelton, and James McDaniel, headed by Probate Judge Jackson Gardner.[36]

On January 20, 1862, the minutes of the Bibb County Commissioners Court record "a special meeting for the purpose of making an estimate of the Volunteers left for the Confederate Army and also the indigent families left without visible means of support." The names of the soldiers they listed are followed in some cases by an estimate of their families' needs, for example:

> Lewis Farley—wife and 1 child needing $67.50 for support twelve months.
> William Hamiker left a mother and 4 children kneeding for support $50.00.

Apparently not all Bibb's remaining farmers continued to cooperate in the war effort, at least in the view of Editor Mason of the *Central Enquirer*. He raised a cry of alarm on December 17, 1863, in an editorial entitled "Farmers." "Now, when our country is in her death struggle," he thought that farmers were expected to do more than any other class of people. He continued:

> They have not, we repeat, done their duty in the present emergency. They have not responded to the appeals of the gov't, the soldiers, the people at

> home in that liberality which they ought to have done. Some time ago an appeal was made in this paper for that gallant company, the Bibb Greys; soon after another was made by Captain Joab Goodson of the 44th Alabama Regiment, and directed contributions of clothing, blankets, &c, to be left at this office. Appeals have been made for our soldiers and their families daily, weekly and monthly, appeals which for eloquence and pathos would ring [*sic*] "iron tears from Pluto's cheek," but have fell as cold as the icy heart that beats in their bosoms. Not a word has been said to us in regard to leaving anything at this office; not even a kind, sympathetic word has been spoken. Capt. Goodson has gone as he came, with the addition of a heavy heart—loaded with grief at the conduct of a people whom he and his comrades are suffering to defend. At the recent battle of Chattanooga the 20th Alabama lost all their clothing. Bibb has two companies in this regiment, and they are now appealing to their friends to have their lost articles replaced. The government can't do it, her resources are too limited. Can we expect independence when we deny those who are trying to achieve it a few of the comforts incident to the wants of a soldier?[37]

Even more than the military reversals, poverty was breaking down morale on the home front. By 1863 the "peace party" was growing throughout the South, and in Bibb men of Union sentiments were beginning to be selected for minor offices. On August 18, 1865, Captain Joab Goodson wrote in alarm to his niece, Nannie Clements: "The most we have to trouble us is the fact that such men as Will Thompson and Tom Dennis are chosen by the people at home to make our laws. We are led to ask the questions, what are we coming to, whither are we drifting? We are fast losing confidence in the patriotism of a great many of the people at home. . . . I am fearful that the people are getting on the wrong track. . . . It makes my heart sick to think how some of our citizens are doing. . . . Is Bibb County for the Union, with the Yankees? God forbid. If so, I am ashamed of the county that gave me birth, but I hope the people generally did not vote for Thompson as a Union man. If this is true, I hope the men will be conscripted, and sent here where they cannot desert."[38]

While this division was mounting as conditions deteriorated, the war came to an end, but not before Bibb had at last been invaded by federal troops. Unfounded rumors reached the county more than once in the spring of 1865. By the last week of March, however, news of the approach of General James H. Wilson's famous Raiders came from an authoritative source, as recorded by Kate Kennedy in Centreville: "O Sister! a negro just arrived from Montevallo with a note from General Pillors [Pillow] saying that the Yankees were positively on their way to Montevallo and be there by noon tomorrow. O I'm perfectly miserable everything is wild with excitement it is no longer a question of doubt—the yanks are really coming but the hardest trial to us is to give up Pa.... he's decided to go and nothing will stop him.... I don't like the way the negroes act—they are flying about the yard with bright beaming countenances—as if some good cheering news had been rec'd. O perhaps it is the novelty of the thing that makes them enjoy it... dont let anything I've said have too much weight. perhaps it will end like the first scare."[39]

In expectation of such an invasion, General Nathan Bedford Forrest had made a reconnoitering expedition through this section of the state and organized home guards to support the troops he had assigned to the county seat. According to tradition, he told an unusually tall schoolmaster that, if he did not join the company, he would take him down to the river and duck him, to which the teacher replied dryly, "It would take a mighty deep hole."[40] Two federal officers' estimate of the force on hand to defend Centreville varied from 150 to 250 "rebels."

During the closing weeks of the war, General Wilson and his 13,500 cavalry troops were moving rapidly through central Alabama seeking to destroy military objectives, including bridges, factories, and especially ironworks, chief of which was the Confederate Arsenal at Selma.[41] The University of Alabama was another target because it was training cadets for the Confederate Army. At Elyton, General Wilson split his forces into three divisions, commanded by Generals Eli Long, Emory Upton, and Edward McCook, respectively. McCook was one of the famous Ohio "Fighting McCooks," numbering fourteen brothers and cousins besides the two fathers.[42] Under Wilson's instructions, McCook detached a brigade under General John T. Croxton to march to Tuscaloosa while the main army hurried toward Selma, burning industries along the way.

On the march from Montevallo down the Selma road, the cavalry Raiders on March 31 reached Brierfield, where they wrecked the furnaces, the rolling mill, and the nearly completed nailery. A detachment under General Philip Roddey attempted to defend the works, but Colonel Fred Benteen's 10th Missouri dug trenches for an attack from a hillside about half a mile away and after a few hours routed the guard and set fire to the plant.[43] The blast furnaces were not located within range of the cannon but sustained considerable damage nevertheless.[44] Not far away, the Little Cahaba, or Brighthope, Furnace suffered the same fate, as did the other ironworks of Bibb and Shelby counties and the Stroup, or Tannehill, Furnace on the Tuscaloosa line. On March 31 Roddey's and Benteen's men clashed in a sharp action at Six Mile Creek, a formidable barrier because it was swollen from recent heavy rains, and the Raiders drove the defenders toward Randolph, where a skirmish took place the following day. Ashby was the scene of another skirmish on the 31st and Ebenezer Church (then in Bibb, on Bolger Creek, north of Plantersville) of a sharp action on the afternoon of April 1 as Forrest, commanding his plucky but inadequate forces, merely delayed Wilson on his way to Selma.[45] Twelve Union dead were buried in Ebenezer churchyard.

Meanwhile when Wilson's men had reached Randolph on the 31st, they "captured a rebel courier, just from Centerville, and from his person took two dispatches" containing important news. From them Wilson learned, as he added in his record, that General W. H. Jackson of the Confederate Army

> ... with his division and all the wagons and artillery of the rebel cavalry, marching from Tuscaloosa via Trion [Vance] toward Centerville, had encamped the night before at Hill's plantation, 3 miles beyond Scottsborough [Scottsville]; that Croxton with the brigade detached at Elyton had struck Jackson's rear guard at Trion and interposed himself between it and the train; that Jackson had discovered this and intended to strike Croxton at daylight April 1.... I also learned that a force of dismounted men were stationed at Centerville, with orders to hold the bridge over the Cahawba at that place as long as possible, but in no event to let it fall into our hands.
>
> With this information in my possession I directed McCook to strengthen the battalion previously ordered to Centerville by a regiment, and to follow at once with LaGrange's entire brigade... with the utmost possible celerity and after seizing the Centerville bridge and leaving it under the protection of a sufficient guard, to cross the Cahawba and continue his march by the Scottsborough road toward Trion... to attack and break up Forrest's force, form a junction with Croxton, if practicable, and rejoin the corps with his entire division by the Centerville road to Selma.[46]

Just before noon on Sunday, April 1, a Confederate courier rode into Centreville from the east, yelling, "The Yankees are coming and Hell's to pay!" A number of residents, seated at their dinner tables, scattered instantly. Lieutenant Graves of the Confederate Army, who was dining at the Kennedy House, ran out and mounted his horse, which was hitched to the gate, and fled into the woods. Young John S. Gardner, at the residence of his father, the probate judge, seized the satchel containing government appropriations for the indigent people of the county and ran into the woods, too. He later reported that he found several other citizens there, some carrying their valuables, others driving their stock, and still others merely seeking personal safety.[47]

In a short time, a cavalry battalion of the 2d Brigade of the 1st Wisconsin Regiment arrived in town, having come at a fast trot from Randolph. Major Stephen V. Shipman, the young Wisconsin architect in command, wrote in his diary after the stress of the day's events:

> I awoke at 6 this morning & was ordered to report with 5 companies.... which I did, and was informed that it was of the utmost importance

> for our forces to get possession of and hold the Bridge across the Cahaba at Centreville. It was already held by from one to two hundred dismounted Cavs. of Forrest's command. I was told the enemy would if possible reach it with———[?] of Chalmers div. which was moving to that point. I must gain it if it was to be done with killing all our horses. I covered the distance 15 miles in 2 hours.
>
> We charged into the town, drove out over 250 rebel soldiers, captured one Captain, 1 Lieut., and twenty-two men. Got possession of the Bridge & threw up hasty breast works. The advance overtook us three and a half hours afterwards. The rebels were driven in all directions, although in line of battle across the streets on Court House square. The Bridge had been fixed with a part of the flooring taken up to prevent our crossing. One Company pursued on the Marion Road. For those needed it was ordered by Genl McCook to remain and hold the Bridge at all Hazards. We discovered Saltpetre cave on the bank of the river and destroyed———[?]. We lost no men in the fight. Armstrong's Brigade is said to be advancing.[48]

The first act of the Raiders, after seizing the bridge, was the usual one of burning cotton. They found bales being held for Confederate tax-in-kind in a store at the corner of East Walnut and Market streets, later the site of Cleveland's Grocery Store, rolled them from the back door down the hill, and set a torch to them.[49] That night, the soldiers camped on the hillside above the bridge while the major occupied quarters at the Kennedy House. There he recorded that he received a dispatch from Colonel Oscar LaGrange about midnight, after which he slept little.

When the remainder of the brigade under General McCook marched into Centreville a few hours after Shipman's battalion, they halted for an hour and then moved up the road toward Scottsville. They camped there that night, not far from the Confederate troops commanded by General William H. Jackson, and seized the opportunity to scour the countryside for supplies, taking horses, meat, and corn from the nearby farmers. When some men of the two armies met at a farmhouse while doing the usual "buttermilk foraging," they agreed to a truce while they shared what the farmer had to offer.[50] McCook's men were repulsed in the skirmish that began shortly after daybreak, and under his orders they retired rapidly toward Centreville, though not before destroying the Scottsville cotton mill. Years later, Mary Jane Stewart Ward, who was sixteen years old at the time of the raid, related hearing the noise of the tearing up of machinery from her home in Cedar Grove.[51]

The federals were pursued by Bell's brigade on the road back to the Centreville bridge across the Cahaba. There Major Shipman stood ready to rip up the decking and burn it as soon as they crossed it but was delayed by the excursion of a thirty-man detail down the Marion road west of the river in search of fresh horses. As the absentees finally raced across, and just as the pursuing Confederate column came into view on the Scottsville road, the work of destruction began.[52] Thus McCook achieved his most important strategic objective: keeping Jackson's division from crossing the Cahaba to join Forrest in the defense of Selma later that day. The burning of the bridge and of all the boats on the river was not completed, however, without skirmishing a body of Confederates who attempted to cross.[53] The Raiders set up cannon on the southeastern side of the hill overlooking the Cahaba, and one of the balls struck the chimney where Mrs. Ben Glass had placed her infant son, Frank, in the family home just west of the bridge, though it did not injure him.[54]

David Kennedy, who had just returned from the cabin of "Uncle Gabe" where he had spent the night after hiding a favorite mare, Prairie Belle, watched the "battle of Centreville" from the family's attic window. From the same vantage point, he saw the Raiders march out of town toward Selma, many riding fresh mounts, one of which he recognized as his father's black horse, Prince. All the invaders were loaded with ham, chickens, and eggs from neighboring plantations. One such soldier was the victim of a Confederate scout's bullet from across the river and was hurriedly buried by his comrades on the hillside where they had slept the night before.[55]

During their brief occupation of Bibb County, the Raiders fanned out to many other communities. According to family tradition, when soldiers made a surprise appearance at the home of David Kersh in Sandy, his daughter, Mrs. John Fondren, stole one of their horses to carry a warning to the neighbors. A young Confederate private named Hogan, at home on sick leave, barely escaped from the Hayes residence at Woodstock as the first of two bands of Raiders arrived, bent on appropriating the best plow horse from the field.[56] When another band attempted to cross the swollen Cahaba at River Bend, Mary Dickerson Pratt had the cables cut and her ferry boat set adrift. As a result, she lost much of her income, for, though the boat was later found at Mobile, it could not be brought back.[57]

Just one week after Wilson's Raiders left Bibb County, General Lee surrendered the remnant of his army at Appomattox. Although the news did not reach the county for several days, undoubtedly the outcome had been expected, and peace, even with defeat, must have been a relief. Yet the division that the conditions of war had created within the county did not heal immediately.

14

CONFLICTS DURING RECONSTRUCTION

DEFEAT IN THE Civil War and the collapse of slavery drastically shook the South's economic and political systems. Because Bibb was outside the Black Belt as well as remote from the power centers of the larger cities, neither the military authorities nor the Freedmen's Bureau paid much attention to it, and it was too poor to attract many Northern political adventurers, usually called "carpetbaggers." The struggle during this trying time was principally internal; it resembled a minor civil war. The division that had begun in the last two years of the war now widened. It arose from time to time between whites and blacks, hill people and valley people, farmers and industrialists, Conservative Democrats and Radical Republicans. As a result, the Reconstruction period was one of the most turbulent decades in the history of the county. Because of the disruption, records are sometimes sketchy, but lively oral traditions abound.

Unfortunately, for two years after the surrender of the Confederacy, the crops were poor throughout Alabama, especially in 1866, when it experienced a severe drought. Destitution was widespread among both races. An official of the Freedmen's Bureau who traveled through Bibb County in January 1866 reported that the suffering of the whites was appalling.[1] This federal agency, presided over in Alabama by the well-intentioned General Wager Swayne (unfairly called "Swine" by Montgomerians), tried to supply rations to starving whites and blacks throughout the state. From November 1865 to September 1866, it issued rations to 166,589 whites and 72,115 blacks.[2] A ration was a week's supply of cornmeal, salt pork, flour, and sugar. Probate judges and selected citizens were expected to determine the distribution in their counties, but the inefficiency and corruption of General Swayne's staff often aborted this arrangement.

During the first year after the surrender, those who owned cotton were likely to have it claimed by so-called cotton agents and cotton spies under federal confiscation laws. Francis S. Lyon, who headed the Canebrake Company when it bought the Brierfield ironworks in 1866, is said to have purchased 384 bales being held for Confederate tax-in-kind. During his absence from Brierfield, a train of army wagons guarded by soldiers carried off 96 bales, which he never recovered because the suspected thief, a man named Ruter, claimed to be a government cotton agent.[3] Some farmers in the Centreville area burned their cotton rather than turn it over to cotton agents. Many leading citizens were in dire straits by 1868, as is evident from the large number of circuit court cases that were continued because of "the bankruptcy of the defendant."[4]

The desperate poverty led to increasing lawlessness. The woods were inhabited by groups of outlaws, thought to be deserters from both armies, who had become cattle thieves. One band lived in the hills in the northern part of the county, a section then referred to as "the Uglies," and another gang in "the Yellow Leaf," a swampy area around Yellow Leaf Creek east of Randolph in what became part of Chilton County in 1868.[5] Bibb residents lived in fear also of the "Blackwell crowd," which operated out of Montevallo immediately after the war and was credited with killing seventeen men. Lawlessness in neighboring Shelby County grew to such an extent that military authorities in Montgomery threatened to send "a mounted force to summary arrest and punish all offenders."[6]

One cause of lawlessness was the disarray in county government in 1865. After the military authorities in Montgomery dissolved the existing county administration in May, no courts were held in Bibb until October. Apparently it was expected that order would be maintained by the unit of federal soldiers that, according to local tradition, was stationed in the county seat for two years under the command of a Captain Dodge, who resided at the Kennedy House. The citizens resented these token occupation troops so much, however, that their presence was sometimes an encouragement to crime rather than a deterrent. According to one often repeated story, young Jacob Dennis Mayberry, recently returned from a long army hospitalization in Richmond, became involved in such a heated argument with one of these soldiers at the corner of East Walnut and Market streets that he killed him with the blow of an ax handle. It is said that only the intervention of Josiah S. Kennedy, whose wife had nursed Captain Dodge during an illness at their hotel, saved Mayberry's life.

On August 31, 1865, newly appointed Provisional Governor Lewis E. Parsons sent officers to each county seat to give citizens an opportunity to take the oath of allegiance to the United States. Centreville attorney Thomas J. Smitherman, a former Confederate soldier, was called upon to administer the oath in Bibb.[7] On the same day, the newly qualified voters elected Judge Jackson Gardner to represent them at the state con-

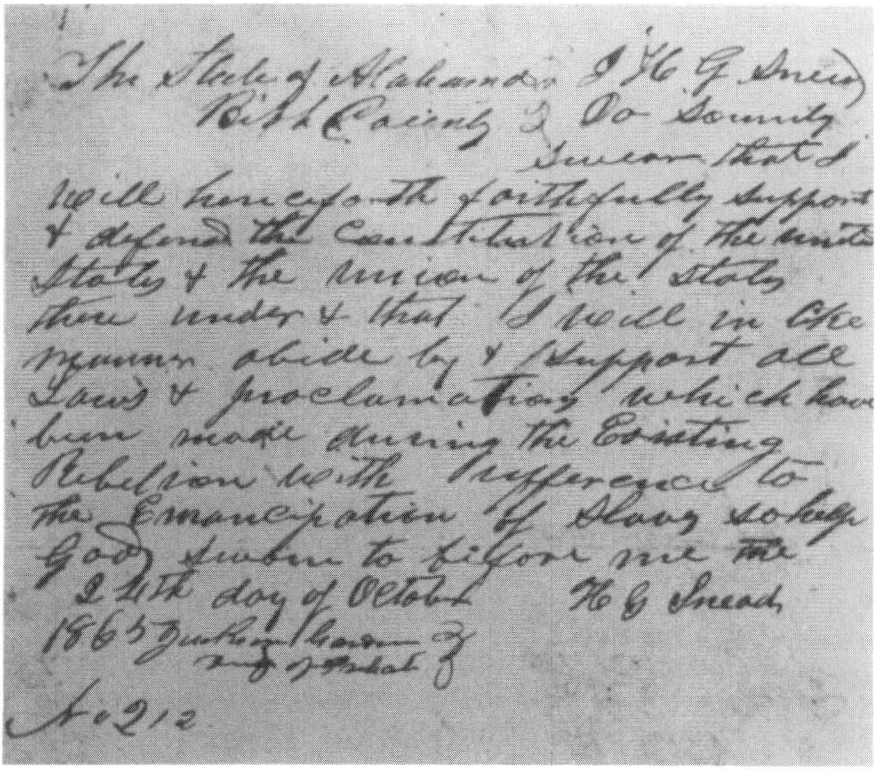

The State of Alabama } H G Snead
Bibb County } Do Solemnly
Swear that I
will henceforth faithfully support
& defend the Constitution of the United
States & the Union of the States
there under & that I will in like
manner abide by & support all
Laws & proclamations which have
been made during the Existing
Rebellion with reference to
the Emancipation of Slaves so help
God Sworn to before me the
24th day of October H G Snead
1865 Jackson Gardner
Judge of Probate
No 212

Oath of allegiance to the United States, signed by Bibb citizens in the fall of 1865, in this case by former Confederate captain Henley G. Snead. (Courtesy of Alabama Department of Archives and History)

stitutional convention that had been called by the governor for September.[8] Except for an undetermined interim after May 1865, in which the office was vacated by order of the federal military government, Gardner served as probate judge from 1856 until his death in 1876.

At some time during the five months in which county records are virtually blank, at least three acting officers were appointed. According to circuit court minutes of October 23, 1865, they were Jackson Gardner as probate judge, his son John S. Gardner as sheriff, and an unnamed "late acting clerk of this court" who had failed to qualify himself for this office, possibly by not taking the oath of allegiance to the United States. Presiding Judge Benjamin R. Saffold, a Republican appointee from Montgomery, found that, in the uncertainty of the situation, the acting probate judge and sheriff had not summoned the necessary jurors, and so he postponed the session until they could do so under his orders. Judge Gardner was bonded in November 1865, with other former officers, all of whom were renamed in the regular election of March 2, 1866. In addition to Judge Gardner, they were William A. Schoolar, clerk of circuit court; A. S. Ward, tax assessor; F. G. Woods, tax collector; and R. H. Oakley, sheriff.[9]

Legislative representatives E. H. Moren and James W. Davis had been reinstated on November 6, 1865.[10] Yet the congressional delegation from Alabama was not permitted seats in the national body, which was now in open rebellion against President Andrew Johnson's Reconstruction policies. Dr. Moren, watching the Washington scene with growing apprehension, commented wryly from the senate chamber in Montgomery: "Our affairs grow more gloomy every day. The Radicals in Congress are disposed to rule with an iron Rod . . . and we will have to grin and bear it."[11]

Meanwhile, in view of the general lawlessness of the times, the state constitutional convention of September 1865 had requested Governor Parsons to authorize the organization of state militia to repress the disorder. The governor shortly afterward called for a military company to be formed in each county, the service to be voluntary and to extend in each case over a period of only six months. The men were to be drilled once a week and called on duty when needed. Colonel S. W. Davidson, Jr., who was placed in charge in Bibb, commissioned W. N. Green as captain to form a company. The sixty-one members Green had enlisted by November 25, 1865, selected Six Mile as their headquarters.[12] The company was broken up into squads of five to ten men each, and each squad took turns at patrolling its own precinct, serving one week at a time. Bibb's men were probably as poorly equipped as were those of Barbour County, where it was reported of the company: "Has no arms, only a few second hand shot guns in a very bad fix."[13] It is impossible to determine how effective these local units were. They served until they disbanded by order of General John Pope when he assumed command of the federal military government in Alabama in the spring of 1867.[14]

During these trying days, race relations grew strained and sometimes hostile. General Swayne of the Freedmen's Bureau, in an attempt to protect the freedmen in the new system of tenant farming, had approved a policy of written labor contracts, but he had warned them to hope for nothing, go to work, and behave themselves.[15] It is doubtful if his astringent words ever reached the freedmen in Bibb. As elsewhere, blacks were probably afraid of being reinslaved by these contracts that few of them could read. They also heard persistent rumors that the U.S. government planned to give each freed family forty acres and a mule.

Freedmen's Bureau agents named Beard and Higginbotham, who were assigned to Bibb in January and February 1866, were suspected of raising other expectations before they were whipped and run out of the county. Two misguided or misunderstood blacks, Tom Johnson and Rube Russell, reportedly walking around dressed in fine clothes paid for by those agents, frightened some Centreville residents into believing that the two planned to "live like white folks and marry white wives." Some white citizens laid this old specter to rest, at least temporarily, by lynching both of them. One morning, passersby observed the body of Johnson hanging from a tree on Market Street, it was reported, and a few mornings later that of Russell on another tree a short distance from Dr. Moren's house. Needless to say, no evidence of the criminals' identity was ever discovered.[16]

One specter was vanquished, but another rose in Bibb as it had a few months earlier in Selma: fear of a black uprising. The severe laws passed by the state constitutional convention of September 1865 in the Black Code are evidence that such fears were statewide. When S. W. Davidson, Jr., questioned a former slave of his, the frightened fellow allegedly acknowledged that a plot was underway to "wipe out Centreville." According to the story, Davidson at once sent to Selma to borrow a hundred rifles. The wagons returned on a Saturday when the town was full of both blacks and whites. As the rifles were unloaded on the square, each was issued to a white man. The tale, probably exaggerated over the years, quotes Davidson as announcing in a loud voice that he was sending for more wagons in order "to haul off the dead niggers so the streets would be clean the next morning for church."[17] The news of the guns, if not of the threat, is said to have spread like wildfire and was credited with preventing the rumored insurrection.

Many white residents placed little faith in the courts while they were presided over by appointees of the provisional government in Montgomery. Friction must have erupted between the circuit judge and the county authorities because Probate Judge Gardner and William Oakley were each fined $25 for contempt in the 1866 fall term of circuit court.[18] A tradition has survived of a case against an accused lyncher, J. T. Miller, in which the judge was seen to pen his sentence while local attorney Newton Suttle was still in the act of presenting his defense. Federal soldiers summoned from Marion reportedly prevented Miller's rescue from jail by a mob, after which he is said to have stabbed himself with a pocket knife.[19]

Available court records of the period scarcely bear out the charge of partiality to the blacks, but they do provide glimpses into their lives at this time of adjusting to their new status as freedmen. Most of them still lacked the identification of a surname. At the spring term of circuit court in 1866, presided over by Republican appointee Judge Benjamin Saffold of Montgomery, three freedmen named simply Wade, Bird, and John were charged with stealing a bale of cotton and were sentenced to the penitentiary for two years. At the same time, four others, listed only as David, Jack, Alec, and George, against whom the charge is not specified, escaped more lightly with only a fine of $5 for George. Isaac Fondren was summoned into court with the advantage of both a surname and two securities, members of the Fondren family, but, when he and his white sponsors failed to appear, the judge threatened them with a $400 fine if they were absent from the next session of court. Two cases that must have caused excitement were dismissed because the witnesses for the prosecution failed to appear. The charge of adultery had been leveled in one case against a white woman and "Wade, a freedman," and in the other against a white man and "Katy, a freedwoman."[20]

In the spring of 1867, word came of the new congressional Reconstruction plan that was to supersede President Andrew Johnson's more conciliatory policy. New legislation reorganized the ex-Confederate states into five districts with a military commander governing each, disbanded state militia, and required new constitutions to replace those drafted in the fall of 1865. It also enfranchised black males of voting age and disfranchised all citizens unable to take the oath that they had not aided the late rebellion in any way. In each of the new military districts created within the state, a board of three loyal persons—two white and one black—was appointed to manage the registration of voters and the election of delegates to the state constitutional convention. In Alabama's twenty-fourth district, composed of Bibb and Shelby counties, the appointees were Mason J. Gibson, James R. Walker, and John Dozier, none of whom can be identified as Bibb residents.[21] In spite of the more severe requirements for voter qualification, white citizens were in the majority on the new official roll in Bibb County.[22] General Josiah Gorgas was one resident of the county who was awarded amnesty after the summer voter registration was completed. He noted in his diary of September 15, 1867: "The *Proclamation* of *amnesty* just issued by the President includes all except the President and his Cabinet, Governors of States, and officers above the grade of Brig. Genl. So that I am now *amnested*, by taking the oath of allegiance. This measure excites little remark."[23]

One of the first effects of the new order was to increase racial tensions. The suspicions and resentment of whites rose as the freedmen showed signs of more independence. The blacks, for whom it had long been illegal to meet without white supervision, were observed to be starting a movement to withdraw from their former masters' churches and to form congregations of their own. Those churches still tried, though often in vain, to encourage their attendance and to exercise authority, as in the case of Levi Glass. The elders of the Centreville Presbyterian Church reported in the minutes of their session: "Levi Glass, a freedman and a member of this church stands indicted in our circuit court with being accessory to stealing a horse.... After giving security for his appearance at court [he] absconded and left his security to pay his bond.... We have been unable to ascertain his place of residence so as to notify him to come before us to answer these charges.... As he had neglected to attend public worship and had absented himself from the ordinances of the church *for a long time,* therefore, Resolved that the said Levi Glass is hereby expelled."[24]

More significantly, many whites were disturbed by absenteeism from the fields and by noisy night meetings of their former slaves. A group of fearful and resentful white citizens of Centreville, Sandy, and the James community met in the summer of 1867 and set about organizing their own chapter of the Ku Klux Klan.[25] In a county containing a little more than 45 percent blacks, Jamesville, the rich farming area south of the present town of Brent, was the only precinct in which blacks outnumbered whites, and Centreville beat, which included the Sandy community, ranked second in black inhabitants.[26]

Later apologists declared that the purpose of the Klan in Bibb was "to make the Negro get to work in order to sustain himself" and that this altruistic object was achieved by "warnings and a few beatings." They claimed that the organization was composed of leading citizens, that it was not secret nor did its members wear masks, and that it lasted only a short time. In denying responsibility for any act more violent than a beating, they blamed "an organization of similar type" for the lynching in March 1869 of one of Stanhope Conwill's former slaves, who was suspected of robbing and attacking a Sandy woman. It was explained that Conwill was not a planter but a "Negro raiser," whose slaves were rowdier and less well disciplined than others.[27] Because the Klan was organized in the southern part of the county, it obviously had the interests of the farmers at heart, not those of the industrialists. General Josiah Gorgas, presiding over the reorganized Brierfield ironworks, noted that Klan members (possibly from Shelby County) had frightened black workers away from their jobs there on at least two occasions.[28]

Doubtless freedmen, both in factories and on the farms, lived in terror of the vigilantes. News of Klan activity in neighboring Shelby must have been noised about Bibb during this period when the county was dependent on the *Shelby County Guide* to publish its official notices. Residents read in that organ an approving account of a visit by Klan members to the Shelby county seat in November 1868: "About a week ago Saturday night the Ku Klux came into town to regulate matters. They were here from eleven p.m. to three a.m.—five hundred in all. They shot one very bad negro, putting six balls through his head. Many heard the noise, but did not know what was going on. They also hung three or four negroes nearly dead, and whipped others severely in order to make them tell about their nightly meetings, and what their object was in holding the same; also as to who their leaders were.... The strangest thing about those Ku Klux was that they did not hesitate to unmask themselves when asked to do so; and out of the whole party none were identified."[29]

No record is extant of such harrowing experiences for the freedmen of Bibb. The U.S. congressional committee that investigated Klan activities did not include it among the twenty-four counties in which the white-robed terrorists were said to have prevailed.[30] In fact, only one reference to Bibb appears in this tremendous volume of testimony, and it concerns merely a shooting incident in which "the parties all knew each other. They are all now in court on both sides," the witness said.[31]

Another result of congressional Reconstruction was to intensify the political struggle within the county. The party lineup was predictable: the southern section, because of the farming interests, remained chiefly conservative and Democratic; the northern and eastern areas were inclined toward the new Republican party. The latter areas were impoverished by the loss of the cotton mill, ironworks, and other local industries that had given employment to a large class of poor whites. Some of the prominent residents had formerly been drawn to the "peace party" and now believed that success and even survival demanded cooperation with the so-called "carpetbag-scalawag" forces in control in Montgomery. They were probably in agreement with Republican convert John Hardy of Selma that not only their personal fortunes but also the speedy revival of all the state's resources depended on such cooperation, and so they were willing to accept the local stigma attached to such a stand.[32]

Now that the Radical Republican party was entrenched at the state capitol, this new political element began to vie for power with the conservatives. The Randolph precinct, which included the Brierfield community, had the largest population, 2,038 residents, in comparison with 1,285 in the Centreville precinct, the second most populous of the seven beats in the county. The Randolph area, though inhabited by only a small proportion of blacks, possessed power through its Union League, a unit of the secret political organization that sought to influence the black vote throughout the South. General Josiah Gorgas, at Brierfield, commented bitterly in his diary on July 4, 1867: "There was a barbecue at the little Methodist Church, half a mile from here, to which the country people and the negroes flocked. It was a congregation of the 'Union League,' a society which seems to be organized in this hopelessly benighted country out of those who skulked during the War, and are now rampant for the Union." That same month, a Methodist minister reporting on a quarterly conference held by his denomination at Cox Chapel reflected anguish over the current conflicts: "Much confusion amongst us owing to the critical position of affairs which I think has a tendency to cause us to cleve more closely to God and to look to him as there is no humanity in man at these times."[33]

Republicans were more successful in their efforts to represent the county at the capitol than at the courthouse, but competition was keen in both arenas. In the election of October 1867 presided over by federal soldiers dispatched to the polls by Republican appointee Governor W. M. Smith to protect the voting rights of the newly enfranchised freedmen, Jesse W. Mahan of Brierfield was named delegate to the state convention called to set in motion congressional Reconstruction.[34] In his diary of November 14, General Gorgas expressed the conservatives' distaste for this body: "The state convention is sitting at Montgomery—mixed black and white." Mahan also represented Bibb in the state senate until 1874, and P. A. Kendrick, an ally from Randolph precinct, took the county's seat in the lower house for one term before his rival, Thomas J. Smitherman, won it, also for a single term.

Most of the Conservative Democrats who had been returned to their offices at the courthouse on March 2, 1866, later either succeeded themselves or were followed by other members of their party. Yet Republican John R. Atchison of the Randolph precinct won the important office of sheriff and Dr. R. H. McPherson of the same precinct was appointed county superintendent of schools by state authorities. The governor also approved Elijah B. Drennon, apparently an outsider, for the post of tax assessor, an especially unpopular and difficult position during this era of poverty and political discontent. In November 1869 Drennon disappeared suddenly and mysteriously from his Bibb County home.[35] Shortly afterward Republicans of the Randolph beat signed as securities for William R. Gaylord, of Six Mile, as his successor and also for Jesse A. Brown as sheriff.[36]

According to one of the political legends of this time, Democrat Jesse A. Brown resorted to a trick to defeat Republican John Latham. He won the office by publicly professing to be a Republican convert, and then, when chancery court met the following May, refused to call the racially mixed jury expected of a Republican.[37] Perhaps the trick backfired, however, for two years later Latham won the sheriff's office and another Republican, Jonathan Newton Smith of Brierfield, was sent to the legislature with the still unbeaten incumbent, Jesse Mahan.

In 1870, the year of Brown's trickery, E. H. Moren performed a similar service for his party legitimately and on a larger stage. Dr. Moren, a native Virginian who had settled in Centreville in 1851 after graduating from medical college in New York and acting as assistant surgeon in the Mex-

Edward Hawthorne Moren, Centreville physician and for many years state senator, elected lieutenant governor in 1870. Henry Damon Davidson, *Inching Along* (Nashville, Tenn., 1941), p. 27 (Courtesy of Nesbitt B. Wesley)

ican War, also later served as head of the Confederate hospital in Greenville. He was elected in both 1861 and 1865 to represent Bibb and Perry counties in the state senate, where he gave significant leadership in the Committee on Finance and Taxation.[38] Now in 1870 he had been elected lieutenant governor of Alabama. The Republicans admitted his election but contested that of Robert B. Lindsey, the Democratic candidate for governor.

The instant that Moren took the oath of office, he ordered the doors of the senate chamber locked and the vote for governor and other state officials counted. The result was announced and the Democratic candidates were sworn in before anyone could interfere.[39] Moren's quick and decisive action in this moment of crisis eventually prevailed, even though for two weeks former Governor Smith refused to vacate the capitol, summoning federal soldiers from the Montgomery garrison to guard him. During that time of chaos, one legislative house recognized Governor Lindsey and the other former Governor Smith. A writ from the circuit court finally ousted Smith on December 8.[40]

In 1872 Bibb Republicans intensified their campaign. In addition to their own excellent speaker, Reverend P. Adams of Randolph, they brought in outside support in a Republican convert, Congressman Charles Hays, a Greene County planter and former Confederate soldier, who was known to the opposition as "Sidemeat Charlie" because of his appropriations of government bacon to the blacks of his county. The bacon had fallen into his hands when the government was slow to appoint distributing agents.[41]

While Hays was wooing the black vote in a speech in Centreville, the local Democrats are said to have harassed him with the popular opposition tactics of that period.[42] Dr. E. H. Moren, not recognizable to Hays in the muddy farm clothes in which he had been feeding his cattle, frequently called out, "That's a lie!" Hays accepted the heckling good-naturedly, even Moren's outrageous assertion to the blacks in the crowd, when he had the opportunity to make a rebuttal for the Democrats, that not the Republicans but he and his fellow legislator, James W. Davis, had passed the law that freed them. "Charlie himself knows," he declared, "that I wrote that bill and passed it through the Senate after my friend Jim Davis passed it through the House. Didn't you, Jim?" "I did that and more, too," replied Davis. At that point, local fire-eater Jacob Dennis Mayberry, though a cousin of Hays, rose from his seat, flashed a large knife, and said, "Doctor, I can't make a speech, but if there is any fighting to be done, I can do that." According to the five old-timers who attested to the truth of this tale, the crowd cheered, and Hays, deflated but still good-humored, moved on to Brierfield, where he was more successful.[43]

This political tug-of-war also involved the county newspaper. John W. Callahan, Republican publisher of the *Centreville Apprentice*, established by 1869, had encouraged the freedmen to take Hays's advice and vote the Republican ticket. As a result of his editorial, he found it necessary to leave the county in a hurry, according to his brother, Sam Callahan, later of West Blocton. John Connoly, a Democrat, who then took over the *Apprentice,* had his troubles, too. He was criticized by Republicans north of Centreville for not supporting Hays's point of view. After he ignored a note warning him to cease publication, he was threatened by a group of unmasked men who gathered in his yard one evening. He had his gun out, however, by the time they could form a circle in front of him, and so they dispersed quietly. Connoly's paper is said to have endured until 1876, when the press was destroyed by an "unknown party."[44]

The election of 1874 was the last hotly contested race between the rival parties in Bibb. In this year, John Latham, P. A. Kendrick, and L. H. Kinnaird were accused of railroading their county slate of nominees. They denied the slander in written statements they nailed to trees throughout the county and which the Democrats in turn denied and ridiculed in affidavits printed in the county newspaper, to which of course the Republicans no longer had access. Congressman Hays, who was now presiding over government appropriations of army bacon to victims of a recent flood in this district, was accused of holding up those appropriations until just before the election and at that crucial time sending them into Bibb's Republican areas, in some cases many miles from a stream.[45] The Democrats were as usual not without their bag of tricks, too. James W. Davis, who had represented the county in the legislature at intervals for more than a quarter of a century, now refused to run again. But it was said that on the night before the election certain Centreville Democrats, including Dr. Moren, prepared enough tickets to elect Davis and commissioned blacks to carry them to ballot boxes throughout the county. As a result, he won.[46]

This year, the Democrats achieved their first decisive victory in Bibb, as in the state, and they celebrated it by a barbecue and horse race down at the race track below the ferry, which, tradition says, had been the ball field of the Creek Indians. There, as a fitting climax to the day and perhaps the decade, Democrat S. W. Davidson, Jr.'s horse outran Republican P. A. Kendrick's contender in a close race.[47] This year of 1874 was considered by many to be the turning point in political reconstruction in Alabama, though rivalry between the two parties was far from over. In November, Alabamians elected both a Democratic governor, George Smith Houston, and a legislature containing a Democratic majority. Bibb Republicans, who had split from the radical contingent of their party and now called themselves Independents, were planning strategy to retrieve their strength in the county. Democrats could look forward to sending Dr. E. H. Moren to represent the county at the 1875 convention, which would replace the constitution of 1868 with a far more conservative document. More important, because of the lessening of tensions, especially racial and political, citizens could now devote more of their energies to the task of reviving their war-impoverished county both agriculturally and industrially.

15

REVIVAL OF AGRICULTURE AND INDUSTRY

DURING THE DECADES immediately following the Civil War, Bibb Countians continued to experience hard times financially but they gradually adjusted to the revolutionized economy. By the end of the century, they had made fresh attempts in both agriculture and industry and, aided by improved transportation, had begun climbing slowly to a new stability.

It is difficult today to visualize the poverty that prevailed after the war or the determination and resourcefulness that kept many a citizen afloat. Solomon Parker Ward and his wife, Mary Jane Stewart Ward, who lived at Slick, near Eoline, provide an exceptional example of success against the discouraging odds of the time. They were married in 1873, the year of the financial panic and yellow fever epidemic. They possessed then, so they later told their youngest son, only fifty dollars and "an old mule and horse, one of which was blind." By the time of this farmer's death, he and his equally energetic and frugal wife had accumulated 1,200 acres of land, the first tract of which he had the good fortune to inherit through his father's foreclosure of a mortgage. He also owned a country store, a cotton gin, a gristmill, and a small sawmill, operated in the late 1890s to saw lumber for his own home, which became the only painted frame house for miles around, a replacement for the family log house. In addition, he left for each of his twelve children as they came of age $300 in gold, buried in a covered jar close to the chimney under his bedroom.[1]

The large majority of Bibb Countians, like the Wards, earned their living on farms, and there both blacks and whites found the greatest challenge to their powers of adjustment to the new order. The labor of slaves, who had constituted the major part of many farmers' holdings, was now replaced chiefly by that of tenants in the new system of sharecropping, in which the tenant contracted to labor for a share of the crop to be produced. According to some Southern historians, this system was more injurious to the South than slavery had been. It bound the local merchant, the farmer, and the homeless laborer together in a tight bond of credit. (Bibb had no banks until the 1890s, when those institutions took over some of the responsibility and risk of extending credit.) The merchant issued credit to the farmer in the form of supplies for planting the crop and supporting the laborer and his family until cotton should be sold in the fall or winter. At that time, the farmer reimbursed the merchant at a rate of credit determined by his creditor, if necessary draining his resources in the process, because a foreclosed mortgage could ruin him. Although the tenant was furnished a house and had the privilege of felling trees for fuel, the supplies issued him frequently absorbed all the funds realized on the crop, so that he received no cash himself.

A legal contract of the sort initiated by the Freedmen's Bureau and signed by a Bibb farmer and his sharecroppers in January 1879 spells out a typical arrangement of the period:

> State of Alabama
> Bibb County Know all men by these presents that this agreement entered into this first day of January 1879, by and between A. C. Hargrove as Executor of the last Will and Testament of Robert McIlvain dec'd and we the freedmen, whose names are hereunto attached, subscribeth Witnesseth that the said A. C. Hargrove as Executor aforesaid has this day employed the laborers below subscribed, to serve as agricultural laborers for the present year 1879 on the plantation of Robert McIlvain, dec'd, located in this county.
>
> And we, the laborers subscribed, agree that we will be subject to the orders and regulations of the said A. C. Hargrove or his agent for the management and superintendence of said farm, that we will labor faithfully on all week days during such hours as the said A. C. Hargrove or his agt. may prescribe, that we will do the necessary repairing to keep up the farm to make, and take care of the crop, that we will take good and faithful care of all utensils, implements, Wagons, horses, Mules and all other property of whatsoever nature not herein enumerated, that may be submitted to our Care or charge. And it is further agreed and understood, that any of the said laborers failing to comply with the conditions of this agreement are to be promptly discharged.
>
> And it is further agreed and understood, that in consideration of the fulfillment of the above agreement by said laborers A. C. Hargrove, as Executor aforesaid, agrees to give to said laborers one half of all the cotton they may grow and gather and bale, one half of the fodder grown and gathered, and two-fifths of the corn grown and gathered on said farm for the present year. And the said laborers are to pay out of their interest of the Crop for all rations, merchandise, labor wages, or any other advances of whatsoever nature not herein enumerated that may be furnished during the year.[2]

This instrument, witnessed by E. J. Kennedy and D. S. Frazer, was signed by the following sharecroppers, each by means of his mark: Peter Davidson, John Watkins, Dick Davis, Wiot Shropshier, Simon Murphy, Alfred Watkins, Wood Watkins, Jim James, and John Davidson.

Unlike the McIlvain place, the majority of Bibb farms after the war did not require as many as nine sharecropping families to cultivate them, yet neither did most fall into the category of one-mule farms of forty acres. The U.S. census of 1870 lists the number of farms in the county according to their acreage:

81 under 50 acres
112 from 50 to 100 acres
75 from 100 to 500 acres
6 over 500 acres
None over 1,000 acres

Unimproved acres numbered 17,793, woodland 63,931, and U.S. government-owned 40,000 acres. The land being farmed had been diminished during the past decade partly because of the loss of a section on the east to the county of Chilton (originally Baker) when it was created by the legislature in 1868 from parts of Shelby, Autauga, and Bibb. The decline in cotton production was equally marked—from 8,303 in 1860 to 3,974 in 1870, afterward climbing by slow degrees to only 6,535 bales in 1900, according to the U.S. census for those decades. Other reasons accounted for this decrease besides the loss of land to Chilton. The remaining acreage was in many cases unproductive because of erosion resulting from lack of cultivation during the war or, in some instances, subsequent desertion by its impoverished owners. A U.S. Army engineer, while surveying the Cahaba River in the fall of 1874, reported the large area of untended land that was marked "old fields" on his map and commented that the neglect was "due to lack of prosperity."[3]

Emigration did not take as heavy a toll as in the 1840s, but the old pioneer instinct to look westward for a new start influenced several families. In the pioneer fashion in which country folk moved to new homes throughout the century, they loaded their household effects on wagons and drove their cattle with them. One of these families was the Woods clan of Six Mile, some of whose members settled in 1870 in a community called Liberty Hill in Bienville Parish, Louisiana. Frequent reports from F. G. Woods, former Bibb tax collector, appeared in the *Bibb Blade* in the 1880s. Oscar Woods wrote home on October 8, 1880, encouraging further emigration: "This is a poor man's Country the land is in reach of nearly every man improved land is worth one Dollar to five Dollars per acre." The only item that he considered expensive was mules, which sold

Typical moving day scene: The Deason family leaves in the 1890s for a new home in the county, Magnolia Deason and small niece on wagon with household goods, John Owens in charge of the three-yoke team of oxen, Mary Jane Deason tending her cows, which apparently are to be driven by two neighbors, Melford and Rufus Kornegay, mounted on mules. (Courtesy of Allie Dee Stewart)

for $135. But by 1891 he wrote a homesick letter, recalling the old trees around his boyhood home at Six Mile ("that olde Hickory below the gate, that spreading old Red Oake near the olde pine pile and that Big apple tree below the olde garden"), concluding: "Times is pretty hard here with a majority of the people corn is worth a dollar and hard to get."[4]

In an attempt to diversify the crops in worn-out cotton fields, Bibb farmers grew other products also. For example, in 1870, in addition to 3,974 bales of cotton, these included:

Indian corn	82,970 bushels	Potatoes	14,906 bushels
Wheat	6,826 bushels	Butter	7,395 pounds
Oats	13,645 bushels	Wool	3,934 pounds

The value of animals slaughtered was estimated at $273,777. Crops raised on a smaller scale were rye, sugarcane, rice, tobacco, and field peas.[5] Yet a ready market did not exist for all these other products, so the average farmer gave his efforts to cotton and continued to do so for the remainder of the century.

One of the cotton farmer's special problems, not new after the war, was that of transporting his bales to market. The beginning of railroads in the county in the 1850s had excited the hope of quick and easy access to the cotton market in Mobile, but the war put an end to their construction and Wilson's Raiders destroyed the fourteen miles of track already completed. Afterward, while the carpetbag government in Montgomery was plunging the state heavily into debt by underwriting bonds for the bankrupt roads, the Alabama and Tennessee Rivers Railroad was rebuilt through Randolph, along the eastern side of the county, as the Selma, Rome and Dalton, and the Alabama and Chattanooga was constructed across Bibb's northern corner in the mineral district.[6] Yet neither of these routes was convenient for the principal farming area, the southern section. Centreville (population 300) was fifteen rough miles from Randolph (population 200), and the river was easier to navigate than Soap Hill.

Another hope of the times was the conveyance of cotton by steamboat on the Cahaba. A steamboat, which could make the round trip after heavy rains had raised the river, could deliver freight to Selma, on the Alabama nineteen miles above the mouth of the Cahaba, and there make connections with the river traffic to Mobile. This dream of pioneer days received fresh encouragement when the U.S. government, under acts of Congress approved June 23, 1874, and June 17, 1880, conducted two surveys of the Cahaba.[7] The second of the reports, prepared by C. B. Percy, assistant engineer, U.S. Army Corps, on January 1, 1881, completed the full distance to Shades Creek on Bibb's northern boundary. Percy expected that improvement in the river would allow 50,000 bales of cotton to be shipped to Mobile, besides giving the shortest and most economical water route for the county's coal and iron to the Gulf.

Two steamboats, well remembered by older residents early in the present century, made successful voyages from Mobile to Centreville about this time. The tedious progress of the *Ella D.*, whose arrival was expected momentarily through the first months of 1880, was chronicled by the county newspaper week by week. Before New Year's Day, the footbridge across the Cahaba at Centreville had been removed to allow its passage.[8] On April 1 it was reported that the boat had been delayed for some time at Burrough's Landing because its engine was too weak to fight the current. Two weeks later, it was stranded on a sandbar near Jericho, not far below the Bibb County line in Perry. Finally, on April 29, a Centreville correspondent of the *Bibb Blade* wrote:

> On last Friday, the 23rd inst., about 2 o'clock p.m., our town was thrown into general confusion by the shrill whistle of the Ella D. several miles below the ferry. . . . There was a general tramping about in the cane to get aboard,

> and Capts. McNeal and Davidson could not stand this excitement but splashed in, and by hard swimming, boarded the Ella D. anyhow. This took place about ten miles below town, at Cooper's Island, and we learn that Messrs. Ed and J. P. Kennedy followed suit about three miles below the ferry, boarding her in like manner. The brass band, too, met the Ella D. about four miles below the ferry, and swimming the river, boarded her, and on the upper deck discoursed the sweetest music all the way to the wharf.
>
> . . . Capt. Verbeck started with a load of salt, but sold most of it before he got to Centreville. He also brought a great number of sacks, intending to buy cotton seed and ship to Selma and other points, but, having met with misfortune, he arrived too late for the cotton seed market. Capt. Verbeck says that he can carry 100 bales of cotton on board, and little work is required to make it an easy go from this point to Cahaba at low stage. . . .
>
> It is now shown beyond all doubt that the Cahaba River can be navigated by small boats. Centreville, by opening the Cahaba to navigation, could be made one of the best cotton markets in Middle Alabama, because cotton can be shipped from here to Selma or Mobile for about the same cost it takes to get it to any point on the railroad.[9]

The following year, the *Mary D.*, owned by Captain B. P. Mosely of Orrville, was more fortunate. Although its arrival at the Centreville wharf on February 11 was unexpected, it was well timed for the cotton market, for it would carry back a hundred bales, to be picked up between Centreville and Jericho. The *Mary D.* was estimated to be a hundred feet long, about twice the size of the *Ella D.* Like its sister ship, it brought a cargo of a hundred sacks of salt and and sold it all. Also like its predecessor, it offered citizens a Sunday afternoon excursion for a brief distance on the river, probably as in the case of the *Ella D.* with the passengers furnishing the wood for fuel.[10]

Several boats made unsuccessful attempts to navigate the Cahaba in the 1880s. One unidentified craft, described as a small stern-wheel boat of no capacity and having but few horsepower, was said to have endeavored to surmount the Centreville shoals but failed totally. Sandbars were the commonest hazard. On February 6, 1884, the *Bibb Blade* noted that Captain Sam Davidson's boat, the *Duke,* had finally been pulled off a sandbar and now lay in the water near it. The failure of the *Captain Sam* was more disastrous. Constructed by Twig Duke on the Davidson plantation, it was floated to Mobile, where its machinery was installed. But it never completed its return voyage. It, too, ran aground on a sandbar, and, when too much pressure was built up in an attempt to free it, the boiler exploded. At the time of the explosion, Captain English was holding his little daughter by the hand, but afterward, when he was rescued in an unconscious state, her body could not be found.[11]

Although this tragedy seems to have ended steamboating to Centreville, government-supported efforts to make the river safe for navigation continued until 1886 and were resumed for a period in the early 1890s. The sum of $28,989.79 was then spent on this project, but in the end it was frustrated by obstructing railroad bridges in Dallas County.[12]

Even while Bibb farmers continued to cherish the hope of shipping their cotton to market by steamboat, they were still relying on the pioneer method of transportation by flatboat. On the day before the *Mary D.* took a load of bales on board at Centreville, the *Bibb Blade* printed an account of a midwinter flatboat voyage as reported by one of the crew who had recently returned. This large craft apparently could accommodate nearly three times the cargo of the small steamboat:

> The flatboat left the mouth of Schultz Creek, where she was built, with 18 bales of cotton on board, purchased from Mr. E. P. Cruise and his sons. She had an easy run down to Centreville, where she took on about 60 bales, shipped by Messrs. J. D. Cooper, J. T. Avery, Stephen Price, and D. M. James....
>
> [We] dropped down to Dr. Moren's landing and tied up for the night. Here we took on 84 bales from Mr. J. S. Kennedy and some for Mr. Glass ... at Mr. Henry Parker's landing: nearly 60 bales from him, Mr. James and Mr. Peters....Capt. S. W. Davidson's landing—50 bales and six from Mr. H. H. Thompson—Total load 285 bales....
>
> Tied up for the night at the Goodson place.... Next night—after hard pulling at Flat Top Cypress Bend—camped at Coon's landing, opposite Jericho.[13]

The long narrative describes the difficulties of the voyage and names the members of both the white and black crews. After several days, they reached the town of Cahaba safely and from that point shipped the cotton by side-wheel steamer on the Alabama to Selma, accompanying it on board. The cost for this delivery was two dollars per bale, according to B. F. Glass's December advertisement of his projected flatboat trip "at the first rise."[14]

The Cahaba footbridge at Centreville, removed in expectation of the *Ella D.* in early 1880, provided the only crossing except by ferry and by ford after Wilson's Raiders had burned the bridge in April 1865. After the war, George W. Howard and Dr. E. H. Moren, owners of the bridge, established a ferry, run successively by B. F. Glass, Samuel Hall, and Abner Jones.[15] Citizens made a number of abortive attempts to obtain a new toll bridge. They began by reorganizing the Centreville Bridge Company on February 6, 1867.[16] The project was placed in the hands of Howard and Moren, but, for lack of the necessary funds, the act of incorporation was repealed on March 1, 1870, after which another act reorganized the company on February 25, 1871, only to be repealed for the same reason.[17] Bibb Countians continued to cross the Cahaba only by ferry and ford until 1885, when the iron and wood bridge authorized by the county commissioners court on February 25, 1877, and undertaken by an engineer, Major Belton Mickle, was finally completed.[18] It was still being operated as a toll bridge in the 1890s, and it was not replaced by a new structure until 1910.

Although postwar cotton farming, plagued by many problems, including transportation, could not reach the production standards of 1860 by the end of the century, industry fared somewhat better, at least for a time. It is true that it suffered from the demoralization of that era and especially from financial and transportation difficulties at the beginning of the period. Yet it eventually inspired the imagination of outside capitalists and attracted their investments. Although the numerous courageous experiments in iron production were destined to close by the early 1890s, by that time the lumber industry was getting underway and the coal mines were already making a name for the county.

The defeat of the Confederacy had sounded the death knell for most of Bibb's wartime industries, including the Scottsville mill[19] and the Little Cahaba, or Brighthope, Furnace, but the Brierfield ironworks was more fortunate. In 1869 this plant had the only iron foundry in the state that had been rebuilt and put back into operation; it could employ three hundred workers.[20] At the conclusion of hostilities, the federal government had seized the property as contraband of war, and General Wager Swayne, as assistant commissioner for Refugees, Freedmen, and Abandoned Lands, placed a military guard there commanded by a Captain Seaman until its future should be determined.[21] At the public auction in January 1866, its former owner, Colonel C. C. Huckabee, stood up and forbade the sale on the ground that, because Congress had set aside the acts of the Confederate government as null and void, that government could not have been the lawful owner of the property. His claim was not recognized, however, either at the auction or later when his lawsuit reached the U.S. Supreme Court, inasmuch as it was charged that he had used the works for hostility against the United States.[22]

General Josiah Gorgas, former chief of ordnance of the Confederacy, had other plans for the famous ironworks. This Pennsylvania native, who had married the daughter of an Alabama governor and become an ardent Southern convert, visited the plant in the fall of 1865, was favorably impressed by its extensive facilities in spite of their desolation at the time, and decided to buy it. After receiving permission from General Swayne to do so, he and eleven stockholders headed by Francis Strother Lyon formed the Canebrake Company. At the auction, this organization, with a combined capital of $95,000 and with $5,000 in reserve, purchased the wrecked ironworks and their approximately 5,000 acres for $45,000 and

Brierfield Furnace Number 2, as rebuilt after the Civil War. Photographed around 1905. (Courtesy of Martin Everse, director, Brierfield Ironworks Park)

placed Gorgas in charge. He immediately sent Giles Edwards, the Welsh ironmaster, to New York to buy machinery.[23] After expensive rebuilding by Edwards and many frustrations, Gorgas finally put Furnace Number Two in blast on November 2, 1866; the yield at first was only nine tons a day.[24] The adjacent earlier stone stack was not reopened after the war.[25]

In January 1867 Lyon deeded the property to the newly incorporated Brierfield Ironworks, of which Gorgas was named president. To finance this enterprise, Gorgas found it necessary to borrow $5,000 in the name of the company from his wife, Amelia Gayle Gorgas, who was issued a promissory note dated March 1, 1867.[26] Yet this loan by no means solved his problems. He had early estimated his expenses at $10,000 a month,[27] a sum that forced him to borrow until he eventually exhausted his credit. The Selma merchants were too weak financially to assist him. As he made his daily ride to the furnace, sometimes on a lame mule, sometimes on an obstinate white one, his mood alternated between delight in the climate and horror at the prospect of bankruptcy. By January 1868 he was hoping for "the assistance of some Northern men who can command money. We do not like this close association with even good Northerners," the native Pennsylvanian wrote, "but cannot now help it."[28]

Although Gorgas was disappointed in these hopes, he persevered in his struggle at Brierfield until 1869, plagued by high freight rates, difficulty in retaining labor, and too much competition. Then he gave up making pig iron and cotton ties to go into the field of education, nine years later becoming president of the University of Alabama. He leased the Brierfield works on August 2, 1869, to his ironmaster, Thomas Alvis, on the basis of three dollars a ton. Alvis, though beset by most of Gorgas's problems, operated the plant until the effects of the financial panic eventually closed it in the fall of 1873. Recalling the employment the plant had given to many natives, the *Bibb Blade* of January 20, 1881, on announcing an imminent reopening, spoke hopefully of the prospect of a return of the "flush times of 1870."

During the two decades after 1873, the Brierfield ironworks continued to inspire hope in new purchasers, each of whom enjoyed a degree of success for a time, though all their ventures ended in failure. More and more, they suffered from competition of coke-fueled plants in the Birmingham area, where it was said that red ore could be mined more cheaply than brown. William D. and Kearsley Carter of Louisville, Kentucky, bought the furnace in February 1881, later incorporating their organization with capital of $150,000 as the Bibb Furnace Company.[29]

Next a St. Louis railroad official, Major Thomas Peter, excited great expectations for several years after he assumed control in 1882. C. C. Huckabee and Robert McCalley were his associates in the Brierfield Coal and Iron Company, incorporated with capital of $750,000.[30] Major Peter rebuilt the furnace to a height of 55 feet with 12 feet in the bosh; remodeled the rolling mill; and erected a large nailery, coke ovens, and a washer. The nailery failed, however, when the iron cut nail began to be replaced on the market by the steel nail. But Major Peter was persistent. When he lost the works through foreclosure proceedings in 1888, he reorganized his company as the Alabama Iron and Steel Company and reacquired the property, two years later converting the operation back to charcoal. In 1894, the year after another financial panic, he lost the plant to the Southern Mineral Land Company, from which it was bought by Coosa River Newsprint, now known as Kimberly Clark. The furnace was blown out for the last time in 1894 and has never been operated again. Major Peter died two years afterward, apparently a victim of the strain he had undergone at Brierfield.[31] Now, almost a century later, the site of his labors has been transformed into the Brierfield Ironworks Park as a reminder of the role that Bibb County played in the early development of the state's iron industry.

While Major Peter was building up the Brierfield plant in the early 1880s, northern Bibb was experiencing industrial growth inspired by the coming of the Alabama and Chattanooga Railroad. The town of Green Pond owes its early existence to ore mines. A correspondent for this old farming community declared in 1881 that, though nine years earlier the village had no homes and only one business house, now it possessed eight business houses, one wood and iron shop, one flour and corn mill, and two ore mines, as well as a population of 300 people.[32]

The leading spirit of the boom in the Woodstock-Green Pond area was the remarkable Welshman Giles Edwards, who had rebuilt the Brierfield furnace for General Gorgas. Some years afterward, he and his wife settled at Woodstock, where he built his own blast furnace in a location convenient to the new railroad.[33] With Thomas Edwards and Henry DeBardeleben of Birmingham, he formed the Edwards Iron Company, declaring a capital investment of $60,000.[34] According to DeBardeleben, Edwards was not only a good ironmaster but also a geologist, engineer, and expert prospector. This versatile man also subscribed to a Welsh newspaper to the end of his life.[35] His coke furnace, with a stack 70 feet high and 15 feet in the bosh, was first blown in 1880 and was remodeled in 1887 and again in 1890. It used the red hematite ore of that area and in 1890 was reported to possess an annual capacity of 30,000 tons, more than double the tonnage declared by Brierfield.[36] But, like the Brierfield ironworks, it was a casualty of the economic depression of the early 1890s. Edwards himself did not survive that depression, for he died in 1892.[37]

While the iron industry was making a brave struggle, the lumber mills, destined to become the principal business by the middle of the twentieth century, were developing throughout the county. The new Alabama and Chattanooga, today the Southern Railway, was responsible for opening up the timber industry in the heavily forested area of northern Bibb. Probably the first large sawmill in the county was the one W. C. Stewart moved from Ohio to Green Pond in December 1870. Even before Giles Edwards, he brought much-needed employment to this section during the financially depressed Reconstruction period. As an emigrant from a state north of the Mason-Dixon line, Stewart was not popular with everyone at this sensitive time. James H. Green, the large landowner in "Kingdom Beat" who was called "Squire Green," attacked the newcomer in these lines:

> We caution all men to beware,
> For them to have the utmost care,
> For there lives at Green Pond Station
> The vilest man in all creation.
> This old man is a teacher;
> He eats with his Negro brother preacher.[38]

Another citizen, Dr. J. U. Ray, appreciated Stewart more keenly. In 1872, after Ray had bought a large body of land from Green on which to relo-

Bob Hayes's general store, Woodstock. The second story was used for a rooming house. Photographed around 1900. (Courtesy of Thomas W. Burns)

cate Woodstock on the railroad, he persuaded Stewart to move his mill there. Ray first built a post office and then a railroad station, both with lumber from the Stewart mill. Perhaps discouraged by the financial panic of 1873, the Ohio mill owner moved two years later to the new industrial town of Birmingham, founded in 1871. But other sawmills were established, including three operated at nearby Bibbville by Ben Farrah, a Virginian, and one at Day's Crossing, a mile south of Ashby, by Andrew Jackson Day. James Hogan, the principal merchant of Bibbville, was also engaged in the manufacture of lumber and brick.

The first sawmill in the county to use steam power was built about 1880 near the Selma, Rome, and Dalton tracks at Randolph by another Virginian, Captain J. B. Howison. He sold it to his brother, Major A. P. Howison, who had emigrated to Bibb in 1876 and, unlike the captain, settled here permanently. Both brothers were fleeing the family's war-devastated plantation.[39] By his investments in timber acreage, Major Howison became one of the largest landowners in this section of the state. He expanded his sawmill and added others. The rough lumber manufactured in these early mills was planed by hand until 1884, but in that year the major revolutionized the local lumber industry by introducing a mechanical planer.[40]

Along with the sawmills, brick works also prospered, especially on the northern and eastern edge of the county. Late in the century, these included two near Ashby, one that had been established before the Civil War by William Gee Oakley and another after the war by a Northerner named Earker. All their wood molds were filled with clay by hand before it was cured by the heat of the kilns. A related industry of this busy railroad community was the Ashby Clay Company, operated after the end of the century by Clay McPherson Day, who shipped fire clay to Birmingham to line the blast furnaces. Also by the 1890s Cox Station possessed a charcoal-burning industry that shipped charcoal to the Rock Run Iron Company, north of Anniston. Numerous black wood-choppers were employed to provide fuel for around twenty ovens.

Yet none of these industries of the last decades of the nineteenth century made as much impact as the coal mines in the northern section of the county. For half a century after 1880, they were to bring new life and hope.

16

THE COAL-MINING TOWNS

COAL WAS DISCOVERED early in Bibb, reportedly in "the year the stars fell," 1831. Although for many years afterward strip mining helped to supply fuel for the local ironworks and refugees from Mississippi opened shallow underground mines for Confederate coal, not until the 1880s did coal mining become a major industry. It brought dynamic changes to an area where, according to a Six Mile Academy student, "not many years ago our fathers plodded along behind the lazy ox or the more sprightly horse between the plow handles, not dreaming of the wealth that lay beneath their feet."[1] For half a century, the coal mines stimulated prosperity and population growth in the northern part of the county. The numerous ghost towns and the still active municipality of West Blocton are testimony today to the erstwhile impact of this industry.

By 1880 prospectors had come to the rugged hills of northern Bibb searching for coal to fuel the burgeoning iron and steel mills in the new city of Birmingham. They soon located rich seams in what became known as the Blocton and Dailey Creek basins, the latter extending into Shelby County. In 1890 the Blocton Basin, of which Blocton became the center, was 18 miles long, averaged 5¼ miles wide, and its surface totaled 94½ square miles.[2] Among its several workable seams, the Underwood, or Thompson, was one of the richest. It was reported to contain, about 6 feet underground, "a solid bench of five and a half feet of good quality well suited to coking, steam, or domestic purposes."[3] Nearby, the Woodstock, or Gholson, seam averaged 3½ feet of similar quality and offered the advantage of a good roof, a large area of which around Blocton was nearly level.

Four men who saw the possibilities in these heavily wooded hills formed the Cahaba Coal and Mining Company. Signing a petition of incorporation at Woodstock on June 27, 1883, they were Truman and W. F. Aldrich of New York State and Cornelius Cadle, Jr., and Charles Turner, both new residents of Selma. These four were later joined by W. S. Gurnee of New York State. They declared a capital stock of one million dollars, composed of 10,000 shares of $100 each.[4] After purchasing large acreage from Henry DeBardeleben of Birmingham, they dropped their slopes and built a railroad nine miles long to connect their first center of operations with the Alabama Great Southern Railroad (the old Alabama and Chattanooga) at Woodstock. A newspaper announcement headed Gresham and dated February 10, 1884, declared: "The road is now complete, and the company expect to ship coal tomorrow. . . . This place has near 200 inhabitants at present. . . . This bids fair to become another Magic City."[5]

Mines Number 1, 2, and 3 were opened in rapid succession, the first located near the old Blocton railroad depot; the second near Primitive Ridge road, behind the company's commissary; and the third near what was to be called "Dago Hollow," more politely "Little Italy." It is said that the name Blocton, rather than Gresham, was first applied to this mining community by Truman Aldrich when the Number 2 mine produced a block of coal that weighed a ton. (The spelling Blockton has sometimes been used.) By April 23, 1886, Truman Aldrich and Cornelius Cadle, Jr., were giving their address as Blocton, and W. H. Aldrich was listed as a resident of Aldrich.[6] In March 1884 a post office had been established at the Blocton mines and Cornelius Cadle, Jr., appointed as postmaster.[7]

By 1890 seven mines had been opened in the Woodstock and Underwood seams in the Blocton area and a coke oven plant constructed. Numbers 4, 5, and 6 were located on the old Woodstock road and Number 7, one of the largest, near Number 2. The company's mines at both Blocton and Gurnee, across the line in Shelby, had by this time reached a daily capacity of 4,000 tons, exceeded in the state only by the Tennessee Coal, Iron, and Railroad Company's operation at Pratt Mines and Blossburg. The coke ovens numbered 467, and the daily capacity was 600 tons.[8] Shortly afterward, when the Cahaba Company was merged with the large T.C.I. in 1892, expansion of Bibb mines was accelerated, three more slopes being added by 1899, all in proximity to the earlier ones. Number 10 was the last T.C.I. mine opened in Bibb. All these operations were slopes except Number 5, which was a shaft.

The State Inspector of Mines, in his first biennial report at the end of 1894, briefly described four of the T.C.I. mines in Bibb, the only ones that were then working "on account of the dullness of the market and possibly great competition."[9] Slope Number 1, in the Woodstock seam, was driven to the greatest depth, 3,000 feet. Each mine was ventilated by a large fan, twenty feet in diameter except in Number 5, the shaft operation, which was cooled by a ten-foot machine. Each of the slopes employed about 250

Beehive coke ovens, crude structures of stone and earth, at Tennessee Coal and Iron Company's Blocton mines. (Courtesy of Charles E. Adams)

men, but 11 workers were sufficient for the shaft. J. G. Moore was superintendent of the mines.

The company built many facilities for the employees on its Blocton property, including residences for the workers and superintendent; a commissary; school; churches; and eventually a hospital. Only nine of these company buildings remain today, all except one the rental property of the Black Diamond Coal Company. They are the former superintendent's house, now owned and occupied by the David Picketts, and two large and six small workers' houses.

The miners who settled in northern Bibb added variety and color to the county's hitherto fairly homogeneous population. They came not only from this region but also from states as far north as Iowa and from such European countries as Belgium, Italy, Austria, Hungary, and Bulgaria. Some, like the Young and Hillman families, native Pennsylvanians who had emigrated to Blocton by 1888, were seasoned miners. Others, including many Europeans, were novices seeking to better their economic situation. Usually the European men preceded their families and lived in

T.C.I. Company school at Blocton, surrounded by company cottages for the miners. (Courtesy of Charles E. Adams)

stockades on the company ground in Number 3 Town until they had worked long enough to reimburse the managers for their boat fare. Most of them could not speak English at first. When the now-lost 1890 U.S. census for Bibb County was taken, it was necessary for an Italian boy to accompany the census reporter as an interpreter.[10]

Some of these immigrants later laughed about their difficulties. John Samsel declared that he ate ham and eggs in the restaurant until he grew weary of them because they were the only English words he knew. When

"Little Italy," residential and business community of immigrant miner families near Number 3 Mine, Blocton. Photographed by Albert Lebourg. (Courtesy of Charles E. Adams)

these mine workers had not only paid their ocean passage but also accumulated enough cash to purchase tickets for their families, their wives and children followed. Because they, too, usually knew no English, they were sometimes tagged in the manner of Mrs. Rosa Bodnar, who wore this label around her neck: "Deliver to Charles Bodnar, Blocton, Alabama, U.S.A."

These hardy adventurers in a foreign land met a certain degree of hostility on occasion, partly because their religion as well as their language were alien to Bibb. Most of them were professed Roman Catholics in a staunchly Protestant region. On at least one occasion an immigrant family was refused the use of a local church for a child's burial. These Catholics were later allowed their own sanctuary and a graveyard, still called the Catholic Cemetery. As a result of many differences in customs with the natives, they soon drew together for mutual comfort and formed their own community near the Number 3 mine, where most of them worked. In the hollow below present-day Smith Hill and on the opposite hillside, they created a settlement that their American neighbors soon dubbed "Dago Town."[11] Half a century ago, this extensive area was still covered with houses, but in the 1980s the hillside is heavily wooded again. Even Albano Ferrire's large combination store and residence, the last

French immigrant photographer Albert Lebourg on motorcycle in front of his portable tent studio at Marvel. (Courtesy of Charles E. Adams)

ghost on the hill above "Dago Street," has now collapsed.

Miners once operated thriving businesses here, among them Narcisso Nucci's general store and his wife's boarding house, patronized in the early years chiefly by miners whose families had not yet joined them. The newly married Nuccis had come to Blocton in the 1880s from the French island of Corsica, though both of them were originally Italian. They joined with several neighbor families in the community practice of sharing an outdoor oven for baking bread. In 1983 the Nuccis's daughter, Mary Nucci Cinelli, was still a resident of West Blocton, and Albano Ferrire's son, Frank, was its longtime mayor.

In 1903, the year of the Blocton tornado, a disastrous flood also ravaged the Italian community. It swept along the creek-bordered street and destroyed several combination business and residential houses, as reported by the local newspaper:

> Part of [D. Costenallo's] house, occupied by a store house, living upstairs, with all his goods and household goods were completely washed off and his family just escaped in time to save themselves.

> The next in line was S. Costelli, his store and contents was afloat. The porch to his store was carried away and lodged against Joe Maera's store. . . .
> A very pathetic scene: a beautiful little girl with black hair and eyes who could talk the English language well weeping over the loss of her pet organ.[12]

By this first decade of the twentieth century, the Italians had formed a social and literary club, which they called the Prosperity Society of Blocton. The enterprising immigrants who found a certain degree of prosperity in the Blocton mines have now long since passed from the scene, but the picturesque names of many of their descendants remain in the county.

In an attempt to find cheap and adequate labor, T.C.I. not only imported foreigners but also contracted with the state for convict workers. On January 3, 1888, the president of the State Board of Inspectors of Convicts signed an agreement to hire exclusively to T.C.I. at these monthly rates: $18 for first-class convicts, $13.50 for second-class convicts, $9.00 for third-class convicts, and maintenance for fourth-class convicts.[13] In the early years, the company sent the prisoners only to the Pratt Mines, where in 1893–94 they were operating one shaft and two slopes.[14] By the turn of the century, however, in spite of the protests of other labor, convicts were shipped to two of the newest mines in Bibb County: Lucille and Belle Ellen. The procedure of turning convicted men over directly from the county jail soon became routine. The *Centreville Press* of September 9, 1900, noted: "Eighteen prisoners convicted at the recent term of the circuit and county courts were transferred to the mines on Tuesday."

Prisoners were hurried off to this difficult and dangerous life for a variety of law violations. On June 12, 1913, the *Press* observed: "Two negroes just convicted in county court, one for petit larceny, the other for defamation of character, were taken at once to the mines to serve out their sentences." During World War I, the Lucile and Belle Ellen mines depended more than ever on this readily available labor. The conditions under which the inmates lived encouraged manslaughter. In reporting such an event, the *Press* commented: "This is the third murder of convict by a fellow convict in Bibb in the past year."[15]

Child labor played a part, too. The miners were often accompanied down the dark slopes by their young sons because the managers would employ any boy old enough to shovel coal. Richard Moore, still a resident of West Blocton in 1982, began his lifelong mining career in 1907 at the age of thirteen. The hours were long—from six in the morning until four or five in the afternoon. Except during World War I, however, the mines frequently operated no more than two days a week.

Belle Ellen band, sponsored by the mine owners, Bessemer Coal, Iron and Land Company, whose president was L. E. Bruns. (Courtesy of Charles E. Adams)

Some people played on the superstition and naiveté of the men who spent long days underground. In 1908 a boy heard a patent medicine salesman make the following pitch in front of a drugstore in Blocton while displaying several jars purportedly containing tapeworms preserved in wood alcohol: "You men who have to go down into the bowels of the earth to make your living probably have a tape worm like this in your stomach at this minute which is sapping your energy. . . . [This medicine at fifty cents a bottle] will make a new person of you."[16]

The methods of mining were crude by modern standards. Walter Gardner, Jr., who worked in the Piper and Coleanor mines for more than forty years, gives this account of the work as he knew it: "The coal was mined in what was called rooms and walls. A coal-digger was given a room, which usually followed a seam of coal off the mine slope, and he was more or less his own boss. The company paid him a fixed price for each ton of coal he mined, and from this pay he had to furnish his tools and powder. He was also responsible for any timbering necessary to make his room safe and to lay track as it was needed in the room. . . . Several mules were driven in the mine each day to pull the coal cars around inside."[17]

Frequent accidents occurred. Gas explosions were numerous, especially in Numbers 2 and 7, and some were fatal. For example, in the two deaths reported to the state in 1893, Til West was suffocated by gas in a fire on February 14 and R. L. Sims was killed by an explosion on June 22.[18] The miners suffered injuries from a variety of other causes also. The *Blocton Messenger* of March 13, 1903, under the headline "A Bad Day in the Mines," reported: "An Italian got so badly injured in No. 3 mine Wednesday that his leg had to be taken off at once. A boy working in No. 2 mine received a severe injury Wednesday. His arm and shoulder are said to have been broken. Wednesday morning Mr. Jim Dykous was so seriously injured that his right leg had to be amputated immediately.... A large rock fell on his leg crushing it.... Just the day before Mr. Dykous had been injured in the face."

Such accidents resulted in demands for more and better safety measures and, in consideration of the danger, higher wages. Three weeks after recounting the incident of Bob Davidson's becoming paralyzed from rock fall in the Number 2 mine,[19] the local editor, an avowed supporter of labor unions, declared: "The coal miner's wages shouldn't be measured by other classes of labor. The miner risks his life as no other man does. In the morning when he enters the dark hole that carries him away from the light of the world, he knows he is risking his life."[20] At this time, Alabama miners were in session in Birmingham, trying to wrest a more favorable contract from the operators.

The labor union movement reached Blocton in 1894, during the economic depression that drastically reduced miners' wages and those of labor in general. The United Mine Workers encouraged the strike of 1894, which closed T.C.I.'s Pratt mines in Birmingham and eventually its Blocton mines. Numbers 1, 2, 3, and 5 were in operation for part of 1894 but produced little more than half the tonnage of coal that they had the preceding year.[21] This strike, like all others before 1934, failed to bring the benefits the miners hoped for. On April 30, 1896, the editor of the *Blocton Times*, after lamenting the cheapness of labor because of the scarcity of money, noted sympathetically: "The miners in the employ of T.C.I. and R.R. Co. have to suffer a cut of 2½¢ per ton." In that year, the local union received attention and support from a national leader, Eugene V. Debs, who spoke twice to large audiences at the tabernacle in Blocton.[22] By 1900, under the presidency of W. R. Young, Local Number 20 of the United Mine Workers of America was expanding rapidly.

The major strikes in the Bibb mines included not only the summer-long walkout of 1894 but also the strikes of 1904, 1908, and 1920. The 1908 demonstration incited the most violence. When union workers heard that T.C.I. was importing foreign strikebreakers from Birmingham, they dug up crossties on the Louisville and Nashville Railroad tracks near Ashworth Crossing, some three miles from Blocton, to stop the train. They fired into the last two passenger coaches, where they had been notified to expect the strikebreakers. A miner injured his foot by dropping a crosstie on it, thus providing involuntary evidence that was used against his local union in the legal case that followed. Litigation about this incident, in which those arrested were referred to in the press as "the foreigners," was not completed until the following spring. Then it was reported by the *Press* on March 4: "The jury in the case of Boresa Melita, after being out three hours, returned a verdict of guilty and set his punishment of life imprisonment. This is the third of the prisoners that have been tried for shooting up the Blocton train, and all have been found guilty and given life sentences. There are some five or six more charged with the same crime. . . . The state we understand has offered to let the balance plead guilty and receive a sentence of five years."

Around the turn of the century, other mines were established both in and around Blocton. Howell and Jones, fresh from their success in the gold rush of 1897–98 in the Klondyke region of northwestern Canada, sank a shaft on rented T.C.I. property between Smith Hill and McCulley Hill and called it Klondyke. They connected it to "Dago Town" by means of a track laid in the summer of 1903.[23] John Milner opened the Hill Creek mine in West Blocton in 1908 and sold it in 1914 to E. D. Reynolds, W. R. Young, and others.

The *Blocton Messenger,* declaring that no coal was better known abroad than that from Blocton, proclaimed: "These rugged picturesque hills that a few years ago were peopled only by birds and mountain violets are being rapidly covered with pretty mining towns, so new that they smell of the rosin and white wash brush."[24] In another issue, it said, "Many coal mines are in operation, one of the largest in the state now sinking within three miles of Blocton, four slopes and many more contemplated."[25] The names of these numerous mining communities outside Blocton, now ghost towns, make a musical roll call: Belle Ellen, Lucille, Piper, Coleanor, Garnsey, Galloway, Marvel, Moffatt, Masena, Braehead, and many others.

Two of the most prosperous were the twin towns of Piper and Coleanor. Piper was established in 1901 and named for O. H. R. Piper of Memphis, later of Birmingham, who was instrumental in forming the Little Cahaba Coal Company.[26] The mines at nearby Coleanor (Coal-Eleanor), opened shortly before, were owned by the Blocton Cahaba Coal Company, headed in 1901 by Fred M. Jackson. In 1905 the Little Cahaba Coal Company purchased its rival company and J. R. Smith became president, Walter E. Henley vice-president, and Ben J. Sherrod secretary.[27] The new management built tracks from Piper to Coleanor, to which point the Southern Railway had already extended its line. The two towns grew rapidly, eventually reaching a population of approximately 2,500, including some 500 employees of the mines.

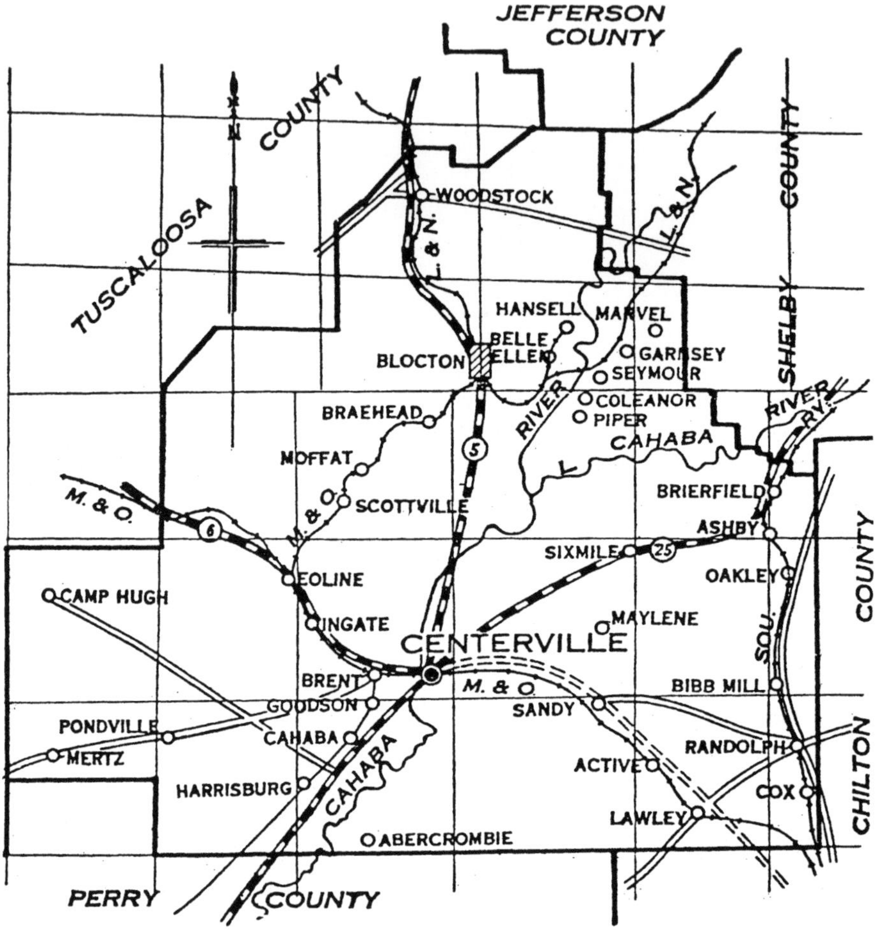

Map of Bibb County during coal-mining era. (Reproduced from an old newspaper print by courtesy of William T. Ogletree)

On the now largely vacant grounds, there stood at this time three churches, a school, three boardinghouses, a barber shop, and offices for a dentist and two physicians, besides more than 500 residences.[28] B. M. Thompson, secretary of the Little Cahaba Coal Company in 1916, recalled that the first postmaster of Piper was J. P. Melvin, the first physician Dr. E. M. Prince, the first merchant John W. Porter, the first preacher Reverend B. T. Cantrell of the Methodist Church, and the first schoolteacher Mrs. A. E. Jemison.[29]

The fastest-growing town in Bibb during the coal-mining era was West

Tipple at Coleanor mine, photographed by Albert Lebourg. Postcard. (Courtesy of Charles E. Adams)

Blocton, the business and residential community adjoining the Blocton mines. West Blocton was first informally called Suttletown, in honor of Julian LaFayette (Fate) Suttle, a native of Sandy, in the southern part of the county, who reportedly established the first business there. In 1889 he formed a partnership with E. N. Cottingham, and in 1892 this firm was dealing in general merchandise and mining supplies.[30] The first house in Suttletown is said to have been a log structure near the present Baptist Church. This area, like the T.C.I. mines, was originally served by the Blocton post office, whose first postmaster was W. L. Pratt, a native of River Bend. Pratt lost the office to C. C. Collier in 1896, when Republican William McKinley succeeded Democrat Grover Cleveland in the U.S. presidency, but Pratt was shortly afterward elected as probate judge, a position he held for most of the rest of his life.

Businesses multiplied in Suttletown through the 1890s in spite of the economic recession. Bibb's first bank, the Blocton Savings Bank, was established in the fall of 1892 (five years before the Bibb County Banking and Trust Company at the county seat), with Irby Morgan, Jr., as president and J. B. Wadsworth as cashier.[31] Many citizens, like William A. Douthit, quickly shifted from one type of enterprise to another. Douthit, a native of Tuscaloosa County, was one of the earliest settlers, arriving in 1883 as the Cahaba Coal and Mining Company was sinking its first slopes. He soon opened a hotel and a bakery, but by 1892 he had sold these and was running a general store.[32]

Most merchants operated general stores, though advertising only one or two departments. Among those advertising at "Suttletown, West Blocton" in 1896 were C. E. Ballard, whose ice cream parlor prided itself on stocking the flavor "phosph ferrone"; F. Hutton, groceries; T. W. McCool, groceries; L. Levine, dry goods; Sachs Brothers, dry goods and clothing. R. H. Hubbard's livery stable claimed to possess "the best buggies, hacks and teams in Blocton." Hubbard had competition from David Frazier, formerly of Centreville, who had opened a similar business in 1892.[33] Dan Belcher operated a meat market, T. V. Quinn advertised as a photographer and John O. Quinn and John Reindel as "tonsorial artists." Suttletown's dentist was Dr. J. I. Logan, and its lawyers were T. S. Dark; R. M. Pendleton, J. M. and B. F. McMaster; Campbell and Thomas; and William J. Bethea, whose partner was W. H. Wright of Birmingham.

All these solicitors of business appealed to the new community through the columns of Guy B. Hard's *Blocton Times.* This newly named successor of his *Intelligencer* was preceded in Blocton journalism by both the *Labor Advocate,* established March 1890, editor unknown, and the *Blocton Courier,* founded in November 1891, edited by Thomas McCumber. *Times* Editor Hard noted, almost as an aside, that the war in Cuba continued, but, like his readers, he felt more interest in the competition between the Blocton baseball club and its rivals. He celebrated its triumphs over Selma, Aldrich, and other towns and applauded the Cadle Silver Cornet Band, which accompanied the team.[34] This baseball team was composed chiefly of railroad employees and was a member of the Southern League of Birmingham.

The rapidly expanding town was incorporated in 1901 as West Blocton, a name that had been preferred by some citizens as early as 1896. Eugene D. Reynolds became its first mayor, assisted by the *Blocton Messenger*'s editor, George D. Rice, as town clerk. By 1903 a number of residents were vying for seats on the town council in a race that was concluded with Dr. L. E. Peacock and Isaac Krentzman (the latter only twenty-five years old) leading the ticket. According to the *Messenger,* the firm of Collier, Glover, and Arnold had opened its law offices and Dr. George W. Randall his office of dentistry. J. H. Deason was offering his services as contractor and builder, and H. C. and W. B. Reynolds had established their general store. T. C. Tuggle, who was to become Bibb's chief photographer, had made a trip to Centreville to take pictures of the new courthouse. The town, full of new faces, attracted business and professional men from all over the county and outside it.

In such a booming community, surrounded by the heterogeneous elements employed in the mines, the mayor and his council were faced with many problems, especially that of preserving order and safety. One com-

Main Street, West Blocton, with kerosene street lamp in foreground, 1909. Some sixty businesses are said to have been located on this street in 1920. Postcard. (Courtesy of Mrs. Effie Ray)

paratively minor difficulty was posed by the popularity of the bicycle, a new phenomenon. Eventually it was deemed necessary to protect pedestrians from its speed on the streets by passing this ordinance: "Be it ordained by the Mayor and Councilmen of West Blocton that any person who rides a Bicycle on the streets . . . at a greater rate of speed than Three Miles an hour, shall on conviction for each offense be fined not less than *One Cent* nor more than *Ten Dollars* or may be imprisoned in the Town Jail or sentenced to Hard Labor for the town. . . . Approved March 3 1903."[35]

Some other encroachments on law and order were more serious. It was not unusual to read among the local newspaper "personals" such an item as "Albert Gilbert, victim of knife stabbing by Tom Thompson of Braehead, is recuperating."[36] The area was known for its frontier violence, frequently growing out of poker games and drunken fights. The court dockets were crowded with cases from the mining communities. A cry was early raised for a term of county court to be held regularly in the Blocton area for the convenience of this part of Bibb. In April 1896 merchant R. B. Wright announced with satisfaction: "Bibb County has leased the second story of the Wright Store House West End Suttletown West Blocton. Court convenes the first Monday in February, April, June, August, October, and December. April and December are regular jury terms. Just downstairs you will find R. B. Wright with a full line of general merchandise."[37] By January 1903 application had been made for a branch of circuit court at West Blocton,[38] granted by July of that year.

The number of murder cases involving citizens of this section in two months of this one year gives evidence of the need for such an arrangement. The *Blocton Messenger* observed: "Our jail is yet full of murderers, though several cases have been disposed of."[39] Some of these crimes reflected the racial tensions of the period. At a time when Deputy Sheriff A. P. Davidson was being tried for killing a black man while making an arrest and William Horton of Belle Ellen was taken into custody for murdering another black named William Cross "for insolence," the *Messenger* called attention sharply to the desirability of more even-handed justice in the courts: "Crimes in Bibb County and especially Blocton have been numerous. But the juries have been as remiss as the people. At the last term of court, every negro was convicted. No white man was convicted."[40] Among the black defendants convicted was Ed Walker, charged with the robbery and murder of Mrs. Castelli and sentenced to hang on April 11, 1903, in "the second legal hanging in Bibb in fifty years."[41]

Yet the most sensational of the Blocton murder cases had nothing to do with race. It gained notoriety partly because it involved two women apparently caught up in an age-old triangle. Mrs. Lilly Gardner allegedly killed Mrs. Mamie Caddell on May 29, 1900, but the case dragged on for more than three years. The *Blocton Messenger* on March 27, 1902, again questioned the justice of the courts: "Why was not the case against Mrs. Lilly Gardner called? . . . She has never yet been tried. She is claimed to be insane. . . . Festus Caddell, who is alleged to be an accessory to the killing of his wife by Mrs. Gardner, has been tried twice. . . . [His case] has been appealed to the Supreme Court for the second time. . . . If the deed was committed by Mrs. Gardner during a moment of frenzy and insanity (as she says, unaided by Caddell), why is the case not disposed of legally?"

When Mrs. Gardner, pleading insanity, was finally tried in the fall term of circuit court the following year, in one of the first murder cases in the new county courthouse in Centreville, she was represented by a battery of legal talent: Colonel Sam Will John of Birmingham, Dan Collier of Tuscaloosa, and the firm of Ellison and Thompson of Centreville. The county seat was crowded with witnesses and spectators for this long-awaited event. The *Messenger* commented that the case had already cost the county thousands of dollars. On September 25, 1903, it reported Mrs. Gardner's acquittal. Festus Caddell, meanwhile, had been meted out a life sentence in the state penitentiary.

In the first decade of the new century, the town continued to experience a population explosion, reaching a total of 892 inhabitants by 1910, when

Centreville could count only 730 and the only other Bibb municipality whose residents were numerous enough to be noted by the U.S. census was West Blocton's neighbor Smith Hill, with 422. Although its citizens were momentarily diverted by the courtroom dramas of the period, they were more concerned with providing the facilities needed by their community. Telephone wires were extended from Centreville in the spring of 1903, after connections with Birmingham had already been established.[42]

But the improvement most agitated for by the local newspaper was the establishment of a public school. "The Town Council has decided that we can no longer go without a school," the editor wrote approvingly. "West Blocton is on record as the only incorporated town in Alabama that has neither church, school, nor postal service of any kind, though all three institutions are less than a mile from town."[43] A bond issue funded the erection of a two-story structure, containing three classrooms, the principal's office, and a cloakroom. In this building, the West Blocton Public School opened on September 10, 1903, with an enrollment of 132 pupils, presided over by Principal A. E. Handley of Gurley. He was assisted by Lula Almon of Moulton in the intermediate department and Mrs. Edward Martin in the primary department. Some of the leaders in this civic movement formed the first board of trustees: F. D. Smith, E. D. Reynolds, Joseph F. Jones, T. C. Wallace, and A. L. Arnold.

Churches soon followed. The first house of worship in the corporate limits of the town is said to have been the synagogue of the considerable Jewish community, the only one of any size in the county, numbering more than twenty families. Most of these families, drawn to the boom town by its commercial opportunities, were refugees from persecutions in Russian-dominated countries, chiefly Poland, though also, in the case of the Krentzmans, Lithuania. Some of these immigrants, like William (Wolf) Israel, were in West Blocton in 1892. Many began business as peddlers but eventually set up general merchandise stores on West Blocton's Main Street. The Hebrew congregation *Ah-Goodies-Ah-Chem* (translated "League of Brothers") was organized on June 5, 1905, accepting the bylaws prepared by a committee composed of Morris M. Odess, Samuel B. Israel, and John B. Krentzman, three young merchants.[44] The building committee, whose members were William Israel, John Krentzman, and Samuel Baer, purchased Lot Number 25 from A. D. Belcher for $100 by a deed filed in the Bibb County Probate Office on July 6, 1905. The synagogue erected on this lot on September 1905 at a cost of around $1,500[45] was a frame building consisting of a sanctuary and a classroom for the children, in which they were taught, among other subjects, Hebrew. Around 1935 it fell into disuse, as the fortunes of the town and the number of Jewish residents declined, and the structure has not survived.

St. Francis Roman Catholic Church and several Protestant facilities had risen on the T.C.I. mining property, but in 1912 the Baptists erected a house of worship within the limits of the new town. Twenty former members of the Blocton First Baptist Church provided the "arm" that created this new congregation.[46] Its first pastor was Frank Willis Barnett, later editor of the *Alabama Baptist.* The Blocton Cumberland Presbyterian Church, created in 1892 by the Green Pond congregation of the same faith, continued to serve West Blocton Presbyterians, but the Methodists, who had first built in the Number 2 Town in 1886, moved their congregation to Number 1 Town, Blocton, in 1900.

West Blocton was now on its way to establishing its own identity, profiting from its proximity to the T.C.I. (later U.S. Steel) mines but living under its own independent government and served by its own institutions. Neither the tornado of 1903, the flood of 1916, nor the much more disastrous fire of July 12, 1927, could hold it back for long. Only the withdrawal of T.C.I. in 1928 began West Blocton's decline from its position as the most prosperous town in the county, Bibb's Magic City. However, unlike most of the other communities that grew up around the mines, it had the vitality to continue on its own power and to remain the chief population center in the northern part of the county when the coal-mining era had passed.

17

THE TURBULENT 1890s

THE 1880s WERE largely uneventful outside the industrial regions of eastern and northern Bibb, and, except for a rare steamboat whistle, time seems almost to have stood still in the county seat. The 1890s, however, brought exciting new events and trends that affected the entire county. These appeared in such diverse areas as crime, politics, and transportation.

Early in the decade, the pioneer violence that had survived in the county came to a traumatic culmination. For some time, organized bands of robbers had operated, mostly unapprehended, and by the 1890s had fostered the name "Bloody Bibb." This epithet is said to have been originated by a newcomer, Frank Connelly, who established the *State Central Express* in Centreville in March 1891. He followed this weekly newspaper in 1895 with the *County Press,* which he published in the Centreville office of the old *Bibb Blade* (founded in 1879 in Six Mile and recently discontinued) and which its subsequent owners, S. F. and L. H. Nunnelee renamed the *Centreville Press.* The epithet was apparently common by October 20, 1892, when Editor S. M. Adams of the *People's Reflector* headed a political article "Bloody and Lawless Bibb."

The most feared gang was that led by Jesse Miller, owner of a twelve-mule farm southeast of Scottsville. Many are the tales told of its daring deeds, some of which after a century have taken on elements of folklore. According to these stories, Jesse Miller and his brother-in-law Peter Dover masterminded the robberies, but in many cases their stooges carried out the evil work. These stooges included both white and black tenants of Miller, and perhaps others. An open letter from an indignant citizen of Scottsville, who signed himself "A Sufferer," lists some of the thefts that were perpetrated in that community.

> Three years ago W. L. Gray's house was broken into by a gang of thieves and $75 worth of goods stolen.
>
> About a year ago a saddle was stolen from the same premises and found in the possession of John Kirkland, a tenant of Jesse Miller.
>
> Three weeks ago a rifle stolen as above was found in the possession of an innocent man and traced to Henry Smith, also a tenant of Jesse Miller. About two or three months ago Edmond Parker's house was broken open and his cotton carried away and traced to Jesse Miller's premises; but the crowning infamy is that this infernal gang of thieves should stoop so low as to rob a poor old widow with a family of small children.
>
> For the last two or three years cattle, swine, sheep, goats and other livestock has disappeared as by magic; we all know what has become of them, but to catch them in the act, "that is the question."[1]

The robbers' chief objectives were cattle and cotton, which they usually tried to take out of the county as quickly as possible. Once when a neighboring farmer, E. P. Burt, was absent from home, the thieves herded cattle into his barn lot temporarily, but the scheme failed when a mob from Blocton threatened Miller.[2] According to tradition, one farmer marked his cotton with pine splinters, which identified it when members of the gang brought it to the Harrisburg gin. Jesse Miller's plots were seldom frustrated, however. He was especially adept at stealing cotton, usually by means of an accomplice. It is said that a black man whom he employed for this purpose always wrapped his wagon wheels in kroker sacks to muffle their noise.[3]

Yet Miller could perform the trick well enough himself. On one occasion, after he had delivered a load of corn as payment for his daughter's tuition and her room and board at the home of the Centreville principal, where she resided during the school term, this ingratiating farmer paid a social call on the principal on his front porch. Then, after taking his leave at dusk, he quietly reclaimed the wagonload of corn from his host's crib on his way home.[4]

In spite of all the circumstantial evidence of their robberies, it was only after the gang members committed murder that they were driven into outlawry. It was rumored that they were quick to exterminate anyone suspected of knowing about their nefarious deeds. On March 27, 1891, only a month after Edmond Parker was robbed of his cotton and Jesse Miller was indicted for grand larceny in the case but not convicted, the *Bibb Blade* reported the disappearance of this "worthy black" and called it "another desperate and heinous crime." Another black man named Lum Miller was thought to have been one of the gang's victims. According to the story, he was murdered on Schultz Creek bridge and the blood stains hacked out of the planks to remove the evidence.[5] For the same reason, Peter Dover reportedly shot Archie Wood from ambush as Wood was opening the gate to his home place not far from Miller's farm. The possession of damaging information was not the only motive for crime, however. Jesse Miller was suspected of setting fire to a farmer's house and causing his death in the conflagration, after the neighbor refused to sell his adjoining farm to Miller.[6]

In the end, it was their elimination of those who knew too much that drove the leaders of the gang into the hands of the law, from which they all too quickly escaped to resume their criminal careers. By January 1884 Peter Dover, sentenced to the state penitentiary for Archie Wood's murder, had fled after one of Bibb's perennial jailbreaks.[7] At one point the *Bibb Blade* reported, almost routinely, "Five prisoners have escaped jail and four more were put in. The Sheriff should fix the fence."

The year 1891 brought the crime wave to a climax. A correspondent of the *Blade* wrote on February 26: "This won't do; it has to stop; if the law is powerless we must look elsewhere for redress.... The people are getting excited and there is no telling what may happen in the near future." As a protest against the lawlessness, citizens held a mass meeting in the county seat at which Centreville mayor Dr. W. J. Nicholson presided, and pledged to protect those who would report violations of the law.[8] Vigilance groups, called "beat clubs," were subsequently organized in each voting precinct, and numerous calls were made, including one from the *Blade* editor, for Sheriff Alonzo Bates's resignation.

Three months later, Jesse Miller, his alleged accomplice George Cook, and Ike Miller, called "Jesse's right-hand man," were arrested for the murder of Miller's tenant Henry Smith, who, according to the *Blade* headline of August 14, "knew too much and was sacrificed for the safety of the gang." Witnesses for the preliminary trial of Miller and Cook were escorted from Blocton by a guard of sixty armed men, an indication of the climate of fear at the time. The prosecution, represented by Sam Will John of Birmingham, County Attorney Thomas J. Smitherman, and Luther Clements, called frightened witnesses to the stand for three days. After their damaging responses, the attorneys for the defense, Hargrove, Logan, and VandeGraff, decided not to introduce any testimony.

On the order of the court, the two prisoners were committed to the Jefferson County jail for safekeeping because the Bibb facility was considered inadequate for such a notorious criminal as Miller. The Blocton Vigilance Committee, which had protected the witnesses on their way to the trial, guarded the prisoners on the twelve-mile trip to the railroad station at Blocton. A week later, Editor Frank Gist noted significantly in the *Blade* that no murder had been committed in Bibb for three weeks.

In another three months, Jesse Miller and George Cook were released from "the safest jail in Alabama" after being tried by Judge Sharp under a writ of habeas corpus.[9] The stories are numerous about what happened to Miller afterward. According to one of these, he was thrown into jail again and threatened by a mob, but he escaped and hid for a time in a cave north of Scottsville, where he was fed by a member of the gang, Jim Morrison. It is a matter of record, however, that on January 2, 1892, Miller and his wife, Amanda, sold for $5,000 a large tract of his land near Scottsville to Theophilus Miller, apparently before leaving the state.[10] On April 27 Sheriff M. J. Latham gave notice through the *Blade* that certain land owned by Miller was to be offered for sale to reimburse the county for delinquent taxes. In an obvious effort to protect his property from the avenging arm of the law, Miller on July 26, 1895, deeded a section of land for $2,000 to his daughter, Grace, a transaction that was "acknowledged by Jesse Miller in due form before R. R. McCulley, justice of peace."[11] This may have been the occasion later recalled by a native Bibb Countian: "When I was a child I remember the report of a surrey coming from Marion to the Courthouse in Centreville. . . . As soon as some business was attended to, it took him back to Marion to catch the train away. Insofar as I ever knew, nobody ever saw him here afterwards or ever knew where he went."[12]

Miller apparently made no more surreptitious appearances before officers of the law, but on October 15, 1900, he gave his son Brooks power of attorney "to look after all my lands in Bibb County."[13] It was suspected that the elder Miller had fled west, possibly no farther than Mississippi, and that he occasionally returned under cover of night to visit his family. For some time, citizens in the Scottsville area remained apprehensive as they drove along the roads through the woods. One of them reported that he was sure he caught a glimpse of the outlaw's sharp eye behind a shotgun carefully aimed over a log, though he dared not take a second look as he drove nervously by.[14]

Although the shadow of Jesse Miller lay longest across the county, the crime that sent the sharpest shock through its citizens in this same bloody year of 1891 was the work of other murderers. In January, Sheriff R. H. Jones (formerly a Bibb resident) returned from Louisiana with a Bibb County prisoner named James Tate. This white tenant farmer had fled the state after allegedly killing his employer, W. B. Head, in an argument on August 29 of the preceding year. As he stepped off the train at Randolph accompanied by the prisoner in handcuffs, Jones was shot down in cold blood.[15] His assassins seized Tate, but how they disposed of him was never known. The only person apprehended, shortly afterward, was a teenage boy whom the men had drafted to hold their horses. Although the grand jury returned indictments for eight or ten suspects, warrants reportedly were not issued promptly and criticism of the county sheriff, Alonzo Bates, mounted. He was accused of being afraid of both the assassins and the Miller gang, not broken up until later in that year. After even the governor questioned his record, the sheriff's force went to work and made several arrests in September,[16] but the suspects remained in hiding and no one was ever convicted of the murder.

Jesse Miller's gang was only one of several bands of desperadoes that roamed the county during the last quarter of the nineteenth century and created a climate in which such murders could be committed unavenged. Because the law enforcement officers were unable to cope with the growing violence, they eventually employed a paid killer from Birmingham, said to have been Henry Coles, detective in the T.C.I.'s Blue Creek district.[17] He first studied the criminals' habits, and, when he was sent to bring in one of them, he used their methods, ambushing and killing them without notice. His work was made easier by the cooperation of the beat vigilance committees. *Blade* editor Frank Gist later declared that this extreme measure was provoked by Bibb's record of "twelve murders in twelve months," concluding that, after the gangs were eliminated, "the Lord took a chastened people back to his bosom."[18] Perhaps it is poetic irony that, when the man who had achieved the end of the gangs by these questionable means returned to Birmingham, he allegedly killed a citizen there, was arrested and jailed, and committed suicide in his cell.[19]

Even while the cold-blooded murders were being brought under comparative control, hot-blooded shootings continued from time to time. One of the most sensational was motivated by a personal quarrel. Dr. Gratton B. Crowe entered the front yard of Ben Glass near Six Mile, called him out on his porch, and in the gun battle that followed shot him fatally, allegedly in self-defense.[20] The bellicose doctor was soon urging violence in political warfare. Politics was a subject of intense interest and often generated more extreme feeling than it had since Reconstruction.

During this decade, the chief political competition in Bibb, as in the rest of Alabama, was no longer between conservative Democrats and Republicans but between the Democratic and Conservative party and the new People's party, whose members were called Populists. The Democratic and Conservative party, by opponents called Bourbon Democrats,[21] represented chiefly the status quo; and the People's party, born largely of discontent in the Farmers' Alliance during this economically depressed period, supported numerous political reforms viewed by the Democrats as unsound.[22] Reuben Kolb was the individual who polarized the two factions within the Democratic party in the state race for governor in 1892 and led the third-party Populist revolt that occurred immediately afterward.

Kolb had ample support in Bibb in 1892 and subsequently; he carried the county in both 1892 and 1894. Because the Farmers' Alliance had already threatened to take over Bibb and Shelby before 1890,[23] support for the reform movement was evidently strong from farmers as well as miners. The clash of opposing forces within the party generated keen excitement in 1892. A young Centreville lawyer who was helping to marshal the vote for Kolb's opponent, incumbent Thomas G. Jones, gave this report of a county mass meeting of the now widely divided Democratic and Conservative party:

> The long expected day dawned fair and bright. The crowd of men began to gather a little after nine. By 10:45 Rev. S. M. Adams called from the porch of the courthouse for all Democrats who endorsed the ticket nominee in March to come up into the courthouse. Maj. A. P. Howison called for all true blue democrats to meet at the Presbyterian Church. Promptly at 11:03 Mr. W. I. Caddell, chairman of the county executive committee, called the meeting to order and nominated Dr. J. W. Brand for chairman. He was elected by acclamation. Dr. Brand in an eloquent speech appealed for Democratic harmony and unity, saying that we came up with olive branches in our hands and oil in our vessels to pour on the troubled waters of the political sea of Bibb County Politics. These sentiments were cheered to the echo. Frank Connelly and Tom McCumber were elected secretaries. Major Howison addressed the meeting in the interest of Pure Democracy and appealed to them to nominate good and pure men for offices, men who would not be controlled by any special class.[24]

The delegates that this conservative faction nominated, said to be uninstructed but actually favoring Jones, were unable to stem the Populist tide of reform. In the August election, the Bibb vote was 1,006 for Jones and 1,603 for Kolb, who ran on an independent ticket after the state Democratic convention nominated Jones. The large majority that Governor Jones won in the Black Belt counties, however, defeated Kolb in the state returns in this hotly contested election, considered by some historians to have been won by stuffed ballot boxes.[25] In the U.S. presidential election in November, Populism again carried Bibb, 1,204 to 1,152 for Weaver against the successful "regular" candidate, Grover Cleveland.

Bibb contributed two Populists who were prominent on the state scene: Reverend Samuel M. Adams and Dr. Gratton B. Crowe, both former Democrats. Adams, a Baptist preacher, was one of three members appointed to the party's platform committee. He had already gained statewide attention as the second president of the Alabama Farmers' Alliance. The *Birmingham Age-Herald,* in reporting his address to that organization on August 26, 1891, when he was introduced by Commissioner of Agriculture Kolb, described him as "cool and dignified in manner and a good talker." When he attempted to succeed Kolb in his state office the following year, however, he was defeated in the August 1 election by a "regular," Hector D. Lane. In the fall of 1892, Adams was rallying support for Kolb for governor by means of his newspaper, the *People's Reflector,* founded in Centreville on September 22. The tone of his editorials opposing "boss rule" was more moderate than that of much of the conservative Democratic press. In this organ and in letters to the *Montgomery Advertiser,* he continued to defend Kolb against the criticism of the *Advertiser,* which denounced both of them as party rebels and ridiculed Adams's biblical quotations.

An equally aggressive Populist on the state scene was Bibb's versatile Dr. Gratton B. Crowe, who lacked political experience. He was born in Marion, Perry County, but came early to Bibb. Without any formal training, he had practiced medicine at Brierfield before the collapse of the ironworks in 1889. Then he went abroad to study his profession at the University of Edinburgh, but returned in time to identify himself with the new reform movement in politics. In 1892 he confined himself to campaigning for the election of Democratic delegates at the state convention in Birmingham.[26]

But by 1894, when Kolb ran for governor a second time, Crowe was on the firing line beside him. It was a year of threatened violence among Populists. On June 28, 1894, the *Mobile Register* reported that Kolb's supporters in Etowah County were drilling twice a week with shotguns, preparing to resist voter fraud in the upcoming election. Dr. Crowe not only advocated violence to combat ballot-box corruption, but also on at least two occasions raised an armed force to seize the state capitol. The first of these abortive attempts occurred when Governor Jones denied the joint Jefferson and People's party the use of the capitol for their convention on November 12, 1894; and the second when, after the contested election, allegedly won by William C. Oates, Kolb tried to enter in order to deliver his inaugural address on December 1. On neither occasion could Dr. Crowe gain enough support from the crowd to attempt his violent tactics.

By 1896, when Kolb was no longer a candidate, a number of local Populist leaders in the state were publishing letters of recantation. Such a letter, addressed to Nelson Fuller, chairman of the executive committee of the People's party in Bibb County, appeared in the *Press* from James G. Oakley of Ashby, close friend of Dr. Crowe. In withdrawing from the party, the writer went on record as favoring the current Democratic tenets of free silver and white supremacy.[27] After the August election, in which Centreville attorney W. W. Lavender defeated six-year incumbent S. M. Adams for the legislature, the *Blocton Times* proclaimed, "We hail with pleasure the return of Democratic supremacy to Bibb County."[28]

Yet, in spite of the waning of Populist strength in Bibb and the rest of Alabama, Dr. Crowe remained loyal through the campaign of 1900, when he was his party's candidate for governor. After his humiliating defeat as a result of polling only 17,543 votes against Democratic candidate William J. Samford, he went abroad another time. On this European visit, he studied geology and came home the following year to exercise his new knowledge in the discovery of mineral resources in Bibb, Jefferson, and neighboring counties. He went out into the field on long prospecting tours, throwing all of his vast energies into this new vocation. By October 9, 1903, the *Blocton Messenger* could say that he was responsible for the development of much of the county's coal and iron. This former physician and politician who had become a coal prospector and mine owner was now a wealthy man. In 1904 he withdrew from the People's Party. Bibb's other leading Populist, S. M. Adams, did also, returning to the right wing of the Democratic party.

The third-party movement made very little news in Bibb after Dr. Crowe's defeat, but another innovation of the 1890s was more enduring. It was also perhaps as supportive of the economy in southern Bibb as Dr. Crowe's mineral explorations were of that in the northern section. A branch of the Mobile and Ohio Railroad, planned as early as 1884,[29] finally arrived in 1898. After the right-of-way had been obtained early in the decade and part of the road graded, the project was temporarily abandoned because of the economic recession following the panic of 1893. But the hope of the new railroad put new life into southern Bibb, especially the county seat. When the work was resumed, laborers were employed to clear the right-of-way that had been surveyed through a thick pine forest from the Cahaba River to Ingate. One eyewitness later recalled that many of the trees felled had been pierced by bullets, supposedly from the guns of desperadoes who a few years earlier had infested these woods.[30] The track was laid at the rate of only two miles a day, but eventually Centreville citizens crowded along it to see the first train arrive. The *Centreville Press* of June 16, 1898, recorded that the first "through train" passed on June 8, 1898.

Residents of the southern half of the county could now ship cotton to market directly by railroad, and, when they wished to visit the outside world, they no longer needed to travel for that purpose to Randolph, a journey from Centreville by horse and buggy for which two hours and thirty-five minutes was considered "fast time."[31] As a result, Randolph gradually lost much of its importance as a railroad town and declined in population. On the other hand, Centreville businessmen were stimulated in this same summer to construct new buildings: the W. W. Yeager two-story brick structure (later known as the Cleveland Grocery Store), the

View of southeast corner of Court Square, Centreville, showing Reynolds general store in left foreground (burned in 1926) and W. W. Yeager hotel and store on right, all three built in 1898; also from left to right, Kennedy house, original Cleveland store (formerly site of black merchant Green Calhoun's store), offices of attorney S. D. Logan and Dr. T. E. Schoolar, and Meigs Drug Store (original location); on hill to rear, 1908 elementary school on left and Davidson-Smitherman-Leggett home on right. Photographed around 1909, probably by T. C. Tuggle. (Courtesy of Sherwood Medders)

first floor to be used for a store, the second for hotel bedrooms, and the large basement for hotel dining room and kitchen; the H. C. and E. B. Reynolds general store, on the opposite corner of East Walnut Street (now the site of Scarbrough Service Station); and the large combination bank and hotel building on the corner of Court Square (now the property of Walter Owens).[32] The "drummers" arriving on the new railroad now had a wider choice of accommodations. In addition to "Miss Sally" Snead's homey old boardinghouse, east of Court Square, they might find quarters in the imposing new hotel-bank building or in "Uncle Billy" Yeager's Centreville Hotel, where he always served tables at breakfast, saying, "Have an egg if you haven't had one."

A new community whose star rose as Randolph's declined was Brent

Snead boardinghouse, Mr. and Mrs. Daniel Snead seated on the porch. The building was located back of present Chism Cleaners off East Court Square; it burned in 1930. (Courtesy of Sherwood Medders)

City. This town was first conceived in the imagination of Brent Armstrong, an engineer who had directed construction of the railroad bridge across the Cahaba. Two miles east of Centreville in the dense pine forest on the Cooper plantation, Armstrong visualized a commercial center for the farmers south of that point. He described his plan to the plantation owners, Jesse Dean and Rhoda Howard Cooper, and gained permission to lay out a town there. At that time, in the woods between the present intersection of Highways 82 and 25 and the residence of James M. and Kay White, there was only a small clearing, the location of a black tenant's cabin.[33] According to tradition, this wooded area was the home of a well-known "blind tiger." The land south of the railroad to a point opposite this clearing was swampy, and the road would have been impassable in winter except for the sand washed onto it from the higher ground.

The map of the survey is signed "D. G. Seymour, C. E., Surveyor of the Map of Brent City, April 9, 1898."[34] It covers only the west side of present Alabama 25 from the street north of the Goodson apartment house to the railroad. All the streets were fifty feet wide and were named by members of the Cooper family, the main thoroughfare being designated Cooper Avenue and the others Raymond, Converse, Wilmoth, Howard, Elizabeth, Nicholson, Franklin, and Grand. Brent Armstrong purchased Lot Number 1 in Block Number 1 in the name of his wife, L. G. Armstrong, from Jesse Dean and Rhoda Howard Cooper on May 11, 1898, for the price of $25. That lot today is the southeastern corner of the Brent Shopping Center parking lot. There, facing Cooper Avenue, Armstrong built his residence, the first house in Brent. On the adjoining lot, facing the railroad tracks, he erected a post office in which he served as Brent's first postmaster, followed in office after his untimely death on August 22, 1899, by his wife for an additional year. The original owners specified one building restriction: no cotton gin or cotton warehouse was to be erected on any lot. They gave a lot to the local Presbyterian congregation, and later their son Howard executed a similar deed of gift to the Baptist Church and their daughter Eva Cooper Ellison to the Methodist Church, as each of these congregations was formed.

Brent grew rapidly, as Armstrong had predicted that it would. S. L. Johnson, who hauled freight from the small house that the Mobile and Ohio Railroad erected west of the tracks, later named the first business buildings as he recalled them:

> A. H. James, a retired farmer from out west of Jamesville, came to Brent and put up the first store, with his home adjoining. This stood about where the Victor Hunt property is now located. He was also Justice of the Peace and one of the most picturesque characters I have ever known. His home and store buildings were very modest, but he said they were good enough for him. I have heard him predict that Brent would be a large town some day.
>
> Lem Elam built a small store on the opposite side of the highway and a little further east. He dealt in feeds and groceries and later had a meat market attached to the business. About 1903 or 1904 a man named Deason built a nice store and home about a hundred yards east of the Elam store, and about the same time one or two small houses were built on the north side of the highway, and slightly west of the Deason store. The pine forest had to be cleared from all the lots on which these homes were built, and the forest still stood all about them.
>
> In one of the years noted above three Thompson brothers came from Toomsooba, Miss., and put up a large saw mill on the west side of the railroad, and about three hundred yards from the crossing. This was the first mill in that section which cut second growth, or what was called short leaf pine. All the timber in the forest described above was of that kind, and the mills had formerly passed this up for the long leaf pine. This mill began at its door and cut far and wide and cleaned the forest out for miles around.[35]

Interior of Brent Mercantile Company's original store, erected in 1910; from left to right: Parker Ward, Birmingham salesman Greer, Wallace Mason, Brady Mitchell, Cross Steele, and Willie Wood, later mayor of Brent. Henry Faucett was founder and first president. (Courtesy of Corrie Faucett Steele)

Memories have differed somewhat concerning the "firsts" of Brent. A. H. James in 1916 credited M. Huey Deason with establishing the first store and himself the second. He also listed Lillie Pratt as the first teacher, J. W. Mitchell as the first resident preacher, and A. W. Walker as the first physician.[36] A. J. Hardin occupied the mayor's office for many years in this new cotton farmers' center. Facilities for these farmers came to the neighborhood, though they were forbidden in the original residential and business section of the town. By the spring of 1900, the Tuscaloosa Cotton Seed Oil Company, whose Brent agent was Huey Deason, was constructing a cotton seed warehouse;[37] and, in the fall of the same year, J. W. Dobbins and Douglas Gilmore were said to be operating their new cotton gin.[38] In the summer of 1903, when Elam and Company was enlarging its store and Maggie Deason was opening her restaurant, Brent had grown to the point of being awarded a railroad station, the welcome assurance of future development. The town was incorporated in 1913, one year after the establishment of the Brent Banking Company.

The new railroad spawned other communities along its path through the woods, besides giving new life to those nearby, like the sawmill village of Pondville. Eoline (named for the daughter of M. and O. Vice-President

Original building of Brent Banking Company, established in 1912 with Henry Faucett as president; destroyed by tornado of 1973. Pictured fourth from right, Andrew J. Hardin, first mayor of Brent; other passersby not identified. (Courtesy of Dan James)

Edward Russell of New Orleans) and Ingate sprang up west of Brent, and Lawley (bearing the name of a local family) and Active, both east of Centreville. Of these, Eoline was the most prosperous. Planted at the juncture of the Blocton branch with the M. and O. line from Artesia, Mississippi, it became a promising little commercial center. In the summer of 1900, it already possessed three stores, a post office, hotel, livery stable, coal chute, telegraph office, water tank, and pumping station,[39] and later, for a brief period, a newspaper, the *Eoline Messenger,* edited and published by the ubiquitous M. Huey Deason.[40] Residents were engaged in farming, sawmilling, lumbering, and coal mining.

In 1906 this community witnessed the beginning of an enterprise that was to be vital to the Bibb economy for most of the new century. The three Belcher brothers, W. E., Addie, and Andrew, established their first sawmill nearby on Bear Creek Road. By 1918 the partnership had been dissolved, and the *Centreville Press* was announcing on January 10: "W. E. Belcher, who lives near Eoline, has 29 fine mules. He will erect a sawmill at Lightsey's Pond. He conducts four sawmills and these mules log the mills." Instead of the pond, a location on the railroad in what is now called Four Points in Centreville was chosen for the erection of a planing mill.

Logging with oxen at Belcher sawmill on Bear Creek Road, near Eoline, 1906. John Thomas Bracknell (front) and Sam Hubbard. (Courtesy of Olon Belcher)

The Belcher-Deal Lumber Company, later W. E. Belcher Lumber Company, had its first office above Meigs Drug Store.

At the end of the turbulent 1890s, when the county's gangs had been driven from the scene and Populism was fading with the defeat of Dr. Crowe for governor, the coming of the long-overdue Mobile and Ohio Railroad through southern Bibb seemed the most permanent and promising event of the decade. The county faced the new century of technology ready for other changes.

18

THE COUNTY SEAT IN THE EARLY 1900s

ALTHOUGH THE COUNTY SEAT became accustomed to the daily hooting of the Mobile and Ohio train, usually greeted by an appreciative group of spectators at the tracks, life remained much quieter than in its more populous industrial neighbor to the north. The contrast between the tempo and tone in Centreville and in the recently incorporated town of West Blocton was underlined, with perhaps condescending kindness, by Editor George Rice of the *Blocton Messenger,* after a visit to the county seat during circuit court week in the spring of 1902: "A few days stay in this little city of romance and refinement, of mossy roofed houses, white-washed fences, green trees and lowing kine—what a panacea for heartache, stomach ache and nervous prostration. We wonder if Drs. Nicholson and Moore ever have to test their skill on those disorders."[1]

Although Editor L. H. Nunnelee of the *Centreville Press* pointed out the unkept condition of the streets, his brother editor magnanimously refused to take comfort, declaring that the absence of a whiskey dispensary, the institution that helped to support West Blocton's improvements, was a blessing. In Centreville, he insisted, he saw "no drunken men walking like they are trying to cross the Cahaba River at a single step and disdaining a foot log." Bibb had been a "dry" county since 1881, when the state legislature had acted upon a proposal drawn up by Dr. J. W. Brand of Randolph, and the rest of the county remained officially dry after West Blocton two decades later petitioned for and won a dispensary. Yet in 1903, under the heading "Centreville Awakening," it was reported that "a mass meeting of Centreville and vicinity had been held for the purpose of devising ways and means by which the prohibition laws of the County might be enforced."[2]

Although it continued to lag behind its rival in municipal developments, Centreville in the early 1900s began to embark on a program of material improvements. These were to include new public and business buildings, new schools for both black and white children, and basic utilities. The new courthouse and jail were the result of countywide dissatisfaction. Bibb's fourth courthouse, built in 1858–59, had long needed renovating or replacing. Two decades earlier, the *Bibb Blade* had implied its condition and the abuse it received: "A skunk was found in the office of the Circuit Clerk at the Courthouse last week. The animal made its escape to its den—somewhere in or under the jail. The Sheriff has been busy preparing for Court. He has had the floor of the Courthouse recovered with fresh sawdust—a good deed."[3] In 1893 the county had given the building a much-needed roof and employed jail prisoners to construct a new cover over the town well in front of it.[4] But these changes, mostly cosmetic, did not discourage plans for a different and more commodious edifice. W. S. Hull was engaged as architect and F. A. Dobson as contractor.

On July 15, 1902, the cornerstone for the present lofty courthouse was laid. The ceremonies were conducted by Dr. R. W. Cunningham, Grand Master of the Grand Lodge of Alabama, and participated in by members of all the Bibb County lodges of Freemasons, as well as by a throng of other citizens.[5] By the following summer, the construction had been completed and the grounds replanted.[6] The hitching posts that had been removed earlier by the mayor had been returned after an outcry from the visiting farmers, who were forbidden to use the young trees for this purpose. The editor of the *Press* congratulated Probate Judge W. L. Pratt because the cost of the new building was only $34,000 and its courtroom provided seats for a hundred or more spectators to attend court sessions.[7] In September 1903, in the first circuit court session held in the new courtroom, it was filled to capacity during the trial of the Gardner murder case.

A new jail was urgently needed also because escapes continued, but the county was compelled to wait for this facility until 1911. When it was finally erected, on the old location west of the courthouse square, it was called the most handsome building in the county. It was constructed of brick, marble, and stone at approximately the same cost as the courthouse, but of the total amount $5,000 was spent on execution fixtures.[8] The jail that it replaced was considered too insecure to hold Tolley Mason, the black man who was convicted of the murder of "Uncle Dick" Meigs in March 1909. Sheriff James G. Oakley took Mason to the state prison in Montgomery to avoid the sort of mob that the following year reportedly overpowered a deputy sheriff at Braehead and lynched his black prisoner, Grant Richardson, who had been arrested on a charge of rape.[9] After the state supreme court refused to commute Mason's death sentence, Sheriff Oakley ordered a scaffold erected in the old jail yard for the execution on August 12, 1910. He refused to admit the morbidly curious crowd of

County officers in 1902 in front of old courthouse: left to right, deputy sheriffs John Reddick and Carlisle Suttle, circuit clerk W. E. Fancher, Sheriff Edgar Crawford, treasurer Nelson Fuller, probate office clerk Theodosia Pratt, Probate Judge W. L. Pratt, and register in chancery L. H. Nunnelee, who was also *Centreville Press* editor and publisher. *Centreville Press*, January 15, 1948. (Courtesy of Jim Oakley, Jr., editor and publisher)

would-be spectators, but several hundred nevertheless climbed to the top of the jailyard fence and watched the hanging.[10] Not even the case of black Alex Hill, hanged in the same jail yard on another hot August day in 1899 for the murder of Mrs. R. H. Hubbard of Eoline,[11] excited such violent racial feeling.

Rape cases, however, aroused the greatest bloodthirstiness. One of the first occupants of the new jail, Josh Wedgewood, a black tramp and escaped convict from outside the county, was hanged on December 22, 1911, from gallows in a cell in order to exclude the excited crowd that clamored to witness his execution. After he had allegedly raped a Filgo girl near Eoline, a mob had hunted him along with bloodhounds brought by the sheriff's department, and he was convicted at a brief special session of circuit court on November 16.[12]

Yet, of all those tried in the new courthouse and executed at the new jail, Clyde Wallace in the next decade probably left the most enduring

Citizens snowballing on lawn of old courthouse during the freeze of 1899, which killed the "China trees" planted there in the 1830s; on right, snow-covered hitching post (in foreground) and town well. (From family collection of author)

West Court Square around 1908: left to right, hotel-bank building, Presbyterian Church, Masonic building, J. T. Casey residence, and new courthouse, with old town well in foreground. Postcard. (Courtesy of Mrs. Albert Perdue)

impression of horror. This yard boy of John Wallace of the Randolph community was accused of raping and murdering Wallace's fourteen-year-old daughter. He was pursued by the customary mob and was sentenced to death on August 17, 1921, after a ten-minute deliberation of the jury, while state troopers dispatched from Montgomery stood on guard to prevent a lynching.[13] Black citizens recall that members of their race were unwelcome in Randolph for many months after this gruesome event. By the next decade, the trap door and all hanging arrangements were removed from the jail in favor of the electric chair in the state prison at Montgomery.

Another county facility that sometimes housed convicted lawbreakers needed improvement but received none. This was the county poorhouse and farm, located a few miles northeast of Centreville off Alabama 25, on property later purchased by C. C. McGraw. Frank Connelly, prominent in Bibb journalism and politics in the 1890s, was fined $1,500 for violation of the county's prohibition laws and in lieu of the fine was sentenced to thirty-nine months in this melancholy place. The governor, however, soon responded to a petition of Connelly's friends to pardon him because of his precarious health, after which he and his family returned to his hometown, Anniston.[14]

Two months before Connelly was freed from this detention house, the

Principals in the execution of Tolley Mason, August 12, 1910, in old jail yard: from left to right, Jefferson County deputy sheriff Etheridge; Bibb deputy Charles Oakley; the condemned man, holding palmetto fan; and Sheriff James G. Oakley; in the background, crowd peering over the high fence. This photograph was made at Tolley Mason's request. (Courtesy of Odie Hubbard)

attending physician, Dr. W. J. Nicholson, in an outburst of indignation described its condition to the public in an open letter to the *Press*. "A glance into Mr. Pippins miserable hut," he wrote, "is enough to melt a heart of stone.... No one can properly feed, clothe and comfortably house these needy ones for the small amount of three dollars and ninety-five cents per month."[15] At this time, the county was accepting the lowest bid for the care of its paupers. They were all kept in one room, both old and young, black and white, while apparently the keeper and his family used the limited remaining quarters. Dr. Nicholson recommended acquiring land nearer the county seat and building good houses, one for the superintendent and others for the inmates, but his plan was never acted on. Certain citizens offered charity to the inmates at Christmas. Judge and Mrs. W. L. Pratt customarily sent a wagon-load of fruit and other good things. By 1918 the *Press* referred to this dreaded house as the "home for the aged and infirm," and to Jim Jones as its "keeper."

Before the courthouse was erected in 1902–3, the county seat possessed three new brick business buildings: the Yeager and Reynolds general stores at Walnut and Market streets, and the combination hotel and bank building erected in 1898, the year after the organization of the town's first bank, Bibb County Banking and Trust Company, at the corner of Walnut and the courthouse square. The remainder of the structures were mostly frame and in many cases antiquated.

While the courthouse was still in process of construction, a disastrous event on unlucky Friday, February 13, 1903, paved the way for a municipal face-lifting. The *Centreville Press* of February 19 carried the news in staccato headlines followed by a story that incidentally gives an index of the businesses on Walnut Street between Market and Cedar:

> On Friday night at 10:30 o'clock the people of Centreville were startled by the ringing of bells and shouts of fire! On looking out of one's window, the whole business part of Centreville was illuminated.
>
> The fire originated in the little colored Restaurant almost in the center of the Block, and when it was discovered it was past saving, and the residents soon saw that the Block was doomed, and set to work to save the balance of the town. The store of S. D. Hall, a corrugated iron building, caught fire a number of times, and only hard and persistent work by the bucket brigade saved the building. A small hydrant on the second floor probably saved the balance of the town. Every glass on the front of the store as well as every one on the south side of the Bank Building, was broken by the extreme heat.
>
> The old warehouse next to Mrs. Davidson's residence caught several times, but there were willing hands to stand the intense heat which was almost unbearable, and dashed water on the burning parts. If the Hall building had burned, the fire would have wiped out the west side of the square and a great many merchants and residents on that side moved out, thinking their property was doomed. The rapidity with which the frame buildings were destroyed was a great advantage, as the buildings across the street would not have stood the intense heat much longer.
>
> The buildings destroyed were as follows: Colored Restaurant, run by Belcher and Martin, owned by M. J. Fuller. Nothing saved.
>
> The Gardner building, owned by Mrs. M. J. Owens, and used as a warehouse by the Centreville Hardware Co. Loss to the company will amount to about $800.
>
> The two-story frame building owned by Hayes Brs., unoccupied.
>
> The residence of Mrs. Amanda Steele. Very little household goods were saved.
>
> The store of J. T. Casey, most of the stock was saved.
>
> D. J. Frazier. Groceries, stock saved.
>
> E. Kennedy. General merchandise, stock saved.

The editor, who revealed that the buildings were uninsured, commented sharply in an editorial in the same issue: "In the absence of Water

Walnut Street, Centreville, looking east, around 1908. The block on the right had been rebuilt after the fire of February 13, 1903. Postcard. (Courtesy of Mrs. Albert Perdue)

Works, or even an Engine and Hose to pump water from the nearby Cahaba River, Centreville lost an entire Block of Business Houses last Friday night, about 12 o'clock, in a little less than an hour and a half." Although they lamented the devastation, citizens were grateful that the still uncompleted courthouse and the county records were not damaged. In a relatively short time, the block was entirely rebuilt, this time of more durable materials.

During this same decade, building projects began just across the river. J. T. Gandy in May 1909 was awarded the contract for the county high school soon to be erected there. The location of the new high school at Centreville, on land purchased from Judge W. L. Pratt, triggered further development of the community. The county surveyor, L. P. Wallace, laid off lots for the Pratt addition just north of the school grounds, and the subdivision named Fairdale was created on part of the 250-acre tract that A. J. Fair bought from Howard Cooper across Walnut Street south of the high school. These were the first major developments since three in the late nineteenth century. W. I. Caddell had opened Aldine on an eastern extension of Walnut Street in 1885. His addition was followed by the Smitherman subdivision, around the large antebellum home on the hill southeast of the business section; and by "Morendia," as Mrs. E. H. Moren

First two-lane bridge across the Cahaba River at Centreville, completed in 1910. (Courtesy of Gesna Hubbard Young)

called the lots she offered for sale around her plantation home just south of town.

As a result of the 1909 additions west of the river, particularly the high school, citizens agitated for a better bridge. On September 15, 1910, the *Press* announced the completion of a new span that provided for two-lane traffic. This bridge, built at a cost of $15,000, replaced the 1885 structure, which was constructed after the original one was destroyed by Wilson's Raiders in 1865.

Of all these projects, the Bibb County High School probably stimulated the most interest, partly because it was introduced as a "plum" to be won in a contest with rival West Blocton. The county obtained its first public high school in 1909 largely through the efforts of its state senator, H. E. Reynolds. As chairman of the Senate Committee on Education, he had managed to persuade the legislature to appropriate the modest sum of $2,000 to each county for the maintenance of a public high school. After the State High School Commission, composed of Governor B. B. Comer, Auditor W. W. Brandon, and State Superintendent of Education H. C. Gunnels, had visited the proposed sites in the competing towns and announced its decision in favor of the county seat, committees appointed at an enthusiastic community meeting began soliciting funds, and by August 19 the *Press* could report that the $10,000 considered necessary for the building had been pledged. Meanwhile Frank Cooper, who had completed his doctorate in Latin and Greek at Johns Hopkins University a year earlier, had accepted the principalship.[16] He was the son of Centreville's retired schoolmaster, Jesse Dean Cooper.

The new building, featuring four large classrooms and an auditorium seating 500, was completed at a cost of $12,000. It was not ready for occupancy by October 4, the date set for the opening, and as a result the first term was begun in the courthouse. In exercises presided over by John T. Ellison, chairman of the County Board of Education, fourteen community leaders rose to make speeches, beginning with Senator Reynolds. After this perhaps trying initiation, thirty-six boys and twenty-eight girls were enrolled as the first pupils.[17] Dr. Cooper was assisted by Harriett Brogdon of Richmond, Virginia, who taught English, history, and advanced Latin, leaving all other subjects to the principal until Lady Portis of Lower Peachtree was added to the faculty for the second term. The following year, Sara Key Bagby of Russell County came to relieve Miss Brogdon of the English instruction.

The first class graduated in 1912, after L. L. Vann had succeeded Dr. Cooper, who had joined the University of Alabama faculty. The three members of this first class were Leta James, Inez McGraw, and Howard Mitchell. The next year the number of graduates rose to sixteen: eleven boys and five girls. By 1916, when J. W. Watson had completed the first three years of his seven-year administration, the school had added a two-story concrete building for manual training, "domestic science," and science laboratories, at a cost of $3,000, and was expecting the state to increase its annual appropriation to $3,000 for the following year.[18]

Meanwhile in 1908, the year before the county high school was located at Centreville, the community had obtained a new elementary school building. After Jesse Dean Cooper retired from the Centreville Male and Female College, which operated departments from primary through college preparatory, an attempt was made to bring it into the public school system. A. F. Harmon graded it during the year he was principal in the old location, later known as the O. C. Oakley residence. But it was ac-

Original Bibb County High School building, erected in 1909, later enlarged by two wings, and now occupied by the Junior High School. (Courtesy of Gesna Hubbard Young)

cepted in the state system only when J. R. Alexander of Anniston began his long and fruitful tenure in 1907. The following year, he moved his pupils into the new brick four-classroom building east of the Smitherman (now Leggett) property, where through the early years he was assisted by such teachers as Lucille Hightower, Jeanette Shapard, Sara Orum, and Janie True. This hilltop structure, later enlarged, was destroyed by fire in February 1958.

During the first decade of the century, while white citizens were gaining both elementary and secondary schools in the state's public school system, members of the black community were struggling to establish a creditable school for their children. The leader in this movement was Henry Damon Davidson, son of former slaves. He was "born in a little log hut on a knoll overlooking the Cahaba River, almost immediately facing the 'big house,' in the 'yard quarters,' on the S. W. Davidson plantation three miles below the town of Centreville, in Bibb County, Alabama, on December 16, 1869."[19] In his youth, the only schools available to his race were held in black churches and rented houses, with one exception in Centreville. While he was clerking in the store of his uncle, Green Calhoun, located on the lot east of the present Dailey-James Hardware Store, he learned that "in another house nearby an old white gentleman called Mr. Stephens kept a Negro school."[20]

Among Davidson's own teachers were Mary Green Calhoun, George Calhoun and his wife, and Reverend A. A. Godwin, none of whose school

Class of 1913, Bibb County High School. Front row, left to right: Alex Gentry, Leonard Harvey, Kate Cleveland, Howard Dunaway, Tom Cleveland; second row: Grace Avery, Harper Stacy, Viola Bolling, William Hayes Mason, Mayfield Ward; third row: Ralph Thomas, Brown Thompson, Essie Rae Gardner, Victor Hunt, Norvia Faucett, Alex Greene. (Courtesy of Mrs. Dalton Murphy)

terms lasted more than three months.[21] With a little assistance from his Calhoun uncles for transportation to Selma, he was able to enter Selma University, later transferring to Payne University, another black college then located in Selma. There he persevered through numerous privations until he graduated in 1893. Years later, in 1934, he won the B.S. degree from the more prestigious Tuskegee Institute by attending summer sessions.

Davidson almost single-handedly established the first reputable school for his race in this area in the fall of 1900. From the beginning of his long career, he envisioned education on the Tuskegee plan for Bibb County's black children, whom he saw "groping in ignorance and illiteracy on the surrounding plantations." He longed to give them a well-balanced education, including intellectual, social, industrial, and religious training.[22] Especially he hoped to emphasize "technical handiwork," beginning with

Henry Damon Davidson, founder and principal of Centreville Industrial Institute, 1900, later Bibb County Training School. Henry Damon Davidson, *Inching Along* (Nashville, Tenn., 1941), p. 173. (Courtesy of Nesbitt B. Wesley)

farming lessons for the boys in the fields and sewing classes for the girls on the porch of the Frazier cottage.

It was not a propitious time in which to solicit funds at home for such an enterprise. The two factions of the Democratic party that arose during the Populist movement had just reunited under the banner of white supremacy. That banner was flown triumphantly during the state constitutional convention of 1901, which dictated new suffrage requirements.[23] The imposition of the cumulative poll tax and the admission of educational tests by the local board of registrars effectively disfranchised most black voters, along with many poor whites.[24] These impediments were viewed by many white citizens, including John T. Morgan, successful candidate for the U.S. Senate in 1900, as one way to clean up election frauds; and on this basis they supported the Black Belt on this measure.

Bibb County's delegates to the convention, J. Fritz Thompson and J. C. James, were "progressives," followers of B. B. Comer during this critical hour. Both in the election of April 23, 1901, calling for the convention, and in that of November 11, approving the new constitution with its disfranchisement provisions, the voters of Bibb County returned a favorable majority, unlike most of the hill counties to the north.[25] The result of the new constitution was to bring an abrupt decline in the registration of voters. In 1896 the county in its eleven beats had possessed 1,986 registered white voters and 1,048 black voters, a ratio of not quite two to one.[26] In the 1904 election in the state as a whole, 23.6 percent of the white male voting population failed to pay the poll tax, and in 1906 only 2 percent of the black males of voting age had been registered, as opposed to 86 percent of the whites.[27]

Henry Davidson was one who fought back against disfranchisement. Although certain "politically reliable" blacks were to be excepted, he did not qualify for that category. Ever since he had come of age a decade earlier, he had been active in the Republican party, which he considered to be the more likely friend of his race. He served first as secretary and later for six years as chairman of the party's county executive committee, unmindful of the sneers of the local newspaper, which reported: "The Republican Convention met at the Court House Saturday. The weather was cool and the aroma did not spread," adding two weeks later that "the Negro Republican Convention" had been held in Blocton.[28]

In his autobiography, the black educator gave an illuminating report of the tactics resorted to by local white Democrats to prevent him from continuing to exercise his right to vote:

> When Alabama, along with other Southern States, decided to eliminate the Negro from politics . . . in 1901, I was determined to hold on to my ballot. So on the day appointed I presented myself to the board for registration. There was a long list of questions to be answered, such as What were the Kentucky Resolutions? Who is the Chief Justice of the Supreme Court of Alabama? What Alabamian was once Vice-President of the United States? and hundreds of others. I was pretty well up on the history of the United States and of Alabama, and they could not turn me down on that plan. It was whispered around town that the chairman of registrars sent hurriedly to one of the other members of the committee, saying, "Hurry with more questions; this 'nigger' has answered all the questions you gave us!"
>
> It was in the afternoon before they had finished with me. Seeing they could not turn me down by questioning (I had heard that Henry Davidson was one of the Negroes picked out for disfranchisement, and had fortified myself against such an act), the chairman told me that I would have to get three prominent white men to endorse me if I expected to vote. (Of course all prominent men had been instructed not to do such a thing.) I went to a few who readily turned me down. I then went to a certain law firm, the members of which were my staunch friends. I said to a certain member, "Mr. A———, you have known me for practically all my life, and you have never known me to go wrong about any matter. I want to vote. Will you endorse me?" "No, Henry," he said; "I have refused my best friend among colored people, and I must refuse you." I turned to another member of the firm and said, "Mr. B———, you have known me for about twenty-five years. You have known me to be an upright, loyal, and honest citizen. I have never been in the courts for crime committed. Will you endorse me as a good citizen so that I may be given the right to vote?" "You have heard what my partner said, Henry. I should like to help you, but my firm will not allow

> me." "I don't want you to endorse me as a firm," I said. "Just endorse me as an individual." Conscience would not let him hold out any longer, so he "gave in." He signed an affidavit as to my good character, and I still have my certificate, of which I am very proud.[29]

Although the political and social climate at this time was not encouraging for the establishment of a school for blacks, Henry Davidson set about the task with the same determination and intelligence that he showed in his effort to retain his suffrage rights. He and his first wife, Lula J. Davidson, opened the Centreville Industrial School, later the Bibb County Training School, in October 1900 in a rented house. After learning that the old Frazier farm of eighty-five acres, which had a five-room cottage and two huts, was to be sold under a mortgage for $1,200, they bought it by making a down payment of $50 and giving a note for $100 to be paid before fall, the final installment to be due two years later.[30] During the first year, one hundred pupils were said to have been enrolled in these quarters, located on the present Centreville Elementary School grounds. After many vicissitudes, Davidson liquidated the debt and had the school deeded to an authorized board of trustees and incorporated in 1903.

Through the years, Davidson continued to wage an uphill battle to build up his school. Like Booker T. Washington, he traveled to the North for support, but without the magic name of Tuskegee he was given a disappointing reception. Except for one benefactor, he found his contributors chiefly on his one trip to the Midwest. Years later, eight individuals in Iowa, three in Nebraska, one in California, and one in Massachusetts were still donating annual amounts varying from $3 to $50. But Emily Howland, of Sherwood, New York, the benefactor of some fifty struggling schools in the South, was his principal resource. She came to Centreville on two occasions to visit the Industrial School and donated one-half the funds required to build Howland Hall, a two-story house erected on the campus to supplement the space in the Frazier cottage. She sent funds when the mortgage was about to be foreclosed, again when new roofs were necessary for the two buildings, and at other times came to the financial aid of the despairing principal.[31]

In 1918, after the deeding of forty acres, including the buildings, to the State Board of Education, the school was accepted as a county training school.[32] As such, it was qualified to receive state aid and also inspired contributions from the Phelps-Stokes Fund, the Rosenwald Fund, and local individuals, all for the erection of its first convenient academic building, constructed in 1921.[33] The purpose of county training schools was to provide model schools for the black race. Through his school, Davidson continued to exert a cultural influence both inside and outside the county.

Each year, he sponsored a field day, to which he invited small schools in Bibb and neighboring counties. He made it a forum for the exchange of ideas as well as an occasion for sports competition.[34] He worked with the annual Black Farm Conference and the Black County Fair in an attempt to encourage improved farming methods as well as home ownership. Through all these mediums, he was a significant force for law and order and for self-respect among his race.

Besides acquiring new facilities for county government, private commerce, and public education, the county seat at the turn of the century was making certain technological advances. It was emerging into the era of telephones, electric lights, and automobiles. The telephone came first. Dr. W. J. Nicholson developed the first local line, which ran to the Jamesville community below Brent. He advertised in the *Press* of January 4, 1900, "Free telephone to residence" for the convenience of his patients. Before other local service was available, the town obtained a long-distance connection with Birmingham in the fall of 1900 and also had the use of a party line to Blocton, built by Suttle and Weaver.[35]

Centreville owed its first electric lights to J. C. Langston. The initial plant, established in 1906 and owned jointly by Langston and John P. Kennedy, was operated by means of a gasoline engine located at the rear of the Kennedy residence.[36] Fuel for this small enterprise was shipped into Centreville in drums. After Kennedy sold his interest to O. C. Oakley, the Centreville Light Company moved its plant in March 1909 to Lightsey's Pond and later, in the second decade of the century, to Blake's Mill, on Schultz Creek. It continued to be powered by Schultz Creek until the Alabama Power Company bought the local company's franchise in 1922 and gave the community its first full-time electricity. The Centreville Light Company was able to furnish power only at night for a limited number of hours, and its customers had to endure many inconvenient interruptions in that power.[37]

Residents of the county seat heard rumors of the new motorized vehicles during the first decade of the century, but the first motorcycle that many of them ever saw was the one received by Boyd Mackey the last week of May 1909, said to be the first in Centreville. The *Press* editor commented, "We now expect one of our citizens to buy an automobile. These cars are going to come and the sooner the better."[38] Only the preceding month Cleveland Mercantile Company had announced that it was expecting a railroad carload of surreys and buggies,[39] and just two years earlier John S. Ward had advertised for a good ox-driver.[40] But change was coming, even though slowly. By October 1910 everybody was running to his front door to watch the progress of Joseph A. Carruth's Model-T Ford, the first automobile in Centreville.[41] Like Mackey's motorcycle, it was noisy enough to be heard some distance

Lightsey's Pond in winter: horse and buggy crossing its bridge, mill house in background. (Courtesy of Sherwood Medders)

away. Its approach had such a disruptive effect on attention in the high school that Dr. Cooper painted the window panes white to discourage his pupils from rushing to them in a body. Schoolmaster Cy Duff was more sympathetic; he joined the race to the door of his one-room black school when "that automatic," as he called it, thundered through Harrisburg.[42] Carruth, by vocation a carpenter, was ahead of his day in looking forward to riding in an airplane, for which prediction many people, including the *Press* editor, ridiculed him.

Near the end of this decade of modern improvements, Bibb took one long backward look at the old days, by paying a nostalgic and affectionate tribute to its Civil War veterans. Half a century after that conflict had erupted, the surviving Confederate soldiers in the county still met annually for a reunion, usually at Scottsville, where various groups honored them with parades, picnics, and oratory. Even the West Blocton dispensary, when it was officially closed, paid the men in gray the courtesy of sending them the stock of whiskey on hand.[43] But the climactic event, shared by the whole county, was the erection of a memorial statue on the courthouse square in 1910. The Leonard Callaway Pratt Chapter of the

J. A. Fair Livery Stable for renting horses and buggies (left) and Sale Stable for buying and selling mules and horses (right), located opposite the present Centreville post office and city hall. Photographed around 1910, probably by T. C. Tuggle. (Courtesy of Sherwood Medders)

United Daughters of the Confederacy (UDC), organized at River Bend in 1906, the only chapter in Bibb at this time, spearheaded this ambitious undertaking, but its members were joined by women from all over the county in the spirit of a crusade. Among their many projects for raising funds the most profitable was the conduct of a "most popular young lady" contest, each vote priced at ten cents.

The pageantry of the unveiling and dedication of the statue of the traditional Confederate soldier on July 22, 1910, was said by an excited reporter to have drawn 4,000 visitors. The chief spectacle of the parade was provided by the twelve most popular young women, each representing a Southern state and each seated by an escort in a buggy decorated in confetti. Evelyn Abney symbolized South Carolina; Nell Steele, Mississippi; Olivia Wallace, Alabama; Annie Weaver, Georgia; Emma Love Riley, Louisiana; Margaret H. Hogan, Texas; Ray Stewart, Virginia; Beulah Avery, Arkansas; Dorothy Smith, North Carolina; Jessie Fondren, Tennessee;

Confederate Monument, unveiled on July 22, 1910; old town well and new courthouse in rear. (Courtesy of Louise Meigs Rogan)

Confederate parade, Miss Arkansas (Beulah Avery) passing in review with escort in decorated buggy. (Courtesy of Mrs. Dalton Murphy)

Delia James, Missouri; Pearl Oglesby, Kentucky. They were preceded by the marshal of the day, L. H. Nunnelee, on horseback, and by two carriages bringing the speakers and the UDC chapter officers, and followed by "some fifty sweet-faced children chanting the old familiar songs of war times, the wagon driven by Capt. J. D. Mayberry drawn by four of his horses. Next more than 100 veterans. Next Uncle West Mayberry the negro servant who went to war with him. Then the UDC members and spectators."[44] The line of parade was more than a mile long.

During the unveiling ceremony, three old citizens were called forward and honored by the rebel yell. They were Mrs. Bettie Howard Smitherman, who had presented the battle flag to the departing Bibb Greys in June 1861, and Phil Vance and Jacob Dennis Mayberry, both members of that first company from Bibb. A total of eight infantry companies and one cavalry unit from the county that saw service during the war were represented at the ceremonies.[45] After Mary Mayberry, UDC chapter president, assisted by Mrs. Phelan Logan, had unveiled the monument, Congressman Oscar W. Underwood presented it for the builder and State Auditor W. W. Brandon received it for the veterans, each delivering a resounding oration.

It was a celebration that Bibb Countians long remembered, one last hurrah for their fathers and grandfathers who fought in the last great

Four actors in drama of dedicating the Confederate Monument: front row, Captain Jacob Dennis Mayberry and daughter, Mary Mayberry, president of the UDC chapter; second row, veterans Phil Vance and Samuel Abney. (Courtesy of Clara Payne Harrell)

war, commemorated now less than a decade before their sons were to march away to another much greater war. The half century of slow recovery and of peace, broken only by the brief clashes in the Philippines and Cuba, was almost over.

19

AT WAR WITH THE KAISER

THE FIRST MAJOR world conflict probably made a deeper impact on Bibb Countians than has any other war except the one they had been commemorating only four years before this conflagration began in Europe. More than the telephone, electric power, or the automobile, it catapulted them into the twentieth century and opened their provincial eyes to the outside world. It was a more personal war than any subsequent conflict has been, not only in the trenches but also at home, where each citizen was expected to become involved in the struggle for victory over the German kaiser, the individual considered responsible for the evil.

In 1916 the roar of the German guns still seemed far away to Bibb Countians. Their ears were tuned to events on the Mexican border, where President Woodrow Wilson on June 18 had ordered the National Guard during a period of tension with the neighbor nation. Mexican outlaws were said to be invading and raiding the United States. By mid-summer, U.S. Marine Willis Rhodes of Ashby, who had joined the service in February, was rushed to San Domingo in an expeditionary force.[1] Two Bibb men, Charles Johnson and Cleve Sessions, immediately enlisted to go to the front with the historic Tuscaloosa Warrior Guards.[2] A black citizen, W. W. Miller, who had fought in the Spanish-American War, proposed to raise a company of his race if the United States declared war with Mexico.[3] Before Christmas, Troop K of the Alabama National Guard Cavalry, composed of Bibb and Perry men and commanded by former Bibb sheriff James G. Oakley, had arrived at San Antonio, ready for action.

Meanwhile President Wilson had been reelected in November over Charles E. Hughes in a campaign that stirred unusual excitement in Bibb, where the guns in Europe were beginning to sound louder. The County Republican Committee, headed by N. C. Fuller, urged: "Vote for Peace, Protection, and Prosperity." However, the Democrats in the county overwhelmed their opponents by a vote of 1,209 to 217 in the November election.[4] As tension with Mexico eased and the situation in Europe worsened, the president in January called General John J. Pershing's troops home from their two-months' tour of duty on the border, leaving Villa and Caranza to settle their differences.

Although they had helped to reelect Wilson because "he kept us out of war," Bibb Countians were apparently ready for the declaration of hostilities with Germany when it came in April. Their personal involvement began with a poll taken by the *Press* in response to Congressman W. B. Oliver's question wired from Washington. When the editor canvassed the streets of Centreville, he found only two men who did not approve the declaration, neither of whom, it was said in extenuation, had read the president's message.[5]

Local patriotism mounted as the U.S. government immediately took precautions to protect certain Bibb facilities from German spies suspected of infiltrating the country. A detachment of the Alabama National Guard Cavalry was stationed at the Mobile and Ohio Railroad bridge at Centreville, and another was dispatched to Blocton to guard the coal mines.[6] Fear of German espionage was strong in the early months of the war. U.S. Congressman Thomas Heflin, popular hitherto for his folksy tales and his humor, turned to grim spy stories as a way to whip up war spirit. In a speech at the Bibb courthouse, entitled "The Causes of the War," he frightened a large audience by relating dramatically how a German spy was detected in the act of slipping poison into beans on the stove of a hospitable Midwestern farm family and afterward at table was required by the father to eat them. ("Stranger, eat beans!")[7]

The county shortly began to organize its resources following directions from the state capitol. In order to make an official count of young men between the ages of twenty-one and thirty-one, conscription registrars were appointed, one for every box in each of Bibb's thirteen precincts. Captain Oakley, home from the Mexican border, was actively recruiting to fill the few vacancies in Troop K, while the *Press* urged, "Join before the draft!" As the enemy sank more ships (sixty-two were noted during one week), the editor denounced German brutality and raised the old Southern bugbear of the abduction of young women. At the same time, he published "The Star-Spangled Banner" and announced the success, "above expectation," of the military registration in Bibb on June 5.[8] The following week, twenty-three recruits in Troop K left for training, the first group to leave Bibb. After a triumphal march from Montgomery to Camp Wheeler at Macon, Georgia, both old and new members of this cavalry unit were transferred to the 117th Field Artillery, and Oakley became captain of Battery B.[9] Most of Bibb's servicemen were inducted into the army; a limited number joined the navy.

Meanwhile, the County Draft Board, whose members were Sheriff John S. Ward, Robert Thrasher, and Dr. L. E. Peacock, had gone into action. In the first drawing, they named only seven men: Willis E. Mitchell, Heiberger; Ben F. Jennette, West Blocton; Grover C. Greathouse, Duncanville; Melvin Ely, Eoline; William Lawrence, Randolph; Sam Hodge Hallman, Centreville; and Henry Holcomb, Centreville.[10] All were sent to Camp Gordon early in September, and the following week the local newspaper reproached the citizens of the county seat for failing to give them a farewell party at the railroad station. For the next fourteen months, farewell parties honored one group of departing soldiers after another. After the departure of forty-four men—forty white and four black—the *Press* noted with satisfaction on October 11: "The people of Centreville tendered the forty white soldiers who left Centreville for Camp Gordon a banquet on the Court House lawn." Afterward, when fifty-six black selectmen were on the point of entraining for Camp Dodge, Iowa, the members of the black community rose to the occasion and "gave them a spread on the Court House lawn."[11]

As the news from Europe grew grimmer and the cost of the war to the nation was said to have mounted to $160 million a day, enlistments were needed on a larger scale. The local editor announced coldly on December 20: "The time for volunteering is over. You will now be called." On January 10, 1918, he said threateningly, "The Bibb County Draft Board has sent out all the questionnaires. Those who don't reply will be listed as deserters and so reported to the government." Beginning in the spring, more and more young men entrained for the various camps, the largest detachment on May 25. On that day, eighty-six Bibb boys were honored at the M. and O. station by the Blocton Band and several patriotic speeches, though nothing was said about entertainment for the twenty-five black draftees slated for departure on the same day.[12] Launched by such festivities, hundreds of Bibb recruits, mostly farm boys who had seldom if ever left the county, were torn from their families and hurried off to be introduced to other regions and other ways of life.

The war changed life at home, too.[13] For one thing, unprecedented emphasis was placed on patriotism. During the first months of the war, many communities held flag-raisings in ceremonies that grew more and more elaborate. Lack of loyalty was not to be tolerated. Black citizens hurriedly gave reassurance of their support, as at the mass meeting they called in the Woodstock-Green Pond area after two members of their race had been lynched near Birmingham for speaking out against the war effort.[14] A minister in Autauga County was immediately asked to resign his pas-

Blocton Band, photographed by T. C. Tuggle in front of T.C.I. office building around 1914. This popular group, sponsored by the company, was dissolved in 1920 as part of the management's strike-breaking efforts. (Courtesy of A. N. Kitchen)

torate after expressing his disapproval of President Wilson's declaration of war in his morning sermon.

It was late in the war before a Bibb County resident was charged with making a similar mistake. In a conversation on the price-fixing of cotton, a farmer of Beat 7, J. E. Perry, vented his honest indignation, and went so far as to compare the president unfavorably with that Satan of the war years, the kaiser. He was reported by an unsympathetic acquaintance and was afterwards arrested and taken to Montgomery by a special agent of the government for questioning, apparently only to be threatened and released.[15] About the same time, less than six weeks before the end of hostilities, a Bibb County Loyalty and Self-Preservation League was organized to compel all men and women between the ages of sixteen and sixty to pledge to work six days a week. Anyone who refused would be issued a "yellow card" and reported to "the main organization."

Although a few individuals may have become fractious late in the conflict, the initial reaction of Bibb citizens was to respond cooperatively in the national crisis. Almost every group or profession wished to "do their bit." Within the first week of the war, the Bibb Medical Association had tendered its services and its members were soon conducting the physical examinations of recruits. Members of the legal profession assisted the men in filling out their draft questionnaires. The bankers took charge of the government's local war loan campaigns. August 24, 1917, was set as registration day for the women of the county, who were urged to choose their line of service. Even the school children became actively involved. When Bibb County High School opened its doors for the fall term in 1918, Principal J. W. Watson introduced a military program, placing the boys in uniform and requesting discarded guns from military schools. Horace Fancher was appointed captain of Company A and W. R. Martin of Company B. These and many other groups stepped forward to be counted.

Several communities moved to organize home guards but soon found that a more urgent need was to ensure an adequate food supply. Mayor W. T. Griffin of West Blocton called prominent citizens to a meeting in his office with two U.S. government representatives, who told them the startling news that in eight months they would be unable to buy flour at any price.[16] After hearing such dire predictions, the county went to work to organize for the emergency, with the constant prodding of its newspapers. As an additional incentive to plant food crops, it was pointed out that the demoralized Russian Army was retreating and leaving thousands of prisoners to the Germans, "who will make them cultivate their gardens."[17] At the same time, county farmers were encouraged to expect loans from the federal government of as much as $50,000, in some cases for as long a period as forty years. By 1918 almost all farmers were trying to learn to raise wheat. They were also urged by Herbert Hoover, federal food controller, to practice conservation, one measure of which, favored by Editor Nunnelee of the *Press,* was "meatless, wheatless menus." Hoover's office also issued such unpopular edicts as the ban in mid-February 1918 on the killing of hens until the egg season was on the wane. Eggs were then selling in the county at the hitherto unheard-of price of 45 or 50 cents a dozen, the price set by the government being 46 cents.[18]

Prices also soared on corn, peas, and other farm products in the spring of 1918, and as a result everybody was expected to plant a "war garden." Governor Charles Henderson proclaimed March 14 Gardening Day and requested all lumber camps, mines, and factories to free their employees for the day in order to plant a garden as a wartime conservation measure. It was noted later that Bibb miners had cooperated well and that Blocton and Garnsey were in the lead. At Blocton 85 percent of the men were said to have planted gardens, the land and fertilizer contributed by Superintendent Stewart, and at Garnsey 90 percent, encouraged by Superintendent Burgess.[19] To grant both farms and factories longer hours of labor, the nation adopted its first daylight-saving schedule on March 31, 1918, to continue until the end of October, but many Bibb farmers resented the "fast time" and some refused to set their clocks forward.

Meanwhile, shortages had become a problem. Some resourceful housewives found substitutes; one example was the velvet bean coffee served by Mrs. Daniel Snead ("Miss Sallie") at her boardinghouse east of Court Square, noted for its price of 25 cents for bed and 25 cents for a meal. By the fall of 1918, no coal was available, and gasoline was so scarce that the state food administrator forbade Sunday "joy riding."[20] The purchase of sugar was restricted to two pounds per person per month, a limit not always easy to enforce. Several Centreville grocers were summoned to Montgomery by the state food administrator and penalized for violating the sugar and flour regulations.[21]

Feeding Bibb in wartime was a problem to be solved only by hard work and self-denial, but financing the war and making supplies for the soldiers were given an extra dimension of excitement through numerous entertainments and contests. In the spring of 1918, when the Germans had started their great offensive on a fifty-mile front in northern France, Bibb County was entering its third national campaign to undergird the war effort by selling Liberty Loan Bonds, which bore 4½ percent interest. The county Liberty Loan chairman, Letcher Melton of the Bibb County Banking and Trust Company, assisted by the Woman's Liberty Loan Committee, filled the month of April with attractions designed to push Bibb "over the top." One such event was the patriotic parade led by Howard Stewart as "Uncle Sam" and Ivey Logan as "Columbia." Afterward at the courthouse, Dr. H. M. Edmonds of Birmingham was the speaker of the evening, climaxing a series of appeals by local patriots. In the enthusiasm of the occasion, the $6,500 that Centreville had been asked to raise was oversubscribed to a total of $11,650.[22] The mining towns topped their large assessments, too, Marvel, for example, subscribing $20,000.[23]

Other features of this campaign included an appeal several days later by Captain Edouard Hirsch of the French Army, twice wounded and recently awarded the Croix de Guerre, and the visit of a train carrying three cars loaded with relics from the French and Belgian battlefields, through which an estimated 1,200 people passed at the Centreville station.[24] But the event that drew the largest crowd was the well-advertised arrival of five "flying machines" distributing Liberty Loan brochures from the air. Editor Sam Allen of the *Blocton Enterprise* expected 5,000 spectators because he believed few had ever seen five airplanes in the sky at the same time. Further excitement was provided when two planes had difficulty in landing for the picnic planned for the aviators. The result of all these efforts was that the county well exceeded its allotment of $66,000.

In the fall, the Fourth Liberty Loan drive was conducted more quietly but just as successfully. Bibb was one of the first Alabama counties to go "over the top," though its assessment had been increased to $110,000 this time. (Community assessments were based on the ratio of taxable values according to county tax records; for example, Centreville $18,000 and Blocton $27,000.) Even the convicts in the Belle Ellen mines subscribed liberally, reportedly donating voluntarily the money they made by working overtime.

Next in importance to the sale of Liberty Loan Bonds in the county was the work of the Red Cross Society, managed chiefly by the women as the financial drives were by the men. This organization aimed to obtain funds to care for wounded soldiers at the front and also to make articles that they might need. In their efforts to collect funds, both the West Blocton and the Centreville chapters were active in presenting entertainments, including a mask party at which the West Blocton Red Cross cleared $32 and a pig auction that netted the Centreville society $65.[25] But their most popular productions were their womanless and manless weddings, at each of which receipts ran between $50 and $100, though the humor far exceeded the financial gain.[26] Meanwhile, the community chapters opened work rooms in Centreville at the courthouse and in West Blocton at the Elks' Hall, where they vied with each other in the number of operating caps, convalescent robes, pajamas, and knitted sweaters and socks they sent to the regional Red Cross headquarters in New Orleans.

While Bibb Countians were so personally involved in all these and other patriotic endeavors, such as collecting a library for the soldiers and supporting the YMCA in its efforts to care for them, they naturally had other concerns during the war years. They were being pressured to consider two upcoming amendments to the U.S. Constitution, one on prohibition of the sale of alcoholic beverages and the other on woman's suffrage. Within the county, the need discussed most urgently was for better roads, "pike roads." Farmers were disturbed by the inexorable march of the Texas boll weevil.

But all these topics became secondary considerations when the epidemic of Spanish influenza broke out in the fall of 1918. Whole families were laid low by this pestilence; at one time, eight members of Roach Kornegay's household were critically ill.[27] By mid-October the schools were closed, many churches soon afterward suspended services, and the black farmers of Bibb County postponed their fall fair. By the end of the year, the disease had abated, but not before taking the lives of a number of the county's most valued citizens. People mourned for them as well as for the soldiers who were victims of flu in the military camps in this country and for those whose deaths in faraway France were increasingly being reported. Families waited anxiously for news from those still in training in this country and from others on the battlefields of Europe—all of them in a strange, new world.

The Rainbow Division, which included the 167th Infantry Regiment, composed of Alabama men, had sailed from England in November 1917. During the crossing, Alabama soldiers reportedly showed their daredevil courage by "shooting craps" despite the constant threat of German submarines. Afterward, Harrison Brister, a black sharpshooter, wrote home, "We took Christmas in Paris."[28]

These early Bibb soldiers, like those who followed them, were soon quartered in French villages, sometimes, like Raymond Blake, in a barn, where they were struck by the picturesqueness and the economy. Their letters home, describing their new world, were often copied in the local newspapers. Milton Edmonds, son of Richard Edmonds of Harrisburg, was delighted by the green, oval-topped hills, the poppies, wheat as high as his head, fertile soil that never eroded and was cultivated by hand, villages where the farmers lived in stone buildings all of the same design and to which quarters for their animals were attached.[29] From "Somewhere in France" F. L. Scarborough commented: "People here do not farm like we do. They raise mostly grain and vegetables. They have lots of Irish potatoes. They are digging them now. They have some apples and plenty of grapes and make lots of wine. They have no corn, no sweet potatoes, very little sugar or syrup. They have some honey and plenty of milk and butter; plenty of beer and whiskey in almost every store. Lots of pretty girls."[30] Ray Griffin, who was quartered "in a nice camp in a town about the size of West Blocton," was impressed by the good hospital, "lots of flowers everywhere . . . great appetite and officers"; his only difficulty was in making Frenchmen understand his sign language.[31] All these soldiers wrote gratefully of the kindness the French people showed them.

In this personal war in which they had all come over "to lick the Kaiser," they were soon moved to the front, where they went "over the top" to dodge the kaiser's artillery fire and sometimes struggle in hand-to-hand combat with "Fritz." Those in the 167th Infantry, Rainbow Division, saw their first real trenches on February 20, 1918, on the Lorraine front, where they fought for 110 days beside the French "Blue Devils." In June the German hordes were said to be forty-five miles from Paris. Writing the following Christmas from Senzig, Germany, Richard A. Jones summarized the subsequent story of the Alabama regiment:

> We stopped the German drive on July 15, when we were carried to Chateau Thierry to help drive the Germans. There the Alabama regiment lost

> nearly one-half of its old men, but we drove them about fifteen miles. We went from Chateau Thierry to the St. Mihiel front near Toulouse. We drove the Germans about fifteen miles and captured many prisoners and much equipment. I am sure you have read in the papers how well the Rainbow Division fought on September 12th. From there we went to the Veschers front in the Argonne Forest and helped drive the Germans back to Sedan and the Meuse river, where the war ended. We then started "hiking" after the Germans and went through Belgium, Luxembourg, to this place. . . . and the people are treating us so nice we don't know what to think of it.[32]

Three days after the battle of September 12, one boy wrote: "I don't see how it can last much longer. I think old Kaiser Bill has begun to realize that Uncle Sam is too much for him."[33]

Many casualties were reported before the final victory. The Germans made prisoners of some Bibb Countians, like Daniel Gallagher of Blocton and Claude Wallace of the Antioch community. Gallagher, son of Neil Gallagher, was captured with twelve other Americans in the front trenches in France in October 1917 and sent to prison at Touschell, West Prussia.[34] He had been wounded three times. George Burdin's nephew, Howard, was one of many who wrote home appreciatively of the Red Cross nurses in army hospitals. "When I came to, after being under the influence of ether for five hours, a real American woman had my hand," he gloated.[35] Concerning Bibb's Dr. William Peters, who attended the Rainbow Division behind the lines, he later wrote: "Captain Peters sure deserves the Croix de Guerre. After I was dressed I sat for three hours watching him dress the others, and all the time the Germans were shelling the first aid station."[36]

Those who survived their wounds gave vivid and sometimes gleeful accounts of the gruesome action they had witnessed or heard about from their comrades, as in the same letter from Lieutenant Burdin: "Then the first advance was through some woods and the Germans had the trees filled with machine guns. They tell me it sure was fun to watch the devils drop to the ground when they were shot. Just like squirrel hunting. One boy from my platoon who was shot twice told me he got about ten out of the trees. The German infantry retreated so fast it was possible to see only the ones who were hiding, hoping to be passed by or captured. We took very few prisoners, among them three women machine gunners who were chained to their guns."

Hubbard Freeman, son of Reverend George W. Freeman, was a hero in at least two actions. In the first, he saved the life of his brother Isaac, who had been shot in the side. Isaac later reported that the Germans and Americans were fighting hand-to-hand in the pitch dark. He and a German were rolling over and over on the ground when his brother, who had been fighting by his side, came to his rescue. After some difficulty in determining which of the two grappling bodies was his brother, Hubbard killed the German. On another occasion, Hubbard was detailed with five other American soldiers to go over the top in order to obtain information for the intelligence department. When they reached the enemy's entrenchments they came upon eleven men, two of whom they killed, taking the other nine as prisoners. Of these, Hubbard killed the two and captured one. For his heroic action he was awarded the Croix de Guerre, the French Medal of Honor, and the Distinguished Service Medal of the United States.[37]

Although Hubbard and Isaac Freeman came marching home together after the war, another pair of brothers, Reuben and Dewey Kornegay, did not. Dewey recovered from his wounds of September 1918, but Reuben did not survive the German shell that fell near him on November 8, only three days before the armistice was signed. His commanding officer paid tribute to his courage in this letter to his parents, Barney and Lera Kornegay:

> In the battles in Champagne, at Chateau Thierry, in the St. Mihiel Salient, and north of the Argonne, he was always in the fighting and never seemed to know the word fear. His recent promotion to corporal was due solely to his exceptionally good conduct under heavy fire.
>
> When our regiment, which was the first to reach the Meuse river, arrived there, it was necessary to send out a patrol to skirt the banks of the river. Reuben was near the head of the patrol when they were sighted by a German battery unknown to them and shelled. Before they had time to take cover a shell hit near by and Reuben was called upon to make the supreme sacrifice. . . .
>
> His death was almost instantaneous and he is now buried at the south edge of a strip of woods one-half a kilometer SE of Pont Magnus overlooking the Meuse river, his grave properly marked.[38]

Many other families in the county received sad letters of this type, for a total of twenty-three Bibb men lost their lives on the battlefront. Their names are engraved on the Veterans' Monument on the courthouse lawn.

On November 11, 1918, the lucky Bibb soldiers who survived "were on the battlefield up to the 11th hour and the 59th minute when the terms of the Armistice forbade any more firing," Rufus Wallace reported after leaving the Verdun front. He added, "Tell Skate to clear my land, I hope to be home in time to make a crop."[39] Most of Bibb's war-weary soldiers, however, headed east instead of west, serving for six months in the American army of occupation in Germany, along with the rest of the 167th Infantry Regiment.

Meanwhile back in Bibb County, where church bells had been rung

World War I soldier Reuben Kornegay, killed in action in France on November 8, 1918. (Courtesy of Mrs. J. D. Owen)

every day at noon to remind the citizens to pray for the success of the armies in the field, armistice had brought a wild celebration. The Belcher lumber mill whistle, church bells, and sirens woke Centreville to the good news on that Monday morning, and later in the day a vast throng of people from all sections of the county assembled to celebrate peace. At Blocton, where dynamite had been discharged and a grand parade held a week earlier after false news of peace, the celebration was renewed in even livelier fashion on November 11.[40] "Blocton and West Blocton went wild," Editor Allen announced. A half-holiday was declared, an even greater parade was arranged, led by the Blocton Band, and in the evening at the brightly lighted pavilion the Italian Band played gay music. The crowd sang such wartime favorites as "Tipperary," "Over There," and

> How you gonna keep 'em down on the farm
> After they've seen Paree?

Other communities throughout the county had their own celebrations, and so did many homes where one or more service stars hung on a simple square in the window. The Draft Board closed its office and the Red Cross its work rooms, Liberty Loan solicitors relaxed and so did war gardeners, and even the League for Loyalty and Self-Preservation gave up its rigorous work requirements for Bibb citizens. The *Press* took one final shot: "The Kaiser is crazy. He should be treated in a mad house."[41]

Now everyone could look forward to the eventual return of the boys from "over there," and make ready to face a postwar period in which life would necessarily be different. In a real sense, the twentieth century had just begun.

CONCLUSION

THE COUNTY PASSED its hundredth birthday in the same year in which the first World War ended, though no one took public note of the centennial. In February, the anniversary month, its residents were absorbed in the action on the Lorraine front, where many of their sons were going into their first trenches. Throughout the remainder of the year, tension mounted until the news of peace came in November. Those on the home front had neither the time nor the inclination to look back to their origins in the pioneer past nor to recall the slow, steady climb their hardy ancestors had made up the economic ladder during the county's first half century.

Nor would they have considered it an appropriate season in which to remember the fratricidal conflict that followed that ascent because they were now singing patriotically of their own sons, "The Yanks are coming!" For most of this generation, which had grown up in the aftermath of Confederate defeat, the struggle back to a measure of security and prosperity during the second half-century of the county's existence had required courage and determination like that of the first settlers. Now that Bibb had recently completed that cycle a second time, perhaps its residents were too close to see it in perspective, though many—both black and white—had kept their sense of humor, as revealed in numerous anecdotes about their experiences during the lean years.

The attempt to recapture the whole story of that first century had to wait until another time. Obviously no such attempt can ever be entirely successful, especially because two large segments of the population, here as elsewhere in Alabama, were inarticulate during most of that period: the blacks and the poor whites. Yet Bibb historians do possess the advantage of fairly complete official records because the courthouse, luckier than those in a number of other Alabama counties, was never burned. Through these records and numerous others of many types, it is possible now to gain a fuller perception of the identity of this county.

Although small and relatively uncelebrated, it has made various contributions to the state. It was influential on the Alabama political scene through such men as Lieutenant Governor E. H. Moren in the Reconstruction period and Samuel M. Adams and Gratton B. Crowe during the Populist revolt. It produced a pioneer black educator in Henry D. Davidson, whose effect in the adjoining counties is yet to be fully assessed.

If its political leadership during its first century was sporadic and its black leadership confined chiefly to one native, the influence of its early experiments in industry was more extensive. The Scottsville cotton factory of 1836 was one of the first in the state, founded two years before Daniel Pratt settled in Prattville, and in the spring of 1865 it was said to be the largest in Alabama. Bibb's ironworks, also among the first, led in the production of iron blooms, along with the forges of Shelby and Talladega, until the Civil War. During the war, they furnished through the Brierfield plant the strongest iron discovered for molding cannon for the Confederate Navy. Coal mining began early during the Civil War, and, when the coal seams were reopened some fifteen years later, the county became an important source of coke for the Birmingham steel mills for nearly half a century. Even before coal mining declined, the timber industry was becoming well known throughout the state, and today it not only furnishes numerous lumber companies in the county but also ships to several large paper mills.

Although Bibb has won distinctions in these areas and perhaps others, it has remained typical of its section of Alabama. Like the surrounding counties, and indeed much of the state, it has made a gradual transition from an agricultural to a predominantly industrial economy. Its story, in keeping with that of most of central Alabama and in contrast with that of the Tennessee valley and of the Black Belt, records the growth of chiefly small farms and, compared with counties like Jefferson, of small industries. Beginning with its early allegiance to Andrew Jackson, the county has usually voted Democratic, but, like some of the surrounding ones, it was capable of turning briefly to the American and Populist parties. Although it often aligned itself with its Black Belt neighbors in the nineteenth century, it almost always cast its majority vote with its twin, Shelby, the county created by the same legislative act in 1818. The history of Bibb suggests many parallels, both economic and political, not only with Shelby but also with the whole of central Alabama.

APPENDIX I

REVOLUTIONARY SOLDIERS WHO SETTLED IN BIBB COUNTY

(Derived from federal pension applications, courtesy of Charles E. Boyd, New York City, with additions from cemetery record, McCord, *Baptists of Bibb County*.)

Agrippa Atkinson
John Blake
David Cammack
Jeremiah Clements
Jonathan Clower (1763–1836), born in Pennsylvania, enlisted in North Carolina.
Charles Coleman, emigrated from North Carolina by 1817, died in 1824 in Greene County.
Zacheus Corley (1762–), moved to Bibb in 1818 from Edgefield District, S.C.
Theophilus Goodwin, a private in the North Carolina Continental Army.
Henry Haggard (1746–), age 94 in 1840; Baptist minister, buried Cahaba Valley Cemetery.
Benjamin Hollingshead (c. 1760–).
Hugh Jones
David Lindsey, died in 1835, buried in Shelby County.
John Mahan (1750–1820), lieutenant Virginia Line troops, buried near Brierfield.
George Mayberry, born Virginia, died 1848 "age about 97 years," buried near Bibb-Perry line.
Richard McCary (1763–1858), died in Choctaw County.
Sabert Oglesby, born in Scotland, died 1831 and buried in Hickman Cemetery; 4th Artillery Regiment, South Carolina.
John Smith (1759–).
William Taber (1761–1844), died in Winston County, Mississippi.
John Wallace (1758–1847), North Carolina troops; buried at Six Mile.
John Edward Ward (1756–1837), buried at Antioch Cemetery.
John Wilson (1760–).

APPENDIX II

COUNTY JURY VENIRE, 1819, 1820, 1821

(Source: Minutes of County Court)

February 1819:
Martin Haggard
Martin Shoultz
Flemmen R. Simmons
James Shaw
Alexander Hamilton
John Henry
George Mayberry
Archimedes Mahan
William Jones
Edward Mahan
Noah Haggard
John Jones
David Lewis
Jonathan A. Thrailkill
Thomas Barnett
Zachariah Canterbury
Thomas Rawling
John Jackson
William Armstrong
Mordecai Lewis
Samuel Wilson
Thomas Gibson
Robert Stacy
James Page
Kinason Shoults
Oliver C. Cleveland
Samuel Canterbury
Ebenezer Leeth, Jr.
Mitchel Roberts
Charles Polak
George Mayberry, Jr.
Jacob Mayberry
Cornelius Cox
John Smitherman
William Frier
William Buckhalter

July 1820:
Francis Carson
William Foshee
John Henry, Sr.
John Moore
William Beaird
Samuel Smitherman
William West
Isaac Turnbow
Jacob Johnson
John Counsell
Thomas Rawling
Mitchel Watkins
John R. Henderson
William Blake
Robert Carson
Thomas Carlton
Jacob Lowdermeck
Gilbert Reynolds
James Sample

February 1821:
William White
Harling Strange
Jesse Horne
John Smith
Thomas White
Michajah Williamson
Isaac Carlton
Grief Johnson
Francis Hicks
John Alphin
Daniel Lewis
William Pounds
John Smitherman
Noah B. Coker
Nathan Taber
Levin Watkins
Samuel Neighbors
Jesse Watkins

APPENDIX III
CHARGE CUSTOMERS OF JAMES C. C. WILEY BEFORE 1829

(Index of account book kept by Wiley in Centreville, used by Dr. David R. Boyd later, from January 1, 1829, now the property of Louise Meigs Rogan, Centreville.)

Adams, George
Adams, William
Avery, Allen
Avery, John
[B's and C's missing]
Davis, J.(?) W.
Duncan, Nelson
Edminson, James
Edmonds, ———
Elam, Hiram
Elam, John
Farr, William
Francis, Gainis (?)
Garner, John
Gordon, Charley
Green, William
Hague, Hiram
Hall, William A.
Hamilton, John
Hank, Robert
Harbin, William B.
Henderson, Lewis
Henry, Hugh
Henry, John
Hill, Alexander
Hill, Claiborne
Hill, George
Hunt, John
James, Frederick
Johnson, Duncan
Johnson, Jacob
Johnson, William
Johnston, Lee
Jones, John
Kellum, Isma
Kellum, Riley
Kellum, Smith
Kennedy, Lewis
Kornegay, Barney
Lightsey, David
Logan, John H.
Owens, Benjamin (?)
Owens, John
Owens, Thomas
Parker, Isaac
Pope, Travis
Porter, James
Quin, John
Risenger, John
Rogers, Lissa (?)
Sawyers, Benjamin
Shamblin, John
Smith, James
Smith, Joshua
Snead, Daniel
Stuart (?), John W.
Summers, John
Terry, Daniel

Tompson, William
Watkins, Jeter
Willson, John M.
Woodruff, Samuel
Wynn, Samuel
Yager, Ezekiel

APPENDIX IV
PATIENTS OF DR. DAVID R. BOYD, 1829 AND HIS SUCCESSOR, 1836

(Index of account book, now the property of Louise Meigs Rogan, Centreville)

1829-:
Adams, George
Adams, Lee
Allen, Drewry
Arnold, William
Baker, Abner
Baldwin, John
Barnes, John
Barr, Jacob
Belcher, Beverly
Berry, Mrs.
Bishop, Allen
Boidston, Levi
Bowden, Bryant
Brown, David L.
Brown, Willis
Caddell, William
Camp, B. L.
Camp, James
Canterberry, Zacheus
Carr, Derastus
Carter, Charles
Carter, Samuel
Cates, Betsey
Cates, John
Cawley (Corley?), Zacheus
Clabough, John
Clark, Alexander
Clark, Daniel
Clark, James B.
Clark, John
Clement, Luallen
Cleveland, Oliver C.
Coker, Noah B.
Coker, William B.
Collier, Charles H.
Cottingham, John
Council, John
Crawford, Robert
Creed, Daniel
Cummins, Malcijah
Cutts, Sherod
Davidson, Samuel W.
Davis, James W.
Davis, Ransome, Jr.
Davis, Willis
Dennis, Abijah
Deshazo, Wilkins
Dominick, Jacob
Doss, Mark W.
Duncan, Richard
Duff, Walter C.
Edminson, James
Edmonds, ———
Elam, Hiram
Elam, John

Falkner, Warren W.
Fergueson, Larkin
Fergueson, Lewis
Fields, Willie H.
Fitz, Reuben
Foley, Needham
Fondern, William A.
Foster, Anderson
Frost, William
Fry, Loderick
Garner, James
Gaskill, Evan
Goodson, John A.
Gordon, Charles
Goss, John
Goss, Matthew
Goss, Samuel
Goss, Thomas
Green, William
Griffin, Benjamin
Griffin, Bird
Hadley, Hubbart
Hall, Winstead
Hamilton, John
Hanks, Robert
Harbin, William B.
Harmon, John
Harmon, William
Harmon, Zach
Harper, Oliver
Harpole, Squire
Hays, James
Henderson, Ichabod
Henderson, Michael
Henry, Hugh
Henry, James
Henry, Jefferson
Henry, John, Jr.
Henry, John, Sr.
Henson, Matthew
Hicks, Frank
Hicks, Alexander
Hill, Alexander
Hill, Claiborne
Hill, James, Jr.
Hill, Jesse
Hill, John, Sr.
Hill, Robert, Jr.
Hinds, Josiah
Hinson, Aaron
Houghton, Edmund
Howard, Edmund
Howard, George
Hunt, John
James, Adam
Jarman, John I.
Johnson, Duncan
Johnson, Hardy, Jr.
Johnson, Jacob
Johnson, Joseph
Johnson, Lee
Johnson, Luke
Johnson, Nancy
Johnson, Solomon
Johnson, William (Haysop)
Jones, Isaac
Kellum, Isma
Kellum, Riley
Kellum, Smith
Kornegay, Barney
Lambden, Levi
Lankston, Isaac
Lathram, ———
Lee, Bryant, Jr.
Lee, Cullen
Lee, Edward
Lee, John
Lee, Hopkins
Lee, Lewis
Lee, William
Leeth, Ebenezer
Lewis, James
Lewis, Jonathan
Lewis, Samuel
Lewis, Willie
Lightsey, David
Lockhart, James
Logan, John H.
Looney, Hugh
Lowe, Lunsford

Lynn, James
McCall, Daniel
McCarver, L. B.
McDaniel, John
McElroy, Ransome
McElroy, William
McEntosh, Daniel
McGuire, Neal
McKee, William A.
McQueen, Malcob
Majure, James
Majure, Nathaniel
Mathis, Moses
Marlin, Peter
Mayberry, George
Mayberry, Jacob
Medders, William
Mitchell, Joseph
Moore, Alfred
Moore, John
Morris, Baylus
Motes, Joshua
Motley, Jacob
Norris, William B.
Owens, Berry
Owens, John
Owens, Thomas
Page, Stewart
Parker, Isaac
Parker, Jesse
Parker, John
Parker, Maves
Parker, Matthews
Parker, Robert
Parkerson, Thomas J.
Pate, Robert
Perkins, Isaac
Perkins, Thadius
Persons, John
Peters, Martin
Pew, Sally
Potts, Henry
Potts, Jonathan
Powell, James M.
Pope, James
Pratt, Absalom
Pratt, Hopkins
Pratt, John
Purtle, George
Purtle, Samuel
Quin, John
Raglin, Benjamin
Rayfield, Daniel
Rayfield, John
Reach, Bailey
Reach, Charles
Reach, Enoch
Reach, Nimrod
Red, Josiah
Risinger, John
Robinson, Alexander
Rogers, Jesse
Rottenberry, Prestley
Saunders, Sherod
Sawyer, William E.
Sexton, Sterling
Shamblin, John
Sherbert, William
Shettlesworth, Martin
Shutts, Ristley (Schultz)
Shutts, Joseph
Shutts, Peter
Shutts, Valentine
Shutts, Valentine, Sr.
Smith, Arch.
Smith, Avington F.
Smith, Clayton
Smith, Henry
Smith, James
Smith, John
Smith, Joshua
Smith, Lewis
Smith, Riley
Smith, Samuel
Smith, William
Sneed, Daniel
Sparkman, William L.
Stacy, Robert
Stanley, Jordan
Starling, Prudence

Stewart, George
Steele, James
Steele, John
Steele, Robert
Stewart, John W.
Stirrell, Alfonzo
Stoutenborough, Anthony
Stover, Josiah
Summers, Thomas
Summers, William
Tabor, William
Tate, Samuel
Tate, Sintha
Tate, William F.
Terry, James
Thomas, Solomon
Thralekill, Jonathan A.
Thompson, Ignatius
Thompson, William
Trucks, George
Tucker, John
Tune, William
Walker, Hiram
Walker, Thomas
Wallace, John
Wallace, Matthew
Wallace, Robert
Watkins, Mitchell
Watkins, Peter
Ward, James
Welden, Daniel
Welden, John
White, Thomas
Whitley, Allen
Whitley, Christopher
Wilson, James
Wilson, John M.
Winn, Samuel
Wolley, Green B.
Wood, Samuel
Wood, William
Woodruff, Nathaniel
Yager, Abijah
Yager, B. Mc.
Yager, Ezekiel
Yager, Mark
Young, Woodson

Patients Added Later (1836)

Birgis, Isaiah
Boyd, Trecy
Brown, Jesse
Carlisle, James
Crawford, Thomas
Davis, Thomas
Defreese, L. B.
Digby, Willey
Foster, Richard
Frost, W. Jacob
Fuller, Mastin I.
Hall, H. William
Hampton, G. W.
Hathcock, Thomas
Hemphill, Hiram
Hurley, William
Hollingshead, Benj.
Jennings, John
Johnston, Redmen
Johnston, Vardy
Jones, Rath
Kennedy, Lewis
Lawrence, Richard
Lewis, Joshua
Logan, Majure
Lucas, Abraham
Mosley, Joab
Nichols, William
Owens, Bird
Owens, Rheubin
Owens, William
Potts, Alfred
Potts, Ann
Roberts, Thomas P.
Robinson, James Sr.
Risinger, George
Rucker, Lindsey
Rucker, Willis
Sinclair, Benjamin
Smith, Joshua
Stringfellow, Joshua
Swindler, ———

Tate, James
Tucker, Howard
Tucker, Ruth
Wagone, ———
Whitehead, Absolom
Whitehead, William
Williams, S. I.
Wood, B. John
Woodruff, Ann
Woodruff, Newton

APPENDIX V
OWNERS OF SLAVES (20 OR MORE) IN 1850

(Derived from *Seventh Census, 1850*)

S. W. Davidson 98
Jacob Mayberry 42
A. K. Harris 44
Elisha King 41
George W. Howard 36
W. C. Duff 31
Charles Collier 27
Alex Avery 20
Henry Avery 22
Pleasant Hill 23
Robert Hill 63
James Hill 25
M. Banks 57
James H. Green 29
O. C. Cleveland 25
William Kinnaird 24
Margaret Goodwin 21
William H. Wilson 21
Joseph Smitherman 20
Enoch Latham 23
T. N. Abney 20
Turner Goodwin 44
William Christian 44
William Y. White 61
James Smelley 20
Joseph Wood 46
Daniel Ward 36

APPENDIX VI
CITIZENS IN CERTAIN VOCATIONS IN 1860

(Compiled from *Eighth Census, 1860*)

Merchants
R. D. Hicks, Randolph
William Hicks, Randolph
W. M. Howard, Centreville
Jacob Kersh, Centreville
J. S. Kennedy, Centreville
J. W. Person, Centreville
Charles Sanford, Centreville
Lucius Winship, Centreville

Lawyers
Zachary Abney, Randolph
Henry Brown, Centreville
W. S. Hornsby, Centreville
Robert McIlvain, Centreville
T. J. Smitherman, Centreville

Overseers
William Acker, Centreville
M. Bankston, Centreville
T. W. Burns, Maplesville
Miller Corley, Centreville
Peter Harris, Six Mile
Alex Hill, Centreville
J. D. Holsemback, Six Mile
Whitney Jones, Maplesville
J. M. McCage, no post office listed
Reuben Owens, Six Mile
Jesse Taylor, Centreville
Wilburn Vance, Oakleyville
M. K. White, Six Mile
Zach Young, Centreville

Physicians
Thomas Broughton, Randolph
James R. Calhoun, Centreville
Alsey Clements, Mars
James W. Crawford, Centreville
Ralph Davis, Six Mile
J. F. Gay, Maplesville
W. C. Jeffries, Centreville
J. S. Johnson, Randolph
R. R. McPhearson, Oakleyville
J. T. McSpadden (dentist), Centreville
Harry O. Melton, Six Mile
D. E. Monore, Mars
E. H. Moren, Centreville
L. Ragland, Scottsville
R. L. Rockett, Scottsville
John M. Shelton, Maplesville
J. W. Spenser, Centreville
J. M Williams, Centreville
Francis Woodruff, Oakleyville
G. W. Yarbour, Centreville

Schoolteachers
William Boling, Centreville
John Campbell, Randolph
Barton B. Carter, Centreville
Eugenia Clabaugh, Maplesville
Isaac M. Clifton, Randolph

R. C. Corley, Centreville
N. B. Dansby, Centreville
Jasper Fair, Centreville
Martha Fuller, Centreville
A. W. Gray, Mars
Eliza Green, Six Mile
Edward Johnson, Randolph
Joseph Johnson, Maplesville
Pinkney Jones, Randolph
D. C. Logan, Randolph
Barton Lowery, Centreville
W. Moncrief, Centreville
Virginia Paschall, Centreville
Walter Paschall, Centreville
William J. Peters, Six Mile
Richard Hopkins Pratt, Centreville
William Pratt, Centreville
Mary A. Steele, Centreville
C. J. Stewart, Centreville
Mark A. Toomey, Affonee
R. D. Tubbs, Scottsville
Isaac Ward, Maplesville
W. C. Ward, Six Mile
Frances Woodruff, Oakleyville
Gef Woodruff, Randolph

APPENDIX VII
MUSTER ROLLS OF CERTAIN CONFEDERATE COMPANIES

(Transcribed from Xerox copies in Alabama Archives and National Archives, Washington)

Company F, 11th Alabama Infantry Regiment

James L. Davidson, Capt.
Joseph Caddell, 1st Lt.
W. J. Suttle, 2nd Lt.
L. A. Winship, 3rd Lt.

Later Officers:

Joseph Caddell, Capt.
W. J. Suttle, 1st Lt.
Zachariah Abney, 2nd Lt.
P. M. Vance, 3rd Lt.

Avery, Arthur
Avery, Henry
Alexander, Abner U.
Arnold, Elbert
Barnes, James B.
Barnes, Martin V.
Barton, Richard
Bolling, William R.
Brazzell, Green C.
Brown, David L.
Brown, Jesse
Brown, William H.
Caldwell, Ben
Campbell, Robert
Carson, M. J.
Childers, William
Chisolm (Chism), J. D.
Conwill, Daniel
Corley, Miller
Davidson, S. W. (Jr.)
Davis, Henry
Davis, John M.
Digby, John H.
Edwards, Perry
Fitts, Oliver
Fondren, John
Franklin, William
Frazier, L. W.
Gardner, Andrew J.
Gardner, Brantley M.
Gardner, John S.
Goodson, Rufus G.
Goodwin, Henry C.

Goodwin, Martin C.
Goss, Stephen
Green, William V.
Griffin, David N.
Griffin, William
Hamilton, John D.
Hardin, Samuel
Henry, J. C.
Henry, Patrick C.
Hill, Alexander P., Sr.
Hill, James, Jr.
Hogan, Marion
Hogan, Richard
Holmes, Jordon
Horn, Leslie L.
James, Absolom
James, Frederick
Jarvis, Carter
Johnson, Oliver C.
Johnston, John W.
Jones, Carter
Kennedy, Josiah M.
Kornegay, Barney K.
Latham, Wesley E.
Lee, Fulton
Leopard, John K.
Lightsey, Daniel
Lightsey, Martin
Lightsey, Moses J.
Lowry, Charles C.
Mayberry, George LaFayette
Mayberry, Jacob D.
McCraw, James D.
Moon, Martin D.
Morrow, Wiley
Moses, John T.
Oldham, Marion
Owen, Thomas
Owen, William R.
Person, James W.
Person, Willie D.
Phillips, Fred M.
Platt, Bryan L.
Potts, Henry
Powell, George M.
Quinn, Chesterfield W.
Rasberry, Newton
Rasberry, William
Raymond, Thomas
Risinger, John
Roberson, Jesse J.
Roper, Thomas F.
Sanford, Benjamin R.
Scroggins, Wiley W.
Simpson, Simri M.
Smelley, James W.
Smelly, John H.
Smith, Carter M.
Smitherman, Newton
Smitherman, Peter
Smitherman, T. J.
Sneed, William J.
Spinks, Jasper
Spinks, Newton
Suttle, James N.
Taylor, George
Taylor, Jacob J.
Taylor, Lewis
Thomas, Elias M.
Thompson, Thomas H.
Wagoner, James M.
Watkins, William
Webb, Columbus
Wilson, William J.
Woodruff, George
Woodward, George
Wooley, Green B.
Wright, Sampson W.

Company B, 20th Alabama Infantry

Jas. W. Dedman, Capt.
T. R. Furguson, 1st Lt.
J. M. Montgomery, 2nd Lt.
W. A. Sandford, 3rd Lt.

F. W. Naince (?), 1st Sgt.
A. S. Evans, 2nd Sgt.
W. S. Campbell, 3rd Sgt.
Jas. Adams, 4th Sgt.
P. M. Farrington, 5th Sgt.
R. Carmy, 1st Corp.
A. Jackson, 2nd Corp.
J. Dubose, 3rd Corp.
W. Freeman, 4th Corp.

A. Attaway
D. M. Atchinson
S. S. Arledge
H. Brado
W. J. Bates
John Brooks
J. M. Byrd
T. M. Burk
B. W. Baxter
Jas. F. Bell
J. B. Barnett
J. J. Bryant
J. Baxley (?)
J. I. Collins
John Campbell
W. P. Cobb
Jas. Cobb
P. R. Crim
W. P. Crim
J. W. Craig
A. Coleman
J. M. Davenport
H. H. Davenport
N. M. Dennis
C. C. Dennis
A. J. Donaghey
J. J. Donaghey
R. B. Edwards
Jas. Edwards
Jasper Farrington
P. B. Gordon
A. H. Gilmer
W. H. Gordon
J. H. Harrell
John Hamilton
H. H. Houston
W. H. Huffman
J. J. Houston
J. W. Jones
John Lowrey, Sr.
W. P. Lewis
R. H. Lewis
John F. Lowery
G. W. Milling
Z. J. Milling
J. Merriwether
J. B. Martin
W. Y. Moore
H. M. Mason
John Y. Moore
W. McGraw
T. McCord
John Nix
W. H. Osborne
J. M. Pickins
W. H. Peeples
Jas. Pelegrene
S. A. Pearson
A. Picken
S. Prescott
A. C. Y. Smith
James Sharp
D. S. Sisk
W. T. Smith
J. Simpson
W. S. Scott
J. D. Standerfer
Jas. M. Scott
M. J. Surles
J. W. Thrash
A. B. Yerrell
D. M. R. Vickers
L. Wainbacher
Jasper Williams
A. C. Ward
H. P. Ward
H. J. Ward
Jas. Wooley

J. L. C. Williams
H. J. Wilson
James Wallace
W. S. Woods

Company D, 20th Alabama Infantry Regiment

1. Pratt, Richard H., Captain
2. Defir, Jown W., 1st Lieut.
3. Glass, William M., 2nd Lieut.
4. Lowery, William F., 2nd Lieut.

1. Paschall, Walter C., 1st Sergt.
2. Trott, Benjamin F., 2nd Sergt.
3. Pratt, Absalom, 3rd Sergt.
4. Arnold, James, 4th Sergt.
5. Fancher, Henry F., 5th Sergt.
6. James, Frederick, 1st Corporal
7. Creel, Jackson, 2nd Corporal
8. Edmit, Blakey, 3rd Corporal
9. Friday, Martin, 4th Corporal
10. Vernon, Jessie, Musician
11. Abston, John N.
12. Abston, George
13. Alexander, John A.
14. Allen, Pleasant
15. Avery, Arthur, Jr.
16. Avery, Able K.
17. Blake, John
18. Boyd, Richard S.
19. Brazell, James B.
20. Brown, Waymon L.
21. Brewer, Henry
22. Burdishaw, Presley
23. Burton, Thomas J.
24. Barius (?), Thomas
25. Brown, Elijah
26. Carter, Samuel P.
27. Carter, John
28. Creel, James F.
29. Creel, John Van B.
30. Camp, James
31. Canterbory, Thomas
32. Canterbory, Samuel
33. Fair, William C.
34. Fair, Pleasant
35. Fair, Andrew
36. Fulgham, James W.
37. Fulton, Robert
38. Gentry, James H.
39. Gray, Wiley A.
40. Gray, William
41. Gray, Lawrence
42. Greathouse, James M.
43. Greathouse, Isaac J.
44. Goodwin, John
45. Horton, Bevil
46. Horton, Noah C.
47. Horton, Alvin W.
48. Harpole, Newton F.
49. Holland, David G.
50. Hagler, John M.
51. Hagler, Thomas C.
52. Harkey, William
53. James, Jasper E.
54. James, Pleasant
55. James, Augustus W.
56. Johnson, Abner
57. Kirbo, William
58. Langston, John M.
59. Langston, Jasper D.
60. Langston, Newton P.
61. Lawsey (?), Isaac N.
62. Litton, Morton C.
63. Long, John W.
64. Lindsey, Middleton
65. Lindsey, Elbert
66. Lee, Nichols
67. McKleroy, James
68. McKleroy, William H.
69. McCuley (?), Robert
70. Mikel, Casper
71. Milum, James
72. Miller, Jessie
73. Miller, Jessie James R.
74. Miller, Joshua E.
75. Marchant, Daniel

76. Meders, James F.
77. Nichols, Daniel N.
78. Pratt, William F.
79. Pender, Thomas
80. Perry, Emmanuel L.
81. Rotenberry, James J.
82. Rotenberry, Columbus
83. Russell, Leon M.
84. Shows, John C.
85. Smith, James M.
86. Smith, Newton
87. Seals, John
88. Steele, Christopher
89. Stewart, Francis
90. Shuttleworth, Merit
91. Shuttleworth, James
92. Shuttleworth, Jackson
93. Summers, John D.
94. Stimpson, George L.
95. Stearett, William
96. Thrasher, John
97. Trott, John C.
98. Taylor, James H.
99. Taylor, John Wesley
100. Thompson, James
101. Underwood, James
102. Wilson, Haymon W.
103. Vernon, Obediah C.

Wallace, Thaddeus, 5th Sergt. (?)
Brassel, Oliver W.

Company F, 20th Alabama Infantry Regiment

Lucius J. Lockett, Capt.
William Shapperd, 1st Lt.
Joseph H. Speek, Lt.
Chapman Spencer, Lt.
Box George, Sgt.
Davis Hugh, Sgt.
Isaac Parish, Sgt.
J. R. R. Arendal, Sgt.
Chester Woods, Cpl.
Uriah Dobbins, Cpl.
J. H. A. Turner, Cpl.

Arendall, John W.
Arnold, Wiman
Belard, Jesse W.
Blackman, Stephen
Broadnax, James
Britt, George
Busart (?) Thomas D.
Burns, Alexander
Crawford, Franklin W.
Crews, Henry R.
Collwin, ——— H.
Clinton, Thos. S.
Crisson, Daniel
Crawford, John W.
Cawdle, William
Colburn, Louis, M.
Dobbins, Wm.
Dinklin, George Y.
Davis, Thos.
Eubanks, Burrell
Eubanks, William B.
Fisher, John W.
Gale, Leonard
George, Jas.
Hogus, John J.
Hopkins, Wm. W.
Horn, Levie L.
Harper, George D.
Henderson, James H.
Johnson, John
Levereth, John W.
Levenbed, Job W.
Lowry, John C.
McGowin, Thos.
Morgan, John
McDivid, Peter
Morrison, ———
Nichols, Wreslee
Petridge, T.
Payne, Charles H.

Peters, Marcus L.
Roberts, Horace R.
Roberts, Thos. J.
Smith, Nathaneal W.
Stokes, James A.
Selz, Rufus A.
Stewart, John
Stewart, Andrew
Stephens, McFields
Smelly, Thos.
Tubb, R. P.
Vaughan, Ausi
Wyers, John H.
Wallace, John
Webb, John T.
Weeks, John
Young, William R.

Company H, 20th Alabama Infantry Regiment

John Peterson, Capt.
S. W. Davidson, Jr., 1st Lt.
W. A. Dockett, 2nd Lt.
W. F. Hobron, Jr., 2nd Lt.
J. F. Perkins, Sgt.
J. R. Taylor, Sgt.
M. A. Toonree, Sgt.
W. M. Belcher, Sgt.
W. K. Moore, Cpl.
E. B. Mayfield, Cpl.
John Mizzer, Cpl.
R. H. Woolley, Cpl.

Avery, S. A. D.
Barner, John
Barnett, James
Barnett, S. T.
Beton, T. J.
Bridwell, Jerry
Brown, R. G.
Codive, D. M.
Codive, J. M.
Colburn, Dan'l
Cunningham, Jas.
Davis, Felix
Davis, S. H.
Davis, William
Duke, J. G.
Duncan, James
Edmonds, J. M.
Edmonds, J. W.
Elam, Isaac
Elam, William B.
Ethridge, G. N.
Fike, W. W.
Fondum, T. B.
Fowler, John W.
Gentry, N. F.
Hobron, Jackson
Hobron, H. N.
Hobron, Handeford
Hobron, William
Harth, Henry
Hartley, J. A.
Holman, Dan'l
Holman, J. Mc.
Holman, E. E.
Hunt, J. T.
Hutchins, Jas.
Jolly, H. S.
Jolly, W. E.
Jones, John
Kinerd, W.
Kinerd, Jas.
Linn, James
Little, W.
Mathis, Williams
McDonald,
McElroy, J. S.
Meggs, James
Mitchell, R. W.
Morton, J. T.
Nichols, F. M.
Parker, Edward

Parker, Thos.
Rains, J. R.
Rutherford, W. C.
Steel, Harvey
Steelman, D. T.
Steelman, J. T.
Steelman, W. Mc
Terry, J. W.
Townsend, R. P.
Tune, Thomas
Watkins, J. B.
Weirs, John
Yeager, D. H. L.
Yeager, E. J.
Yeager, F. S.
Yeager, U. P.
Yeath, Rob't.

Company B, 44th Alabama Infantry Regiment

Jno. H. Jones, Capt.
J. D. Brown, 1st Lt.
Guston Ambrose, 2nd Lt.
Joab Goodson, 2nd Lt.
Felix Woods, Sgt.
S. W. Frederick, Sgt.
Joel B. Lowrey, Sgt.
Lafayette H. Carlton, Sgt.
Pleasant M. Fancher, Sgt.
Algenon P. Wallace, Cpl.
Jas. S. Chesser, Cpl.
Elias M. Mink, Cpl.
D. A. Abston, Cpl.

Abston, Jno. W.
Allen, M. J.
Allen, Drury O.
Allen, Coleman
Ashworth, Marion B.
Bates, Hiram
Bankston, W. L.
Berry, Jas. W.
Blackston, Thos.
Bracknell, Aquilla
Bracknell, Wm.
Brown, Wm. W.
Brown, Dan'l
Bunn, Jas. D. T.
Burns, Hiram L.
Canterberry, Nicholas J.
Canterberry, Jefferson D.
Carlisle, Wm. T.
Clark, Jas. J.
Clark, Travis L.
Campbell, Wm. J.
Deason, James
Deason, Jno. C.
Ellison, James
Fancher, Jas. W.
Fuller, Wm. R.
Fulghum, Anthony
Harkey, Reuben C.
Hubbard, Minor C.
Hubbard, Geo. W.
Hubbard, Calvin
Hubbard, Stephen M.
Jarman, Emanuel W.
Kiser, Paul H.
Little, Jasper J.
Lowrey, S. D.
Lucas, Rufus
Martin, Allen
McElroy, Wm. W.
Martin, Godfrey
McCulley, Jason
Massey, Jno. J.
Meadows, M. V.
Merriwether, Robt. T.
Mitchell, Geo. H.
Moore, Thompson
Nash, Jno. W.
Nelson, Wm. H.
Nelson, Jas. J.
Nelson, Dan'l. C.

Nolen, Myrick
Norwood, Samuel
Owen, Henry
Perry, Levin
Perry, Jas. C.
Perry, Milton W.
Perry, Wm. B.
Pierson, Wm.
Pratt, Marshall J.
Pritchard, Norris
Ratliff, Evan
Reach, Jas. C.
Reach, Theophilas
Seaman, Edw.
Sherbert, Wm. F.
Sherbert, Jno. B.
Sherbert, N. A.
Smith, Chas. C.
Smith, Wm. Riley
Smith, Eli
Smith, Wm. Redman
Stalkman, John
Stevens, Wm. D.
Tate, Jas. M.
Vernon, Thos. J.
Wagoner, Elisha J.
Ward, Jno. P.
Williams, Jas. H.
Williams, Elias M.
Windham, M. J.
Woods, Robt. E.
Thompson, Nathan
Cobb, Saml. C.
Colbert, Thos. W.
Gandy, Harvey M.

Company F, 44th Regiment Alabama Infantry

H. C. Snead, Capt.
W. D. Oakley, 1st Lt.
J. S. Haraldson, 2nd Lt.
Pressley Arnold, 3rd Lt.
John J. Persons, 1st Sgt.
Charles J. Stewart, Sgt.
Henley D. Lightsey, Sgt.
David M. Corley (?) Sgt.
John L. Adams, Cpl.
Wilson L. Kersh, Cpl.
John M. Oakley, Cpl.
L. W. Frazier, Cpl.
John D. McKinney, Cpl.

Henry Avery
William Avery
A. D. Avery
J. Arnold
D. W. Atcherson
B. T. Bailey
Emsley Bearden
Hardy Bearden
John H. Bolander
William Bolander
Elias H. Corly (Cosby)
Charles Cosby (Corly)
Collumbus Cosby (Corly)
Allen Carter
Henry Cash
W. D. Champion
John W. Clark
William Clark
J. S. Cleveland
E. M. Cousson
Henry Cutts
John Cutts
James A. Defir
John W. Defir
Sam C. Dudley
John T. Edwards
Levy Edwards
S. R. Edwards
Isaac Elam
Cecil Fair

Thomas Fletcher
A. J. Fondren
Samuel Fulton
William Fulton
Allen Gentry
James Gentry
L. R. Hall
J. C. Hardy
Robert S. Harris
Joseph Helton
A. M. Hill
Lewis Horn
William Hornsby
Thomas Hunicutt
E. L. Johnston
Philip R. Johnson
James A. Jones
J. R. C. Jones
Collumbus James
Lewis King
Jim Krout
J. E. Lawrence
W. S. Lawrence
T. N. Lawrence
Joseph Latham
Alexander Lindsey
Hiram C. McKinney
J. M. McSpadden
John E. Mason
Racy Maness
James Mathes
Levie Morris
Fielding Oakley
Calvin Oldham
M. G. Oldham
William Ponder
Kinchen Ponder
Green Rasbery
L. K. Russel
C. L. Stewart
J. W. Stewart
R. E. Stewart
W. D. Scott
Bengiman Scott
G. W. Stockman
J. A. Smith
A. J. Stringfellow
John W. Terry
A. W. Thompson
N. H. Thompson
Jackson Trucks
D. D. Trucks
F. M. Trucks
G. W. Threadgill
L. L. Wyatt
Thomas Walker
J. M. Wilson
J. M. West

Company G, 44th Alabama Infantry Regiment

Tho. C. Daniel, Capt.
B. W. Brown, 1st Lt.
W. A. Dunklin, 2nd Lt.
Jno. W. Lawrence, 3rd Lt.
M. J. Williams, 1st Sgt.
W. P. Becker, 2nd Sgt.
L. A. Cockrell, 2nd Sgt.
S. E. Macon, 2nd Sgt.
D. G. Wilson, 3rd Sgt.
Jno. C. Phillips, 5th Sgt.
A. L. McLean, 1st Cpl.
R. P. Haralson, 2nd Cpl.
J. E. McCraw, 3rd. Cpl.
R. E. Perry, 4th Cpl.

John H. Allen
John P. Allen
E. M. Byone
Jno. Belvin
Thos. Boothe
M. P. Brewer
J. G. Brown

W. R. Bugg
J. W. Culp
Wm. A. Culp
M. T. Cox
Jno. Campbell
H. W. Coffy
H. J. Cole
R. H. Croswell
J. W. Dunn
J. T. Dunklin
F. F. Dunklin
D. E. Dunlop
J. W. Edwards
B. L. Edwards
Z. Edmonds
D.(?) H. Friday
W. B. Fisher
Jas. J. Garrett
E. M. Garett
M. L. Goodwin
M. G. Goodwin
Thos. H. Hendrix
Isaac Hicks
G. E. Hicks
Elijah Headley
E. S. Headley
Isa. Headly
John Headly
Lindsy Henly
G. B. Henly
C. E. Hudson
Joseph Harper
W. G. Jones
M. G. Jones
W. E. Lewis
T. H. B. Littleton
Samuel Lindey
W. L. Laurence
W. R. Langford
C. C. Lee
J. B. Lassiter
W. B. Milton
W. O. Milton
Joseph Moore
B. C. Mize
S. J. Matthews
David Mitchel
W. N. Martin
D. W. Neal
J. P. Pattillo
J. A. F. Pyson
Enoch Parker
J. W. Parker
William Shearer(?)
E. R. Shearer
P. H. Shivers
R. S. Smith
Starling J. Shaver
D. P. Scoggins
Staples Smitherman
J. A. Samples
W. J. Samples
George Samples
H. H. Sturgis
H. G. Thompson
J. T. Thrasher
B. A. Thrasher
Fred Voegelin
Eli Wallis
J. Q. Wilson
W. M. Walker
W. H. Whatly
R. L. Woodward
Jno. J. White
P. C. Wallis
Jno. H. Williams
J. E. Yarbrough
Jno. Boyd
Jno. Harrison
J. W. Lapsley
G. M. McConnico
A. W. McGill
Jno. J. Porter
Robert Sharp
A.(G?) L. Stewart
R. Roberson

Company H, 44th Alabama Infantry Regiment

Francis M. Goode, Capt.
Joseph S. Johnson, 1st Lt.
H. J. Callen, 2nd Lt.
B. C. Barrett, 3rd Lt.
Joshua O. Johnston, 4th Lt.
Joel T. Lawhorn, 1st Sgt.
David E. Johnston, 2nd Sgt.
Robert D. Smitherman, 3rd Sgt.
John S. Gardner, 4th Sgt.
David N. Wells, 5th Sgt.
James E. Elliott, 1st Cpl.
William E. Long, 2nd Cpl.
Noah B. Hicks, 3rd Cpl.
James M. Barnes, 4th Cpl.

Samuel Abney
Edmond J. Atchinson
Gardner Bowling
Richard Belvin
Green Baity
Levi Banks
Isiah Belvin
James M. Burke
William H. Bankston(?)
——— Banks
William F. Chambers
Edward E. Cothren
David O. Conwill
John C. Conwill
Pinkney Cost
Bailey Cost
Thomas J. Creel
William J. Creel
Solomon J. Z. Champion
James R. Dean
Christopher C. Deadwilder
Stephen D. Dudley'
James Edwards
Edward Fulgham
John R. Fulgham
Richard W. Fowler
Frances M. Fancher
John R. Gray
James F. Gray
Larence Gray
Alfred M. Galaway
John M. Gothard
Little P. C. Horn
William Henderson
Jordon Horn
Rainder B. Hardin
David Joiner
John W. Kornegay
Silas P. Kornegay
Joab M. Langston
A—— Langston
Daniel C. Langford
George A. Leach
William Lawhorn
James T. Murphy
Theopholus Miller
——— McGraw
——— M. Martin
Abraham Moore
——— McCary
M—— Mosley
William B. McCary
Robert L. Moore
James Pickett
Joshua H. Petway
L. ?ma Ragsdale
Matthew Robinson
Isaac Robinson
Ivin Raglin
Alexander Raglin
Blanton B. Riggins
Henry F. Rottenbery
Andrew D. Smith
Thomas Smitherman
Isaac Smith
Luke Smith
Joseph Smith
Wilson Smelley
Jasper M. Wylie
James F. W. . . .

David Waldrup
Jacob Walker
Elfonzo F. Webb
John H. Ward

Company A, 62nd Alabama Infantry Regiment

J. L. Davidson, Capt.
Jas. A. McCaw, 1st Lt.
Wm. C. Ward, 2nd Lt.
William D. Moseley, Jr., 2nd Lt.
William D. McLaughlin, 1st Sgt.
Robert D. Hill, Sgt.
David M. Scott, Sgt.
Fleming G. Cocke, Sgt.
Frank B. Watkins, Sgt.
Geo. W. Ware, Cpl.
Jno. Atcherson, Cpl.
Davie A. J. Whatley, Cpl.
Augustus M. Ward, Cpl.

Lee Avery
William A. Barnett
John D. Brazeel
George W. Broadhead
Thomas B. Burns
William Caldwell
David W. Campbell
John P. Cash
John M. Cates
Jas. T. Casey
William A. Cook
Thomas J. Cox
William M. Crop
George W. Cooper
Ezekiel Dumlap
William E. Dye
James Y. Fancher
Pleasant H. Fancher
Josiah Fenington
William T. Foster
John W. Gardner
Bayless E. Grace
William R. Hanson
Andrew W. Hays
John M. Hays
Thomas Hamric
John Jarman
William Honeycut
Thomas G. Kennedy
Columbus P. Lee
Ephraim Lemley
William J. Floyd (Lloyd?)
Martin W. Moore
Robert McMullin
Thomas Milam
George Muncher
John Palmer
Jacob Perkins
Pink Posey
Alexander Rachels
J. M. Reach, Sr.
J. M. Reach, Jr.
A. H. Reese
James M. Reed
Gabriel M. Richards
William A. Rogers
Samuel D. Sherburt
Wm. J. Smitherman
James B. Shons
Robert Shropshear
William Stephens
Jere T. Stewart
Albert Tidwell
Wiley Troff
Munroe T. Wallace
James Walker
James J. Ward
Augustus Wilson
James P. Williams
Joseph F. Wood
William Womack
Robert T. Wilcox
Robert M. Yeager

Company A, 9th Alabama Cavalry Regiment
Clanton's Brigade

T. L. Faulkner, Capt.
W. C. C. Cleveland, 1st Lt.
B. W. Brown, 2nd Lt.
T. W. Hutchinson, 3rd Lt.
C. F. James, 1st Sgt.
H. A. Gorden, 2nd Sgt.
J. N. C. Brown, 3rd Sgt.
G. W. Marshall, 4th Sgt.
E. W. Hicks, 1st Cpl.
Jesse Miller, 2nd Cpl.
Dank Goodson, 3rd Cpl.
J. M. Vance, 4th Cpl.

Avery, A.
Bains, Alexander
Battles, J.
Bolden, B. (Bolding?)
Bolden, W. L.
Booth, C. M.
Brown, I. (?) D.
Brown, J. D.
Brown, T. R.
Caffee, John
Carow (?), J. H.
Carter, W. A.
Christian, Billy
Clifton, Charly
Cochran, Perry
Collier, J. K.
Cover, W. M.
Crow, J. B.
Davis, J. L.
Debardelabon, Dan
Denison, John
DeJarnett, M.
Deramus, L. Y.
Dobbins, John W. (Winslow)
Durden, John
Edmonds, Sam
Ellis, A. D.
Frazier, N. W.
Goldson, G. W.
Goldson, W. G. M.
Goldson, J. S.
Goldson, W. L.
Goldson, W. P.
Goodson, E. B.
Goodson, John
Goodson, W. F.
Goodwin, Billy
Hall, G. W.
Hall, G. N.
Hamilton, Jas.
Hasmer, Joe
Hendricks, J.
Hicks, R. R.
Howard, T. G.
Howard, T. H.
Hudson, Thomas
Hutchinson, Thomas
Hutchinson, W. H.
James, C. F.
Jones, D. M.
Jones, T. J.
Kersh, A. J.
Kicker, T. J.
Latham, Z. B.
Lawrence, W.
Lewis, H. D.
Lewis, J. W.
Long, J. O.
Mason, E.
Mason, Sim
Masle (?) D.
McCord, S. S. B.
McGuire, M.
McSpadden, John T.
McWilliams, O. H.
Miller, E.
Miller, J.
Moore, W. D.
Moses, W. B.
Murphy, B. J.
Murphy, W. T.
Parker, R. W.

Parker, Thomas
Pearce, Steve
Pearson, Lawson
Perry, Calvin
Peters, T. W.
Potts, T. D.
Price, T. H.
Quinn, J. C.
Raglin, B. F. (Ragland)
Rice, L. S.
Ricks, Jas.
Ricks, Jesse
Robbins, J. D.
Robison, Ike
Rolen, A. L.
Rolen, J. M.
Smelley, Will
Smith, E.
Smith, Oscar
Smith, T. W.
Snead, D. B.
Stanley, J. W.
Steel, N. Y.
Stoutenmire, M. F.
Thomas, L. J.
Tucker, A. J.
Turner, E. W.
Wallace, D. A.
Warters, W. B.
Weldon, James
Wells, J. W.
West, P.
Whetstone, William
Wilkins, J. E.
Williams, L.
Woolley, M. L.
Zimmerman, G. L.

APPENDIX VIII
BIBB'S STATE MILITIA ROLL, NOVEMBER 25, 1865

(Original in Alabama Archives)

1. W. N. Green, Capt.
2. L. C. Wallace, 1st Lieut.
3. F. M. Fancher, 2nd Lieut.
4. H. C. Fancher, 3rd Lieut.
5. L. Carleton, 1st Serg.
6. T. M. Fancher, 2nd Serg.
7. James Wyatt, 3rd Serg.
8. A. M. Ward, 4th Serg.
9. B. Eddins, 5th Serg.
10. J. D. Farrington, 1st Corp.
11. E. B. McGuire, 2nd Corp.
12. W. E. Smith, 3rd Corp.
13. John Litton, 4th Corp.

14. E. W. Jarmin
15. Thomas Litton
16. Joseph Litton
17. James Cottingham
18. John Jarmin
19. L. P Wallace
20. T. C. Baronett
21. W. M. Thomas
22. L. E. Starr
23. W. J. Hawkins
24. Jack Cottingham
25. John Martin
26. Robt. E. Woods
27. L. M. Russell
28. D. L. Russell
29. J. P. Ward
30. D. W. Ward
31. A. D. Lightsey
32. Eli Snow
33. B. Farrington
34. E. W. Lemley
35. E. H. Mulky
36. H. H. Splawn
37. Samuel Miles
38. F. G. Carleton
39. Jeff Snow
40. J. L. Campbell
41. L. H. Campbell
42. Reuben Owen
43. J. H. Woods
44. N. B. Cooper
45. W. G. Johnson
46. S. A. Edins
47. B. V. Colwell
48. A. J. Adams
49. S. M. Doak
50. Robt. Goode
51. Hines Gentry
52. J. M. Robeson
53. William Thompson
54. Henry Ward
55. Walter Fancher
56. Coleman Dennis
57. J. D. Smith
58. Adolphus Sims
59. Aaron Campbell
60. James Trucks
61. W. D. Woods

APPENDIX IX

BUSINESS AND PROFESSIONAL DIRECTORY OF BLOCTON, 1905–1906

(Source: *Young and Co.'s Business and Professional Directory of Cities and Towns Throughout Alabama, 1905–1906*)

Abston, S. F. Co., furniture and undertakers
Avery, John, grocery and restaurant
Baer, Joe, dry goods and shoes
Bishop, E. M., lawyer
Blocton Savings Bank, capital $25,000
Borum, Thomas I., jeweler
Carlton, M., tailoress
Carlton, M. W., grocery
Curtis, C. J., physician
Dark, T. S., lawyer
Davie, J. B., general merchandise
Douthit House, J. W. Stewart, prop.
Dunnabie, Robert, grocery
Dyer, W. A., blacksmith
Dycus, J. B., blacksmith
Fikes, W.C.T., shoemaker
Frederick, Louis, meat market
Gentry, A. H., justice of peace
Green Bros. Drug Co., druggists
Greene, C. H. and Bros., sawmill
Harris, T. T., men's furnishings, millinery
Harvey, W. A., druggist
Hubbard, R. H., livery, Blocton depot
Head, T. F., physician
Israel, W., dry goods, groceries, etc.
James, J. T., general merchandise
Keith, R. B., barber shop
Kinard, J. C., groceries
Krentzman, J., dry goods, medicine
Lee, S. A., groceries
Logan, W. R., lawyer
McCool, T. S. and Sons, general mdse.
McElroy, L., mineral water bottler
Mills, J. D., shoemaker
Odess, M. M., dry goods and shoes
Ogletree, H. C., general mdse., undertaker
Peacock, L. E., physician
Perry, W. W., millinery, dry goods
Price, S. W., pool room, restaurant
Reynolds, H. C. & W. B., general mdse.
Rice, C. H., publisher *Blocton Messenger*
Schauer, M. A., general merchandise
Smith, H., groceries
Smith, F. D., E. D., L. G., hardware
Sparks, W. D., general merchandise
Trigg, A. W., physician
Tuggle, T. C., photographer
Vickery, T. J., gunsmith
Walters and Gamble, millinery

Ward, Ed, barber
Watkins, W. L., groceries
West Blocton Dispensary, A. C. LaGrone, mgr.
West Blocton Opera Room, J. W. Stewart, mgr.

APPENDIX X

MAYORS OF WEST BLOCTON

(Courtesy of A. N. Kitchen and Mrs. Lemuel Parker)

1901–04	E. D. Reynolds
1904–06	L. E. Peacock
1906–08	W. H. Logan
1908–10	Yancey S. Smith
1910–12	M. C. Davie
1912–14	T. A. McCool
1914–16	W. H. Wright
1916–19	W. T. Griffin
1919–20	M. C. Davie
1920–21	E. M. Bishop
1921–24	W. H. Wright
1924–30	M. C. Davie
1930–32	T. A. McCool
1932–44	W. R. Ray
1944–47	Dave Evans
1948–49	J. W. Randall
1950–51	V. Y. Foster
1952–58	Ben Stanley
1959–60	R. G. Moore
1961–64	Floyd T. Morrison
1965–	Frank T. Ferrire

APPENDIX XI

COUNTY JUDGES, 1818–1982

(Compiled by Mrs. Josiah Kennedy from courthouse records)

May 1818 term: John Canterbury, Chief Justice; John Cates and James Smith, Justices Quorum.
February 1819: John Canterbury, C. J.; Henry W. Stevens, Littlepage Sims, James Smith, J. Q.
August 1819: Gabriel Benson, C. J.; John Cates, Henry W. Stevens, James Smith, J. Q.
April 1820: Andrew W. Luck, C. J.; Agrippa Atkinson, John Cates, Charles Densorf, James Smith, J. Q.
1821–23: Andrew W. Lusk, County Judge
1823–July 1836: Thomas Crawford
July 1836–January 1837: Hiram Hemphill
January 1837–January 1843: J. E. Summers
January 1843–January 1849: William C. Henry
January 1849–October 31, 1849: William Caddell
November 1, 1849–May 19, 1850: H. D. Calhoun
May 20, 1850–May 19, 1856: John N. Suttle
May 1856–April 1876: Jackson Gardner
April 1876–November 1880: Thomas J. Smitherman
November 1880–November 1892: John S. Gardner
November 1892–July 31, 1895: M. Y. Hayes
August 1895–February 16, 1896: James L. Davidson
February 1896–November 1898: N. H. Thompson
November 1898–April 1915: William Luther Pratt
April 1915–January 1923: William J. Nicholson
January 1923–January 1948: William L. Pratt
January 1948–January 1972: George Harper Stacy
January 1972–January 1975: Fred H. Davis
January 1975–January 1977: William T. Vanderford
January 1977– : George Allen Desmond

APPENDIX XII

COUNTY SHERIFFS, 1818–1982

1818 Andrew Henshaw
1819 John Henry
1822 Hugh Henry
1825 William E. Lawler
1828 James W. Davis
1831 Robert Parker
1834 Thomas P. Roberts
1837 Edward Lee
1840 John W. Suttle
1843 Robert Parker
1852 Jackson Gardner
1855 William A. Schoolar
1858 Richard H. Oakley
1861 William D. Oakley
1864 Richard H. Oakley
1865 Richard H. Oakley
1868 John R. Atkinson
1870 Jesse A. Brown
1872 John Latham
1875 C. F. James
1877 Charles C. Collier
1880 Noah B. Coker
1884 John Latham
1888 Alonzo Bates
1892 M. J. Latham
1896 Robert Vance
1900 E. H. Crawford
1904 E. H. Crawford
1907 James G. Oakley
1911 Charles L. Oakley
1915 John S. Ward
1919 R. H. Wood
1923 John S. Ward
1927 B. F. Griffin
1931 John S. Ward
1935 R. Jackson Gardner
1939 Vernon T. Harris
1943 Vernon T. Harris
1947 James F. Johnson
1951 Joel I. McCalla
1955 Carl A. Griffin
1959 Harold (Duck) Dailey
1963 Harold Dailey
1967 Harold Dailey
1971 Harold Dailey
1973 Jack Lee
1975 Glenn M. Smitherman
1979 Glenn M. Smitherman

APPENDIX XIII
REPRESENTATIVES IN TERRITORIAL AND STATE LEGISLATURE, 1818–1982

Senate
1818–19 Littlepage Sims
1819–20 Littlepage Sims
1821–22 Charles A. Dennis
1822–23 Jack Shackelford
1825–26 D. Sullivan
1828–29 Thomas Crawford
1831–32 Joab Lawler
1832–33 Alexander Hill
1834–35 David R. Boyd
1835–36 James Hill
1837–38 James Hill
1840–41 Daniel E. Watrous
1843–44 Daniel E. Watrous
1847–48 James M. Nabors
1849–50 Daniel E. Watrous
1853–54 Jack F. Cocke
1857–58 Jack F. Cocke
1861–62 Edward H. Moren
1865–66 Edward H. Moren
1868 J. W Mahan
1871–72 J. W. Mahan
1872–73 R. W. Cobb
1874–75 R. W. Cobb
1875–76 R. W. Cobb
1876–77 A. C. Hargrove
1878–79 A. C. Hargrove
1880–81 A. C. Hargrove
1882–83 A. C. Hargrove
1884–85 E. H. Moren
1886–87 W. C. Cross
1888–89 A. C. Hargrove
1890–91 W. T. Downey
1892–93 W. T. Downey
1894–95 W. F. Hogue
1896–97 W. F. Hogue
1898–99 J. G. Moore
1899 J. G. Moore
1900–01 J. G. Moore
1903 William Francis Hogue
1907 H. E. Reynolds
1909 H. E. Reynolds
1911 W. J. Vaiden
1915 Howard Cooper
1919 J. Marvin Moore
1923 G. W. Randall
1927 J. Marvin Moore
1931 Howard Cooper
1935 Judson C. Locke
1939 Howard Cooper
1943 T. J. Jones
1947 Howard Cooper
1951 Judson C. Locke
1955 H. P. James
1959 Norman Crawford
1963 H. P. James
1967 Walter Givhan
1971 Walter Givhan

1975 Walter Givhan
1979 Richard Shelby

House of Representatives
1819–20 Jonathan Jones
1820–21 Gabriel Benson
1821–23 Jonathan Jones
1823–24 Charles A. Dennis, Alexander Hill
1824–25 Jonathan Jones, Alexander Hill
1825–27 Jonathan Jones
1827–28 James B. Clark
1828–29 James B. Clark, Alexander Hill
1829–30 James B. Clark, Jonathan Jones
1830–31 James B. Clark, David R. Boyd
1831–32 David R. Boyd, Julius Goodwin
1832–34 James W. Davis, John E. Summers
1834–35 David E. Davis, Hopkins Pratt
1835–36 David E. Davis, Robert Parker
1836–37 John Williams, William Christian
1837–38 James W. Davis, Robert Parker
1838–39 John E. Summers, L. Kennedy
1839–40 John Williams, Frederick James
1840–41 David E. Davis, S. W. Davidson
1841–42 David E. Davis, Ezekiel Henry
1842–43 Pleasant Hill, Kenneth Morrison
1843–44 Pleasant Hill, David E. Davis
1844–45 Kenneth Morrison, B. L. Defreese
1845–46 Robert Hill
1847–48 James W. Davis
1849–50 O. S. Quinn
1851–52 James W. Davis
1853–54 James W. Davis, Charles P. Findley
1855–56 E. H. Bernhard, J. W. Crawford
1857–58 Robert Parker
1859–61 S. W. Davidson, Jr.
1861–63 Henry D. Calhoun
1863–67 James W. Davis
1868–70 P. A. Kendrick
1870–72 T. J. Smitherman
1872–73 J. N. Smith
1874–76 J. W. Davis
1876–77 J. S. Harnsberger
1878–79 J. D. Cooper
1880–81 R. C. Caffee
1882–83 E. H. Moren
1884–85 I. N. Suttle
1886–87 James W. Brand
1888–89 Samuel M. Adams
1890–91 Samuel M. Adams
1892–95 Nelson Fuller
1896–97 W. W. Lavender
1898–99 Charles Collier
1900–01 John T. Wilson
1903 Jasper Fritz Thompson
1907–09 Jerome Fuller
1911 W. W. Lavender
1915 J. B. Davie
1919–31 N. E. Stewart
1935 L. S. Moore
1939–47 J. Fred Wood
1951 R. C. Bamberg
1955–59 Virgis M. Ashworth
1963 Fred H. Davis
1967–Walter Owens

NOTES

Chapter 1

1. Harry Toulmin, comp., *Digest of the Laws of the State of Alabama* (Cahaba, 1823), pp. 87–88. Georgia also has a Bibb County, of which the city of Macon is county seat.

2. The texts of both treaties are recorded in Charles A. Kappler, ed., *Indian Affairs: Laws and Treaties* (Washington, 1903), vol. 2.

3. *Acts Passed at the First Session of the General Assembly of the Alabama Territory in the Forty-second Year of American Independence [1817–1818]* (St. Stephens, 1818), p. 30. This series of volumes is hereafter cited as *Acts of Alabama.*

4. Toulmin, *Digest,* pp. 88–89.

5. Ibid., p. 97.

6. *Acts of Alabama* (Tuscaloosa, 1831), p. 9.

7. "Examination and Survey of Cahaba River, Alabama," *Annual Report of the Chief of Engineers, U.S. Army, 1875* (Washington, 1875), p. 11.

8. Blanche E. Dean, Amy Mason, and Joab L. Thomas, *Wildflowers of Alabama and Adjoining States* (University, Ala., 1973), p. 96.

9. Ross Clark, "Woody Plants of Alabama," *Annals of the Missouri Botanical Garden* 58 (1971): 192.

10. Thomas Wilson, "Outdoors," *Centreville Press,* March 12, 1981.

11. Dean et al., *Wildflowers,* p. 26.

12. Saffold Berney, *Handbook of Alabama* (Montgomery, 1892), p. 270.

13. U.S. Public Land Survey of Alabama, Field Notes, Office of Alabama Secretary of State, Xerox copy in the office of Hammermill Paper Company, Centreville.

14. John A. Swanton, *Indians of the Southeast United States,* Smithsonian Bulletin Number 137 (Washington, 1946), pp. 22, 26.

15. Kappler, *Indian Affairs,* 2:62.

16. Howard F. McCord, *Baptists of Bibb County* (Privately printed, 1979), p. 136.

17. Thomas P. Clinton, "Early History of Tuscaloosa," *Alabama Historical Quarterly* 1 (Spring 1930): 144, locates Black Warrior Town 1½ miles west of Tuscaloosa.

18. Swanton, *Indians of the Southeast,* pp. 245-46.

19. Ibid., p. 249.

20. Thomas McAdory Owen, *History of Alabama and Dictionary of Alabama Biography* (Chicago, 1921), vol. 1, p. 131. Albert S. Gatchet discovered another Upper Creek town of this name on a small eastern tributary of the Tallapoosa River. See his "Towns and Villages of the Creek Confederacy," *Publications of the Alabama Historical Society,* 1 (1900): 399, 407.

21. W. P. Wallace, "Reminiscences," *Blocton Enterprise,* May 24, 1917.

22. David Crockett, *Narrative of the Life of David Crockett,* 5th ed. (Philadelphia, 1834) pp. 83–84.

23. Swanton, *Indians of the Southeast,* p. 244.

24. Bobby Roy Elam, Brent, possesses a considerable collection of Indian relics found in Bibb County.

25. "Map of Alabama constructed from surveys in General Land Office with Other Documents by John Melish, entered . . . October 29, 1818. Improved in 1819."

26. Owen, *Alabama,* 1:131.

27. See Henry S. Halbert and T. H. Ball, *The Creek War of 1813 and 1814,* ed. Frank L. Owsley, Jr. (University, Ala., 1969); and James W. Holland, "Andrew Jackson and the Creek War: Victory at the Horseshoe," *Alabama Review* 21 (October 1968): 243–75.

28. Andrew Jackson, *Correspondence of Andrew Jackson,* ed. John Spencer Bassett (Washington, 1926), vol. 1, p. 508.

29. "Letters of General John Coffee to His Wife," *Tennessee Historical Magazine* 2 (December 1916): 275.

30. Kappler, *Indian Affairs,* 2:62.

31. Owen, *Alabama,* 2:1243. For further insights into the Creek Indians and their way of life, see Thomas S. Woodward, *Woodward's Reminiscences of the Creek or Muscogee Indians* (Tuscaloosa, Ala., 1939).

32. Ethel Armes, *The Story of Coal and Iron in Alabama* (Birmingham, 1910), p. 23.

33. *Centreville Press,* April 13, 1911.

34. Ibid., April 24, 1913.

35. Owen, *Alabama,* 1:188. See also Henry S. Halbert, "Choctaw Indian Names in Alabama and Mississippi," *Transactions of the Alabama Historical Society, 1898–1899,* 3 (1900): 64–77.

36. William A. Reed, *Indian Place Names in Alabama* (Baton Rouge, La., 1937), p. 3.

37. Ibid., p. 35.

38. Ibid., p. 47.

Chapter 2

1. Clarence Edwin Carter, comp. and ed., *Territorial Papers of the United States,* vol. 18, *Alabama* (Washington, 1952), p. 72.

2. U.S. Public Land Survey, Field Notes, Office of Alabama Secretary of State.

3. Unsigned statement ca. 1900 on early Bibb settlers addressed to Dr. Thomas M. Owen, Bibb County Vertical File, Alabama Department of Archives and History, hereafter referred to as Alabama Archives.

4. Carter, *Territorial Papers,* 18:70.

5. See Thomas Perkins Abernethy, *The Formative Period in Alabama* (Montgomery, 1922), map, plate 4, p. 164. No official record of the native states of Bibb's residents is available before the U.S. census of 1850. At that time, among states outside of Alabama, South Carolina led with 724 natives, followed by Georgia with

408, and North Carolina with 406. The other principal contributors were Tennessee, 248; Virginia, 68; Mississippi, 20. Information compiled by Charles E. Boyd, New York City, and quoted with his permission.

6. Armes, *Story of Coal and Iron,* p. 23.

7. For example, the descendants of Oliver Cromwell Cleveland of the Tennessee Militia; Jim Garner, South Carolina Militia; Simeon E. Sims and Thomas A. Lawrence, Alabama Militia. See Bibb County Land and Patent Books, Probate Office.

8. James Mayfield Ward, *The Noble Family of Ward* (Privately printed, 1970), p. 18.

9. See Peter J. Hamilton, "Indian Trails and Early Roads," *Publications of Alabama Historical Society,* 1 (1900): 422–29; and Abernethy, *Formative Period,* chapter 8.

10. Charles E. Boyd, *Haysop: A Church, a Community, a People* (Birmingham, 1979), p. 126.

11. Owen, *Alabama,* 2:1243. On patterns of migration and settlement, see also Frank L. Owsley, *Plain Folk of the Old South* (Baton Rouge, La., 1949).

12. Gideon Lincecum, "Autobiography," *Publications of the Mississippi Historical Society,* 8 (1904): 467–68.

13. Fletcher Green, ed., *The Lides Go South and West* (Columbia S.C., 1952), p. 6.

14. Ibid., p. 5.

15. B. F. Riley, *History of Conecuh County, Alabama* (Columbus, Ga., 1881), p. 67.

16. Philip Henry Gosse, *Letters from Alabama* (London, 1859) p. 88.

17. Bibb County Administrators' Account Book C, 1821–31.

18. W. Stanley Hoole, ed., "Elyton, Alabama, and the Connecticut Asylum: The Letters of William H. Ely, 1820–1821," *Alabama Review* 3 (July 1950): 64.

19. Charle Collier Dailey, *The Dailey Dozen* (Privately printed, 1975): pp. 15–16.

20. Frederick Lee Olmsted, *A Journey in the Back Country* (1860; reprinted., New York: Shocken Books, 1970), p. 205.

21. Dailey, *Dailey Dozen,* p. 16.

22. Carter, *Territorial Papers,* 18:437.

23. Ibid.

24. W. P. Wallace to Thomas M. Owen, June 29, 1899, Bibb Vertical File, Alabama Archives.

25. Bibb County Deed Book A, p. 65.

26. Minutes of Cahaba County Orphans' Court, May 1818.

27. Unsigned letter to Thomas M. Owen, ca. 1900, Bibb Vertical File, Alabama Archives.

28. Ibid.

29. Carter, *Territorial Papers,* 18:343.

30. Hamilton, *Marion County Journal,* November 28, 1974.

Chapter 3

1. Carter, *Territorial Papers,* 18:344.

2. See "Register of Gubernatorial Appointments," *Alabama Historical Quarterly* 6(1944): 149–51.

3. *Facts about Shelby County,* brochure, n.d., Shelby County Historical Society and Shelby County Commissioners.

4. Riley, *Conecuh County,* pp. 29, 46.

5. Toulmin, *Digest,* p. 121.

6. Cahaba County Court Minutes, November 1818.

7. Joseph G. Baldwin, *Flush Times of Alabama and Mississippi* (1855; reprint ed., New York, 1957), p. 43.

8. Bibb County Court Minutes, February 1821.

9. Carter, *Territorial Papers,* 18:343–44.

10. "Register of Gubernatorial Appointments," 6:151.

11. Carter, *Territorial Papers,* 18:446–47.

12. Cahaba County Court Minutes, May 1818.

13. Minutes of Bibb County Court of Commissioners of Roads and Revenues, May 7, 1827.

14. Jasper E. James Diary, December 13, 1858, in the possession of James M. White, Brent.

15. Cahaba County Court Minutes, May 1818.

16. By 1866 the common charge for overnight accommodations in northern Bibb was $3. Gorgas Diary, Gorgas Papers, University of Alabama Library.

17. Henshaw to Governor Bibb, July 28, 1818, Carter, *Territorial Papers,* 18:384.

18. See Walter M. Jackson, *Alabama's First United States Vice-President, William Rufus King* (Decatur, Ala., 1952)

19. Information from documents in the possession of a descendant, Vera Hicks, Centreville. See also Bibb Vertical File, Alabama Archives.

20. Cahaba County Court Minutes, November 1819.

21. Bibb County Court Minutes, March 1822.

22. Ibid., January 1822.

Chapter 4

1. Certificate 748, in the possession of E. D. Clouse, Woodstock.

2. Bibb County Land Grants and Patents, I.

3. See Gordon T. Chappell, "John Coffee: Land Speculator and Planter," *Alabama Review* 22 (January 1968): 24–43.

4. Edward Kennedy to Thomas M. Owen, Centreville, March 10, 1917, Bibb Vertical File, Alabama Archives.

5. *American State Papers 1789–1838, Public Lands* (Washington, 1832–61), vol. 1, pp. 409–10, 561. These papers reveal the story of his abortive adventure and its consequences.

6. Edward Kennedy to Owen, Bibb Vertical File, Alabama Archives.

7. *Public Statutes at Large of the U.S.A. from Organization of Government to March 3, 1845,* vol. 6 (Boston, 1848), chapter 77. For a comprehensive discussion of such land claims, see David Lightner, "Private Land Claims in Alabama," *Alabama Review* 20 (July 1967): 187–204. Lightner believes that a lenient Congress honored many inadequately supported claims.

8. Opinion of William Wirt, February 21, 1823, *American State Papers, Public Lands,* 2:161–63.

9. NE ¼ Section 26, Township 23, Range 9 East. See Bibb County Land Grants and Patents, I.

10. Carter, *Territorial Papers,* 18:67.

11. Abernethy, *Formative Period,* p. 74.

12. John Logan's name appears in an 1828 listing in Dr. David R. Boyd's Account Book, in the possession of Louise Meigs Rogan, Centreville.

13. *Acts of Alabama* (Tuscaloosa, 1827), pp. 72–74.

14. Letter of July 22, 1820, mailed from the state capital, Cahaba, quoted in Hoole, "Elyton, Alabama," 3:54.

15. The north-south postal route was authorized by an act of Congress on May 13, 1820, and the east-west route by an act on May 8, 1822. See *Public Statutes at Large* 3 (Boston, 1856): 581, 705.

16. Bibb County Administrators' Accounts, Book C, pp. 50–51.

17. "Unpublished Letter from General Jackson," *Birmingham Age-Herald,* July 7, 1889.

18. Owen, *Alabama,* 1:204.

Chapter 5

1. Owen, *Alabama,* 2:1242; Margaret Pace Farmer, *One Hundred Fifty Years in Pike County, Alabama* (Anniston, 1973), pp. 13, 16, 35.

2. S. A. Townes, "The History of Marion" (Marion, Ala., 1844), reprinted in *Alabama Historical Quarterly* 14 (1952): 185–86.

3. Toulmin, *Digest,* pp. 120–21.

4. Ibid., p. 139.

5. McCord, *Baptists of Bibb,* p. 89.

6. *Annals of Congress, 18th Congress, First Session, 1823–1824* (Washington, 1856), p. 77.

7. *Acts of Alabama* (Cahaba, 1825), pp. 64–65.

8. SE ¼ Section 29, Township 23, N., Range 11 East. See Bibb County Land Grants and Patents, I.

9. *Acts of Alabama* (Tuscaloosa, 1828), pp. 24–28.

10. This document is preserved in Alabama Archives. Quotations appear in Peter A. Brannon, "Building of Bibb County Court House, 1829–1830," *Montgomery Advertiser,* August 22, 1937. A summary of its contents may also be found in Ulysses Huey Abrams, *A History of Early Bibb County, Alabama,* ed. Mattie Sandford Johnson (Huntsville, 1981), pp. 99–100.

11. NE ¼ Section 25, Township 23 North, Range 9 East. See Bibb County Land Grants and Patents I.

12. MS notes of a descendant, Dovie Casey, in the possession of Lillian Tibbs, Red Eagle community.

13. *Acts of Alabama* (Tuscaloosa, 1832), pp. 50–51.

14. Anne Royall, *Southern Tour* (Washington, 1831), vol. 2, p. 184.

15. *Centreville Press,* May 18, 1899.

16. Typescript, Kennedy Papers. This family collection of historical papers and memorabilia, carefully preserved by Mrs. J. P. Kennedy, and in part written by her, is now in the possession of Mrs. Josiah Kennedy. The latter has identified the original lots with their present occupants. Through her efforts, this historic business section is now listed on the National Register of Historic Places. The Enoch Carson lot is still occupied by a descendant, J. T. Fuller, Jr.

17. John G. Aiken, comp., *Digest of the Laws of Alabama* (Philadelphia, 1833), p. 72.

18. Centreville Press, February 19, 1903. The fire, discovered at midnight on Friday, February 13, destroyed this entire block on the south side of Market Street. See chapter 18, pp. 205–206, of this history.

19. The dates of the Henry-Kennedy and Davidson-Smitherman-Leggett houses are reported in the MS notes of Mrs. J. P. Kennedy, Kennedy Papers.

20. *Historic Preservation,* compiled and published by West Alabama Planning and Development Council, Tuscaloosa, June 1974.

21. "Antiquities of Bibb," *Centreville Press,* April 1, 1900.

22. John Morgan Green, "History of the Farm," MS in the possession of E. D. Clouse, Woodstock, who bought the house and farm in 1946.

23. As told to the author by her father, John T. Ellison.

24. Jasper E. James Diary, May 7, 1858.

Chapter 6

1. A humorous tribute to this dish, entitled "Bacon and Greens, by Green Pease Bacon, Esq.," actually Bakus W. Huntington, a Sumter County lawyer, was published in the short-lived Alabama literary magazine *The Southron,* in 1839. Today, the verses are more readily available in Arthur Palmer Hudson, *Humor of the Old Deep South* (New York, 1936), pp. 274–75.

2. Dr. William J. B. Owings, "Doctoring in Bibb County," *Sparrow Hawk* (published quarterly by Bibb County Junior High School) 3 (Summer 1978): 22.

3. S. A. Townes, "The History of Marion," *Alabama Historical Quarterly* 14 (1952): 203.

4. Bibb County Administrators' Accounts, Book C, 1821–31.

5. Ibid.

6. Baldwin, *Flush Times,* p. 34.

7. Record Book, Bibb County Circuit Court, 1826–36, Spring Term 1830.

8. Records of the Centreville Presbyterian Church, October 17, 1830, March 10, 1832. MS filed in church office.

9. Record Book, Bibb County Circuit Court, 1826–36, Fall Term 1830.

10. Ibid., Spring Term 1830.

11. *Seventh Census, 1850.*

12. *Acts of Alabama* (Tuscaloosa, 1835), p. 75.

13. Marion E. Lazenby, *History of Methodism in Alabama and West Florida* (Nashville, Tenn., 1960), p. 72.

14. Willis Brewer, *Alabama: Her History, Resources, War Record, and Public Men from 1540 to 1872* (Montgomery, 1872), p. 135.

15. This ledger, in the possession of Louise Meigs Rogan, Centreville, covers chiefly the years 1829–36, but some bills are carried over from as early as 1824.

16. J. Marion Sims, *The Story of My Life* (New York, 1884), p. 175.

17. Dr. Boyd's Account Book, September 11, 1830.

18. McCord, *Baptists of Bibb,* p. 175.

19. Record Book, Bibb County Circuit Court, 1826–36, Fall Term 1826.

20. Ibid., Fall Term 1831.

21. *Seventh Census, 1850.*

22. Dailey, *Dailey Dozen,* pp. 17–18.

23. Daniel S. Gray, comp., *Autauga County: The First Hundred Years, 1818–1918* (Prattville, Ala., 1972), p. 16.

24. Hosea Holcomb, *History of the Rise and Progress of the Baptists in Alabama* (Philadelphia, 1840), p. 217.

25. Kennedy Papers. Flavius Josephus was a first-century Jewish historian.

26. *Memorial Record of Alabama* (Chicago, 1893), p. 480.

27. Crawford Papers, Alabama Archives.

Chapter 7

1. Anson West, *History of Methodism in Alabama* (Nashville, Tenn., 1893), p. 347.

2. *Eighth Census, 1860.*

3. McCord, *Baptists of Bibb* gives a complete list of Bibb Baptist churches as well as a comprehensive cemetery record for the county. B. F. Riley, *A Memorial History of the Baptists of Alabama* (Philadelphia, 1923), remains the best account of the Baptist church in the state as a whole during the nineteenth century.

4. McCord, *Baptists of Bibb,* p. 133.

5. For a history of Haysop, see Boyd, *Haysop.*

6. Minutes of Enon Baptist Church, July 1836. Original minutes from 1819 are in the People's Bank, Centreville; Xerox copies are in the possession of David Weaver, River Bend community, and the Samford University Library, Birmingham.

7. Letter to *Bibb Blade,* quoted in *Centreville Press,* June 11, 1936.

8. Minutes of Enon Baptist Church, January 1839, May 1840.

9. Ibid., August 1844.

10. Ibid., September 1841, June 1843.

11. Ibid., June 1871, August 1871.

12. McCord, *Baptists of Bibb,* p. 6.

13. West, *Methodism,* p. 145.

14. Ibid.

15. Frank Gist to *Bibb Blade,* quoted in *Centreville Press,* June 11, 1936.

16. Lazenby, *Methodism in Alabama and West Florida,* p. 445.

17. Quarterly Conference Minutes of Centreville Circuit, April 18, 1835. Orig-

inal MS minutes are preserved in Alabama Archives, and a Xerox copy is in Huntingdon College Library, Montgomery; excerpts are reprinted in Abrams, *History of Early Bibb County,* pp. 71–91. Centreville Church disbanded by 1860, reorganized in 1889, and rebuilt on the same lot, aided by the Sandy Church.

18. Minutes of Enon Baptist Church, June 1825, August 1825.

19. Minutes of Centreville Circuit, June 27, 1840.

20. Ibid., December 3, 1842.

21. Bibb County Deed Book E, p. 341.

22. C. H. Motley, "Sandy Chapel," *Centreville Press,* November 30, 1910.

23. Minutes of Centreville Circuit, October 14, 1837, September 21, 1844.

24. Ibid., May 13, 1837.

25. Records of Centreville Presbyterian Church, February 7, 1824. MS minutes from 1824, church office. On the Presbyterian denomination in this general area, see Walter E Posey, *The Presbyterian Church in the Old Southwest* (Richmond, Va., 1952).

26. John R. Williams, ed., "Frontier Evangelist: The Journal of Henry Bryson," *Alabama Historical Quarterly* 42 (1980): 27.

27. Letter to Thomas M. Owen, unsigned, Bibb Vertical File, Alabama Archives.

28. Records of Centreville Presbyterian Church, August 23, 1868.

29. *Seventh Census, 1850.*

30. Letter from Mrs. R. H. Hickman, Green Pond, *Centreville Press,* June 22, 1936.

31. Brief history preceding minutes of church session of April 1871. Original MS minutes from 1871 are in Alabama Archives; a Xerox copy is in the possession of Mrs. R. V. Colley, Green Pond.

32. James Hugh Blair Hall Papers, Alabama Archives.

33. Records of Pleasant Hill Church from 1849, original MS in the possession of Cobbett Cox, Eoline community.

34. James Hugh Blair Hall Papers.

35. Records of Pleasant Hill Cumberland Presbyterian Church, June 1, July 3, 1850.

Chapter 8

1. For an account of the origin of the sixteenth section clause, see W. G. Clarke, *History of Education in Alabama* (Washington, 1889), p. 217. Chapter 3 of part 4 gives a brief history of public schools in Alabama. A fuller discussion of education in the state prior to 1860 may be found in A. B. Moore, *History of Alabama and Her People* (Chicago, 1927), chapter 11.

2. *Seventh Census, 1850.*

3. A typical account book, kept by J. C. Hicks when he was coprincipal of the school in Centreville, is in the possession of his daughter, Vera Hicks, Centreville.

4. Jasper E. James Diary, November 29, 1857.

5. Dailey, *Dailey Dozen,* pp. 22–23. Compare with Philip Henry Gosse, *Letters from Alabama, U.S.A* (London, 1859), pp. 43–44.

6. Dailey, *Dailey Dozen,* pp. 22–23.
7. Bibb County Deed Book G, p. 78.
8. Record Book, Bibb County Circuit Court, 1826–36, Fall Term 1826.
9. Alice Lee Little Meigs has written a well-documented account of these academies and of four others that originated after the Civil War. "Early Academies of Bibb County, Alabama" (M.A. thesis, University of Alabama, 1947).
10. Typescript copy, Kennedy Papers.
11. Howard F. McCord, "History of Friendship Lodge," filed in minutes of lodge.
12. Minutes of Friendship Lodge, Number 83, May 3, 1851.
13. Eliza McNeil Kennedy to Louisa Kennedy, November 1852, Kennedy Papers.
14. *Seventh Census, 1850.*
15. Ibid.; *Eighth Census, 1860.*
16. Mrs. J. P. Kennedy, MS notes, Kennedy Papers.
17. Ibid.
18. Ibid.
19. A. W. Hayes, "The Green Pond School," Xerox copy of transcript in the possession of Mrs. Thomas M. Nicholson, Centreville.
20. Minutes of Cold Water Lodge, No. 148, Book 1, p. 21.
21. Bibb County Deed Book G, p. 591.
22. The account book is in the possession of Howard F. McCord, Centreville.
23. Six Mile *Bibb Blade,* August 6, 1883.
24. *Centreville Press,* June 11, 1936.
25. Ibid. George Leith was already a Bibb settler in June 1829, according to Dr. David R. Boyd's Account Book.
26. Ray M. Atkinson and G. Benton Towry, *Richard Hopkins Pratt and the Six Mile Academy* (Birmingham, 1960), p. 57 (appendix A).
27. *Eighth Census, 1860.*

Chapter 9

1. The definitive study of slavery in Alabama is James B. Sellers, *Slavery in Alabama* (University, Ala., 1950). Chapters 4 through 8 describe the life and legal status of slaves.
2. See Harold Wilson, "Basil Manly, Apologist for Slavocracy," *Alabama Review* 15 (January 1962): 38–53.
3. Bibb joined the Black Belt counties in this vote. See map derived from the Senate Journal record, 1826, in Abernethy, *Formative Period,* p. 192.
4. West, *Methodism,* pp. 647–48.
5. Donald E. Collins, ed., "A Georgian's View of Alabama in 1836," *Alabama Review* 25 (July 1972): 221.
6. *Marion Standard,* April 9, 1909.
7. J. M. Brown of Sandy, quoted by Harwell Jones, "History of Reconstruction in Bibb County" (M.A. thesis, University of Alabama, 1932), p. 69.
8. *Acts of Alabama* (Cahaba, 1825), p. 64.
9. Record Book, Bibb County Circuit Court, 1826–36, Fall Term 1830.

10. Judgments Rendered, Bibb County Circuit Court, 1840–59.

11. Ibid.

12. Ibid.

13. Bibb County Administrators' Accounts, Book C, 1821–31.

14. Bibb County Circuit Court Minutes, Book D, 1840–47.

15. Judgments Rendered, Bibb County Circuit Court, 1859–66.

16. Complete Record, Bibb County Circuit Court, 1843–47.

17. John Morgan Green, "History of the Farm," MS in the possession of E. D. Clouse, Woodstock.

18. Voucher in George Mayberry estate settlement papers, March 24, 1851, in the possession of the author.

19. Centreville *Central Enquirer,* May 12, 1860.

20. George Mayberry estate settlement papers.

21. Ruth Tucker estate settlement papers, in the possession of the author.

22. Greensboro *Alabama Beacon,* January 5, 1855.

23. Bibb County Administrators' Accounts, Book C. A Perry County settler was hiring out a man slave at a dollar a day in 1839, as reported in his accounts. See Weymouth T. Jordan, *Hugh Davis and His Alabama Plantation* (University, Ala., 1948), pp. 79–81, for Davis's practices in hiring.

24. Tuscaloosa *Independent Monitor,* October 15, 1857.

25. *Alabama Code* (Montgomery, 1852), pp. 237–40.

26. *Reports of Cases Argued and Determined in the Supreme Court of Alabama,* 39 (Montgomery, 1868): 96.

27. Ibid., 35, 415–19.

28. Henry Damon Davidson, *Inching Along* (Nashville, Tenn., 1944), p. 5.

29. A search through the original WPA slave narratives in Alabama Archives failed to reveal any interviews with Bibb County ex-slaves. But see E. A. Botkin, ed., *Lay My Burden Down* (Chicago, 1945), for the testimony of those elsewhere.

30. "Slavery during the Civil War," *Sparrow Hawk* 3 (Summer 1978): 11–12.

31. Ibid., p. 13. See Jordan, *Hugh Davis,* p. 99, on Davis's punishment of slaves.

32. "Slavery during the Civil War," 3:13. She is probably quoting "Aunt Rachel" Howard, former slave of George Howard, who lived to an advanced age into the twentieth century.

33. Moren Letters, Alabama Archives.

34. Kennedy Papers.

35. For Dr. Boyd's Account Book, see chapter 6.

36. Minutes of Enon Baptist Church.

37. Records of Centreville Presbyterian Church.

38. Mrs. J. P. Kennedy, "History of Centreville," *Centreville Press,* July 27, 1950.

39. Minutes of Mount Zion Baptist Church, May 1863. Xerox copy of original minutes is in the possession of Mrs. Cleveland Stewart, Centreville.

40. Ibid., August 1859.

41. Ibid., May 1861.

42. Bibb County Deed Book F, p. 435.

43. James E. Sellers, "Free Negroes of Tuscaloosa County before the Thirteenth Amendment," *Alabama Review* 23 (April 1970): 110–27.

Chapter 10

1. Bibb County Court Execution Docket and Fee Book, 1840–50. A. B. Moore, *The History of Alabama and Her People* (Chicago, 1927), pp. 238–45, gives a useful summary of events connected with the bank crisis.
2. Kennedy papers.
3. Boyd, *Haysop,* p. 84.
4. Miriam and Parker Steele, *The Steeles of Bibb County* (Privately printed, 1979), pp. 8, 9, 12.
5. LaFayette *East Alabamian,* August 11, 1843.
6. Tuscaloosa *Independent Monitor,* November 9, 1847.
7. Ibid., November 23, 1847.
8. Brewer, *Alabama,* pp. 588–89.
9. Tuscaloosa *Independent Monitor,* July 6, 1848.
10. Jasper E. James Diary, April 11, 1858.
11. *DeBow's Review,* December 18, 1858, p. 717.
12. Tuscaloosa *Independent Monitor,* reprinted in *Selma Press,* May 5, 1838.
13. *DeBow's Review,* December 18, 1858, p. 717.
14. Ibid., p. 718.
15. *Seventh Census, 1850.*
16. Armes, *Story of Coal and Iron,* p. 61.
17. Ibid., p. 62, repeats the family legend that the original Tannehill was a foundling adopted by a Scottish family at age two and named for the hill on which he was found while they were rounding up some calves.
18. *Eighth Census, 1860.*
19. Armes, *Story of Coal and Iron,* p. 72.
20. Ibid.
21. Ibid., p. 74.
22. Miss A. E. Mahan, quoted by S. M. Mahan, Jr., in "A Brief History of Bibb Furnaces," 1955, typescript, Bibb County High School Library.
23. Armes, *Story of Coal and Iron,* p. 71.
24. Ibid., p. 76.
25. *DeBow's Review,* October 1851, p. 717. The other high furnace was at Polkville, in Benton (now Calhoun) County. Tannehill, just across the Bibb line in Tuscaloosa County, claims to have gone into blast in 1855.
26. Armes, *Story of Coal and Iron,* p. 75.
27. Voucher dated April 1, 1849, George Mayberry estate settlement papers.
28. Bibb County Tax Reports, 1858.
29. *Seventh Census, 1850.*
30. Minutes of Commissioners' Court, Bibb County, November 20, 1854.
31. *Seventh Census, 1850.*
32. *Eighth Census, 1860.*

Chapter 11

1. "Examination and Survey of Cahaba River, Alabama," pp. 13–14.

2. J. W. Scruggs, Jr., comp., *Alabama Steamboats, 1819–1869* (Privately printed, n.d. [c. 1953]).

3. Donald E. Collins, ed., "A Georgian's View of Alabama in 1836," *Alabama Review* 25 (July 1972): 222.

4. Bibb County Administrators' Court, 1858–65.

5. Minutes of Commissioners' Court, Bibb County, November 20, 1854.

6. *Eighth Census, 1860.*

7. Fragment of Union Springs newspaper, probably the *Gazette,* established in 1858, quoting the Centreville *Central Enquirer* of 1858, in the possession of the author.

8. Charles E. Boyd, comp., *Centreville Press,* November 14, 1974.

9. This letter is in the possession of the author.

10. Edward Kennedy to Thomas M. Owen, August 11, 1916, Bibb Vertical File, Alabama Archives.

11. Amanda Suttle to unnamed family member, November 1852, Kennedy Papers.

12. William Garrott Brown, *History of Alabama* (New York, 1900), p. 208. See N. P. Renfro, Jr., *The Beginning of Railroads in Alabama* (Auburn, Ala., 1910).

13. *Selma Free Press,* August 4, 1837.

14. See the author's *Early Alabama Publications* (University, Ala., 1947), chapter 1.

15. L. H. Nunnelee to Thomas M. Owen, April 2, 1903, Bibb Vertical File, Alabama Archives. For a town-by-town listing of Bibb newspapers, see the author's *History and Bibliography of Alabama Newspapers in the Nineteenth Century* (University, Ala., 1954).

16. The counties in the 3d Congressional District were Autauga, Bibb, Dallas, Jefferson, Lowndes, Perry, and Shelby.

17. John Witherspoon DuBose, *The Life and Times of William Lowndes Yancey* (New York, 1892), p. 137.

18. Ibid.

19. Ibid., p. 189.

20. *Centreville Press,* September 18, 1913.

21. On the activities of the American party in Alabama, see Lewy Dorman, *Party Politics in Alabama from 1850 to 1860* (Wetumpka, Ala., 1935), chapters 6 and 7.

22. G. Ward Hubbs has collected and annotated Barr's stories under the title *Rowdy Tales from Early Alabama* (University, Ala., 1981). The first tale, "Salted Him," describes a shrewd Bibb farmer's annual shopping visit to Tuscaloosa in pioneer days.

23. Jasper E. James Diary, August 4, 1858. See also DuBose, *Life and Times of Yancey,* chapter 17.

24. *Eighth Census, 1860.*

25. Ibid.

26. S. K. J., "Colonel John G. Barr," New York *Spirit of the Times,* October 23, 1858, copied from Centreville *Enquirer.*

27. They were Dr. J. W. Crawford, S. W. Davidson, J. S. Kennedy, and Robert Hill.

28. Voucher in George Mayberry estate settlement papers.

29. Jasper E. James Diary, August 14, 1857, January 3, June 13, 1858.

30. Traditionally one of the beautiful virgins in the Muslim Paradise.

31. Unnamed daughter of Josiah S. Kennedy to her sister, Kennedy Papers.

32. The other possible exception is Jack, who cannot be identified. Lucius Winship, third lieutenant of that company, died at Orangeburg, S.C., on January 5, 1863. The others survived the war.

Chapter 12

1. J. M. Brown, untitled MS on Civil War memories, Xerox copy in the possession of the author.

2. Brewer, *Alabama*, pp. 63, 137.

3. Except for Calhoun and Pickens, Bibb and Shelby were the two most northern counties that voted to send secessionist delegates. Southern Alabama was secessionist except for Conecuh. Malcolm C. McMillan, ed., *The Alabama Confederate Reader* (University, Ala., 1963), map opposite p. 71.

4. See Alto L. Gardner and Nathan Stott, "William Lowndes Yancey: Statesman of Secession," *Alabama Review* 15 (July 1962): 190–202; DuBose, *Life and Times of Yancey*, chapter 24; and Malcolm C. McMillan, *Constitutional Development in Alabama, 1798–1901* (Chapel Hill, N.C., 1955), chapter 6.

5. See Thomas C. DeLeon, *Four Years in Rebel Capitals* (Mobile, 1892), pp. 23–24.

6. Mrs. J. P. Kennedy, "History of Centreville."

7. Walter L. Fleming, *Civil War and Reconstruction in Alabama* (New York, 1905), p. 231.

8. Josiah McNeil Kennedy to his brother Archibald, June 23, 1861, Kennedy Papers.

9. Thomas J. Smitherman to Judge Jackson Gardner, January 10, 1862, in the possession of Louie Waller, Miami, Florida.

10. Brewer, *Alabama*, p. 607.

11. Ibid., p. 622.

12. William Kennedy to an unnamed sister, September 11, 1861, Kennedy Papers.

13. Brewer, *Alabama*, p. 636.

14. Ibid., p. 655.

15. W. R. Young, "The Lawrences," Xerox typescript of family records, p. 81, in the possession of the author.

16. Brewer, *Alabama*, p. 674.

17. Ibid., p. 687.

18. Margaret Ham, "The Personal Side of the War," as told by her great-aunt, Mrs. Logan, in the *Bibb Eagle*, published by the Bibb County Heritage Association, February 1977.

19. September 13, 1861, Jasper E. James Letters, in the possession of James M.

White, Brent. Jasper's brother Monroe, his cousin Willie Nichols, and his young uncles Pleasant and Arthur James. Monroe, Willie, and Pleasant all died in the Confederate service the following winter and spring.

20. October 8, 1861, Jasper E. James letters.

21. December 25, 1861, ibid.

22. W. Stanley Hoole, ed., "The Letters of Captain Joab Goodson," *Alabama Review* 10 (April 1957): 138.

23. Ibid.

24. Jasper James to Alexander Hill James, July 22, 1862, February 8, 1863.

25. Jasper Fair to N. E. Fair, December 14, 1862, in the possession of Mrs. Dan Cottingham, Centreville.

26. Jasper James to Mr. and Mrs. A. H. James, July 22, 1862.

27. Ibid., August 10, 1864.

28. Jasper Fair to N. E. Fair, December 14, 1862.

29. Irving Ragland to Nancy Ragland, August 1862, in the possession of David Bailey, Centreville.

30. Ham, "Personal Side of the War."

31. Hoole, "Letters of Captain Joab Goodson," 10: 132, 133.

32. Ibid., p. 145.

33. McMillan, *Alabama Confederate Reader,* p. 200.

34. Hoole, "Letters of Captain Joab Goodson," 10 (July 1957): 217.

35. Jasper James to A. H. James, February 8, 1863.

36. *Memorial Record of Alabama,* p. 498.

37. Jasper James to Mr. and Mrs. A. H. James, May 2, 1863.

38. Hill James to A. H. James, August 12, 1863, Jasper E. James Letters.

39. William Kennedy to his sister, Mobile, September 11, 1861, Kennedy Papers.

40. Jasper James to A. H. James, January 10, 1862.

41. Ibid., January 26, February 8, 1863.

42. McMillan, *Alabama Confederate Reader,* p. 325.

43. Bessie Martin, *Desertion of Alabama Troops from the Confederate Army* (New York, 1932), p. 258.

44. Daniel Lightsey to John W. Suttle, June 7, August 1, 1862, Letters to John W. Suttle, 1858–64, in the possession of Howard F. McCord, Centreville.

45. Fleming, *Civil War and Reconstruction,* p. 110.

46. Jasper Fair to N. E. Fair, December 14, 1862.

47. Centreville *Central Enquirer,* December 17, 1863.

48. Edward Kennedy's letter is summarized in one written by one sister to another, Centreville, June 24, 1864, Kennedy Papers.

49. Josiah McNeil Kennedy to a sister, Yorktown, April 20, 1862, Kennedy Papers.

50. Ibid.

51. Hoole, "Letters of Captain Joab Goodson," 10: 134.

52. Hill James to Mr. and Mrs. A. H. James, September 4, 1864, Jasper E. James Letters; Hoole, "Letters of Captain Joab Goodson," 10: 225.

Chapter 13

1. Daniel Lightsey to John W. Suttle, August 2, 1862, Letters to John W. Suttle.
2. Fleming, *Civil War and Reconstruction* p. 105. See Albert B. Moore, *Conscription and Conflict in the Confederacy* (New York, 1924).
3. *Memorial Record of Alabama,* p. 489.
4. Kate Kennedy to Annie Kennedy, July 5, 1864, Kennedy Papers.
5. Mrs. Jasper Langston, *Centreville Press,* March 14, 1934.
6. Ham, "Personal Side of the War."
7. Mrs. J. P. Kennedy, "History of Centreville," MS notes, Kennedy Papers.
8. Ham, "Personal Side of the War."
9. *Centreville Press,* October 1, 1914.
10. Armes, *Story of Coal and Iron,* p. 172.
11. "Antiquities of Bibb," *Centreville Press,* January 25, 1900.
12. *Alabama Blast Furnaces* (Woodward Ala., n.d.), p. 46.
13. Josiah Gorgas Diary, Sunday (no day or month), 1866, Gorgas Papers, University of Alabama Library.
14. Armes, *Story of Coal and Iron,* pp. 171–72.
15. DeLeon, *Four Years in Rebel Capitals,* p. 55. See Walter W. Stephens, "The Brooke Guns from Selma," *Alabama Historical Quarterly* 20 (Fall 1958): 462–75.
16. Armes, *Story of Coal and Iron,* p. 186.
17. Ibid., p. 151.
18. B. F. Oglesby, typescript on memories of the Civil War, Kennedy Papers.
19. Eugene A. Smith, *Geological Survey of Alabama* (Montgomery, 1890), p. 109.
20. William Garrett, *Public Men of Alabama* (Atlanta, 1872), p. 724.
21. Kennedy Papers.
22. Fleming, *Civil War and Reconstruction,* p. 173.
23. A. W. Hayes, "Reminiscences of the War between the States," typescript, in the possession of Mrs. Thomas M. Nicholson, Centreville, pp. 6–7.
24. Green, "History of the Farm."
25. McMillan, *Alabama Confederate Reader,* p. 323.
26. Lucille Griffith, *Alabama: A Documentary History to 1900* (University, Ala., 1968; rev. ed. 1972), p. 439.
27. Moren Letters, Alabama Archives.
28. McMillan, *Alabama Confederate Reader,* p. 322.
29. Fleming, *Civil War and Reconstruction,* p. 172.
30. Jasper James to A. H. James, January 26, 1863, Jasper E. James Letters.
31. Margaret Kennedy to a sister, July 5, 1864, Kennedy Papers.
32. Hayes, "Reminiscences of the War," p. 6.
33. Ella Loon, *Salt as a Factor in the Confederacy* (New York, 1933), p. 4. See also T. J. Krouse, "Clarke County Salt Works," *Alabama Historical Quarterly* 20 (Spring 1958): 95–100.
34. A. H. James to Lucinda Summers James, Jasper E. James Letters.
35. Fleming, *Civil War and Reconstruction,* p. 197.
36. Centreville *Central Enquirer,* December 17, 1863.

37. Ibid.

38. Hoole, "Letters of Captain Joab Goodson," 10: 146–47. E. H. Moren and James W. Davis, both loyal to the Confederacy, were elected to the state legislature from Bibb in 1861 and again in 1865. Possibly Thompson and Dennis were justices of the peace or constables, but their names do not appear in the records of bonded officers of the county. See McMillan, *Alabama Confederate Reader*, chapter 17.

39. Kate Kennedy to Annie Kennedy, n.d., Kennedy Papers.

40. Mrs. J. P. Kennedy, MS notes, Kennedy Papers. Possibly the man Forrest addressed was DeWitt Logan, a schoolteacher who was locally known for his height. On General Forrest, see Robert S. Henry, *"First with the Most" Forrest* (Indianapolis, 1944).

41. One of the liveliest and best-informed accounts of this episode is James Pickett Jones, *Yankee Blitzkrieg: Wilson's Raid through Alabama and Georgia* (Athens, Ga., 1976).

42. James H. Rodabaugh, "The Fighting McCooks," *Civil War History* 3 (1957): 287–90.

43. William F. Scott, *The Story of a Cavalry Regiment* (New York, 1893), p. 445.

44. Mahan, "Brief History of Bibb Furnaces," pp. 7–8.

45. *Montgomery Daily Mail*, April 2, 1865.

46. *The War of the Rebellion: A Compilation of the Official Records of the Union and Confederate Armies* (Washington, 1880–1901), ser. 1, vol. 49, pt. 1, p. 358.

47. MS notes of Mrs. J. P. Kennedy, whose husband recalled these events of his childhood, Kennedy Papers.

48. Stephen V. Shipman Diary, April 1, 1865, Shipman MSS, State Historical Society Library, Madison, Wisconsin.

49. David Kennedy, "Personal Recollections of Wilson's Raiders in Bibb County," typescript ca. 1915, Kennedy Papers.

50. John Milton Hubbard, *Notes of a Private* (St. Louis, 1913), p. 187.

51. Ward, *The Noble Family of Ward*, p. 51.

52. Shipman Diary, April 2, 1865.

53. *War of the Rebellion*, ser. 1, vol. 49, pt. 1, p. 428.

54. The house, the present residence of Mrs. Dan Cottingham, has been considerably altered, but the mark on the chimney is still visible.

55. Kennedy, "Wilson's Raiders."

56. Hayes, "Reminiscences of the War," p. 8.

57. Cary McCord, "The Pratt Family," typescript in the possession of Howard F. McCord, Centreville.

Chapter 14

1. Fleming, *Civil War and Reconstruction*, p. 280.

2. Elizabeth Bethel, "The Freedmen's Bureau in Alabama," *Journal of Southern History* 14 (February 1948): 84.

3. Jones, "Reconstruction in Bibb," p. 5. This thesis is valuable for its record of interviews conducted in the winter of 1931–32 with the following elderly citizens,

who recalled events of the Reconstruction period: J. P. Kennedy, J. M. Brown, Will Jones, Fred Jones, Andrew Kersh, John McDaniel, and Mrs. Robert McCalley. On cotton frauds, see Richard W. Griffin, "Cotton Frauds and Confiscations in Alabama, 1863–1866," *Alabama Review* 7 (October 1954): 265–76.

4. Minutes of Circuit Court, Bibb County, 1860–73, Fall Term 1868.

5. Jones, "Reconstruction in Bibb," pp. 65–66.

6. Montgomery *State Sentinel*, June 17, 1867. A man named Jim Cobb was hanged by a Chilton gang from "a leaning apple tree" and then shot, according to T. E. Wyatt, *Chilton County and Her People* (Clanton, 1940; rev. ed., 1950, 1976, Carlos W. Wyatt). For an account of lawlessness and political revolt in Tuscaloosa and other counties west of Bibb, see John L. Hunnicutt, *Reconstruction in West Alabama* (Tuscaloosa, 1959).

7. Jones, "Reconstruction in Bibb," p. 2.

8. Brewer, *Alabama*, p. 137.

9. Bibb County, Bonds of County Officers, 1853–73.

10. Brewer, *Alabama*, p. 137.

11. E. H. Moren to Frances Davidson Moren, February 3, 1866, Moren Papers.

12. Clyde E. Wilson, comp., "State Militia of Alabama, June 21–December 18, 1865," *Alabama Historical Quarterly* 14 (1952): 307.

13. Ibid., p. 306.

14. Montgomery *Daily State Sentinel*, May 18, 1867.

15. Bethel, "Freedmen's Bureau," 14: 111–12.

16. Jones, "Reconstruction in Bibb," pp. 3–4.

17. Ibid., pp. 67–68.

18. Minutes of Circuit Court, Bibb County, 1866–73. William Oakley was a former sheriff of the county.

19. Jones, "Reconstruction in Bibb," p. 2.

20. Minutes of Circuit Court, Bibb County, 1866–73, Fall Term 1868, Spring Term 1869.

21. Order of Third Military District Headquarters, Atlanta, May 21, 1867, Military Records, Alabama Archives.

22. Fleming, *Civil War and Reconstruction*, p. 494.

23. Gorgas Diary, Gorgas Papers.

24. Records of Centreville Presbyterian Church, September 25, 1870.

25. Jones, "Reconstruction in Bibb," p. 68.

26. *Ninth Census, 1870.*

27. Jones, "Reconstruction in Bibb," p. 68.

28. Josiah Gorgas to Francis S. Lyons, February 22, 1867, Gorgas Papers.

29. Columbiana *Shelby County Guide*, December 3, 1868.

30. *Report of the Joint Select Committee to Inquire into the Condition of Affairs in the Late Insurrectionary States* (Washington, 1872), vol. 8, p. 73.

31. Ibid., vol. 8, p. 1986.

32. Montgomery *Daily State Sentinel*, January 30, 1868. See Sarah Van Woolfolk, "Five Men Called Scalawags," *Alabama Review* 17 (January 1964): 45–55. In Bibb, there are no legends of the personal chastisement of scalawags and consequent

punishment, as in Greene County, where a military court released guilty Eutaw citizens with shaved heads, said to be "better than no heads at all" by the *Shelby County Guide,* April 30, May 7, 1868.

33. Minutes of Methodist Quarterly Conference, Randolph Circuit, July 20, 1867.

34. See McMillan, *Constitutional Development,* chapter 12, for an account of the convention. Horace M. Bond questions the large number of carpetbaggers usually said to have been delegates. *Negro Education in Alabama* (1939; reprint ed., New York, 1969), chapter 5.

35. *Centreville Apprentice,* quoted in Columbiana *Shelby County Guide,* November 23, 1869.

36. Bibb County, Bonds of County Officers, 1853–79.

37. Jones, "Reconstruction in Bibb," p. 13.

38. Owen, *Alabama,* 4:1238.

39. John T. Ellison, "City of Centreville: Short Sketches of Old Settlers and Prominent Citizens," Centreville *County Press,* June 17, 1896.

40. Brewer, *Alabama,* p. 73.

41. Fleming, *Civil War and Reconstruction,* p. 783.

42. For the Democrats' weapon of heckling, see H. E. Sterkx, "William C. Gordon and Reconstruction in Bullock County," *Alabama Review* 15 (July 1962): 68.

43. Jones, "Reconstruction in Bibb," p. 16.

44. Ibid., p. 12.

45. See Edward Williamson, "The Alabama Election of 1874," *Alabama Review* 15 (July 1962): 218.

46. Jones, "Reconstruction in Bibb," p. 16.

47. Ibid., p. 17.

Chapter 15

1. Ward, *The Noble Family of Ward,* p. 52.

2. Article of Agreement between A. C. Hargrove as Executor of the Last Will of Robert McIlvain and Farm Laborers, Kennedy Papers.

3. *Annual Report of Chief of Engineers, U.S. Army, 1875,* p. 16.

4. Oscar Woods to A. L. Arnold, Arnold Scrapbook, in the possession of Mrs. Theo Arnold Eady, Centreville.

5. *Ninth Census, 1870.*

6. Brewer *Alabama,* p. 136. See Albert B. Moore, "Railroad Building in Alabama during the Reconstruction Period," *Journal of Southern History* 1 (November 1935): 421–41.

7. Saffold Berney, *Handbook of Alabama* (Birmingham, 1892), p. 516.

8. Six Mile *Bibb Blade,* January 1, 1880.

9. Signed S. D. L., probably Stephen Douglas Logan, a young Centreville lawyer.

10. Six Mile *Bibb Blade,* February 17, 1881.

11. *Selma Times,* quoted by John P. Kennedy, "Steamboating on the Cahaba," *Centreville Press,* undated clipping, Kennedy Papers. Possibly this was Captain C. J. English, who in 1868 was "captain of a 'safe packet' named 'The Virginia,'

which goes from Montgomery to Selma three times a week . . . as regular as pig's tracks." Columbiana *Shelby County Guide,* April 30, 1868.

12. Berney, *Handbook of Alabama,* p. 516.

13. Six Mile *Bibb Blade,* February 16, 1881.

14. Ibid., December 1, 1881.

15. Jones, "Reconstruction in Bibb," p. 45.

16. *Acts of Alabama* (Montgomery, 1867), p. 347.

17. Jones, "Reconstruction in Bibb," p. 46.

18. Ibid.; note of a daughter of J. S. Kennedy, Kennedy Papers.

19. Its owner, the Tuscaloosa Manufacturing Company, after reorganizing in 1877, opened a new factory at Cottondale, Tuscaloosa County.

20. Joseph Hodgson, *Alabama Manual and Statistical Register for 1869* (Montgomery, 1869), p. 105.

21. Gorgas Diary, January 21, 1866.

22. Armes, *Story of Coal and Iron,* p. 172 ff.

23. Gorgas Diary, February 1, 1866.

24. Ibid., November 16, 1866.

25. *Alabama Blast Furnaces,* p. 48.

26. Bibb County Deed Book J.

27. Gorgas Diary, July 1, 1866.

28. Ibid., January 3, 1868.

29. Petition dated November 26, 1881, Register of Bibb County Incorporations, 1879–89.

30. Petition of incorporation dated April 10, 1882, ibid.

31. Armes, *Story of Coal and Iron,* pp. 325–28.

32. Six Mile *Bibb Blade,* February 24, 1881. The iron industry in Alabama as a whole began a period of expansion in 1880. Before 1900, around forty new blast furnaces were erected, according to Bradford C. Colcord, *The History of Pig Iron Manufacture in Alabama* (Woodward, Ala., 1950), p. 10. See also Robert H. McKenzie, "Reconstruction of the Alabama Iron Industry," *Alabama Review* 25 (July 1972): 178–91.

33. Berney, *Handbook of Alabama,* p. 465.

34. Petition of incorporation, June 16, 1875, Register of Bibb County Incorporations, 1879–89.

35. Armes, *Story of Coal and Iron,* p. 230.

36. Berney, *Handbook of Alabama,* pp. 465–67.

37. Woodstock *Bibb County Democrat,* May 15, 1892.

38. Jones, "Reconstruction in Bibb," p. 37.

39. *Memorial Record of Alabama,* p. 487.

40. Six Mile *Bibb Blade,* March 20, 1884.

Chapter 16

1. Nettie Pratt, "Bibb County, A Desirable Place of Habitation," Six Mile *Bibb Blade* clipping ca. 1885, Arnold Scrapbook.

2. Smith, *Geological Survey of Alabama,* p. 113.
3. Ibid., p. 114.
4. Register of Bibb County Incorporations, 1879–89.
5. Six Mile *Bibb Blade,* February 20, 1884.
6. Register of Bibb County Incorporations, 1879–89.
7. Six Mile *Bibb Blade,* March 26, 1884.
8. Berney, *Handbook of Alabama,* p. 474.
9. *First Biennial Report of the State Inspector of Mines for the Years Beginning December 31, 1892, and Ending December 31, 1894* (Montgomery, 1895), p. 20.
10. Dailey, *Dailey Dozen,* p. 31.
11. "Dago" from the Spanish *Diego* ("James") was a term that had long been used contemptuously of Spaniards, Portuguese, and Italians.
12. *Blocton Messenger,* March 6, 1903.
13. Printed agreement, Governors' Papers, Alabama Archives. This aspect of the T.C.I. operation is omitted in a brief history of the company, Robert Gregg, *Origin and Development of T.C.I. and C. Company* (New York, 1958).
14. *First Biennial Report of the State Inspector of Mines,* p. 7.
15. *Centreville Press,* April 24, 1913.
16. Dailey, *Dailey Dozen,* pp. 25–26.
17. "Bygone Days," *Centreville Press,* June 12, 1980.
18. *First Biennial Report of the State Inspector of Mines,* pp. 52, 53.
19. *Blocton Messenger,* June 12, 1903.
20. Ibid., July 3, 1903.
21. *First Biennial Report of the State Inspector of Mines,* pp. 58, 59, 73. See David Ward, *Labor Revolt in Alabama: The Great Strike of 1894* (University, Ala., 1965).
22. *Blocton Times,* May 21, 1896.
23. *Blocton Messenger,* May 29, 1903.
24. Ibid., January 16, 1903.
25. Ibid., March 27, 1903.
26. B. M. Thompson to Thomas M. Owen, August 10, 1916, Bibb Vertical File, Alabama Archives.
27. Walter Gardner, Jr., "Bygone Days," *Centreville Press,* June 5, 1980.
28. Ibid., April 17, 1980.
29. B. M. Thompson to Thomas M. Owen, August 10, 1916, Bibb Vertical File, Alabama Archives.
30. *Memorial Record of Alabama,* p. 497 (where Cottingham is misspelled).
31. *Blocton Courier,* November 25, 1892.
32. *Memorial Record of Alabama,* p. 482.
33. Ibid., p. 483.
34. *Blocton Times,* April 30, 1896.
35. *Blocton Messenger,* March 6, 1903.
36. Ibid., March 13, 1903.
37. *Blocton Times,* April 30, 1896.
38. *Blocton Messenger,* January 16, 1903.
39. Ibid., March 13, 1903.

40. Ibid., March 20, 1903.
41. Ibid., May 1, 1903.
42. Ibid., March 27, 1903.
43. Ibid., February 13, 1903.
44. The original MS of the bylaws is in the possession of Elmo Ellis, Atlanta.
45. *Blocton Enterprise,* August 4, 1910.
46. McCord, *Baptists of Bibb County,* p. 154.
47. *Blocton Enterprise,* August 4, 1910.

Chapter 17

1. Centreville *Blade-Enterprise,* February 26, 1891. The widow, Frank Perry, of the Scottsville community, was robbed of her entire peanut crop.
2. Interview with Burt's son, I. L. Burt of West Blocton, December 6, 1979.
3. Interview with I. L. Burt.
4. As told to the author by her grandfather, Jesse Dean Cooper, the host who was robbed.
5. Ward, *The Noble Family of Ward,* p. 56.
6. As told to the author by her mother, Eva Cooper Ellison.
7. Benjamin Caddell to James Palmer, Pondville, January 4, 1884, Caddell Letters, in the possession of Mrs Albert Perdue, Brent.
8. Centreville *Bibb Blade,* May 22, 1891.
9. Ibid., November 6, 1891.
10. Bibb County Deed Book A-5, p. 435.
11. Bibb County Deed Book C-1, p. 29.
12. Ward, *The Noble Family of Ward,* p. 56.
13. Bibb County Deed Book 4, p. 524.
14. The individual involved told this story to the author many years ago.
15. Letter from John H. Wood, Centreville *Bibb Blade,* June 3, 1891.
16. Centreville *Bibb Blade,* September 11, 18, 25, 1891.
17. Interview with Jack Lawrence, formerly of West Blocton, July 20, 1979.
18. Centreville *Bibb Blade,* quoted in *Centreville Press,* June 11, 1936.
19. *Centreville Press,* June 11, 1936.
20. Centreville *State Central Express,* April 7, 14, 1892.
21. For the background of this term, see Allen J. Going, *Bourbon Democracy in Alabama, 1874–1890* (University, Ala., 1951).
22. See William Warren Rogers, *The One-Gallused Rebellion: Agrarianism in Alabama, 1865–1896* (Baton Rouge, La., 1970); and John B. Clark *Populism in Alabama* (Auburn, Ala., 1927).
23. Sheldon Hackney, *Populism to Progressivism in Alabama* (Princeton, 1969), p. 10.
24. John T. Ellison Diary, 1892–95, Alabama Archives.
25. See Charles G. Summersell, "The Alabama Governor's Race in 1892," *Alabama Review* 8 (January 1955): 5–35.
26. John T. Ellison Diary, September 14, 1892.

27. *Blocton Times,* July 30, 1896.
28. Ibid., August 6, 1896.
29. Benjamin Caddell to James Palmer, Pondville, April 4, 1884, Caddell Letters.
30. As told by Jewell V. Woolley, formerly of Brent, to the author.
31. John T. Ellison Diary, April 3, 1892.
32. *Centreville Press,* June 23, 1898.
33. S. L. Johnson, "Brief History of Bibb County," *Centreville Press,* April 1, 1948.
34. Bibb County Deed Book A-9, p. 531.
35. Johnson, "Brief History of Bibb County."
36. A. H. James to Thomas M. Owen, August 1, 1916, Bibb Vertical File, Alabama Archives.
37. *Centreville Press,* May 21, 1900.
38. Ibid., September 27, 1900.
39. Ibid., June 7, 1900.
40. Issue of June 17, 1910, Alabama Archives Newspaper Collection.

Chapter 18

1. *Blocton Messenger,* April 24, 1902.
2. Ibid., June 12, 1903.
3. Six Mile *Bibb Blade,* February 12, 20, 1880.
4. Centreville *County Press* June 1, 1893.
5. Howard F. McCord, "History of Friendship Lodge, No. 83," filed in minutes of the lodge, Centreville.
6. *Blocton Messenger,* August 21, 1903.
7. *Centreville Press,* February 19, 1903.
8. Ibid., June 18, 1936.
9. Ibid., March 25, 1909, October 13, 1910.
10. Ibid., August 14, 1910.
11. Ibid., August 5, 1899. Hill had aimed his gun at her husband, who was demanding that he repay a loan by working for him.
12. *Centreville Press,* November 23, 1911.
13. Ibid., August 11, 18, 1921.
14. Ibid., March 1, 1900.
15. Ibid., January 11, 1900.
16. Ibid., April 8, 1909.
17. Ibid., October 7, 1909.
18. *Bibb County High School Catalog, 1916–1917.*
19. Davidson, *Inching Along,* p. 1.
20. Ibid., p. 6.
21. Ibid., p. 26. For a statewide study, see Bond, *Negro Education.*
22. Davidson, *Inching Along,* p. 39. This was the ideal of Booker T. Washington, expressed in *Up from Slavery* (New York, 1901). See Daniel Walden, "The Contemporary Opposition to the Political and Educational Ideas of Booker T. Washington," *Journal of Negro History* 45 (April 1960): 103–15.

23. See Bond, *Negro Education,* chapter 12.
24. See McMillan, *Constitutional Development,* chapters 14–19.
25. Hackney, *From Populism to Progressivism,* appendix IV.
26. *Blocton Times,* May 28, 1896.
27. Hackney, *From Populism to Progressivism,* p. 206. See Walter B. Jones, "The Constitutional Convention of 1901 and Poll Taxes," *Alabama Historical Quarterly* 10 (Winter, 1948): 16–25.
28. *Centreville Press,* April 19, May 3, 1900.
29. Davidson, *Inching Along,* pp. 73–74.
30. Ibid., p. 39.
31. *Twenty-Ninth Annual Report and Catalogue, 1928–1929, Centreville Industrial Institute and Bibb County Training School.*
32. Davidson, *Inching Along,* p. 175.
33. On the Phelps-Stokes and Rosenwald funds, see Bond, *Negro Education,* pp. 264–69, 274–80.
34. Davidson's brother-in-law became principal of the Shelby County Training School, according to Nesbitt B. Wesley, Centreville, former principal of the Bibb County Training School.
35. Mrs. J. P. Kennedy, "History of Centreville."
36. *Centreville Press,* January 2, 1958 (obituary of J. C. Langston).
37. Ibid., March 25, April 8, 1909.
38. Ibid., May 29, 1909.
39. Ibid., April 8, 1909.
40. Ibid., January 7, 1907.
41. Ibid., October 27, 1910.
42. Interview with Bessie Tubbs, Centreville, February 19, 1982.
43. *Centreville Press,* January 21, 1909.
44. Ibid., July 28, 1910.
45. *Blocton Enterprise,* August 4, 1910.

Chapter 19

1. *Centreville Press,* July 27, 1916.
2. Ibid., July 6, 1916.
3. Ibid., July 13, 1916.
4. Ibid., November 16, 1916.
5. Ibid., April 12, 1917.
6. Ibid.
7. Ibid., November 20, 1917. The newspaper account of the speech does not repeat this propaganda tale, but some Centreville citizens still remember it vividly. Ralph M. Tanner, "Senator Tom Heflin as a Story-Teller," *Alabama Review* 15 (January 1962): 54–60, omits the war propaganda of the popular raconteur.
8. *Centreville Press,* June 7, 1917.
9. Ibid., October 11, 1917.
10. Ibid., September 6, 1917.

11. Ibid., November 1, 1917.
12. *Blocton Enterprise,* May 30, 1918.
13. See David M. Kennedy, *Over Here* (New York, 1980).
14. *Centreville Press,* May 10, 1917; *Birmingham News,* April 7, 8, 1917.
15. *Centreville Press,* September 26, 1918.
16. *Blocton Enterprise,* May 10, 1917.
17. *Centreville Press,* August 2, 1917.
18. Ibid., February 21, 1918.
19. Ibid., May 2, 1918.
20. Ibid., September 5, 1917.
21. Ibid.
22. Ibid., April 11, 1918.
23. *Blocton Enterprise,* April 18, 1918.
24. Ibid.
25. Ibid., February 28, 1918; *Centreville Press,* October 10, 1918.
26. *Centreville Press,* December 20, 1917; *Blocton Enterprise,* November 15, 1917, March 7, 1918.
27. *Centreville Press,* October 10, 1918.
28. Ibid., July 11, 1918. For an early, and somewhat chauvinistic, history of the 167th Regiment, see William Henry Amerine, *Alabama's Own in France* (New York, 1919).
29. *Centreville Press,* October 24, 1918.
30. Ibid., December 12, 1918.
31. *Blocton Enterprise,* November 21, 1918.
32. *Centreville Press,* February 13, 1919. For a grimmer account from a British soldier's point of view, see H. Stuart Dolden, *Cannon Fodder* (Poole, Dorset, 1980), chapter 25.
33. *Centreville Press,* November 14, 1918.
34. Ibid., November 8, 1917, March 28, 1918.
35. Ibid., May 23, 1918.
36. Ibid., July 27, 1918.
37. Ibid., February 27, 1919. Amerine, *Alabama's Own,* pp. 97–98, telescopes these two incidents into one and leaves Isaac Freeman out of the story.
38. *Centreville Press,* January 23, 1919.
39. Ibid., January 16, 1919.
40. *Blocton Enterprise,* November 7, 14, 1918.
41. *Centreville Press,* November 21, 1918.

BIBLIOGRAPHY

I. Primary Materials

Manuscripts

Alabama-West Florida Conference of Methodist Church. Quarterly Conference Minutes of Centreville, later Randolph, Circuit, 1835–70. Alabama Department of Archives and History, Montgomery, hereafter referred to as Alabama Archives.

Arnold, A. L. Scrapbook in possession of Albert Eady, Centreville.

Boyd, David R. Physician's Account Book, 1829–36. Heritage Room, Brent-Centreville Public Library, Centreville.

Brown, J. M. Untitled MS on Civil War memories. Xerox copy in possession of author.

Caddell, Benjamin. Letters. In possession of Mrs. Albert Perdue, Brent.

Centreville Presbyterian Church. Records, 1824–1900. Filed in the church office.

Crawford, Thomas. Crawford Papers. Alabama Archives.

Ellison, John T. Diary, 1892–95. Alabama Archives.

Enon Baptist Church. Minutes, 1819–1900. In possession of People's Bank, Centreville.

Freemasons' Cold Water Lodge, Number 148, Green Pond. Minutes from 1851. In possession of the lodge.

Gorgas, Josiah. Diary. Gorgas Papers, University of Alabama Library, University, Alabama.

Green, John Morgan. "History of the Farm." In possession of E. D. Clouse, Woodstock.

Green Pond Presbyterian Church. Minutes from April 1871. Alabama Archives.

Hall, James Blair. Hall Papers. Alabama Archives.

Hayes, Andrew Wilson. "The Green Pond School." Xerox copy of typescript in possession of Mrs. Thomas M. Nicholson, Centreville.

———. "Reminiscences of the War between the States." Typescript in possession of Mrs. Thomas M. Nicholson, Centreville.

Hicks, J. C. Teacher's Account Book, 1890s. In possession of Vera Hicks, Centreville.

James, Jasper E. Diary, 1850s. In possession of James M. White, Brent.

———. Letters, 1861–64. In possession of James M. White, Brent.

Jones, Harwell. "History of Reconstruction in Bibb County." M.A. thesis, University of Alabama, 1932.

Kennedy Papers. Miscellaneous collection of family papers and local memorabilia. In possession of Mrs. Josiah Kennedy, Centreville.

Letters, miscellaneous: Ragland, in possession of David Bailey, Centreville; Fair, in possession of Mrs. Dan Cottingham, Centreville; Smitherman, in possession of Louie Waller, Miami.

Letters to Thomas M. Owen. Bibb County Vertical File, Alabama Archives.

Letters to J. W. Suttle, 1858–64. In possession of Howard F. McCord, Centreville.

McCord, Carey. "The Pratt Family." Typescript in possession of Howard F. McCord, Centreville.

McCord, Howard F. "History of Friendship Lodge." Filed in minutes of lodge, Centreville.

Mahan, S. Michael, Jr. "A Brief History of Bibb County Furnaces." Typescript, 1935. Bibb County High School Library, Centreville.

Meigs, Alice Lee Little. "Early Academies of Bibb County, Alabama." M.A. thesis, University of Alabama, 1947.

Military Records, 1861–65. Alabama Archives.

Moren, Edward Hawthorne, Letters, 1860–86. Alabama Archives.

Mount Zion Baptist Church. Minutes from 1859. Xerox copy in possession of Mrs. Cleveland Stewart, Centreville.

Pleasant Hill Cumberland Presbyterian Church. Records from 1849. In possession of Cobbett Cox, Eoline community.

Shipman, Stephen V. Diary. Shipman MSS, Wisconsin Historical Society Library, Madison, Wisconsin.

Suttle, J. W. Account Book, 1860s. In possession of Howard F. McCord, Centreville.

United States Public Land Survey of Alabama, Field Notes. Office of Alabama Secretary of State, Montgomery.

Vertical File, Bibb County. Alabama Archives.

Bibb County Official Records

Administrators' Court Account Books, 1821–31, 1858–65.

Bonds of County Officers, 1824–39, 1839–53, 1853–73. 3 vols.

Circuit Court: Record Books, 1821–58 (15 vols.); Judgments Rendered, 1840–59, 1859–66; Minutes, 1840–47, 1860–73; Fee Book, 1824–49.

County Court (later Commissioners' Court of Roads and Revenues): Minutes, 1818–37; Record, 1821–50 (9 vols.), 1876–93; Execution Docket and Fee Book, 1824–49.

Deed Books A, E, F, G, A-9, 4.

Land Grant and Patent Books, Vol. I.

Orphans' Court: Minutes, Book A, 1818–29; Book C, Administrators' Accounts, 1821–31; Book B, Administrators' Accounts, 1831–45, 1858–65.

Register of Incorporations, 1879–89 (with Bonds of County Officers, 1853–79).

Tax Assessment Records: Real Estate, 1853; Personal Property, 1854, 1855, 1856, 1858 (4 vols.); Real and Personal Property, 1867.

Government Documents

Aiken, John G., comp. *Digest of the Laws of Alabama.* Philadelphia: Alexander Tower, printer, 1833; For sale by D. Woodruff, Tuscaloosa, Alabama, 1833.

Alabama, Department of Mines. *First Biennial Report of the State Inspector of Mines for the Years Beginning December 31, 1892, and Ending December 31, 1894.* Montgomery: n.p., 1895.

Alabama, General Assembly. *Acts Passed at the First Session of the General Assembly of the Alabama Territory in the Forty-second Year of American Independence [1817–1818].* St. Stephens: printed by Thomas Eaton, 1819.

———.*Acts Passed at the Sixth Annual Session of the General Assembly of the State of Alabama [1824–1825]* Cahaba: William B. Allen, state printer, 1825.

———. *Acts Passed at the Ninth Annual Session of the General Assembly of the State of Alabama [1827–1828].* Tuscaloosa: Henry and McGuire, state printers, 1828.

———. *Acts Passed at the Twelfth Annual Session of the General Assembly of the State of Alabama [1830–1831].* Tuscaloosa: Wiley, McGuire, and Henry, state printers, 1831.

———. *Acts Passed at the Thirteenth Annual Session of the General Assembly of the State of Alabama [1832–1833].* Tuscaloosa: May and Ferguson, state printers, 1833.

———. *Acts Passed at the Sixteenth Annual Session of the General Assembly of the State of Alabama [1834–35].* Tuscaloosa: David Ferguson, state printer, 1835.

———. *Acts of the Session of 1866–7 of the General Assembly of the State of Alabama.* Montgomery: Reid and Screws, state printers, 1867.

———. *Code of Alabama.* Montgomery: Brittan and DeWolf, state printers, 1852.

Alabama, Supreme Court. *Reports of Cases Argued and Determined in the Supreme Court of Alabama.* Vol. 39. Montgomery: Barrett and Brown, 1868.

Toulmin, Harry, comp. *Digest of the Laws of the State of Alabama.* Cahaba: Ginn and Curtis, 1823; J. and J. Harper, New York, printers.

United States, Army Engineer Corps. *Annual Report of the Chief of Engineers, U.S. Army, 1875.* Washington: Government Printing Office, 1875.

United States, Bureau of the Census. *Seventh Census of the United States: 1850.* Washington: Robert Armstrong, public printer, 1853.

———. *Eighth Census of the United States: 1860.* Washington: Government Printing Office, 1864.

———. *Ninth Census of the United States: 1870.* Washington: Government Printing Office, 1872.

United States, Congress. *American State Papers, 1789–1838, in Relation to the Public Lands.* 8 vols. Washington: Duff Green, 1834; Gales and Seaton, 1834–61.

———. *Annals of Congress, 18th Congress, First Session, 1823–1824.* Washington: Gales and Seaton, 1856.

———. *Indian Affairs: Laws and Treaties.* Edited by Charles J. Kappler. 5 vols. Washington: Government Printing Office, 1903–41.

———. *Public Statutes at Large from the Organization of Government in 1789 to March 3, 1845.* Edited by Richard Peters, Vol. 3 [*Public Acts, 13th–17th Congress, 1813–23*]; vol. 6 [*Private Acts, 1st–28th Congress, 1789–1845*]. Boston: Charles C. Little and James Brown, 1856, 1848.

———. *Report of the Joint Committee to Inquire into the Condition of Affairs in the Late Insurrectionary States.* Vol. 8, *Alabama.* Washington: Government Printing Office, 1872.

United States. *The Territorial Papers of the United States.* Compiled and edited by Clarence Edwin Carter. Vol. 18, *The Territory of Alabama, 1817–1819.* Washington: Government Printing Office, 1952.

United States, War Department. *The War of the Rebellion: A Compilation of the Original Reports of the Union and Confederate Armies.* 129 vols. Washington: Government Printing Office, 1880–1901.

Newspapers

Alabama Beacon, Greensboro.
Alabama Intelligencer, Tuscaloosa
Bibb Blade, Six Mile, later Centreville.
Bibb County Democrat, Woodstock, later Centreville.
Bibb County News, Centreville.
Birmingham Age-Herald, Birmingham.
Birmingham News, Birmingham.
Blade-Enterprise, Centreville.
Blocton Courier, Blocton.
Blocton Enterprise, West Blocton.
Blocton Messenger, West Blocton.
Blocton Times, Blocton.
Cahawba Press and Alabama Intelligencer, Cahaba.
Central Enquirer, Centreville.
Centreville Press, Centreville.
County Press, Centreville.
East Alabamian, LaFayette.
Eoline Messenger, Eoline.
Eutaw Whig and Observer, Eutaw.
Independent Monitor, Tuscaloosa.
Marion Standard, Marion.
Montgomery Advertiser, Montgomery.
Montgomery Daily Mail, Montgomery.
People's Reflector, Centreville.
Selma Free Press, Selma.
Selma Times, Selma.
Shelby County Guide, Columbiana.
State Central Express, Centreville.
State Sentinel, Montgomery.
Tuscaloosa News, Tuscaloosa.

Books and Pamphlets

Baldwin, Joseph G. *Flush Times of Alabama and Mississippi.* 1855. Reprint. New York: Sagamore Press, 1957.

Barr, John Gorman. *Rowdy Tales from Early Alabama.* Edited by G. Ward Hubbs. University, Ala.: University of Alabama Press, 1981.

Berney, Saffold. *Handbook of Alabama.* Birmingham: Roberts & Son, 1892.

Botkin, E. A., ed. *Lay My Burden Down.* Chicago: University of Chicago Press, 1945.

Crockett, David. *Narrative of the Life of David Crockett.* 5th ed. Philadelphia: E. L. Carey and A. Hart, 1834.

Dailey, Charles Collier. *The Dailey Dozen.* N.p. [Birmingham]: Printed for Mattie Wyatt Cost, 1975.

Davidson, Henry Damon. *Inching Along.* Nashville, Tenn.: National Publications Company, 1944.

DeLeon, Thomas C. *Four Years in Rebel Capitals.* Mobile: Gossip Printing Company, 1890.

Dolden, A. Stuart. *Cannon Fodder: An Infantryman's Life on the Western Front, 1914–1918.* Poole, Dorset, U.K.: Blandford Press, 1980.

Froost, Lewis. *Letter of the Chief Engineer in Relation to the Alabama and Tennessee Railroad.* Selma: Reporter Office, 1850.

Gosse, Philip Henry. *Letters from Alabama (U.S.).* London: Morgan and Chase, 1859.

Green, Fletcher M., ed. *The Lides Go South and West.* Columbia, S.C.: University of South Carolina Press, 1952.

Hamilton, William T. *The Duties of Masters and Slaves; or Domestic Servitude as Sanctioned by the Bible.* Mobile: F. H. Brooks, 1845.

Henry, Robert S. ed. *As They Saw Forrest: Recollections and Comments of Contemporaries.* Jackson, Tenn.: McCowat, Mercer Press, 1956.

Hodgson, Joseph. *Alabama Manual and Statistical Register for 1869.* Montgomery: printed for Joseph Hodgson, editor of Montgomery Mail, 1869.

Hubbard, John Milton. *Notes of a Private.* 1909. Reprint. St. Louis: Nixon-Jones Printing Company, 1913.

Hunnicutt, John L. *Reconstruction in West Alabama.* Tuscaloosa: Confederate Publishing Company, 1959.

Jackson, Andrew. *Correspondence of Andrew Jackson.* Edited by John Spencer Bassett. 7 vols. Washington: Carnegie Institution, 1926–33. Reprint (7 vols. in 6). New York: Kraus, 1969.

Langston, Fern, comp. *Echoes of Six Mile.* Montevallo, Ala.: Privately printed, 1981.

McMillan, Malcolm C., ed. *Alabama Confederate Reader.* University, Ala.: University of Alabama Press, 1963.

Milburn, William Henry. *Ten Years of Preacher Life.* New York: Darby and Jackson, 1859.

Olmsted, Frederick Lee. *A Journey in the Back Country.* 1860. Reprint. New York: Shocken Books, 1970.

Royall, Anne. *Mrs. Royall's Southern Tour.* Vol. 2. Washington: Privately printed, 1831.

Sims, J. Marion. *The Story of My Life.* New York: D. Appleton, 1884.

Washington, Booker T. *Up from Slavery.* New York: A. L. Burt Company, 1901.

Woodward, Thomas S. *Reminiscences of the Creek or Muskogee Indians.* Montgomery: Barrett and Wimbish, 1939.

Articles

["Alabama Blast Furnaces"], *DeBow's Review,* October 1851.

Collins, Donald E., ed. "A Georgian's View of Alabama in 1836." *Alabama Review* 25 (July 1972): 218–26.

Dieteritt, John H., ed. "Letters of General John Coffee to His Wife, 1813–1815." *Tennessee Historical Magazine* 2 (December 1916): 246–94.

Dubose, John Witherspoon. "Recollections of the Plantation." *Alabama Historical Quarterly* 1 (Spring 1930): 63–75.

"1830 Census of Bibb County." Transcribed from microfilm by Mrs. Charles E. Norton. *Alabama Genealogical Society Magazine* 1 (January 1967): 26–28; (April 1967): 18–34; (July 1967): 5–13.

Gardner, Walter, "Bygone Days." *Centreville Press,* June 12, 1980.

Ham, Margaret. "The Personal Side of the War." As told by Mrs. Eugenia Pratt Logan, *Bibb Eagle,* published by the Bibb County Heritage Association, February 1977.

Hoole, W. Stanley, ed. "Elyton, Alabama, and the Connecticut Asylum: The Letters of William H. Ely, 1820–1821." *Alabama Review* 3 (July 1950): 36–69.

———. "The Letters of Captain Joab Goodson." *Alabama Review* 10 (April 1957): 126–53; (July 1957): 171–215.

[Jennings, S. K.]. "Colonel John Barr." New York *Spirit of the Times,* October 23, 1958.

Lincecum, Gideon. "Autobiography." *Publications of the Mississippi Historical Society,* 8 (1904): 467–468.

"Register of Gubernatorial Appointments, Civil and Military: Territory of Alabama, February 9, 1818–November 14, 1819; State of Alabama, December 14, 1819–October 4, 1822." *Alabama Historical Quarterly* 6 (Summer1944): 122–328.

["Scottsville Cotton Mill"]. *DeBow's Review,* December 18, 1858.

"Unpublished Letter from General Jackson." *Birmingham Age-Herald,* July 7, 1889.

Wilson, Clyde E., comp. "State Militia of Alabama, June 21–December 18, 1865." *Alabama Historical Quarterly* 14 (1952): 301–30.

Wallace, W. P. "Reminiscences." *Blocton Enterprise,* May 24, 1917.

Williams, John R., ed. "Frontier Evangelist: The Journal of Henry Bryson." *Alabama Historical Quarterly* 42 (1980): 5–39.

II. Secondary Materials

Books and Pamphlets

Abernethy, Thomas Perkins. *The Formative Period in Alabama.* Montgomery: Brown Printing Company, 1922.

Abrams, Ulysses Huey. *A History of Early Bibb County, Alabama.* Edited by Mattie Sandford Johnson. Huntsville: Xerox edition by Mrs. Johnson, 1981.

Alabama Blast Furnaces. Woodward, Ala.: Woodward Iron Company, n.d.

Amerine, William Henry. *Alabama's Own in France.* New York: Eaton and Gattinger, 1919.

Armes, Ethel. *The Story of Coal and Iron in Alabama.* Birmingham: Chamber of Commerce, 1910.

Atkinson, Ray M., and G. Benton Towry. *Richard Hopkins Pratt and the Six Mile Academy.* Birmingham: Banner Press, 1960.

Bond, Horace M. *Negro Education in Alabama.* 1939. Reprint. New York: Octagon Books, 1969.

Boyd, Charles E. *Haysop: A Church, a Community, a People.* Birmingham: Banner Press, 1979.

Brant and Fuller, comps. *Memorial Record of Alabama.* 2 vols. Madison, Wis.: Brant and Fuller, 1893.

Brewer, Willis. *Alabama: Her History, Resources, War Record, and Public Men.* Montgomery: Barrett and Brown, 1872.

Brown, William Garrott. *History of Alabama.* New York: University Publishing Company, 1900.

Clark, John B. *Populism in Alabama.* Auburn, Ala.: Auburn Printing Company, 1927.

Clarke, W. G. *History of Education in Alabama.* Washington: Government Printing Office, 1889.

Clinton, Matthew W. *Tuscaloosa, Alabama: Its Early Days, 1816–1865.* Tuscaloosa: Zonta Club, 1958.

Colcord, Bradford C. *The History of Pig Iron Manufacture in Alabama.* Woodward, Ala.: Woodward Iron Company, 1950.

Connelly, Thomas L. *Autumn of Glory: The Army of Tennessee, 1862–1865.* Baton Rouge, La.: Louisiana State University Press, 1972.

Coulter, E. Merton. *The Confederate States of America, 1861–1865.* Baton Rouge, La.: Louisiana State University Press, 1950.

Dean, Blanche E., Amy Mason, and Joab L. Thomas. *Wildflowers of Alabama and Adjoining States.* University, Ala.: University of Alabama Press, 1973.

Dorman, Lewy. *Party Politics in Alabama from 1850 to 1860.* Wetumpka, Ala.: Wetumpka Publishing Company, 1935.

DuBose, John Witherspoon. *The Life and Times of William Lowndes Yancey.* 2 vols. 1892. Reprint. New York: Peter Smith, 1942.

Ellison, Rhoda Coleman. *Early Alabama Publications: A Study in Literary Interests.* University, Ala.: University of Alabama Press, 1947.

———. *History and Bibliography of Alabama Newspapers in the Nineteenth Century.* University, Ala.: University of Alabama Press, 1954.

Facts about Shelby County. Brochure. N.p.: Shelby County Historical Society and Shelby County Commissioners, n.d.

Farmer, Margaret Pace. *One Hundred Fifty Years in Pike County, Alabama, 1821–1971.* Anniston, Ala.: Higginbothem, 1973.

Fleming, Walter L. *Civil War and Reconstruction in Alabama.* New York: Columbia University Press, 1905.

Garrett, William. *Public Men of Alabama.* Atlanta: Plantation Publishing Company, 1872.

Going, Allen J. *Bourbon Democracy in Alabama, 1874–1890.* University, Ala.: University of Alabama Press, 1951.

Gray, Daniel S., comp. *Autauga County: The First Hundred Years, 1818–1918.* Prattville, Ala.: Autauga County Prattville Public Library, 1972.

Gregg, Robert. *Origin and Development of the T.C.I. and R. Company.* New York: Newcomen Society of England, American Branch, 1948.

Griffith, Lucille. *Alabama: A Documentary History to 1900.* University, Ala.: University of Alabama Press, 1968; rev. ed. 1972.

Hackney, Sheldon. *Populism to Progressivism in Alabama.* Princeton, N.J.: Princeton University Press, 1969.

Halbert, Henry S., and T. H. Ball. *The Creek War of 1813–1814.* Edited by Frank L. Owsley, Jr. University, Ala.: University of Alabama Press, 1969.

Henry, Robert S. *"First with the Most" Forrest.* Indianapolis: Bobbs-Merrill, 1944.

Historic Preservation. N.p.: compiled and published by West Alabama Planning and Development Council, June 1974.

Holcomb, Hosea. *History of the Rise and Progress of the Baptists in Alabama.* Philadelphia: King and Bird, printers, 1840.

Horne, Stanley. *The Decisive Battle of Nashville.* Baton Rouge, La.: Louisiana State University Press, 1956.

Jackson, Walter M. *Alabama's First United States Vice-President, William Rufus King.* Decatur, Ala.: Decatur Publishing Company, 1952.

Jones, James Pickett. *Yankee Blitzkrieg: Wilson's Raid through Alabama and Georgia.* Athens, Ga.: University of Georgia Press, 1976.

Jordan, Weymouth T. *Antebellum Alabama Town and Country.* Tallahassee, Fla.: Florida State University, 1957.

———. *Hugh Davis and His Alabama Plantation.* University, Ala.: University of Alabama Press, 1948.

Kennedy, David M. *Over Here.* New York: Oxford Press, 1980.

Lazenby, Marion Elias. *History of Methodism in Alabama and West Florida.* Nashville, Tenn.: Parthenon Press, 1960.

Letford, William, comp. *Alabama Congressional and Legislative Representation, 1819–1960, with Maps.* Publication of Alabama Department of Archives and History. Montgomery: Walker Printing Company, n.d. [c. 1961].

Loon, Ella. *Salt as a Factor in the Confederacy.* New York: Columbia University Press, 1933.

McCord, Howard Floyd. *Baptists of Bibb County.* N.p.: privately printed, 1979.

McMillan, Malcolm C. *Constitutional Development in Alabama, 1798–1901.* Chapel Hill, N.C.: University of North Carolina Press, 1955.

Martin, Bessie. *Desertion of Alabama Troops from the Confederate Army.* New York: Columbia University Press, 1932.

Moore, Albert B. *Conscription and Conflict in the Confederacy.* New York: Columbia University Press, Macmillan Company, agent, 1924.

———. *History of Alabama and Her People.* Chicago: American Historical Society, 1927.

Owen, Thomas M. *History of Alabama and Dictionary of Alabama Biography.* 4 vols. Chicago: S. J. Clarke Publishing Company, 1921.

Owsley, Frank L. *Plain Folk of the Old South.* Baton Rouge, La.: Louisiana State University Press, 1949.

Pickett, Albert J. *History of Alabama and Incidentally of Georgia and Mississippi, from the Earliest Period.* Birmingham: Webb Book Company, 1896.

Posey, Walter E. *The Presbyterian Church in the Old Southwest.* Richmond, Va.: John Knox Press, 1952.

Reed, William A. *Indian Place Names in Alabama.* Baton Rouge, La.: Louisiana State University Press, 1937.

Renfro, N. P., Jr. *The Beginning of Railroads in Alabama.* Auburn, Ala.: Alabama Polytechnic Institute Historical Studies, 1910.

Riley, Benjamin F. *History of Conecuh County, Alabama.* Columbus, Ga.: Thomas Gilbert, 1881.

———. *A Memorial History of the Baptists of Alabama.* Philadelphia: The Judson Press, 1923.

Rogers, William Warren. *The One-Gallused Rebellion: Agrarianism in Alabama, 1865–1895.* Baton Rouge, La.: Louisiana State University Press, 1970.

Scott, William F., *The Story of a Cavalry Regiment.* New York: G. P. Putnam's, 1893.

Scruggs, J. Hubert, Jr., comp. *Alabama Postal Roads with Maps.* N.p.: privately printed, n.d. [ca. 1953].

———, comp. *Alabama Steamboats, 1819–1869.* N.p.: privately printed, n.d. [ca. 1953].

Sellers, James B. *Slavery in Alabama.* University, Ala.: University of Alabama Press, 1950.

Smith, Eugene A. *Geological Survey of Alabama.* Montgomery: Brown Printing Company, 1890.

Steele, Miriam and Parker. *The Steeles of Bibb County.* N.p.: privately printed, 1973.

Swanton, John A. *Indians of the Southeast United States.* Washington: Smithsonian Institution, 1946.

Ward, David. *Labor Revolt in Alabama: The Great Strike of 1894.* University, Ala.: University of Alabama Press, 1965.

Ward, James Mayfield. *The Noble Family of Ward.* N.p.: privately printed, 1970.

West, Anson. *History of Methodism in Alabama.* Nashville, Tenn.: Barbee and Smith, 1893.

Wyatt, T. E. *Chilton County and Her People.* Clanton: Union Banner Press, 1940; rev. ed., Carlos W. Wyatt, 1976.

Young, William Raymond. *The Lawrences.* N.p.: Xerox edition by W. R. Young, 1975.

Articles

"Antiquities of Bibb." *Centreville Press,* January 25, April 1, 1900.

Bethel, Elizabeth. "The Freedmen's Bureau in Alabama." *Journal of Southern History* 14 (February 1948): 49–92.

Boyd, Charles E. "Early Bibb County Postmarks." *Centreville Press,* November 14, 1974.

Brannon, Peter A. "Building of Bibb County Court House, 1829–1830." *Montgomery Advertiser,* August 22, 1937.

Catts, Samuel Walker. "Wilson's Raid and Other Recital." *Alabama Historical Quarterly* 5 (Winter 1943), 430–37.

Chappell, Gordon T. "John Coffee: Land Speculator and Planter." *Alabama Review* 22 (January 1969): 24–43.

Clark, Ross C. "The Woody Plants of Alabama." *Annals of the Missouri Botanical Garden* 58 (1971): 99–242.

Clinton, Thomas P. "Early History of Tuscaloosa." *Alabama Historical Quarterly* 1 (Summer 1930): 169–178.

———. "The Military Operations of General John T. Croxton in West Alabama, 1865." *Transactions of the Alabama Historical Society* 4 (1904): 449–63.

Ellison, John T. "City of Centreville: Short Sketches of Old Settlers and Prominent Citizens." Centreville *County Press* June 17, 1896.

Gardner, Alto L., and Nathan Stott. "William Lowndes Yancey: Statesman of Secession." *Alabama Review* 15 (July 1962): 190–202.

Gatchet, Albert S. "Towns and Villages of the Creek Confederacy." *Publications of the Alabama Historical Society* 1 (1900): 386–415.

Griffin, Richard W. "Cotton Frauds and Confiscations in Alabama, 1863–1866." *Alabama Review* 7 (October 1954): 265–76.

Halbert, Henry S. "Choctaw Indian Names in Alabama and Mississippi." *Transactions of the Alabama Historical Society, 1898–1899,* 3 (1900): 64–77.

Hamilton, Peter J. "Indian Trails and Early Roads." *Publications of Alabama Historical Society,* 1 (1900): 422–29.

Holland, James W. "Andrew Jackson and the Creek War: Victory at the Horseshoe." *Alabama Review* 21 (October 1968): 243–75.

Johnson, S. L. "Brief History of Bibb County." *Centreville Press,* April 1, 1948.

Jones, Walter B. "The Constitutional Convention of 1901 and Poll Taxes." *Alabama Historical Quarterly* 10 (Winter 1948): 16–25.

Kennedy, Mrs. J. P. "History of Centreville." *Centreville Press,* July 27, 1950.

Krouse, T. J. "Clarke County Salt Works." *Alabama Historical Quarterly* 20 (Spring 1958): 95–100.

Lightner, David. "Private Land Claims in Alabama." *Alabama Review* 20 (July 1967): 187–204.

McKenzie, Robert H. "Reconstruction of the Iron Industry in Alabama, 1865–1880." *Alabama Review* 25 (July 1972): 178–91.

Moore, A. B. "Railroad Building in Alabama during the Reconstruction Period." *Journal of Southern History* 1 (November 1935): 421–41.

Motley, C. H. "Sandy Chapel." *Centreville Press,* November 30, 1910.

Myers, John B. "The Freedman and the Law in Post-Bellum Alabama, 1865–1867." *Alabama Review* 23 (January 1970): 56–74.

Owen, Thomas McAdory. "Indian Tribes and Towns in Alabama." *Alabama His-*

torical Quarterly 12 (1950): 118–241, reprinted from Owen. *History of Alabama and Dictionary of Alabama Biography.*

Owings, William J. B. "Doctoring in Bibb County." *Sparrow Hawk* 3 (Summer 1978): 22.

Rodabaugh, James H. "The Fighting McCooks." *Civil War History* 3 (1957): 287–90.

Rogers, William Warren. "Farmers Alliance in Alabama." *Alabama Review* 15 (January 1962): 5–18.

Sellers, James B. "Free Negroes of Tuscaloosa County before the Thirteenth Amendment." *Alabama Review* 23 (April 1970): 110–27.

Stephen, Walter W. "The Brooke Guns from Selma." *Alabama Historical Quarterly* 20 (Fall 1958): 462–75.

Townes, S. A. "The History of Marion" (1844). Reprinted in *Alabama Historical Quarterly* 14 (1952): 171–215.

Walden, Daniel. "The Contemporary Opposition to the Political and Educational Ideas of Booker T. Washington." *Journal of Negro History* 45 (April 1960): 103–15.

Williamson, Edward C. "The Alabama Election of 1874." *Alabama Review* 17 (July 1964): 210–18.

Wilson, Harold. "Basil Manly, Apologist for Slavocracy." *Alabama Review* 15 (January 1962): 38–53.

Wilson, Thomas. "Outdoors." *Centreville Press,* March 12, 1981.

Woodward, Joseph H. "Alabama Iron Manufacturing." *Alabama Review* 7 (July 1954): 199–208.

Woolfolk, Sarah Van. "Five Men Called Scalawags." *Alabama Review* 17 (January 1964): 45–55.

INDEX

(The lists of names in the Appendixes have been omitted from the Index.)